Foundations of
anthropological
theory

Foundations of Anthropological Theory

Blackwell Anthologies in Social & Cultural Anthropology

Series Editor: Parker Shipton, Boston University

Drawing from some of the most significant scholarly work of the 19th and 20th centuries, the *Blackwell Anthologies in Social and Cultural Anthropology* series offers a comprehensive and unique perspective on the ever-changing field of anthropology. It represents both a collection of classic readers and an exciting challenge to the norms that have shaped this discipline over the past century.

Each edited volume is devoted to a traditional subdiscipline of the field such as the anthropology of religion, linguistic anthropology, or medical anthropology; and provides a foundation in the canonical readings of the selected area. Aware that such subdisciplinary definitions are still widely recognized and useful – but increasingly problematic – these volumes are crafted to include a rare and invaluable perspective on social and cultural anthropology at the onset of the 21st century. Each text provides a selection of classic readings together with contemporary works that underscore the artificiality of subdisciplinary definitions and point students, researchers, and general readers in the new directions in which anthropology is moving.

Series Advisory Editorial Board

Fredrik Barth, *University of Oslo and Boston University*
Stephen Gudeman, *University of Minnesota*
Jane Guyer, *Northwestern University*
Caroline Humphrey, *University of Cambridge*
Tim Ingold, *University of Aberdeen*
Emily Martin, *Princeton University*
Sally Falk Moore, *Harvard Emerita*
Marshall Sahlins, *University of Chicago Emeritus*
Joan Vincent, *Columbia University and Barnard College Emerita*

1. *Linguistic Anthropology: A Reader,* Second Edition
    Edited by Alessandro Duranti
2. *A Reader in the Anthropology of Religion*, Second Edition
    Edited by Michael Lambek
3. *The Anthropology of Politics: A Reader in Ethnography, Theory, and Critique*
    Edited by Joan Vincent
4. *Kinship and Family: An Anthropological Reader*
    Edited by Robert Parkin and Linda Stone
5. *Law and Anthropology: A Reader*
    Edited by Sally Falk Moore
6. *The Anthropology of Development and Globalization: From Classical Political Economy to Contemporary Neoliberalism*
    Edited by Marc Edelman and Angelique Haugerud
7. *The Anthropology of Art: A Reader*
    Edited by Howard Morphy and Morgan Perkins
8. *Feminist Anthropology: A Reader*
    Edited by Ellen Lewin
9. *Ethnographic Fieldwork: An Anthropological Reader*
    Edited by Antonius C. G. M. Robben and Jeffrey A. Sluka
10. *Environmental Anthropology*
    Edited by Michael R. Dove and Carol Carpenter
11. *Anthropology and Child Development: A Cross-Cultural Reader*
    Edited by Robert A. LeVine and Rebecca S. New
12. *Foundations of Anthropological Theory: From Classical Antiquity to Early Modern Europe*
    Edited by Robert Launay

Forthcoming

Psychological Anthropology: A Reader on Self in Culture
Edited by Robert A. LeVine

A Reader in Medical Anthropology: Theoretical Trajectories, Emergent Realities
Edited by Byron J. Good, Michael M. J. Fischer, Sarah S. Willen, and Mary-Jo DelVecchio Good

Foundations
of Anthropological Theory

*From Classical Antiquity
to Early Modern Europe*

Edited by

Robert Launay

A John Wiley & Sons, Ltd., Publication

Library of Congress Cataloging-in-Publication Data
Foundations of anthropological theory : from classical antiquity to early modern Europe / edited by Robert Launay.
p. cm. – (Blackwell anthologies in social & cultural anthropology ; 12)
Includes bibliographical references and index.
ISBN 978-1-4051-8776-3 (hardcover : alk. paper) – ISBN 978-1-4051-8775-6 (pbk. : alk. paper)
1. Anthropology–History. 2. Anthropology–Philosophy. 1. Launay, Robert, 1949–
GN17.F68 2010
301.01–dc22
2009045861

A catalogue record for this book is available from the British Library.

Set in 9/11pt Sabon by SPi Publisher Services, Pondicherry, India.
Printed in Singapore by Ho Printing Singapore Pte Ltd

01   2010

For Cecile and Claire

Contents

Acknowledgments   x
Note on the Text   xii

Introduction   1
Robert Launay

Part I   The Ancient World   29

1   The Histories of Herodotus   31
    Herodotus

2   Germany   39
    Tacitus

Part II   The Middle Ages   47

Section II   (a) European Travelers   49

3   The Travels of Marco Polo   51
    Marco Polo

4   The Travels of Sir John Mandeville   63
    John Mandeville

Section II   (b) The Muslim World   71

5   Travels in Asia and Africa, 1325–1354   73
    Ibn Battuta

6   The Muqaddimah   84
    Ibn Khaldun

Part III   The Renaissance   **93**

7   History of a Voyage to the Land of Brazil, otherwise Called America   95
    Jean de Léry

8   Of Cannibals   106
    Michel de Montaigne

9   Method for the Easy Comprehension of History   114
    Jean Bodin

10 Letter to Joseph Scaliger   125
    Henri Lancelot Voisin de la Popelinière

Part IV   The Seventeenth Century   **127**

Section IV   (a) Jesuits and the Comparative Perspective   **129**

11 Natural and Moral History of the Indies   131
    José de Acosta

12 Relation of What Occurred in New France, in the Year 1634   143
    Paul Le Jeune

13 Memoirs and Remarks ... Made in Above Ten Years Travels
    through the Empire of China   151
    Louis Le Comte

14 Customs of the American Indians Compared with the Customs
    of Primitive Times   159
    Joseph François Lafitau

Section IV   (b) Globetrotters   **171**

15 Travels in Persia, 1673–1677   173
    John Chardin

16 A New Voyage Round the World   183
    William Dampier

Part V   The Enlightenment   **193**

Section V   (a) The Quarrel of the Ancients and the Moderns   **195**

17 Of Heroic Virtue   197
    William Temple

18 Of the Origin of Fables   207
    Bernard le Bovier de Fontenelle

Section V   (b) Putting Words in Their Mouths: Dialogues and Letters   **215**

19 New Voyages to North America   217
    Baron de Lahontan

20 Persian Letters   225
    Montesquieu

21 The *Supplément au Voyage de Bougainville*   228
    Denis Diderot

Section V (c) Universal History: France   **241**

22 The Spirit of Laws   243
    Montesquieu

23 A Discourse on Inequality   251
    Jean-Jacques Rousseau

24 The Philosophy of History   260
    Voltaire

25 The A, B, C   265
    Voltaire

Section V (d) Universal History: Scotland   **271**

26 Lectures on Jurisprudence   273
    Adam Smith

27 An Essay on the History of Civil Society   277
    Adam Ferguson

Author Index   289
Subject Index   291

Acknowledgments

Herodotus, *The Histories of Herodotus* (excerpts), translated by Henry Cary, New York: D. Appleton and Company, 1899.

Tacitus, *Germania* (excerpts), from *The Complete Works of Tacitus*, translated by Alfred John Church and William Johnson Brodribb, New York: Modern Library, 1942. (The Church and Brodribb translation was originally published in London by Macmillan in 1875.)

Marco Polo, *The Travels of Marco Polo* (excerpts), revised from Marsden's [d. 1836] translation and edited with Introduction by Manuel Komroff, New York: Boni and Liveright, 1926.

John Mandeville, *The Travels of John Mandeville* (excerpts), translated by C.R.W.D. Moseley, London: Penguin Books, 1983.

Ibn Battuta, *Travels in Asia and Africa, 1325–1354* (excerpts), translated by H.A.R. Gibbs, London: Routledge and Kegan Paul, 1929.

Ibn Khaldun, *The Muqaddimah* (excerpts), translated by Franz Rosenthal, Princeton, NJ: Princeton University Press, 1967 [copyright Bollingen Foundation].

Jean de Léry, *History of a Voyage to the Land of Brazil* (excerpts), translated by Janet Whatley, Berkeley and Los Angeles: University of California Press, 1990.

Montaigne, "Of Cannibals" (complete), from *The Essays of Michel de Montaigne*, translated by George B. Ives, New York: Heritage Press, 1946 [the translation was first published by Harvard University Press in 1925].

Jean Bodin, *Method for the Easy Comprehension of History* (excerpts), translated by Beatrice Reynolds, New York: Columbia University Press, 1945.

Henri Lancelot Voisin de la Popelinière, "Letter to Joseph Scaliger" (complete), original translation by Robert Launay; French text reprinted in George Huppert, *The Idea of Perfect History*, Urbana, IL: University of Illinois Press, 1970.

José de Acosta, *Natural and Moral History of the Indies* (excerpts), edited by Jane E. Mangan, translated by Frances M. López-Morillas, Durham, NC: Duke University Press, 2002.

Paul Le Jeune, "Relation of What Occurred in New France, in the Year 1634" (excerpts), from *Jesuit Relations and Allied Documents*, vol. 6, edited by Reuben Thwaites, Cleveland, OH: Burrows Brothers, 1901 [online].

Louis Le Comte, *Memoirs and Remarks Made in above Ten Years Travels through the Empire of China* (excerpts), London: Olive Payne, 1738, spelling edited and modernized by Robert Launay.

Joseph François Lafitau, *Customs of the American Indians Compared with the Customs of Primitive Times* (excerpts), edited and translated by William Fenton and Elizabeth Moore, 2 vols., Toronto: The Champlain Society, 1974.

John Chardin, *Travels in Persia 1673–1677* (excerpts), New York: Dover Publications, 1988 (republication of London: Argonaut Press 1927), spelling edited and modernized by Robert Launay.

William Dampier, "A New Voyage round the World" (excerpts), in *A Collection of Voyages*, 4 vols., London: James and John Knapton, 1729 [online], spelling edited and modernized by Robert Launay.

William Temple, "Of Heroic Virtue" (excerpts), in *Five Miscellaneous Essays*, edited by Samuel Holt Monk, Ann Arbor, MI: University of Michigan Press, 1963.

Bernard le Bovier de Fontenelle, "Of the Origin of Fables" (complete), translated by Robert Launay.

Baron de Lahontan, *New Voyages to North America* (excerpts), reprinted from the English edition of 1703 by Reuben Thwaites, Chicago: A.C. McClurg and Co., 1905.

Montesquieu, *Persian Letters* (excerpts), translated by John Davidson, London: privately printed, 1892.

Denis Diderot, "The *Supplément au Voyage de Bougainville*" (excerpts), in *Political Writings*, translated and edited by John Hope Mason and Robert Wolker, Cambridge: Cambridge University Press, 1992.

Montesquieu, *The Spirit of Laws* (excerpts), translated by Thomas Nugent, revised and edited by J.V. Prichard, London: George Bell and Sons, 1878.

Jean-Jacques Rousseau, *A Discourse on Inequality* (excerpts), translated by Maurice Cranston, London: Penguin Books, 1984.

Voltaire, *The Philosophy of History* (excerpts), translated by Robert Launay.

Voltaire, "The A, B, C or Dialogues between A, B, C" (excerpts), in *Political Writings*, edited and translated by David Williams, Cambridge: Cambridge University Press, 1994.

Adam Smith, *Lectures on Jurisprudence* (excerpts), edited by R.L. Meek, D.D. Raphael, and P.G. Stein, Oxford: Oxford University Press, 1978.

Adam Ferguson, *An Essay on the History of Civil Society* (excerpts), Philadelphia: A. Finley, 1819.

Note on the Text

In this volume, note should be made of the following original features: in several places in the text, the translators or editors have inserted the page number of the original French or Latin text in square brackets in the English text. We have retained this as an aid to the user.

Introduction

Robert Launay

The modern discipline of anthropology emerged in the second half of the nineteenth century, heralded by a rapid spate of publications following on the heels of Charles Darwin's *Origin of Species* in 1859. In 1860, Herbert Spencer published his seminal essay "The Social Organism" outlining a comparative framework for evaluating societies in terms of their complexity. In 1861, Henry Sumner Maine's *Ancient Law* sought the foundations of Roman jurisprudence by attempting to reconstruct its predecessors, relying extensively on Sanskrit legal texts. By 1865, with the publication of books by John McLennan, John Lubbock, and E.B. Tylor, a growing corpus of texts heralded the birth of a new subject.[1]

The central premise of this body of work was hardly new: modern Europe had allegedly emerged slowly from "savage" beginnings to resemble "Oriental" societies before blossoming in the classical societies of Greece and Rome, the direct antecedents of our own mature modernity. (Fortunately, terms such as "savage" and "Oriental" have disappeared from contemporary anthropological discourse.) For example, the German philosopher Georg Wilhelm Friedrich Hegel wrote in 1830 that "Europe is absolutely the end of History, Asia the beginning."[2] Asian societies represented the furthest horizon of Hegel's attention. He had no interest whatsoever in any other part of the non-European world. "Savages" were presumably beyond the pale of History (with a capital "H") and beneath notice. What distinguished the Victorian anthropologists from their immediate predecessors such as Hegel was their dogged quest for origins. This led them to take the study of non-European societies – the more "savage" the better! – entirely seriously. Seen in this light, "other" – non-European – societies emerged as theoretically important for understanding "Society" in general.

It is this consistent emphasis on others – or, more sententiously, "the Other" – which distinguishes anthropology from other approaches to the study of society, of history, or more generally of human nature. Anthropology is not simply a discourse about others; more important, it is a theoretical discourse, insisting on the idea that it is essential to understand others if we are to understand the world, human society, and ultimately ourselves. Such a premise is by no means self-evident. René Descartes'

Discourse on Method, written in 1637, called for radical philosophical introspection; the different opinions and practices he witnessed in his youthful travels, he confessed, were only sources of confusion. Even Aristotle, who adopted a thoroughly empirical and comparative perspective in his *Politics*, restricted the scope of his inquiry to the government of city-states, drawing almost all of his examples (with the notable exception of Carthage) from the Greeks. After all, for examples of government, of society, of human nature, why look further away than home? Even so, the Victorian anthropologists were hardly the first to insist on the importance of looking afar. Moralists, historians, and of course travelers, each in different ways and for different purposes, explored the implications of human differences.

This anthology presents a small sample of this vast literature. The bulk of the selections are from early modern Europe, from the sixteenth to the eighteenth centuries. From the very beginning of the discipline, anthropologists have given some acknowledgment to their predecessors. Tylor was particularly well read in this domain, and he gave generous credit to the efforts of eighteenth-century writers, some of them now quite obscure. In 1893, as part of his doctorate, Emile Durkheim wrote a short treatise (in Latin!) on Montesquieu's contribution to the discipline of sociology. In the twentieth century, E.E. Evans-Pritchard included chapters on Montesquieu and Adam Ferguson in his unfinished history of anthropology. A.R. Radcliffe-Brown and Sol Tax credited the Jesuit Joseph Lafitau with the "discovery" of classificatory kinship terminology some hundred years before Morgan. All of these authors were engaged in the project of formulating a universal history. This project of a universal history was fundamental to the writings of nineteenth-century theorists such as Comte, Hegel, and Marx, not to mention the Victorian anthropologists. But such a project was first formulated, not in the eighteenth century, but rather two centuries before, particularly in France. Later, the project owed a tremendous debt to the Jesuits, who were responsible for educating those very Enlightenment authors who fulminated against them. The Jesuit project was not (at least primarily) to write universal history but rather to bring about universal conversion to Roman Catholicism, but the comparative approach which they adopted for this purpose was consistently integrated into currents of Enlightenment discourse.

From the sixteenth through the nineteenth centuries, a proper education required the mastery of the Latin, if not the Greek, classics. Classical antiquity was consequently central to any project of universal history. When McLennan published his book *Primitive Marriage* in 1865, critics were quick to point out that, in the absence of any mention of classical antiquity, the work was of limited relevance and interest; he retorted by publishing an article on "Kinship in Ancient Greece" the following year. Consequently, the anthology begins with two classical authors, one Greek and one Roman. This is not to suggest that they were the first to reflect on the problem of "others" and of human differences. However, they provided an invariable point of reference for subsequent European thinkers.

In between the ancient world and the Renaissance, I have included a few medieval writers. Marco Polo is justifiably a familiar name, although John Mandeville represents a very different, and for a long time just as influential, approach to a similar subject. But Europe was in every sense a backwater at the time, and I have also juxtaposed by way of comparison two North African authors: Ibn Battuta, who traveled and wrote about many of the same places as Marco Polo, as well as West Africa and the East African coast; and Ibn Khaldun who formulated a sophisticated project of universal history centuries before such a project was even conceivable in Europe.

Classical Antiquity

Herodotus, the earliest of the authors included in this collection, was simultaneously historian, moralist, and traveler. His *Histories*[3] (c. 440 BCE) relate the story of the Persian Wars, of the expeditions mounted by various Persian emperors in order to subdue a motley group of Greek city-states at odds with one another and torn by internal factional rivalries. The aim of the work is to explain how and why, against all odds, the Greeks successfully resisted the superpower in their corner of the world, an empire which had subdued Babylon and Egypt, not to mention Asia Minor (modern Turkey). In fact, various Greek city-states had also colonized Asia Minor, and this is how they ran afoul of Persian imperial ambitions. But Herodotus did not limit himself to accounts of heroic battles and (less heroic) diplomatic maneuvering. In the first few books, he described in considerable detail the various peoples and places who fell under the aegis of Persian domination, or who resisted Persian incursions: Persia, Mesopotamia, Egypt, Asia Minor, and Scythia (central Asia) among others. According to Herodotus, these descriptions were based on his own observations and investigations in the course of his extensive travels, during which he elicited accounts of the Persian Wars as well as the more distant past.

These descriptions set the stage for the events narrated in the rest of the work, but they served a broader and more important purpose: to determine what distinguished the Greeks from other peoples and allowed them to resist the Persians, whereas mighty empires such as Egypt were easily subdued. Herodotus rejected out of hand any simplistic assertion of Greek superiority over "barbarians" – a term applied to all those whose language was unintelligible, in other words, not Greek. In a famous anecdote, Herodotus deflated Greek pretensions, telling how the Persian emperor Darius confronted the Greek delegation with the Callatiae, who ate their dead rather than cremating them; the Greeks were predictably appalled, but the Callatiae were just as horrified by the funeral practices of the Greeks. Everyone, Darius (and Herodotus) concluded, is convinced that their own customs are the best. By and large, Herodotus declined to judge the customs of others. Somewhat puckishly, he catalogued all the ways in which Egyptian practices ran contrary to those of the rest of the world, but he did not condemn or even disparage the Egyptians in the process.

Clearly, Herodotus was fascinated by the sheer diversity of human customs. As the anecdote suggests, he was particularly attentive to funeral practices, describing Egyptian techniques of mummification in considerable detail. In a similar vein, he systematically noted various forms of worship, detailing the sorts of temples found among various peoples, the nature of the priesthood, and modes of ritual observances, especially sacrifice. More broadly, he related dynastic histories, sexual mores, marriage practices, and any other particularities which caught his attention. His account of matrilineal kinship and inheritance among the Lycians of Asia Minor – for Herodotus, simply one more example in his panoply of the variety of customs – was of particular interest among eighteenth- and, above all, nineteenth-century theorists. For the Jesuit Father Lafitau (see below), the fact that the Iroquois had a similar kinship system suggested a common origin, the hypothesis that native Americans were Lycians who had migrated through Asia across Siberia to the Americas. In 1861, J.J. Bachofen, a contemporary of the Victorian anthropologists, contended that the Lycian example demonstrated that the Greeks and

other European peoples had passed through a matrilineal stage before acceding to
the (supposedly) superior institutions of patriarchy.

Of the various peoples Herodotus described, his accounts of Egypt and Scythia were
especially elaborate. Aside from the fact, according to Herodotus, both peoples were
particularly averse to adopting foreign customs, they otherwise embodied two opposite
poles in the spectrum of human diversity. The Egyptians were an ancient – for
Herodotus, the oldest – empire. (The Persians were very recent upstarts.) Their monuments were remarkable; Herodotus was predictably impressed by the pyramids.
However different they may have been from the Greeks, Herodotus clearly admired
their wisdom and their piety. The Scythians, on the other hand, were pastoral nomads.
As Herodotus noted, they moved their houses with them. For Greeks whose cultural
and political life centered on the *polis*, the city-state, such impermanence was thoroughly unsettling. Yet, precisely because of their mobility, the Scythians were the only
people aside from the Greeks who successfully repelled all Persian attempts to subdue
them, defeating two separate expeditions and killing one Persian emperor in the process. The Egyptians, however wise and venerable, were no match for the Persian army.
Admittedly, this polarity between great urban empires on one hand, the unsettled (and
unsettling) ways of nomads on the other, was only implicitly sketched by Herodotus.
The descriptions of Egypt and Scythia appear in separate sections of the *Histories*.
There is little reason to believe that it was his intention to contrast these particular
peoples to one another. Yet this polarity was, in one form or another, to dominate
European ways of thinking about others until the nineteenth century, if not until now.

Herodotus' anecdote about the Greeks and the Callatiae, along with his matter-of-
fact manner of narrating radical differences in customary practice, has sometimes
been interpreted as an early example of cultural relativism, of the doctrine that one
should never judge one culture from the standpoint of another. Herodotus was nothing if not a moralist, and the *Histories* are full of anecdotes meant to convey a specific
message. This particular anecdote is too often taken out of its context, which recounts
the madness of the Persian emperor Cambyses. Cambyses had deliberately destroyed
Egyptian temples. Was his affliction punishment from the gods, or was he already
mad to tear temples down? For Herodotus, however differently people worshiped the
gods, these gods still punished misdeeds, especially impiety. "Custom" – funeral rites,
sacrificial rituals, even rules of marriage and inheritance – was morally neutral for
Herodotus. However fascinating, it was irrelevant in evaluating the moral superiority
of one people over another. Rather, the domain of politics and government determined the moral worth of different peoples. The cruel antics of Cambyses were symp-
tomatic of a system of despotism, where subjects were subjected, in every sense of the
word, to the whims of the ruler, even a madman. In a broader sense, the pretensions
of an absolute ruler already constituted a form of madness, the overweening pride
which the Greeks called *hubris*, and which, sooner or later, would bring down the
vengeance of the gods. Greek citizens, on the other hand, were subject to the rule of
law. (However, many residents of a city-state might not be citizens; indeed, Herodotus
himself, a native of Halicarnassus in Asia Minor, lived as a foreigner, and not as a
citizen, in Athens.) It is precisely, he suggested, because the rule of law granted freedom to citizens that the Greeks were prepared to mount such a heroic resistance.

But this rule of law was not simply a feature of the Greek character. Aside from
describing the dizzying variety of customs around the Mediterranean, the *Histories*
relate how Greek city-states, most notably Athens, liberated themselves from the

rule of "tyrants," military strong men who ruled as dictators. Freedom and the rule of law were subject to threats from within the city-state just as much as from empires abroad. They could be achieved and maintained only through hard, painful, and often heroic struggle. If, for Herodotus, "custom" was irrelevant for determining the worth of Greeks as compared to "barbarians," this was because such an emphasis on custom would lead to a conviction of the intrinsic superiority of the Greeks. Ultimately, Herodotus' vision, while it was a celebration of the Greek victory over the Persians, also contained the seeds of a deeper pessimism about the sustainability of the very freedom which allowed their victory.

Herodotus was probably not the first and certainly not the last author in classical antiquity to describe different, "barbarian" societies in detail, though – at least in terms of writings that have survived – he undoubtedly remains the most comprehensive and thoughtful. Among the Romans, Julius Caesar left a cursory and self-serving description of the Gauls in his account of their conquest in 58 BCE. Somewhat later, in 98 CE, the Roman historian **Tacitus** wrote a short volume on the Germans[4] which ultimately served as the pre-eminent model of the genre among modern Europeans from the sixteenth to the nineteenth centuries. (The intelligentsia of early modern Europe invariably read Latin, but much more rarely ancient Greek. Herodotus was already available in translation in the sixteenth century, but Roman authors, Tacitus among them, were an essential part of their educational curriculum in adolescence.)

Tacitus' description of the Germans was admittedly somewhat peripheral to his historical writing, which related the first two centuries of the Roman Empire. Tacitus' wry irony made it clear, in his sardonic account of the vices of the Roman emperors, that he did not consider this history a particularly glorious one. Along with other historians writing in the early years of the empire, he was a member of the senatorial elite who deplored their political marginalization. They harbored a nostalgia for the bygone glories of the Roman Republic. For Romans, Germans were the arch-barbarians, those who, unlike the Celtic Gauls, Britons, and Iberians, successfully resisted conquest. (Rome established a series of colonies along the Rhine – the city of Cologne takes its name from the Latin *colonia* – but most of German territory remained outside of Roman control.) Tacitus' account was remarkably sympathetic to the Germans, a luxury he could afford. In his day, the Germans were not yet a direct menace to Rome, though they could still, for time to time, inflict crushing (and embarrassing) defeats on Roman legions. Granted, Tacitus' Germans were far from perfect. They shirked from hard labor, drank to excess, and gambled recklessly. On the other hand, they were unflinchingly courageous in battle, steadfastly honest, generous, free from avarice, and faithful to their spouses. In other words, for Tacitus, the Germans came far closer to incarnating the old Roman republican virtues than did his own Roman contemporaries. As with Herodotus, the "barbarians" constituted a vantage point for Tacitus to evaluate the moral worth of his own society, though Tacitus' savage irony precluded the kind of impartiality which Herodotus proclaimed.

Europeans and Muslims in the Middle Ages

The encroachment of the "barbarians" in the centuries that followed rendered an attitude like that of Tacitus untenable. The removal of the Roman Empire's capital to Constantinople, the dissolution of the Western empire, and the rise of Islam, while they never left Western Europe entirely isolated, certainly relegated it to the very periphery, with the notable exceptions of Muslim lands, Spain and (initially) Sicily. When Western Europe began to expand economically and demographically in the eleventh century, its interest in the rest of the world initially took the form of the Crusades, though the rival maritime powers of Venice and Genoa were quick to seize on the commercial advantages of trade with the rest of the world. It is no accident that the most famous travel book of the Middle Ages, **Marco Polo**'s account of his travels[5] (1298), was the work of a Venetian. It is important to point out that his was hardly the first such book, nor even the first description of Cathay. The sudden and spectacular expansion of the Mongols in the thirteenth century was simultaneously a cause for alarm and for optimism in Western Europe. After all, aside from China – at the time well beyond the European purview – it was the Muslim heartlands which felt the brunt of the Mongol incursions. The Papacy, envisioning the conversions of the Mongol lords to Christianity, imagined that the Islamic realms would thus be caught in a vice. Various friars – William of Rubruck, Odoric of Pordenone, John of Plano Carpini – were sent as emissaries and missionaries, and they left relatively detailed accounts of their travels. Their accounts were in Latin, for all intents and purposes accessible only to churchmen and clerks.

Marco Polo's account, by contrast, was written in the vernacular, in French – not Italian – the international courtly language of the time. It was the product of the accidental collaboration between Marco Polo, then prisoner of the Genoese, and Rustichello of Pisa, author of (apparently mediocre) medieval romances, who rightly saw in Marco's story his greatest opportunity to produce a "bestseller." As such, the work was one of the very first travel books of the Middle Ages to be explicitly aimed at a lay audience. If certain of the book's details are the products of Rustichello's literary imagination, many of the descriptions are convincing as eyewitness accounts. The work is remarkably free from moralizing, although this is also true of some of Marco's predecessors, for example, William of Rubruck. The tone alternates between deadpan descriptions and a sense of wonder at the marvels of a radically foreign world. This world included both pastoral nomads (the Mongols, notably) and vast empires; China was far larger, wealthier, more populous, and safer to travel than anywhere in Europe, or even in the European imagination. Indeed, Marco earned the nickname "Marco millions" on his return, on the suspicion that his description of China must have been radically exaggerated. However, what was unexpected for Marco's audience is very different from nowadays. Marco's claim that he saw a unicorn (perhaps a rhinoceros?) came as no surprise to his readers; this was precisely the sort of marvel to be found at the ends of the earth. On the other hand, the claim that the Chinese used paper money rather than gold and silver, and that ordinary townspeople actually ate meat and fish at the same meal,[6] were considered frankly incredible.

Sir John Mandeville's travels[7] (c. 1356), although they were also written in French for a lay audience and included accounts of a journey to Cathay and the Indies, were radically different from Marco Polo's. First of all, it is not certain that Mandeville ever existed, in which case he can hardly have traveled to any of the places he described. Many, if not all, of the details in his book can be traced to other sources. For many contemporaries, this actually made Mandeville's book seem more reliable; the details could actually be confirmed in other accounts, although this included cannibal giants with only one eye (shades of Homer!), men who hopped about on one leg, or people without heads whose faces were on their chest. Even so, the author (or authors) of the book was certainly convinced that this portrayal of the world was fundamentally accurate. This world, by the way, was round (educated people in the Middle Ages were not flat earthers!). Jerusalem was both at the center and the apex of the globe. The first half of the book relates the journey to the Holy Land, the second from Jerusalem to the Indies and to Cathay – in other words, from one end of the world to the center, and from there to the opposite end. The people at this other end were our opposites in every sense. Note that, as in *Gulliver's Travels* (did Jonathan Swift read Mandeville?), this presents a conundrum: they might be much bigger or much smaller, much richer or much poorer, much better or much worse. Mandeville explored all these and other ways in which humans could be different but, unlike Marco, with a moral edge. Marco wrote at the end of the thirteenth century, at the tail end of a long period of European prosperity and expansion. By Mandeville's time in the middle of the fourteenth century, Europe was in the midst of a dismal economic, political, religious, and demographic crisis. With the onset of a mini-ice age, global cooling resulted in failed harvests and recurrent cycles of famine. Saint John of Acre, the last stronghold of the Crusaders in the Holy Land, fell to the Muslims. The Popes left Rome to settle in Avignon. The Hundred Years' War between England and France began. Worst of all, the bubonic plague ravaged Europe (and the Muslim lands as well), killing off as much as a fourth of the population. For Mandeville, the situation was the direct result of Christendom's spiritual disintegration. As a masterful touch of irony, he put his virulent critique in the mouth of the Sultan of Egypt. The splendor of Cathay and the order that reigned there, but also the virtuous ascetic piety of the Indian "Bragmins," served as bitter reminders that pagans and even Muslims (but not Jews!) might be worthier than Christians.

The Muslim contemporaries of Marco Polo and Mandeville were far more centrally located within the global economy of the Eastern Hemisphere. **Ibn Battuta**'s extensive travels[8] (1356–1358) took him even further afield than Marco Polo – and, it might be added, he could write them down himself. As a jurist, a man of learning, he was at home anywhere within the Muslim world. He was a member of an extensive Islamic network. In China, he met a fellow Moroccan whose brother he later ran across in West Africa. Compared to the view from Europe, it was a small world indeed. His learning qualified him for employment in any of the Muslim courts he might visit, usually a great advantage – unless, of course, he fell out of favor with the ruler. Even in China, there existed a large Muslim community of merchants who welcomed him, though by his own admission he felt less at ease in a non-Muslim realm. Still, his description of China is remarkably matter-of-fact. Like Marco Polo, he was struck by the circulation of paper currency and the use of coal for heating. Both Marco Polo and Ibn Battuta visited the bustling city of Kinsai (modern Hangzhou); I have included both descriptions for the purposes of comparison.

Ibn Khaldun's voluminous *The Muqaddimah* (1377),[9] his philosophy of history, is a remarkable work, not only for its time but for any era. In it, he theorized the dichotomy between pastoral nomads and urban monarchies, a dichotomy only sketched out by Herodotus and noted in passing by Marco Polo. These different ways of life entailed different values and behaviors. Pastoral nomadism required personal courage and fortitude as well as an ethos of group feeling, a fierce attachment to bonds of kinship in order to mobilize warriors for offense and defense. Urban life, on the other hand, fostered specialization, the development of sophisticated craftsmanship and of learning, at the expense of group solidarity. In urban societies, warfare, too, was the business of specialists. These differences, he speculated, accounted for the life span of dynasties. When nomads managed to unite, they were poised to overthrow the reigning dynasty, protected only by professional soldiers rather than by the majority of subjects. Once the new rulers acceded to power, they adapted to urban ways in a few generations, coming to resemble the very dynasty they had overthrown and setting the stage for the next wave of nomads. Ibn Khaldun's project had no immediate successors, either in the Muslim world or in Europe. It was to be another two centuries before Europeans would, in very different circumstances, begin to elaborate their own schemes of universal history.

The Renaissance

By the sixteenth century, European constructions of time and space had altered radically. Most obviously, the "discovery" of the New World and the opening of a sea route around the Cape of Good Hope to South and East Asia meant that Europeans no longer occupied the periphery of the world. Jerusalem forever lost its place at the center of the universe in favor of a far more Eurocentric vision, graphically embodied in Mercator's maps. At the same time, humanists, first in Italy and later throughout Western Europe, "discovered" classical antiquity. Of course, Medieval Europeans were well aware of the Greeks and Romans: Aristotle, Alexander the Great, and a motley assortment of Roman emperors are all mentioned by Mandeville. But for Mandeville and his contemporaries, Greece and Rome were part of a broader generic "past," more pious and heroic but otherwise not very different from the present. For the humanists, the achievements of the Greeks and Romans in the domains of learning, the arts, and even (despite the fact that they were "pagans"!) in morality were unsurpassed if not unsurpassable. The adoption of the printing press in the mid-fifteenth century made such classical learning accessible to an ever greater number of people. At the same time, it fostered the development of a burgeoning literature of travel to distant places. Literature of discovery became such a popular genre that it quickly gave rise to whole anthologies, the first edited by Ramusio in Venice (1550–1559), followed by De Bry (beginning in 1590) in Germany and Hackluyt in England (1598–1600). Last but not least, printing also enabled the spread of the Reformation. Books were still a luxury, but they ceased to be very literally precious commodities. The idea that every Christian believer should own a copy of the Holy Bible in his or her own language, which he (or even she) could read and interpret without the aid of the clergy, was hardly conceivable without printing.

These developments also provoked new divisions in Europe, pitting Catholic and Protestant camps against one another as well as fostering rival imperial ambitions with the aim of controlling strategically important commerce with the Americas and with Asia. These divisions were felt particularly in France, where Protestant and Catholic factions vied for influence and whose imperial pretensions initially lagged far behind those of Spain and Portugal. Admiral Coligny, one of the principal leaders of the Huguenots, attempted to address both problems simultaneously by establishing a colony, Antarctic France, in what is now Brazil, in the bay of modern Rio de Janeiro, under the noses of the Portuguese. French traders had already established a foothold in the region, specializing in the export of Brazil wood, a tropical wood used to produce a red dye. These traders, much like the *voyageurs* in Canada a century or two later, settled down among the local population, learning the language, taking native wives, and establishing alliances with "friendly" Tupi villages. In 1555, Coligny sent vice-admiral Nicolas Durand de Villegaignon, a man he considered sympathetic to the Huguenot cause, to establish the colony. Villegaignon's puritan views led him to condemn all sexual relations between French men and Tupi women on pain of death, radically alienating the established traders, not to mention his all-male crew. He promptly sent off to Jean Calvin in Geneva for a contingent of impeccably moral Protestant families to set a good example. Once the Protestants arrived, Villegaignon engaged them in a vitriolic theological dispute, resulting in the execution of a few of the Protestants. The others fled, taking refuge for a year among the local Tupi until they found a passage back to France. Even though the Tupi were cannibals, the Protestants found them considerably more congenial than Villegaignon. Under conditions such as these, it is hardly surprising that the colony was a short-lived experiment.

Years later, in the midst of the long and bloody Wars of Religion in France (1562–1598), **Jean de Léry**, one of these Protestants, published his account of the Tupi (1578) among whom he had sojourned.[10] While this was not the only published description of the native Brazilians, it stands out not only for the wealth of detail but for its sympathetic yet unsentimental appreciation of Tupi culture. A few years later, **Michel de Montaigne** devoted one of his *Essays* (1580) – a literary genre he invented – to a short description of the Tupi.[11] He deliberately and provocatively labeled them "cannibals," a term usually reserved for the enemies of the French, who allegedly harbored a vicious taste for human flesh. Their allies, called "anthropophagi," only ate their enemies as a form of revenge, a perfectly respectable motive, fully consistent with the code of honor characteristic of Renaissance nobility. Montaigne ironically compares the "cannibals" to his own society, which was still in the throes of a civil war fought over theological issues which, he wryly noted in another essay, few of the combatants actually understood. Montaigne played with the meanings of "barbarian" and "savage." He pointed out that, among the ancient Greeks, "barbarian" originally meant "foreign." He suggested that his own society was far more barbaric – cruel and immoral – than cannibal "barbarians," and that difference is not necessarily a sign of inferiority. Similarly, the word "*sauvage*" in French can mean either "savage" or "wild"; the undomesticated "savages," he suggests, are far closer to Nature than we are. For Montaigne, the "cannibals," like the Greeks and the Romans, constituted yardsticks by which we could measure the depths of our own mediocrity.

In fact, the French Wars of Religion not only pitted Protestants against Catholics. The Catholics themselves were bitterly divided, and the ultra-Catholic League rose in open revolt against King Henry III, at one point driving him out of Paris, on the grounds that his party was seeking a compromise. This dismal state of affairs led to a radically new project in the fields of law and history, in an attempt to free them from the domain of theology and thus the hegemony of the Catholic Church. Such a project was obviously attractive to Huguenot intellectuals, but also to Catholics in the King's party anxious to maintain their distance from Rome. It was inspired by the work of fifteenth-century Italian humanists, who had critiqued medieval scholastic law, predicated on the existence of a single universal code of law, compiled in the reign of the emperor Justinian (from 527–565 CE). Paradoxically, to the extent that the meaning of key Latin terms was obscure, medieval jurists were able to interpret the law in different, indeed contradictory, ways. The humanists, in their attempt to use their knowledge of philology to clarify the meaning of the law, came instead to the conclusion that it was a hopeless hodgepodge. Based on differences in style and vocabulary in different parts of the text, they were able to demonstrate that this supposedly unitary law was a collage of edicts promulgated at different times under different circumstances for different purposes. A century later, French theorists carried this critique a step further. One Huguenot historian suggested that the idea that a single law could be applicable in all times and places was as absurd as the suggestion that a single medicine could cure all illnesses.[12] From these premises, there emerged a project of comparative history for the purposes of determining which institutions were appropriate under which circumstances.

Arguably the most brilliant of these historical and legal thinkers was **Jean Bodin**[13] (1530–1596), best known for his elaboration of the modern concept of sovereignty. Among his other accomplishments was an unpublished (and, at the time, thoroughly unpublishable) series of dialogues in which seven sages, each an adherent of a different religion (a Catholic, a Lutheran, a Calvinist, a Jew, a Muslim, a skeptic, and an adherent of "natural religion"), debate theology with one another, with no single speaker ever gaining the upper hand. (Bodin also published a tract *On the Demonology of Witches*, in which he argued that witchcraft was real and witches should be eliminated; atheists were also beyond the scope of his tolerance.) Bodin's comparative framework, first elaborated in his *Method for the Easy Comprehension of History* (1566) relied heavily on the theory of climates, a legacy from Aristotle which held considerable sway until the end of the eighteenth century if not later. Cold climates, he argued, caused the body to generate internal warmth, stimulating physical size, strength, manual dexterity, and the capacity to drink like a fish. External heat generated smaller, weaker bodies with little tolerance for alcohol. However, since the mind developed in inverse proportion to the body, people in colder climates tended to be dull-witted and brutish while southerners were clever, but apt to compensate for their physical weakness by devising crafty and underhanded schemes. Residents of temperate climates, intelligent enough to formulate wise policies and strong enough to implement them, were the ideal rulers.

Not surprisingly, thinkers who employ this perspective always situate themselves in the temperate zone, and Bodin was no exception. However, his formulation was anything but mechanically Eurocentric. In the first place, European powers were divided among climactic zones, with Germany an example of a "cold" society and Spain of a "hot" one. Significantly, Bodin, who read widely in the contemporary literature of travel as well as in history, extended the temperate zone from France through Asia, including Turkey, Persia, and China in the optimal zone. But Bodin's scheme was further complicated by the assertion that, just as the mind is superior to the body, so hot climates are superior to cold ones, as the birthplace of all philosophies and religions. He noted with approval the religiosity of Abyssinia (modern Ethiopia) and Morocco. He was far more disparaging of Germany than of Asia and Africa (though, unlike Montaigne, he was distinctly unimpressed by Native Americans); the Holy Roman Empire, he commented, bore no comparison to Abyssinia or China. Even so, he admitted that Germany and even Scandinavia had produced notable scholars, showing that the effects of climate were never absolutely determinate.

The project of writing universal history was ultimately responsible for a letter in 1604 from the Huguenot historian **La Popelinière**[14] (1541–1608) to his colleague Joseph Scaliger in Holland that contains the first grant proposal in the history of anthropology. La Popelinière lamented that accounts of distant lands, whether American "savages" or Asiatic civilizations, were the products of unschooled observers, adventurers with other preoccupations than the disinterested pursuit of knowledge. He asked Scaliger to put in a good word with the Dutch East India Company so that he might accompany them abroad on a mission far worthier (in his opinion!) than base mercantile pursuits. Predictably, his proposal fell on deaf ears.

The Jesuit Contribution

The promising and ambitious project of comparative history found little echo in the seventeenth century. With the rise of absolute monarchies, rulers were hardly sympathetic to theories which suggested that different forms of government might be suited to different times and places. They much preferred to assert the Divine Right of Kings and to suggest that their legitimacy rested on invariant grounds; but even such influential theorists as Thomas Hobbes (1588–1679) and John Locke (1632–1704), whose theories of the social contract contradicted any notion of divine right, framed their arguments in terms of deductive principles rather than taking into account the variety of human societies.

The Jesuits were the unlikely torch bearers of the comparative approach in the seventeenth century, though of course their aims were radically different from the sixteenth-century jurists and historians. The Jesuits were ultimately concerned with converting unbelievers, whether Protestants in Europe or the various peoples of Asia and the Americas. (With the important exception of Ethiopia, Africa was largely outside their purview.)

The Jesuits were not by any means the only order concerned with converting the rest of the world of unbelievers. However, perhaps because the Jesuit order was so new – it was established by Ignatius de Loyola (1491–1556) in 1540 – its methods differed significantly from their established rivals, such as the Franciscans and Dominicans. In Mexico, where the Jesuits were latecomers, Diego de Landa, Bernardino de Sahagun, and Diego Duran had already compiled extensive information about the civilizations which they were attempting to evangelize. They demonstrated an impressive command of the local languages, Maya and Nahuatl, and also a remarkable knowledge of native society, especially religion. Some of them felt deep sympathy for the native population; Sahagun even compiled and translated an account of the Spanish conquest in Nahuatl, from the Mexican point of view. However, their ultimate goal was to understand the local religion in order to suppress it thoroughly, to recognize it even in concealed form. (Even so, pre-Columbian practices survived by being incorporated into Mexican Catholic ritual, for example, on the Day of the Dead.) Their rich descriptions were only contained in manuscripts, for the eyes only of fellow missionaries or, occasionally, of powerful patrons back home.

The Jesuits, on the other hand, almost immediately seized on the advantages of publishing their accounts. Their descriptions capitalized on the popularity of travel literature, served as propaganda. They sought to stir the hearts of young men (the Jesuits, unlike other orders, had no female counterparts) to join the order and devote their lives to the missionary endeavor. At the same time, they also aimed at the pocketbooks of older and wealthier potential patrons; such patrons could also intercede on their behalf in European courts. Thus, in the sixteenth century, the Jesuit **José de Acosta** published the fullest and most influential account of the empires of Mexico and Peru, *Natural and Moral History of the Indies*[15] (1590). If he and other Jesuits were largely responsible for collecting information about Peru, his description of Mexico relied mostly on materials which the Franciscans had gathered, but had disdained from publishing. Acosta, like his Franciscan colleagues, characterized much of indigenous religion as the work of the Devil. But there were aspects of these religions, especially the belief in a supreme creator, that Acosta acknowledged as divinely inspired, and on which the Catholic missions could build. Even more important, Acosta suggested that missionaries needed to adapt different strategies to different kinds of populations, that they could not use the same approaches towards the subjects of powerful and sophisticated empires such as Mexico and Peru as towards the "savage" Chichimecs, for example, of the northern deserts of Mexico. While he conceded that "savages" might need to be converted by force, he countered that peoples such as the Mexicans and Peruvians had to be swayed by persuasion. It was precisely for the purposes of effective persuasion that the Jesuits needed to understand the societies in which they operated. These were the strategies that the Jesuits were to employ in India and in China, in North and in South America, all the while publishing descriptions of these distant societies while painting the missionaries in a heroic light.

The operations of the Jesuit missions in New France (modern Quebec) and in China are cases in point. Originally, the evangelization of New France had been confided to the Recollets, a branch of the Franciscans. As their numbers were insufficient, they called on the Jesuits for reinforcement, a move they were later to regret bitterly. When the British briefly took control over the colony, all French missionaries were expelled. When France regained control, the Jesuits managed to obtain exclusive rights to preach there. Unlike the Recollets, the Jesuits immediately set out to publish annual *Relations*, accounts of the triumphs and tribulations of the mission in the form of letters.

Among the earliest of these relations is the account of **Paul Le Jeune**, the mission's first superior, of his attempt to follow a Montagnais hunting band in the winter of 1634.[16] He camped with a band led by the brother of a young man, Pierre Pastedechouan, who had been converted to Christianity and sent to France to be educated. The Jesuits expected that he would return to New France and teach them his language. However, dissatisfied by his treatment, he abandoned his new faith and returned to live with his brother, earning him the epithet "the Apostate" in Le Jeune's relation. Le Jeune was particularly anxious to avoid another brother of "the Apostate," a shaman he called "the Sorceror" and who was Le Jeune's rival for the spiritual leadership of the group. To Le Jeune's great dismay, "the Sorceror" joined the group anyway. The winter was a particularly hard one, with some bands actually starving to death, and Le Jeune provided a particularly vivid account of how a hunting band could cope under such difficult circumstances. His relationship with the Montagnais was tortuous. He admired their intelligence, the richness of the language, their generosity, and their heroic stoicism in the face of adversity. But he deplored their tendency to make a mockery of everything, especially because he was usually the butt of their jokes and insults. His account is particularly rich in examples of how the natives, especially "the Sorceror," talked back. For example, Le Jeune, who (unlike later Jesuits) misunderstood the basis of matrilineal kinship, taunted "the Sorceror" by suggesting that his sister's sons were his heirs only because he could never be certain of his wife's fidelity. "The Sorceror" aptly retorted that the French ungenerously loved only their own children, while the Montagnais loved them all. A century later, such exchanges would provide a literary model for dialogues between "savages" and Europeans, where the "savages" consistently got the upper hand.

Le Jeune's experience that winter led him to the conclusion that attempts to convert nomadic hunters were a lost cause unless they could be compelled to settle down. Le Jeune had higher hopes for the mission of his colleague, Jean de Brébeuf, among the settled Huron, the principal allies of the French in the region and middlemen in the fur trade. Although the mission to the Huron eventually met with considerable success, the Huron were ultimately massacred or driven out by their Iroquois enemies and rivals.

At the same time, the Jesuits were also attempting to gain a foothold in China. As among the Montagnais and the Huron, they were determined to integrate themselves into Chinese society, although their movements were closely restricted by Chinese officialdom. Initially, they sought to emulate the appearance and behavior of Buddhist monks, the closest approximation they could find to Catholic priests. As it turned out, Buddhist monks were not very highly regarded in Chinese society, and this was not an effective way to win friends and influence people in high places. At the beginning of the seventeenth century, Matteo Ricci had the insight that it would be more profitable to adopt the manner and the mannerisms of the mandarins, the Chinese literati who occupied the ranks of officialdom. Undaunted by the prospect of mastering the Confucian classics so thoroughly that he could enter into conversations with Chinese scholars on an equal footing, Ricci earned the respect of the elite so effectively that the Jesuits at last gained access to the Imperial Throne. (The Emperor was not actually present on that occasion, but this was still an especially high honor, and a token of his influence at court.) The rivals of the Jesuits – initially the Franciscans and Dominicans, later the French Missions Etrangères (Foreign Missions) – accused them of making unacceptable compromises in order to win elite converts. They called into question the appropriateness of the Jesuit translation of "God" and, perhaps more aptly, their condoning of rites commemorating Confucius, not to mention the ancestors, rites which were obligatory for Chinese officials, Christian or not. The Quarrel of the Chinese Rites reached the attention of the Pope as well as Louis XIV of France. **Louis Le Comte**'s elaborate description of China (1697)[17] was intended as a polemical defense of the Jesuit position. Like many of his predecessors, he nearly made a saint of Confucius and argued that the rites honoring him as well as lineage ancestors were just tokens of respect, not a form of worship. (Indeed, the book was condemned by the Sorbonne for certain of its passages about Chinese religion.)

For Le Comte and the Jesuits, the longevity and stability of the Chinese Empire (dynastic revolutions notwithstanding) were absolutely remarkable, dwarfing the achievements of Rome, until then the unchallenged European yardstick for durability. In fact, this longevity was theologically embarrassing. Chinese chronicles dated the Empire to before the beginning of the world, according to accepted Biblical calculations. Worse yet, this account was accompanied by dates for solar and lunar eclipses which Jesuit astronomers and mathematicians could verify, leading the Jesuits to readjust their assessment of the world's creation in order to fit the Chinese data. Le Comte's suggestion that the underpinnings of this stability are the rules which govern everyday behavior, notably codes of filial piety and politeness, is an early example of sophisticated sociological reasoning.

The Jesuit descriptions of the peoples whom they were attempting to convert were very widely read in Europe, well beyond the confines of Roman Catholic believers. The seventeenth-century German philosopher Gottfried Wilhelm Leibniz, for example, Protestant though he was, corresponded actively with the Jesuits about China and actively took their side in the Rites controversy.[18] These contrasting portraits of the "savages" of New France, on one hand, the vast and stable empire of China, on the other, clearly demarcated the poles of European discourse about "others." Until the end of the eighteenth century, it was impossible to write about China without in one way or another taking the Jesuit descriptions into account. Indeed, the Jesuits continued their active program of publication until the suppression of the order in 1773. Each year, they published a carefully edited selection of *Edifying and Curious Letters* from missionaries throughout the world. These were kept in the libraries and avidly read by such major Enlightenment thinkers as Montesquieu, Turgot, and Voltaire,[19] who nonetheless employed their descriptions in order to construct thoroughly secular versions of universal history.

Partly in response to such secularist theorizing, Father **Joseph François Lafitau** undertook a religiously informed project of universal history, *Customs of the American Indians Compared with the Customs of Primitive Times*[20] (1724), basing himself on his own and his fellow Jesuits' experiences among the Iroquois. Specifically, he compared the customs of "American savages" to those of the "earliest times" – that is to say, peoples described in the Bible or by the Greeks and the Romans. (Lafitau accepted Biblical chronology. For him, such peoples were indeed very "early" in the history of the universe.) He stressed the parallels between the matrilineal kinship system of the Iroquois and their neighbors (which Lafitau understood far more thoroughly and judiciously than Le Jeune), and that of the Lycians described by Herodotus. On these grounds, he suggested that the New World had been populated by migrations from Eurasia across Siberia into North America, a hypothesis unjustly ridiculed by Voltaire.

Lafitau's contention was that, in the earliest beginnings, human institutions followed divine laws, but that only the Hebrews, the Chosen People, kept the memory of these laws intact. Among the world's other peoples, these laws suffered distortion and degeneration, though not without retaining a significant residue of divine inspiration which could serve, in the end, to lead these peoples back to the truth as Lafitau understood it. This represented a very different comparative approach from that of Acosta, one and a half centuries earlier. For Acosta, the asceticism of the Aztec priests, who would endure rigorous fasts and draw copious blood by pricking themselves with maguey thorns, simply demonstrated the Devil's lack of imagination, his propensity to mimic valid religious practices for perverse purposes. For Lafitau, similar rites in the Ancient World or in North America were testimonies of the divine spark, embodying sacred truths rather than parodying them. Similarly, the scrupulous avoidance of marriage between relatives among the Iroquois was a testimonial to divine inspiration. (The ease with which they obtained divorce, on the other hand, proved that their marriage practices were still short of perfection.) His description of

Iroquois government took pains to show that, even in the absence of centralized authority, the "savages" were capable of maintaining order.

Secular Travelers

While the Jesuits adroitly exploited the European taste for travel literature, they hardly enjoyed a monopoly. The corpus rapidly expanded throughout the seventeenth and eighteenth centuries, generating new and ever fatter anthologies. Many of these books were translated with amazing rapidity, especially into English, French, German, and Dutch. For instance, Samuel Johnson's literary career began with a commission to produce an English translation of a French translation of the Portuguese account of the journey of the Jesuit friar Jeronimo Lobo to Ethiopia. Many of these works contained substantial information – or misinformation – about the lands and peoples visited (sometimes very briefly, sometimes for much longer periods of time). However, in spite of La Popelinière's impassioned plea, there was no travel simply for the purpose of gathering information, whether geographical, geological, botanical, zoological, or anthropological, until the second half of the eighteenth century, with the Pacific voyages of Bougainville and Captain Cook.

It is only possible to include a few examples from this voluminous literature. **John Chardin** was a Huguenot jeweler who traveled from France through Turkey and the Caucasus to Persia. His clients included the Sultan of Persia, but also Louis XIV. His description of Persia[21] (1686) was long considered authoritative, and it was one of Montesquieu's principal sources for his *Persian Letters* as well as for *The Spirit of Laws*. Though he provided a quite comprehensive description of Persia, it was his depiction of Persia as a despotic society under the arbitrary rule of the Sultan that most fired the theoretical imaginations of Montesquieu among others.

William Dampier was perhaps the most colorful of all the seventeenth-century travelers, beginning his career as a buccaneer in the Caribbean before sailing around the world, sometimes by jumping ship or even by mutiny. He was a keen observer and a vivid writer. His *A New Voyage Round the World* (1697)[22] furnished descriptions of all sorts of peoples, ranging from native Australians (New Holland was the name for the northern part of Australia at the time) to the realm of Tonkin (the northern part of Viet Nam). His attitude was by and large quite broad-minded and often skeptical. Narrating how he jumped ship and escaped to an island whose inhabitants had a reputation for ferocity, he explains why he suspected such accounts were exaggerated; he noted that, in his travels, reports alleging that peoples were cannibals had turned out to be erroneous, and he even expressed doubts about the very existence of the practice.

Ancients and Moderns

The comparative project initially formulated by French historians in the sixteenth century lay dormant for most of the seventeenth century, but it was revived in rather unusual circumstances by the recital of a long poem to the French Academy in 1687. Charles Perrault, now best known for his charming and witty volume of *Mother*

Goose Tales, shocked part of the audience by suggesting that the accomplishment of France under Louis XIV had even surpassed those of the ancient Greeks and Romans. The ensuing polemic, the Quarrel of the Ancients and the Moderns, excited the enthusiasm of the leading literary and intellectual personalities of France and ultimately England on one side or the other.[23]

Bernard le Bovier de Fontenelle, a brash young author, vigorously defended the claims of the Moderns. Though not a scientist himself, he was throughout his career a staunch proponent of scientific knowledge, committed to explaining new discoveries in ways which were not only comprehensible but entertaining to lay readers. For example, his *Dialogues on the Plurality of Worlds* explained the principles of Copernican astronomy in witty and elegant prose. Science, as a cumulative enterprise which developed by correcting the errors of the past, embodied the superiority of the Moderns over the Ancients. This disembodied form of knowledge was never the property of any one people. Just as the French had now surpassed the Athenians, Fontenelle playfully imagined a time in which [Native] Americans, at the forefront of scientific knowledge, would look to Europeans with misplaced reverence as Ancient sages.

On the English side, **William Temple**, an elder statesman best known as the first patron of Jonathan Swift, set out to rebut Fontenelle's essay. For Temple, knowledge was not radically disembodied. If different plants could flourish in different soils and climates, so might different ideas in different times and places. In any case, the first formulations of these ideas were the best. Not only were the Ancients superior to the Moderns, but the earliest Ancients the best of all, even if their knowledge is now lost to us because they rightly preferred oral to written transmission of knowledge. Temple even suggested that the original sources of Ancient learning lay in Asia rather than in Europe, that the true wellsprings of Ancient wisdom were to be found in India and China. This debate between Temple and Fontenelle about whether knowledge was unitary and disembodied or whether it was multiple and embedded in specific cultural and historical contexts was taken up, a century later, by Immanuel Kant and his erstwhile student Gottfried Herder;[24] arguably, it still finds echoes in some of the postmodern critiques of abstract rationality.

In an essay "Of Heroic Virtue,"[25] one of several which he published along with his rejoinder to Fontenelle in 1692, Temple demonstrated even more forcefully that the kind of admiration he harbored for the ancient Greeks and Romans extended well beyond the confines of Europe. Rejecting examples of heroic societies, not only from Greece and Rome but also from Egypt and Mesopotamia, as too familiar, he chose four more distant examples from each of the cardinal directions, north, south, east, and west. Revealingly, his examples from north and south, the Scythians (whom he considered to be the ancestors of the Norsemen) and the Arabs, were initially pastoral nomads remarkable for their extensive military conquests. From the east and the west, he chose China and Peru, great empires who, in his opinion, especially exemplified good government. Temple made it quite clear that he much preferred the virtue of good government in China and Peru to the heroism of Scythian or Arabian military conquest. It is no accident that the Scythians and Arabs were far closer to Europe than the Chinese and Peruvians. Temple, who was severely critical of his own society, clearly admired most those peoples furthest away in space, like the Peruvians or Chinese, or in time, like the ancient Greeks and Romans.

Fontenelle's essay "Of the Origin of Fables,"[26] written in the heat of the Quarrel, remained unpublished until 1724, after passions had died down. Fontenelle was certainly not the first to suggest parallels between classical mythology and that of Native Americans. The Franciscan friar Bernardino de Sahagun, for example, had categorized Aztec divinities as the Mexican Venus, Jupiter, or Hercules, lumping them all into the category of "pagan" religions, inventions of the Devil. Lafitau more generously saw such parallels as reflections of an original divine revelation, and thus products of a common origin. Fontenelle, on the other hand, sought an explanation in terms of modes of human thought, universal properties of humanity rather than inventions of God or the Devil. His suggestion that some myths were explanations of natural phenomena, which seems so horribly hackneyed to modern readers, was actually remarkably novel. Until that time, myths were perceived either as allegories or as garbled accounts of historical events. He even went so far as to suggest that myth was, like science, an attempt to explain the unknown in terms of known phenomena. At the same time, he also suggested that myth was a product of rhetoric, the fruit of the storyteller's desire to please in light of the expectations of the audience. Such embellishment, repeated and exaggerated each time the story was told anew, quickly distorted whatever true events the story may have originally told beyond all recognition. Ultimately, he used classical mythology as a weapon for ridiculing the reverence which the partisans of the Ancients lavished on the Greeks and the Romans. More generally, the survival of myths embodied for Fontenelle an uncritical acceptance of the authority of the past. In contrast, a scientific approach continually called into question its own conclusions.

Literary Others: Dialogues and Letters

The Quarrel of the Ancients and Moderns was fought out in literary genres – poems, satires, and essays. In the eighteenth century, these and other genres might take their inspiration from travel literature; Jonathan Swift's *Gulliver's Travels* and Voltaire's *Candide* parodied contemporary travel literature as a form of sharp satire. However, both of these books reflected the rules of the genre, portraying the world through the eyes of the European traveler, even as they undermined the central character's authority to understand the world he was witnessing. At the same time, there developed another means of subverting the genre of travel literature, one which purported to portray Europeans through the eyes of foreign "others."

One of the pioneers of the genre was the **Louis-Armance, Baron de Lahontan,** who served as an officer in New France at the end of the seventeenth century and published a volume of *New Voyages to North America*[27] (1703) which began as a conventional travel book only to end on a highly unusual note. The book is in three parts. The first tells the story of the author's real and exaggerated explorations. The second part, still following established conventions, is a description of the natives of New France, an amalgam of Algonquians and Huron. In this section, he furnished a sharp critique of previous missionary accounts, whether by the Jesuits or the Recollets (who had been allowed back into the colony). The Jesuits, he suggested, were all too eager to promote the success of their mission by asserting that the Indians were anxious to accept the Christian faith; the Recollets, wanting to disparage the Jesuit claims, tended to portray the Indians as recalcitrant brutes. Neither depiction, he argued, gave justice to the critical intelligence of the Indians, who would give polite (and meaningless) public assent to the missionaries while privately – if one came to know them well and earn their trust – evincing sharp skepticism, impressing Lahontan with their extraordinary ability to argue their point.

Such dialectical aptitude provided the basis for the third and most singular part of Lahontan's book, a series of dialogues between himself and Adario, "a savage of good sense and who has traveled widely." The character of Adario, it has been suggested, is loosely based on the Huron chief Kandiaronk, "the Rat." In the dialogues, the character of Lahontan is the straight man, resolutely advocating the truths of Roman Catholic Christianity and the superiority of European civilization, while Adario persistently and ruthlessly deflates all of his arguments. Of course, the character of Adario, not Lahontan, is the author's real mouthpiece. Adario is the advocate of "natural" religion and society as opposed to the artificial and debased religion and society of Europe. The Jesuits, Adario ironically suggests, are far too intelligent to believe the nonsense they tell us. Money and the desire for unnecessary luxuries are sources of corruption. Europeans need the law to punish the wicked, Adario argues, only because they are otherwise incapable of living virtuous lives as do the Algonquian and Huron; in any case, this law only provides the occasion for chicanery and for the oppression of the weak by the powerful.

These dialogues furnished a model for Enlightenment authors (Voltaire, among others) throughout much of the eighteenth century. One of the last – and perhaps the most original – was **Denis Diderot**'s *Supplement to the Voyage of Bougainville*.[28] The work, written in 1771 or 1772, remained unpublished in Diderot's lifetime, although it circulated in manuscript form in literary circles. In his youth, Diderot had been imprisoned for a few days in the dungeon of Vincennes as a result of one of his publications, an experience he was not anxious to repeat. The work is (loosely!) based on a real scientific expedition, one of the earliest, a voyage to the Pacific undertaken by Louis-Antoine de Bougainville in 1766. As a result of this journey as well as those of Captain Cook, the Polynesian islanders came to replace Native Americans as the prototype for literary "savages." Diderot focused on Bougainville's idyllic (and idealized) description of Tahiti as a kind of natural paradise, especially combined with Tahitian practices of sexual hospitality. The structure of the relatively short piece is complex, consisting of dialogues within dialogues. In the course of a conversation, two Frenchmen, A and B, turn their attention to Bougainville's travels, commenting on two (unknown) episodes in Tahiti. The first is an old man's "farewell," a bitter harangue against the French crew who have abused the generous hospitality of the Tahitians and who have claimed French sovereignty over the island. The speech is a fierce and eloquent denunciation of colonialism.

After this harangue there follows a lighter dialogue between the Tahitian Orou (who has conveniently sailed on a French ship and speaks fluent French!) and his guest, the ship's chaplain. To the chaplain's dismay, Orou offers him the companionship of his wife or one of his daughters for the night, failing to understand the grounds on which the chaplain alleges that he must refuse this hospitality. (Another of Diderot's unpublished works, a ferocious condemnation of religious celibacy, tells the story of a young woman confined against her will as a nun in a convent.) As is the convention in such dialogues, the "savage" Orou proves a far subtler dialectician than the poor chaplain, who is no match, either for Orou's rhetoric or for the charms of his wife and daughters. Orou argues for a code of "natural" sexual freedom, a code which admittedly owes a great deal more to Diderot's imagination than to Tahitian sexual mores; Orou's apology for incest is as un-Tahitian as possible! Orou's argument is remarkably utilitarian. Free love is good for the nation by providing more children to defend it and produce its wealth. In the bargain, it fosters a general love for all children rather than exclusive affection for one's own descendants. Free love, much like the free trade advocated by the French political economist François Quesnay (a contributor to Diderot's *Encyclopedia*), was a force for the general good. It is not clear how seriously Diderot took his own argument. A and B ultimately suggest that, like the chaplain, we should behave like the Tahitians in Tahiti and like the French in France.

Witty dialogues were the obvious means of putting words into the mouths of literary "savages" like Adario and Orou, advocates of a "natural" philosophy, religion, and way of life which challenged the wisdom of "civilized" society. On the other hand, the opinions of Asian characters – Turks, Persians, or Chinese for example – could just as easily be expressed as letters, a form which characterized many of the novels of the late seventeenth and of the eighteenth centuries. The first novel to express a foreign character's opinion in epistolary form was Giovanni Marana's *Letters of a Turkish Spy* (1684) whose hero comments on events in Europe while falling in love and out-witting attempts to unmask him. (The events in question were situated far enough in the past to ensure that the author would not be accused of expressing seditious opinions.)The book attempted to convey an outsider's perspective on European politics and society, although the spy's foreignness was not nearly as convincing as his disguise. Even so, the novel was extremely successful, generating several sequels and a host of imitators in England and France. These included Oliver Goldsmith's *Citizen of the World* (1760), the ruminations of a Chinese mandarin in London, and Françoise de Graffigny's strikingly original *Letters of a Peruvian Woman* (1747), which tells the story of an Inca noblewoman kidnapped by the Spanish and rescued by a dashing French naval officer who falls hopelessly in love with her. She writes letters to the man she loves and never expects to see again, first by tying knots in bits of string (a fanciful interpretation of Peruvian *quipus*) and only later, when she runs out of string, in the French which she has learned in the interim. The novel is far more successful than *The Turkish Spy* in conveying the slow and sometimes painful process of learning another culture, as the heroine slowly and hesitatingly learns her way in French society without ever giving up her own values.

However, the most famous of these exotic epistolary novels was unquestionably **Montesquieu**'s *Persian Letters*,[29] whose success quickly eclipsed Marana's. Unlike most other such novels, it is told from the point of view of several narrators, jumping back and forth between the European travels of two Persians, Usbeck and Rica, and Usbeck's harem back in Persia. The tone shifts accordingly, from a satire on European (especially French) society to philosophical musings to high melodrama. Montesquieu uses the foreignness of his urbane Persian travelers to provide a detached and ironic view of the foibles of Parisian high society. The Persian visitors, unfamiliar with French ways, manage to exoticize them, as Montesquieu adroitly turns the tables on the conventions of travel literature.

The Revival of Universal History

Enlightenment writers were not simply interested in non-European others as characters (all too often stock characters) in sophisticated literary games. Those very same thinkers – Montesquieu, Voltaire, Diderot, in particular – who playfully peopled their dialogues and novels with diverse exotic figures also devoted serious attention to non-Europeans in other contexts. Such peoples figured prominently in their different attempts to formulate a comparative philosophical history of human institutions. Just as the dialogues and letters featuring eloquent "savages" and urbane Asians provided a vehicle for casting a critical eye on European institutions, a comparative history furnished a means for evaluating modern Europe's place compared to past societies as well as to distant contemporaries.

Such a project of comparative history had its origin, as we have seen, in the sixteenth century. In the seventeenth century, its major exponent was, paradoxically enough, a churchman, Cardinal Jacques-Bènigne Bossuet, whose *Discourse on Universal History* (1681) was intended as a testimony to divine providence. A century later, Voltaire lambasted Bossuet's history for its Eurocentrism, most notably for its omission of any reference to China. Voltaire's own *Essai sur les mœurs* (1756) (which might be translated as an "Essay on Customs," bearing in mind that the "essay" consists of two thick volumes) was intended as a secular alternative to Bossuet. It is important to note that Bossuet's history, however Eurocentric, included two long chapters on Egypt and Babylon, a testimony to the enduring legacy of Herodotus, but also an indication that these two empires had yet to be fully exoticized in the European imagination. Like Greece and Rome, they remained a part of the relatively familiar realm of the Ancients. Indeed, Bossuet's comparatively flattering description of the order and stability of the Egyptian empire reads almost like a model for the court of Louis XIV.

By the eighteenth century, the project of universal history was largely secular (though, as we have seen with Lafitau, not entirely so). **Montesquieu**, in his encyclopedic *The Spirit of Laws*[30] (1748), was particularly responsible for resurrecting the project. The central contention of the work is that different kinds of societies require different kinds of laws. This, we have seen, was the very premise of the sixteenth-century French legal historians, whose ideas had remained in abeyance for over a century. The book, as Voltaire was quick to point out, was voluminous and more than occasionally disorganized, given its lofty ambitions. Montesquieu attempted to assess the impact of climate, topography and religion among other factors on the system of government. The central thread of the book, however, was a tripartite typology of governments and the different principles which animated them. Montesquieu identified these three types of governments as republics, monarchies, and despotisms. In a monarchy, the ruler was nonetheless constrained by the rule of law, whereas the despotic regime depended on the arbitrary whims of the ruler. Ideally, a republic and its laws were animated by "virtue." Montesquieu, whose *Persian Letters* had been censured by the Church, insisted that he was referring only to civic virtue, to the personal commitment of citizens to uphold the order of the republic, and not to morality in general. (Montesquieu's attempt to deflect clerical criticism was ultimately unsuccessful. The work was eventually placed on the Index of Forbidden Books.) A monarchy, on the contrary, was driven by the principle of honor, on the defense of privileges appropriate to each rank of society. Honor was, in particular, the ethos of the aristocracy, but it is important to point out that the upper ranks of the bourgeoisie could buy an aristocratic title. Such prerogatives included, not only the right to inherit judicial office but also to buy or sell it; Montesquieu himself had inherited and ultimately sold his office in order to finance his Parisian lifestyle. For Montesquieu, virtue was totally out of place in a monarchical system. As for despotisms, they were ruled by fear.

Montesquieu's paradigm of despotism was modeled on his understanding of Asian empires, notably Persia, as described by Chardin. Despite his initial assertion that each system of government needed to be understood in its own terms, he clearly considered despotic authority detestable. Despotism reduced all subjects to slavery. (Despite the fact that he was from Bordeaux, a town whose prosperity in Montesquieu's time relied as much on the slave trade as on the wine trade, he vigorously denounced the enslavement of Africans.) Its moral equivalent in terms of gender relations was the "domestic slavery" of the harem, an institution which admittedly exercised an erotic fascination in the European imagination and whose prevalence was radically exaggerated by Montesquieu and others.

Ultimately, for Montesquieu, the central question was how to counteract the dangerous concentration of power in central authority, as embodied by the monarch. For Europe, he suggested, the aristocracy constituted the only viable alternative to a republican government, which required the cultivation of civic virtue, unlikely in the France of Louis XV! In any case, it was, he argued, only sustainable in relatively small nations (like Holland and Switzerland). The ethos of status honor, with all the prerogatives it entailed, however unjust and immoral it might appear in the abstract, reinforced the power of an aristocracy which, in defense of its own privileges, could constitute a counterbalance to the abuse of centralized royal authority. Montesquieu pointed to the absence of a hereditary aristocracy in Asian "despotic" empires as evidence. If the rule of law in republics was the result of the deliberate vigilance of its citizenry, in monarchies it was the unintended consequence of the self-interested maneuvers of an aristocracy whose ranks, it should be emphasized, were never entirely closed.

Montesquieu, unlike many of his contemporaries, was quite uninterested in "savages." He declined to speculate about the origins of government in general terms, though he devoted considerable attention to the specific feudal origins of the French monarchy. In contrast, such questions were absolutely central to **Jean-Jacques Rousseau**, the other great political thinker of the French Enlightenment. In his *A Discourse on Inequality* (1753),[31] he attempted to trace the origins of private property and of government by speculating about humanity in the State of Nature. Attempts to postulate a "State of Nature" had already characterized social contract theories in the seventeenth century, specifically those of Thomas Hobbes and John Locke. For Hobbes, such a state entailed an anarchic free-for-all, an infernal war of every man against every man whose only viable remedy was the surrender of liberties to a sovereign authority. For Locke, on the other hand, the State of Nature embodied the "natural" rights to life, liberty, and property; sovereign authority was legitimate only insofar as it protected these rights.

Rousseau's portrayal was even more radical: humans in their "natural" state were entirely devoid of society and culture. Obviously, Locke's "natural" rights – indeed, any rights at all – are eminently social. Rousseau understood that even Hobbes' nightmarish vision of universal warfare was grounded in human desires to possess more than their fellows; however, the very notion of "possession," much less any accompanying desires, was also intrinsically social and cultural. Rousseau, unlike Hobbes, also understood that "savages" could not possibly exemplify a State of Nature; "savages," like us, were definitely social beings.

Obviously, despite Rousseau's eloquent plea for more judicious, philosophically informed descriptions of non-Europeans, his depiction of asocial, acultural humans living in a "natural" state could only be purely speculative. Such humans lived alone, feeding themselves and fending off wild beasts. Children left their mothers as soon as they were able, never to return nor in any way to acknowledge any enduring bond. Sexual urges were assuaged and the reproduction of the species ensured by random coupling, in the absence of any cultural criteria of beauty or even physical attractiveness. Such humans were not inclined to violence. At worst, a stronger individual would snatch a meal from a weaker fellow he met at random, but the loser would just wander off to procure a replacement. They were, of course, literally incapable of harboring grudges. They did, however, harbor a "natural" empathy for their fellows, the ability to understand in a visceral way another's suffering. Reveling in someone else's misfortune was a distinctly social vice. Most of all, they had no language, and consequently no means of transmitting any acquired knowledge from one individual, much less from one generation, to another. Any invention, any discovery, died with its discoverer. Such individuals were radically amoral, incapable of either good or evil, because morality is distinctly social. However, it also followed that they were naturally equal. Inequality, in other words, was also a social product.

Rousseau's State of Nature can be understood as a sort of thought experiment, an attempt to separate the "natural" from the social and cultural aspects of human existence. Rousseau carefully avoided any assertion that this was an attempt to reconstruct the earliest origins of humanity. On the other hand, any such assertion would have run directly afoul of clerical authorities who insisted on Biblical creation. Diderot's brief imprisonment demonstrated to his contemporaries that this could be a dangerous strategy. On the other hand, Rousseau's categorization of "savagery" as a sort of mid-point, a compromise between the State of Nature and the depravity of contemporary Europe, suggests that he may well have taken his construct of natural humanity as historically accurate. The State of Nature was, after all, one of total and radical ignorance. Savages could enjoy the real benefits of human society, not least fellowship and love, without the misery and enslavement of the poor masses, the boundless appetite for unhealthy luxuries and frivolous pastimes of the wealthy few that characterized Rousseau's world. The price of such happiness was, Rousseau also suggested, stupidity. The practice among some Native Americans of flattening the skulls of children at birth, a practice which Rousseau was convinced also stunted their mental faculties, was not necessarily baneful in his opinion. It is clear, in any case, that Rousseau never subscribed to any notion of the "noble savage," a phrase he never used.[32] Echoing Lahontan among others, Rousseau suggested that the roots of human inequality lay in private property, in the imposition of "mine" and "thine." Human "improvements" in the arts and sciences led directly to moral degeneracy. The discovery of iron technology, he suggested, was a particularly unfortunate invention, providing tools not only for increased agricultural productivity but also for warfare. Plowshares could too easily be turned into swords.

Voltaire's reputation as a thinker has certainly suffered from comparison to intellectual heavyweights like Montesquieu and Rousseau. He had no grand scheme to offer, and could easily sacrifice consistency for the sake of a *bon mot*, an elegant witticism. Yet he was a sharp and perceptive, if not always a very fair, critic of the grand schemes of his contemporaries. For example, in his *The Philosophy of History*

(1765)[33] his argument that Lafitau put far too much emphasis on superficial resemblances between ancient peoples and Native Americans in order to posit a common historical origin is absolutely sound, even if Lafitau's hypothesis that the Americas were originally peopled by Eurasians crossing through Siberia turned out to be correct. (His suggestion that the presence of humans in the New World could simply be taken for granted, on the other hand, was not particularly astute, to say the least. Worse, by suggesting a polygenetic origin of mankind, it bolstered racist ideologies.) His critique of Rousseau, echoed by many of his contemporaries, was that humans were essentially – one might even say naturally – social creatures. At the very least, this correctly implied that the earliest humans never lived in conditions approaching Rousseau's State of Nature. On the other hand, it did not necessarily invalidate the utility of Rousseau's scheme as a thought experiment, a yardstick by which to measure the costs and benefits of human material and intellectual "progress."

In any case, Voltaire, like Montesquieu but unlike Lafitau and Rousseau, was never really very interested in "savages." He was, of course, always willing to use (or misuse) "savages" for the purposes of irony. For example, he suggested that European peasants, rather than the Huron or the Iroquois, were the true "savages" – a witticism which transparently revealed Voltaire's bourgeois class biases. Elsewhere, notably in his universal history, the *Essai sur les mœurs*, he demonstrated that he was generally unimpressed by the achievements of Native Americans, except perhaps the Peruvians. But, in spite of Voltaire's real admiration for Montesquieu, his criticisms were particularly astute. He expressed them on several occasions, for example, in a philosophical dialogue between three Englishmen, A, B, and C (published in 1768).[34] In particular, Voltaire argued that there never existed any form of government such as despotism as Montesquieu had characterized it. In the first place, it was obviously impossible to administer any realm simply in accordance with the whims of a single ruler; there had to exist an administrative machinery independent of the ruler's direct control. What is more, Voltaire quite correctly pointed out that China, Persia, and Turkey, the very regimes which Montesquieu claimed embodied despotism as a system of government, were all subject to the rule of law, laws which constrained the ruler as well as his subjects. Voltaire particularly admired China, accepting the Jesuit descriptions of the empire at face value despite his virulent anticlericalism. Voltaire's critique stemmed partly from his adamant opposition to the aristocracy. For Montesquieu, the aristocracy constituted a counterweight against centralized royal authority; Voltaire, on the other hand, backed the monarchy opposition to the privileges of the aristocracy. Montesquieu considered the absence of a hereditary aristocracy in the Asian empires, to be a fatal flaw. For Voltaire, on the contrary, it constituted a powerful demonstration that aristocracy was in no way essential for good government.

In such ways, these grand visions of universal history addressed the relationship between private property and social inequality as well as the wellsprings of good and bad government. But at the same time, they reflected the personal involvement of their authors in the partisan politics of contemporary France. Similar debates took place outside France, especially in Great Britain. Of course, the nature of partisan politics was not identical; in Britain, central authority was embodied by the Prime Minister as well as (and sometimes rather than) the King. Partisan divisions were expressed in terms of "court" and "country," which only sometimes corresponded to the opposition between the Whig and Tory parties. At other times, factions within the Whig

Party opposed to the ruling clique also constituted a "country" constituency. Both Montesquieu's and Voltaire's ideas were significantly influenced by their respective journeys to England. Montesquieu drew some of his inspiration for his critique of despotic centralized authority from "country" rhetoric against the incipient tyranny of the "court" party. (The same rhetoric later underpinned the arguments of those American colonists who declared independence from British "tyranny.")

In the eighteenth century, Britain was unquestionably the greatest economic and military power in Europe, one that (in different ways) constituted a model of government and society for both Montesquieu and Voltaire. Even so, Paris remained the intellectual capital of the Enlightenment. British writers invariably took the opinions of leading French thinkers into account, all the while developing their own distinctive approach. Curiously enough, although London remained the capital of British *belles lettres*, Scotland was the most vibrant center of philosophy of all sorts, including social and political. David Hume was the most prominent figure of the Scottish Enlightenment, but his close friend **Adam Smith** was hardly a negligible thinker in his own right. While Smith is mostly remembered for *The Wealth of Nations*, he was a polymath whose interests were by no means restricted to political economy. He also wrote on morality and astronomy, and gave lectures on the subject of jurisprudence at the University of Glasgow. These unpublished lectures in 1762 and 1763[35] addressed a problem which had already been formulated by Montesquieu and, before him, the French jurists in the sixteenth century: what is the correspondence between the laws and the form of society? At the outset of his lectures, he traced the progressive development of society from "savagery" to civilization, in terms of different means of livelihood: hunting, pastoralism, agriculture, and commerce. He was consequently among the very first to formulate a framework which was to underpin evolutionary thinking in anthropology in the nineteenth century and beyond.[36] In particular, he pointed out the relationship between modes of livelihood and the origins of social inequality. Unlike hunting, he argued, pastoralism generated inheritable and divisible forms of wealth in the form of livestock. It was possible for some pastoral nomads to accumulate large herds whereas others possessed few or even no animals, generating a new form of division in society, however unstable in its beginnings, between the wealthy and powerful and the poor and weak.

Smith's colleague **Adam Ferguson**, the only highlander in this generation of Scottish intellectuals, was to develop the political implications of "progress" in his *An Essay on the History of Civil Society* (1767).[37] The Iroquois, as described by Lafitau, constituted Ferguson's paradigm of "savagery." He was, in fact, quite aware that the Iroquois did not subsist on hunting alone, that they also tilled the soil and lived in settled villages. More important, however, was that they did not accumulate forms of wealth which generated significant inequality. As equals, he argued, they had an equal stake in the preservation of their own society. In the absence of centralized authority, they were able to muster warriors effectively for attack and for defense. In spite of their emphasis on personal courage, they were careful to make every attempt to minimize the loss of even one of their party on any expedition; the population was sufficiently small to make the loss of any warriors, even in a successful expedition, a significant blow. In important respects, the Iroquois embodied the kind of commitment to "civic virtue" which Montesquieu had argued was typical of republican government.

Ferguson is often cited as an early apostle of the doctrine of "progress" but, in fact, his *Essay* is as concerned with the prospect of decadence as it is with progress. For Ferguson, the problem lay in the progressive elaboration of the division of labor, rather than in the development of private property *per se*. As the division of labor increased, so individuals were focused on the particularities of their own occupation, and not the interest of society as a whole. Warfare became the occupation of a specialized portion of the population, and the life of the individual soldier increasingly expendable. Worse, this specialization increasingly reduced the mass of citizens into automatons that mechanically followed the instructions of their superiors. The ordinary infantryman, for example, had much less autonomy and indeed less knowledge of the campaign than an Iroquois warrior, just as the ordinary laborer was employed in ceaseless drudgery, physically and mentally stunted as compared with an ordinary "savage." To the extent that, in contemporary society, fewer and fewer individuals had any real say in managing society or any real stake in its maintenance, such a system was easily susceptible to turning into a kind of "despotism" abhorred by Montesquieu, a government by and for the wealthy and powerful minority. For Ferguson, the "progress" of humanity's rise from "savagery" was achieved only at a considerable cost for society as a whole and for the mass of its individual members.

By the end of the eighteenth century, such pessimism became increasingly rare, displaced by a faith, not only in the unstoppable march of human progress but of Europe's indubitable place at the forefront. Until then, if European conquest and colonization seemed unstoppable in the New World, the situation had been quite different in Asia where, despite European outposts, India and China remained economic, if not political, giants. Until very late in the century, European supremacy could not be taken for granted but, once it was established, European self-confidence apparently knew no bounds. Universal history was written as the history of the emergence of European supremacy, retrospectively understood as an inevitable outcome. "Savages" and Asians were the doomed losers in the race. "Noble savages" – Walter Scott's Highlanders as well as Fenimore Cooper's Mohicans – were literary figures of nostalgia, bearers of a romantic aura of doomed nobility. It was out of the question, however, that such "others" might seriously lead Europeans to call into question the values of their own society.

The Legacy of the Forerunners

While the discipline of anthropology constitutes a distinctly modern approach to understanding "others," it should be clear in retrospect that many of its key issues were also central to the concerns of earlier – sometimes much earlier – European thinkers. It is not helpful to think of modern anthropology as the inevitable end result of these early approaches. This is a certain recipe for reading these works outside of the historical contexts in which they were written, as if they were only crude approximations (some cruder than others!) of modern anthropological knowledge. The selections in this anthology (not to mention the countless other writings which could just as easily have been included) need to be understood in their own terms and in their own contexts. Yet, unless we are prepared to treat them as relics, we must take into account the ways in which they address questions which have not ceased to be contemporary.

From the outset, in the writings of Herodotus, we see a preoccupation, not only with the differences between "others" and "ourselves," but with differences between different categories of "others." From the standpoint of the Greeks, the city-state – the *polis* – constituted the natural unit of "politics." Great empires like Egypt and Persia, on one hand, nomadic pastoralists like the Scythians, on the other, constituted the opposite poles of a spectrum in which the Greeks occupied the middle. In any case, this contrast between vast empires and nomadic herders (and later hunters) remained a leitmotif of European (and Islamic) writing about "others." Admittedly, Marco Polo was more inclined to gawk at the magnificence of China than at their nomadic Mongol conquerors; differences are, after all, always relative. Ibn Khaldun was the first, however, to theorize the implications of these differences between modes of livelihood in a systematic fashion; indeed, he was certainly unmatched in this regard by European writers until the eighteenth century. It is true that, as early as Acosta in the late sixteenth century, the Jesuits also took such differences into account, but this was more specifically in order to gauge the different ways in which they could win converts in different kinds of societies. Sir William Temple moralized these differences, preferring the stable government of empires over the conquering zeal of nomads. But it was not until the Scots, Adam Smith and Adam Ferguson, that Europeans systematically theorized the broader social implications of different economic systems. It is no accident that Karl Marx expressed his admiration of Ferguson in a footnote to the first volume of *Capital*.

Herodotus was primarily concerned, however, with differences between political systems rather than modes of livelihood or even the scale of societies. His paradigm of Persian "despotism" was eventually to resonate with certain seventeenth-century travelers – Chardin among others – and especially in the writings of numerous Enlightenment thinkers in France and Britain, beginning with Montesquieu who, like Herodotus before him, contrasted the rule of law with subjection to the personal whims of an absolute ruler. However, there remained a question unanswered – indeed unasked – by Herodotus: under what conditions do republics, despotisms, or other political systems emerge and flourish? Again, Ibn Khaldun was perhaps the first to attempt to frame an answer in sophisticated theoretical terms, albeit in a way which was not directly applicable to the European context. In Europe, sixteenth-century French legal historians were the first to frame the question in comparative terms, even if their answers (for example, Bodin's theory of climates) seem archaic in retrospect. For very different reasons, the Jesuits pursued the same line of inquiry, furnishing remarkably functionalist analyses of the moral underpinnings of the Chinese empire (Le Comte) or the effectiveness of Iroquois government in the absence of central authority (Lafitau). Montesquieu's reformulation of the sixteenth-century comparative project ensured that this continued to be a central problem in Enlightenment thought.

Herodotus also introduced the notion that "others" – "barbarians" no less – might constitute a moral yardstick by which we might evaluate ourselves. Tacitus' ironic twist, his suggestion that the "barbarians" might actually be better people than "we" are, was an even more prevalent paradigm. Mandeville put his virulent critique of the decadence of Christendom in the mouth of the Sultan of Egypt, and his portrayal of the "natural" piety of Indian "pagans" was quite deliberately intended to put his fellow Christians to shame. Mandeville may not have self-consciously modeled his argument on Tacitus; the same could not be said of Montaigne's essay "Of Cannibals," replete with classical allusions. Montaigne, in turn, was unquestionably a model for subsequent writers: Lahontan, Rousseau, Diderot, and even Adam Ferguson.

It would be silly, of course, to suggest that all lines of inquiry can be traced back in some form or another to Herodotus. The question of what was "natural" to human beings was not one which preoccupied Herodotus. In fact, it had a special Christian resonance; "natural" human understanding and behavior existed in contraposition to Divine revelation. Mandeville's righteous "pagans" were, admittedly, theologically problematic, and controversial in his own time. Jesuits like Acosta and Lafitau were subtler theologians, concerned with discerning the presence or absence of the divine spark in the practices of non-Christian peoples. However, the problem of human "nature" and of "natural" humans was by no means the sole prerogative of churchmen. The amalgamation of the "savage" and the "natural," first formulated by Montaigne in the form of a play on words,[38] came to constitute a stock conceit of the eighteenth century. Lahontan's and Diderot's "natural" dialecticians are Huron or Tahitian. In a far less playful vein, Rousseau attempted to explore humanity in a State of Nature abstracted from social and cultural biases.

One way or the other, all these thinkers suggested in the strongest possible terms that the economic, political, intellectual, and moral dimensions of humanity were not exhausted, and could not be entirely understood, simply with reference to ourselves alone. Differences between human societies were deeply significant, although there was certainly no consensus about how and why. Admittedly, "others" were a convenient vehicle for Europeans to think and talk about themselves. Whether one considered China to be an abhorrent example of despotic rule or a model of orderly government said as much about one's factional political affiliations in France or Britain as it did about China. But these debates about China (to stick to this one example) were not just European exercises in navel gazing in disguise. Such debates incited a quest for knowledge about "others" which could on occasion transcend the very terms of the original debate. La Popelinière's and Rousseau's eloquent pleas for travel to remote places and unfamiliar peoples for the sake of knowledge alone, rather than for conquest, monetary gain, or the conversion of souls, were not to be fulfilled until much later. These pleas certainly did not bring anthropology into being. But they contributed to the forging of a niche which anthropology came to occupy.

NOTES

1 For the emergence of anthropology in Victorian England, see J.W. Burrow, *Evolution and Society: A Study in Victorian Social Theory*, Cambridge: Cambridge University Press, 1996; George W. Stocking, *Victorian Anthropology*, New York: Free Press, 1987; Henrika Kuklick, *The Savage Within: The Social History of British Anthropology, 1885–1945*, Cambridge: Cambridge University Press, 1991.
2 Georg Wilhelm Friedrich Hegel, *The Philosophy of History*, translated by J. Sibree. New York, Dover Publications, 1956.
3 Chapter 1.
4 Chapter 2.

5   Chapter 3.
6   In the Middle Ages, fish was served instead of meat in wealthy households on fast days, on Friday or during Lent.
7   Chapter 4.
8   Chapter 5.
9   Chapter 6.
10 Chapter 7.
11 Chapter 8.
12 For a comprehensive account of the legal and historical thought of sixteenth-century France, see George Huppert. *The Idea of Perfect History: Historical Erudition and Historical Philosophy in Renaissance France*, Urbana, IL: University of Illinois Press, 1970.
13 Chapter 9.
14 Chapter 10.
15 Chapter 11.
16 Chapter 12.
17 Chapter 13.
18 Gottfried Wilhelm Leibniz, *Writings on China*, translated by Daniel J. Cook and Henry Rosemont, Jr., Chicago and La Salle, IL: Open Court, 1994.
19 Michèle Duchet, *Anthropologie et histoire au siècle des Lumières*, Paris: Albin Michel, 1971, pp. 76–9.
20 Chapter 14.
21 Chapter 15.
22 Chapter 16.
23 For recent assessments of the quarrel, see Joseph Levine, *The Battle of the Books: History and Literature in the Augustan Age*, Ithaca, NY: Cornell University Press, 1991; Joan DeJean, *Ancients Against Moderns: Culture Wars: The Making of a Fin de Siècle*, Chicago: University of Chicago Press, 1997.
24 For the political and cultural ideas of Kant and Herder, see Sankar Muthu, *Enlightenment Against Empire*, Princeton, NJ: Princeton University Press, 2003; John H. Zammito, *Kant, Herder, and the Birth of Anthropology*, Chicago: University of Chicago Press, 2002.
25 Chapter 17.
26 Chapter 18.
27 Chapter 19.
28 Chapter 21.
29 Chapter 20.
30 Chapter 22.
31 Chapter 23.
32 Ter Ellingson (*The Myth of the Noble Savage*, Berkeley, CA: University of California Press, 2001) refutes this allegation in great detail, demonstrating how racist ideologues in the nineteenth century used the accusation to discredit Rousseau's ideas.
33 Chapter 24.
34 Chapter 25.
35 Chapter 26.
36 Ronald L. Meek, *Social Science and the Ignoble Savage*, Cambridge: Cambridge University Press, 1976.
37 Chapter 27.
38 The word *sauvage* in French can mean either "savage, ferocious" or "wild, undomesticated" (and, by implication, "natural").

Part I
The Ancient World

1

The Histories of Herodotus

Herodotus

I now proceed to give a more particular account of Egypt; it possesses more wonders than any other country, and exhibits works greater than can be described, in comparison with all other regions; therefore more must be said about it. The Egyptians, besides having a climate peculiar to themselves, and a river differing in its nature from all other rivers, have adopted customs and usages in almost every respect different from the rest of mankind. Among them the women attend markets and traffic, but the men stay at home and weave. Other nations, in weaving, throw the wool upward; the Egyptians, downward. The men carry burdens on their heads; the women, on their shoulders. They ease themselves in their houses, but eat out of doors; alleging that, whatever is indecent, though necessary, ought to be done in private; but what is not indecent, openly. No woman can serve the office for any god or goddess; but men are employed for both offices. Sons are not compelled to support their parents unless they choose; but daughters are compelled to do so, whether they choose or not. In other countries the priests of the gods wear long hair; in Egypt they have it shaved. With other men it is customary in mourning for the nearest relations to have their heads shorn; the Egyptians, on occasions of death, let the hair grow both on the head and face, although accustomed to shave. Other men live

apart from beasts, but the Egyptians live with them. Others feed on wheat and barley, but it is a very great disgrace for an Egyptian to make food of them; but they make bread from spelt, which some call zea. They knead the dough with their feet; but mix clay and take up dung with their hands. The Egyptians are circumcised. Every man wears two garments; the women, but one. Other men fasten the rings and sheets of their sails outside; but the Egyptians, inside. The Grecians write and cipher, moving the hand from left to right; but the Egyptians, from right to left: and doing so they say they do it right-ways, and the Greeks left-ways. They have two sorts of letters, one of which is called sacred, the other common.

They are of all men the most excessively attentive to the worship of the gods, and observe the following ceremonies: they drink from cups of brass, which they scour every day; nor is this custom practised by some and neglected by others, but all do it. They wear linen garments, constantly fresh washed, and they pay particular attention to this. They are circumcised for the sake of cleanliness, thinking it better to be clean than handsome. The priests shave their whole body every third day, that neither lice nor any other impurity may be found upon them when engaged in the service of the gods. The priests wear linen only, and shoes of byblus, and are not permitted to wear

Herodotus, *The Histories of Herodotus*, trans. Henry Cary, New York: D. Appleton and Company, 1899, pp. 97–100, 113–15, 166–8, 226–7, 230–5.

any other garments, or other shoes. They wash themselves in cold water twice every day, and twice every night; and, in a word, they use a number of ceremonies. On the other hand, they enjoy no slight advantages, for they do not consume or expend any of their private property; but sacred food is cooked for them, and a great quantity of beef and geese is allowed each of them every day, and wine from the grape is given them; but they may not taste of fish. Beans the Egyptians do not sow at all in their country, neither do they eat those that happen to grow there, nor taste them when dressed. The priests, indeed, abhor the sight of that pulse, accounting it impure. The service of each god is performed, not by one, but by many priests, of whom one is chief priest; and, when any one of them dies, his son is put in his place. The male kine they deem sacred to Epaphus, and to that end prove them in the following manner: If the examiner finds one black hair upon him, he adjudges him to be unclean; and one of the priests appointed for this purpose makes this examination, both when the animal is standing up and lying down; and he draws out the tongue, to see if it is pure as to the prescribed marks, which I shall mention in another part of my history. He also looks at the hairs of his tail, whether they grow naturally. If the beast is found pure in all these respects, he marks it by rolling a piece of byblus round the horns, and then having put on it some sealing earth, he impresses it with his signet; and so they drive him away. Any one who sacrifices one that is unmarked is punished with death. In this manner the animal is proved. The established mode of sacrifice is this: having led the victim, properly marked, to the altar where they intend to sacrifice, they kindle a fire. Then having poured wine upon the altar, near the victim, and having invoked the god, they kill it; and after they have killed it, they cut off the head; but they flay the body of the animal: then having pronounced many imprecations on the head, they who have a market and Grecian merchants dwelling among them, carry it there, and having so done, they usually sell it; but they who have no Grecians among them, throw it into the river: and they pronounce the following imprecations on the head: "If any evil is about

to befall either those that now sacrifice, or Egypt in general, may it be averted on this head." With respect, then, to the heads of beasts that are sacrificed, and to the making libations of wine, all the Egyptians observe the same customs in all sacrifices alike : and from this custom no Egyptian will taste of the head of any animal. But a different mode of disembowelling and burning the victims prevails in different sacrifices. I proceed therefore to speak of the practice with regard to the goddess whom they consider the greatest, and in whose honour they celebrate the most magnificent festival. When they have flayed the bullocks, having first offered up prayers, they take out all the intestines, and leave the vitals with the fat in the carcass; and they then cut off the legs and the extremity of the hip, with the shoulders and neck, and having done this, they fill the body of the bullock with fine bread, honey, raisins, figs, frankincense, myrrh, and other perfumes; and after they have filled it with these, they burn it, pouring on it a great quantity of oil. They sacrifice after they have fasted; and while the sacred things are being burned they all beat themselves; and when they have done beating themselves, they spread a banquet of what remains of the victims.

All the Egyptians sacrifice the pure male kine and calves, but they are not allowed to sacrifice the females, for they are sacred to Isis; for the image of Isis is made in the form of a woman with the horns of a cow, as the Grecians represent Io; and all Egyptians alike pay a far greater reverence to cows than to any other cattle. So that no Egyptian man or woman will kiss a Grecian on the mouth, or use the knife, spit, or caldron of a Greek, or taste of the flesh of a pure ox that has been divided by a Grecian knife. They bury the kine that die in the following manner: the females they throw into the river, and the males they severally inter in the suburbs, with one horn, or both, appearing above the ground for a mark. When it is putrefied and the appointed time arrives, a raft comes to each city from the island called Prosopitis; this island is in the Delta, and is nine schceni in circumference: now in this island Prosopitis there are several cities; but that from which the rafts come to take away the bones of the oxen is called Atarbechis; in it a Temple of Venus has been erected. From this city, then, many persons go about to other towns; and having dug up the bones, all carry them away, and bury them in one place; and they bury all other cattle that die in the same way that they do the oxen; for they do not kill any of them. All those who have a temple erected to Theban Jupiter, or belong to the Theban district, abstain from sheep, and sacrifice goats only. For the Egyptians do not all worship the same gods in the same manner, except Isis and Osiris, who, they say, is Bacchus; but these deities they all worship in the same manner.

[...]

Their manner of mourning and burying is as follows: When in a family a man of any consideration dies, all the women of that family besmear their heads and faces with mud, and then leaving the body in the house, they wander about the city, and beat themselves, having their clothes girt up, and exposing their breasts, and all their relations accompany them. On the other hand, the men beat themselves, being girt up, in like manner. When they have done this, they carry out the body to be embalmed. There are persons who are appointed for this very purpose; they, when the dead body is brought to them, show to the bearers wooden models of corpses, made exactly like by painting. And they show that which they say is the most expensive manner of embalming, the name of which I do not think it right to mention on such an occasion; they then show the second, which is inferior and less expensive; and then the third, which is the cheapest. Having explained them all, they learn from them in what way they wish the body to be prepared; then the relatives, when they have agreed on the price, depart; but the embalmers remaining in the workshops thus proceed to embalm in the most expensive manner. First they draw out the brains through the nostrils with an iron hook, taking part of it out in this manner, the rest by the infusion of drugs. Then with a sharp Ethiopian stone they make an incision in the side, and take out all the bowels; and having cleansed the abdomen and rinsed it with palm-wine, they next sprinkle it with pounded perfumes. Then having filled the belly with pure myrrh pounded, and cassia, and other perfumes, frankincense excepted,

they sew it up again; and when they have done this, they steep it in natrum, leaving it under for seventy days; for a longer time than this it is not lawful to steep it. At the expiration of the seventy days they wash the corpse, and wrap the whole body in bandages of flaxen cloth, smearing it with gum, which the Egyptians commonly use instead of glue. After this the relatives, having taken the body back again, make a wooden case in the shape of a man, and having made it, they inclose the body; and thus, having fastened it up, they store it in a sepulchral chamber, setting it upright against the wall. In this manner they prepare the bodies that are embalmed in the most expensive way. Those who, avoiding great expense, desire the middle way, they prepare in the following manner: When they have charged their syringes with oil made from cedar, they fill the abdomen of the corpse without making any incision or taking out the bowels, but inject it at the fundament; and having prevented the injection from escaping, they steep the body in natrum for the prescribed number of days, and on the last day they let out from the abdomen the oil of cedar which they had before injected, and it has such power that it brings away the intestines and vitals in a state of dissolution; the natrum dissolves the flesh, and nothing of the body remains but the skin and the bones. When they have done this they return the body without any further operation. The third method of embalming is this, which is used only for the poorer sort: Having thoroughly rinsed the abdomen in syrmaea, they steep it with natrum for the seventy days, and then deliver it to be carried away. But the wives of considerable persons, when they die, they do not immediately deliver to be embalmed, nor such women as are very beautiful and of celebrity, but when they have been dead three or four days they then deliver them to the embalmers; and they do this for the following reason, that the embalmers may not abuse the bodies of such women; for they say that one man was detected in abusing a body that was fresh, and that a fellow-workman informed against him. Should any person, whether Egyptian or stranger, no matter which, be found to have been seized by a crocodile, or drowned in the river, to whatever city the body may be carried the inhabitants are by law compelled to have the body embalmed, and, having adorned it in the handsomest manner, to bury it in the sacred vaults. Nor is it lawful for any one else, whether relatives or friends, to touch him; but the priests of the Nile bury the corpse with their own hands, as being something more than human.

They avoid using Grecian customs; and, in a word, the customs of all other people whatsoever. ...

Cambyses is said, even from infancy, to have been afflicted with a certain severe malady, which some called the sacred disease. In that case, it was not at all surprising that when his body was so diseased his mind should not be sound. And toward the other Persians he behaved madly in the following instances: for it is reported that he said to Prexaspes, whom he highly honoured, and whose office it was to bring messages to him, and whose son was cupbearer to Cambyses, and this is no trifling honour, he is reported to have spoken as follows: "Prexaspes, what sort of man do the Persians think me? and what remarks do they make about me?" He answered, "Sir, you are highly extolled in every other respect, but they say you are too much addicted to wine." Prexaspes said this of the Persians, but the king, enraged, answered as follows: "Do the Persians indeed say that, by being addicted to wine, I am beside myself, and am not in my senses? Then their former words were not true." For, on a former occasion, when the Persians and Crœsus were sitting with him, Cambyses asked what sort of man he appeared to be in comparison with his father Cyrus; they answered that he was superior to his father, for that he held all that Cyrus possessed, and had acquired besides Egypt and the empire of the sea. Crœsus, being present, not being pleased with this decision, spoke thus to Cambyses: "To me now, O son of Cyrus, you do not appear comparable to your father, for you have not yet such a son as he left behind him." Cambyses was delighted at hearing this, and commended the judgment of Crœsus. Therefore, remembering this, he said in anger to Prexaspes : "Observe now yourself, whether the Persians have spoken the truth, or whether they who say such things are not out of their senses; for if I shoot that son of yours who

stands under the portico, and hit him in the heart, the Persians will appear to have said nothing to the purpose; but if I miss, then say that the Persians have spoken truth, and that I am not of sound mind." Having said this, and bent his bow, he hit the boy; and when the boy had fallen, he ordered them to open him and examine the wound; and when the arrow was found in the heart, he said to the boy's father, laughing: "Prexaspes, it has been clearly shown to you that I am not mad, but that the Persians are out of their senses. Now tell me, did you ever see a man take so true an aim?" But Prexaspes, perceiving him to be out of his mind, and being in fear for his own life, said, "Sir, I believe that a god himself could not have shot so well." At that time he committed such an atrocity; and at another time, having, without any just cause, seized twelve Persians of the first rank, he had them buried alive up to the head.

While he was acting in this manner, Crœsus the Lydian thought fit to admonish him in the following terms: "O king, do not yield entirely to your youthful impulses and anger, but possess and restrain yourself. It is a good thing to be provident, and wise to have forethought. You put men to death who are your own subjects, having seized them without any just cause; and you slay their children. If you persist in such a course, beware lest the Persians revolt from you. Your father Cyrus strictly charged me to admonish you, and suggest whatever I might discover for your good." He then manifested his good-will in giving this advice; but Cambyses answered: "Do you presume to give me advice, you, who so wisely managed your own country; and so well advised my father, when you persuaded him to pass the river Araxes, and advance against the Massagetæ, when they were willing to cross over into our territory? You have first ruined yourself by badly governing your own country, and then ruined Cyrus, who was persuaded by your advice. But you shall have no reason to rejoice; for I have long wanted to find a pretext against you." So saying, he took up his bow for the purpose of shooting him; but Crœsus jumped up and ran out. Cambyses, when he was unable to shoot him, commanded his attendants to seize him, and put him to death. But the attendants, knowing his temper, concealed

Crœsus for the following reason, that if Cambyses should repent, and inquire for Crœsus, they, by producing him, might receive rewards for preserving him alive; or if he should not repent, or regret him, then they would put him to death. Not long afterward Cambyses did regret Crœsus, and the attendants, knowing this, acquainted him that he was still living; on which Cambyses said: "I am rejoiced that Crœsus is still alive; they, however, who saved him shall not escape with impunity, but I will have them put to death." And he made good his word.

He, then, committed many such mad actions, both against the Persians and his allies, while he stayed at Memphis, both opening ancient sepulchres, and examining the dead bodies; he also entered the Temple of Vulcan, and derided the image, for the image of Vulcan is very like the Phœnician Pataici, which the Phœnicians place at the prows of their triremes. For the benefit of any one who has not seen them, I will describe them; it is a representation of a pigmy. He likewise entered the temple of the Cabeiri (into which it is unlawful for any one except the priest to enter), and these images he burned, after he had ridiculed them in various ways: these also are like that of Vulcan; and they say that they are the sons of this latter. It is then in every way clear to me that Cambyses was outrageously mad; otherwise he would not have attempted to deride sacred things and established customs. For if any one should propose to all men to select the best institutions of all that exist, each, after considering them all, would choose their own; so certain is it that each thinks his own institutions by far the best. It is not therefore probable that any but a madman would make such things the subject of ridicule. That all men are of this mind respecting their own institutions may be inferred from many and various proofs, and among them by the following: Darius having summoned some Greeks under his sway, who were present, asked them for what sum they would feed upon the dead bodies of their parents. They answered that they would not do it for any sum. Darius afterward having summoned some of the Indians called Callatians, who are accustomed to eat their parents, asked them in the presence of the Greeks, and who were informed of what

was said by an interpreter, for what sum they would consent to burn their fathers when they die. But they, making loud exclamations, begged he would speak words of good omen. Such, then, is the effect of custom: and Pindar appears to me to have said rightly, that "custom is the king of all men."

[...]

The Euxine Sea, to which Darius led an army of all countries, except the Scythians, exhibits the most ignorant nations: for we are unable to mention any one nation of those on this side the Pontus that has any pretensions to intelligence; nor have we ever heard of any learned men among them, except the Scythian nation and Anacharsis. By the Scythian nation one of the most important of human devices has been contrived more wisely than by any others whom we know; their other customs, however, I do not admire. This most important device has been so contrived that no one who attacks them can escape; and that, if they do not choose to be found, no one is able to overtake them. For they, who have neither cities nor fortifications, but carry their houses with them, who are all equestrian archers, living not from the cultivation of the earth, but from cattle, and whose dwellings are wagons – how must not such a people be invincible, and difficult to engage with? This device has been contrived by them, as the country is fit for it, and the rivers aid them: for the country, being level, abounds in herbage and is well watered: and rivers flow through it almost as numerous as the canals in Egypt. Such of them as are celebrated and navigable from the sea I will mention: the Ister, that has five mouths; then the Tyres, the Hypanis, the Borysthenes, the Panticapes, the Hypacyris, the Gerrhus, and the Tanais.

[...]

Thus the Scythians are provided with these celebrated rivers. The grass that grows in Scythia is the most productive of bile for cattle of any with which we are acquainted; and when the cattle are opened one may infer that such is the case.

Thus the greatest commodities are furnished them in abundance. Their other customs are established as follows: They propitiate the following gods only: Vesta, most of all; then Jupiter, deeming the Earth to be the wife of Jupiter; after these Apollo, and Venus Urania, and Hercules, and Mars. All the Scythians acknowledge these; but those who are called Royal Scythians sacrifice also to Neptune. Vesta, in the Scythian language, is named Tabiti; Jupiter is, in my opinion, very rightly called Papæus; the Earth, Apia; Apollo, Œtosyrus; Venus Urania, Artimpasa; and Neptune, Thamimasadas. They are not accustomed to erect images, altars, and temples, except to Mars; to him they are accustomed. The same mode of sacrificing is adopted by all, with respect to all kinds of victims, alike, being as follows: The victim itself stands with its fore feet tied together; he who sacrifices, standing behind the beast, having drawn the extremity of the cord, throws it down; and as the victim falls he invokes the god to whom he is sacrificing; then he throws a halter round its neck, and having put in a stick, he twists it round and strangles it, without kindling any fire, or performing any preparatory ceremonies, or making any libation, but having strangled and flayed it he applies himself to cook it. As the Scythian country is wholly destitute of wood, they have invented the following method of cooking flesh: When they have flayed the victims, they strip the flesh from the bones, then they put it into caldrons made in the country, if they happen to have any, which very much resemble Lesbian bowls except that they are much larger; having put it into these, they cook it by burning underneath the bones of the victims. If they have no caldron at hand, they put all the flesh into the paunches of the victims, and having poured in water, burn the bones underneath: they burn very well, and the paunches easily contain the flesh stripped from the bones; thus the ox cooks himself, and of all other victims each cooks itself. When the flesh is cooked, he that sacrifices, offering the first fruits of the flesh and entrails, throws it before him. They also sacrifice other cattle, chiefly horses.

In this manner, then, and these victims, they sacrifice to the other gods; but to Mars, as follows: In each district, in the place where the magistrates assemble, is erected a structure sacred to Mars, of the following kind: bundles of fagots are heaped up to the length and breadth of three stades, but less in height; on the top of this a square platform is formed; and three of the sides are perpendicular, but on the fourth it

is accessible. Every year they heap on it one hundred and fifty wagon-loads of fagots, for it is continually sinking by reason of the weather. On this heap an old iron scimetar is placed by each tribe, and this is the image of Mars; and to this scimetar they bring yearly sacrifices of cattle and horses; and to these scimetars they offer more sacrifices than to the rest of the gods. Whatever enemies they take alive, of these they sacrifice one in a hundred, not in the same manner as they do the cattle, but in a different manner; for after they have poured a libation of wine on their heads, they cut the throats of the men over a bowl; then having carried the bowl on the heap of fagots, they pour the blood over the scimetar. This then they carry up; but below at the sacred precinct, they do as follows: having cut off all the right shoulders of the men that have been killed, with the arms, they throw them into the air; and then, having finished the rest of the sacrificial rites, they depart; but the arm lies wherever it has fallen, and the body apart. Such, then, are the sacrifices instituted among them. Swine they never use, nor suffer them to be reared in their country at all.

Their military affairs are ordered as follows: When a Scythian overthrows his first enemy, he drinks his blood; and presents the king with the heads of the enemies he has killed in battle: for if he brings a head, he shares the booty that they take; but not if he does not bring one. He skins it in the following manner: Having made a circular incision round the ears and taking hold of the skin, he shakes from it the skull; then having scraped off the flesh with the rib of an ox, he softens the skin with his hands; and having made it supple, he uses it as a napkin; each man hangs it on the bridle of the horse which he rides, and prides himself on it; for whoever has the greatest number of these skin napkins is accounted the most valiant man. Many of them make cloaks of these skins, to throw over themselves, sewing them together like shepherd's coats; and many, having flayed the right hands of their enemies that are dead, together with the nails, make coverings for their quivers: the skin of a man, which is both thick and shining, surpasses almost all other skins in the brightness of its white. Many, having flayed men whole, and stretched the skin on wood, carry it about on horseback.

Such usages are received among them. The heads themselves, not indeed of all, but of their greatest enemies, they treat as follows: Each, having sawn off all below the eyebrows, cleanses it, and if the man is poor, he covers only the outside with leather, and so uses it: but if he is rich, he covers it indeed with leather, and having gilded the inside, he so uses it for a drinking-cup. And they do this to their relatives if they are at variance, and one prevails over another in the presence of the king. When strangers of consideration come to him, he produces these heads, and relates how, though they were his relatives, they made war against him, and he overcame them, considering this a proof of bravery. Once in every year the governor of a district, each in his own district, mingles a bowl of wine, from which those Scythians drink by whom enemies have been captured: but they who have not achieved this do not taste of this wine, but sit at a distance in dishonour; this is accounted the greatest disgrace: such of them as have killed very many men, having two cups at once, drink them together.

Soothsayers among the Scythians are numerous, who divine by the help of a number of willow rods, in the following manner: When they have brought with them large bundles of twigs, they lay them on the ground and untie them; and having placed each rod apart, they utter their predictions; and while they are pronouncing them, they gather up the rods again, and put them together again one by one. This is their national mode of divination. But the Enarees, or Androgyni, say that Venus gave them the power of divining. They divine by means of the bark of a linden tree: when a man has split the linden tree in three pieces, twisting it round his own fingers, and then untwisting it, he utters a response. When the King of the Scythians is sick, he sends for three of the most famous of these prophets, who prophesy in the manner above mentioned; and they generally say as follows, that such or such a citizen has sworn falsely by the royal hearth, mentioning the name of the citizen of whom they speak: for it is a custom with the Scythians in general to swear by the royal hearth when they would use the most solemn oath. The person who, they say, has sworn falsely is immediately seized and brought forward; and when he is come, the prophets charge him with being clearly proved by their prophetic art to have sworn falsely by the royal hearth, and for this reason the king is ill. He denies it, affirming that he has not sworn falsely, and complains bitterly. On his denial, the king sends for twice as many more prophets; and if they also, examining into the prophetic art, condemn him with having sworn falsely, they straightway cut off his head, and the first prophets divide his property between them; but if the prophets who came last acquit him, other prophets are called in, and others after them. If, then, the greater number acquit the man, it is decreed that the first prophets shall be put to death. They accordingly put them to death in the following manner: When they have filled a wagon with fagots, and have yoked oxen to it, having tied the feet of the prophets and bound their hands behind them, and having gagged them, they inclose them in the midst of the fagots; then having set fire to them, they terrify the oxen, and let them go. Many oxen therefore are burned with the prophets, and many escape very much scorched, when the pole has been burned asunder. In this manner, and for other reasons, they burn the prophets, calling them false prophets. The king does not spare the children of those whom he puts to death, but kills all the males, and does not hurt the females. The Scythians make solemn contracts in the following manner with whomsoever they make them: Having poured wine into a large earthen vessel, they mingle with it blood taken from those who are entering into covenant, having struck with an awl or cut with a knife a small part of the body; then, having dipped a scimetar, some arrows, a hatchet, and a javelin in the vessel, when they have done this, they make many solemn prayers, and then both those who make the contract and the most considerable of their attendants drink up the mixture.

The sepulchres of the kings are in the country of the Gerrhi, as far as which the Borysthenes is navigable. There, when their king dies, they dig a large square hole in the ground; and having prepared this, they take up the corpse, having the body covered with wax, the belly opened and cleaned, filled with bruised cypress, incense, and parsley and anise-seed, and then sewn up again, and carry it in a chariot to another nation: those who receive the corpse brought to them do the same as the Royal Scythians; they cut off part of their ear, shave off their hair, wound themselves on the arms, lacerate their forehead and nose, and drive arrows through their left hand. Thence they carry the corpse of the king to another nation whom they govern; and those to whom they first came accompany them. When they have carried the corpse round all the provinces, they arrive among the Gerrhi, who are the most remote of the nations they rule over, and at the sepulchres. Then, when they have placed the corpse in the grave on a bed of leaves, having fixed spears on each side of the dead body, they lay pieces of wood over it, and cover it over with mats. In the remaining space of the grave they bury one of the king's concubines, having strangled her, and his cup-bearer, a cook, a groom, a page, a courier, and horses, and firstlings of everything else, and golden goblets; they make no use of silver or brass. Having done this, they all heap up a large mound, striving and vying with each other to make it as large as possible. When a year has elapsed, they then do as follows: Having taken the most fitting of his remaining servants; they are all native Scythians; for they serve him whomsoever the king may order, and they have no servants bought with money; when, therefore, they have strangled fifty of these servants, and fifty of the finest horses, having taken out their bowels and cleansed them, they fill them with chaff, and sew them up again. Then having placed the half of a wheel, with its concave side upper-most, on two pieces of wood, and the other half on two other pieces of wood, and having fixed many of these in the same manner, then having thrust thick pieces of wood through the horses lengthwise, up to the neck, they mount them on the half-wheels; and of these the foremost part of the half-wheels supports the shoulders of the horses, and the hinder part supports the belly near the thighs, but the legs on both sides are suspended in the air: then having put bridles and bits on the horses, they stretch them in front, and fasten them to a stake; they then mount upon a horse each, one of the fifty young men that have been strangled, mounting them in the following manner: When they have driven a straight piece of wood along the spine as far as the neck, but a part of this wood projects from the bottom, they fix it into

a hole bored in the other piece of wood that passes through the horse. Having placed such horsemen round the monument, they depart.

Thus they bury their kings. But the other Scythians, when they die, their nearest relatives carry about among their friends, laid in chariots; and of these each one receives and entertains the attendants, and sets the same things before the dead body, as before the rest. In this manner private persons are carried about for forty days, and then buried. The Scythians, having buried them, purify themselves in the following manner: Having wiped and thoroughly washed their heads, they do thus with regard to the body: when they have set up three pieces of wood leaning against each other, they extend around them woollen cloths; and having joined them together as closely as possible, they throw red-hot stones into a vessel placed in the middle of the pieces of wood and the cloths. They have a sort of hemp growing in this country very like flax, except in thickness and height; in this respect the hemp is far superior: it grows both spontaneously and from cultivation; and from it the Thracians make garments, very like linen, nor would any one who is not well skilled in such matters distinguish whether they are made of flax or hemp, but a person who has never seen this hemp would think the garment was made of flax. When, therefore, the Scythians have taken some seed of this hemp, they creep under the cloths, and then put the seed on the red-hot stones; and this being put on, smokes, and produces such a steam that no Grecian vapour-bath would surpass it. The Scythians, transported with the vapour, shout aloud; and this serves them instead of washing, for they never bathe the body in water. Their women, pouring on water, pound on a rough stone pieces of cypress, cedar, and incense tree; and then this pounded matter, when it is thick, they smear over the whole body and face: and this at the same time gives them an agreeable odour, and when they take off the cataplasm on the following day they become clean and shining.

They studiously avoid the use of foreign customs; not only, therefore, will they not adopt those of each other, but least of all Grecian usages.

2

Germany

Tacitus

4. For my own part, I agree with those who think that the tribes of Germany are free from all taint of inter-marriages with foreign nations, and that they appear as a distinct, unmixed race, like none but themselves. Hence, too, the same physical peculiarities throughout so vast a population. All have fierce blue eyes, red hair, huge frames, fit only for a sudden exertion. They are less able to bear laborious work. Heat and thirst they cannot in the least endure; to cold and hunger their climate and their soil inure them.

5. Their country, though somewhat various in appearance, yet generally either bristles with forests or reeks with swamps; it is more rainy on the side of Gaul, bleaker on that of Noricum and Pannonia. It is productive of grain, but unfavourable to fruit-bearing trees; it is rich in flocks and herds, but these are for the most part undersized, and even the cattle have not their usual beauty or noble head. It is number that is chiefly valued; they are in fact the most highly prized, indeed the only riches of the people. Silver and gold the gods have refused to them, whether in kindness or in anger I cannot say. I would not, however, affirm that no vein of German soil produces gold or silver, for who has ever made a search? They care but little to possess or use them. You may see among them vessels of silver, which have been presented to their envoys and chieftains, held as cheap as those of clay. The border population, however, value gold and silver for their commercial utility, and are familiar with, and show preference for, some of our coins. The tribes of the interior use the simpler and more ancient practice of the barter of commodities. They like the old and well-known money, coins milled, or showing a two-horse chariot. They likewise prefer silver to gold, not from any special liking, but because a large number of silver pieces is more convenient for use among dealers in cheap and common articles.

6. Even iron is not plentiful with them, as we infer from the character of their weapons. But few use swords or long lances. They carry a spear (*framea* is their name for it), with a narrow and short head, but so sharp and easy to wield that the same weapon serves, according to circumstances, for close or distant conflict. As for the horse-soldier, he is satisfied with a shield and spear; the foot-soldiers also scatter showers of missiles, each man having several and hurling them to an immense distance, and being naked or lightly clad with a little cloak. There is no display about their equipment: their shields alone are marked with very choice colours. A few only have corslets, and just one or two here and there a metal or leathern helmet. Their horses are remarkable neither for beauty nor for fleetness. Nor are

Tacitus, *Germania*, in *The Complete Works of Tacitus*, trans. Alfred John Church and William Jackson Brodribb, New York: The Modern Library, 1942, pp. 710–22.

they taught various evolutions after our fashion, but are driven straight forward, or so as to make one wheel to the right in such a compact body that none is left behind another. On the whole, one would say that their chief strength is in their infantry, which fights along with the cavalry; admirably adapted to the action of the latter is the swiftness of certain foot-soldiers, who are picked from the entire youth of their country, and stationed in front of the line. Their number is fixed, – a hundred from each canton; and from this they take their name among their countrymen, so that what was originally a mere number has now become a title of distinction. Their line of battle is drawn up in a wedge-like formation. To give ground, provided you return to the attack, is considered prudence rather than cowardice. The bodies of their slain they carry off even in indecisive engagements. To abandon your shield is the basest of crimes; nor may a man thus disgraced be present at the sacred rites, or enter their council; many, indeed, after escaping from battle, have ended their infamy with the halter.

7. They choose their kings by birth, their generals for merit. These kings have not unlimited or arbitrary power, and the generals do more by example than by authority. If they are energetic, if they are conspicuous, if they fight in the front, they lead because they are admired. But to reprimand, to imprison, even to flog, is permitted to the priests alone, and that not as a punishment, or at the general's bidding, but, as it were, by the mandate of the god whom they believe to inspire the warrior. They also carry with them into battle certain figures and images taken from their sacred groves. And what most stimulates their courage is, that their squadrons or battalions, instead of being formed by chance or by a fortuitous gathering, are composed of families and clans. Close by them, too, are those dearest to them, so that they hear the shrieks of women, the cries of infants. *They* are to every man the most sacred witnesses of his bravery – *they* are his most generous applauders. The soldier brings his wounds to mother and wife, who shrink not from counting or even demanding them and who administer both food and encouragement to the combatants.

8. Tradition says that armies already wavering and giving way have been rallied by women who, with earnest entreaties and bosoms laid bare, have vividly represented the horrors of captivity, which the Germans fear with such extreme dread on behalf of their women, that the strongest tie by which a state can be bound is the being required to give, among the number of hostages, maidens of noble birth. They even believe that the sex has a certain sanctity and prescience, and they do not despise their counsels, or make light of their answers. In Vespasian's days we saw Veleda, long regarded by many as a divinity. In former times, too, they venerated Aurinia, and many other women, but not with servile flatteries, or with sham deification.

9. Mercury is the deity whom they chiefly worship, and on certain days they deem it right to sacrifice to him even with human victims. Hercules and Mars they appease with more lawful offerings. Some of the Suevi also sacrifice to Isis. Of the occasion and origin of this foreign rite I have discovered nothing, but that the image, which is fashioned like a light galley, indicates an imported worship. The Germans, however, do not consider it consistent with the grandeur of celestial beings to confine the gods within walls, or to liken them to the form of any human countenance. They consecrate woods and groves, and they apply the names of deities to the abstraction which they see only in spiritual worship.

10. Augury and divination by lot no people practise more diligently. The use of the lots is simple. A little bough is lopped off a fruit-bearing tree, and cut into small pieces; these are distinguished by certain marks, and thrown carelessly and at random over a white garment. In public questions the priest of the particular state, in private the father of the family, invokes the gods, and, with his eyes towards heaven, takes up each piece three times, and finds in them a meaning according to the mark previously impressed on them. If they prove unfavourable, there is no further consultation that day about the matter; if they sanction it, the confirmation of augury is still required. For they are also familiar with the practice of consulting the notes and the flight of birds. It is peculiar to this people to seek omens and

monitions from horses. Kept at the public expense, in these same woods and groves, are white horses, pure from the taint of earthly labour; these are yoked to a sacred car, and accompanied by the priest and the king, or chief of the tribe, who note their neighings and snortings. No species of augury is more trusted, not only by the people and by the nobility, but also by the priests, who regard themselves as the ministers of the gods, and the horses as acquainted with their will. They have also another method of observing auspices, by which they seek to learn the result of an important war. Having taken, by whatever means, a prisoner from the tribe with whom they are at war, they pit him against a picked man of their own tribe, each combatant using the weapons of their country. The victory of the one or the other is accepted as an indication of the issue.

11.　About minor matters the chiefs deliberate, about the more important the whole tribe. Yet even when the final decision rests with the people, the affair is always thoroughly discussed by the chiefs. They assemble, except in the case of a sudden emergency, on certain fixed days, either at new or at full moon; for this they consider the most auspicious season for the transaction of business. Instead of reckoning by days as we do, they reckon by nights, and in this manner fix both their ordinary and their legal appointments. Night they regard as bringing on day. Their freedom has this disadvantage, that they do not meet simultaneously or as they are bidden, but two or three days are wasted in the delays of assembling. When the multitude think proper, they sit down armed. Silence is proclaimed by the priests, who have on these occasions the right of keeping order. Then the king or the chief, according to age, birth, distinction in war, or eloquence, is heard, more because he has influence to persuade than because he has power to command. If his sentiments displease them, they reject them with murmurs; if they are satisfied, they brandish their spears. The most complimentary form of assent is to express approbation with their weapons.

12.　In their councils an accusation may be preferred or a capital crime prosecuted. Penalties are distinguished according to the offence. Traitors and deserters are hanged on trees; the coward, the unwarlike, the man stained with abominable vices, is plunged into the mire of the morass, with a hurdle put over him. This distinction in punishment means that crime, they think, ought, in being punished, to be exposed, while infamy ought to be buried out of sight. Lighter offences, too, have penalties proportioned to them; he who is convicted, is fined in a certain number of horses or of cattle. Half of the fine is paid to the king or to the state, half to the person whose wrongs are avenged and to his relatives. In these same councils they also elect the chief magistrates, who administer law in the cantons and the towns. Each of these has a hundred associates chosen from the people, who support him with their advice and influence.

13.　They transact no public or private business without being armed. It is not, however, usual for anyone to wear arms till the state has recognised his power to use them. Then in the presence of the council one of the chiefs, or the young man's father, or some kinsman, equips him with a shield and a spear. These arms are what the "toga" is with us, the first honour with which youth is invested. Up to this time he is regarded as a member of a household, afterwards as a member of the commonwealth. Very noble birth or great services rendered by the father secure for lads the rank of a chief; such lads attach themselves to men of mature strength and of long approved valour. It is no shame to be seen among a chief's followers. Even in his escort there are gradations of rank, dependent on the choice of the man to whom they are attached. These followers vie keenly with each other as to who shall rank first with his chief, the chiefs as to who shall have the most numerous and the bravest followers. It is an honour as well as a source of strength to be thus always surrounded by a large body of picked youths; it is an ornament in peace and a defence in war. And not only in his own tribe but also in the neighbouring states it is the renown and glory of a chief to be distinguished for the number and valour of his followers, for such a man is courted by embassies, is honoured with presents, and the very prestige of his name often settles a war.

14.　When they go into battle, it is a disgrace for the chief to be surpassed in valour, a disgrace for his followers not to equal the valour of the chief. And it is an infamy and a reproach for life to have survived the chief, and returned from the field. To defend, to protect him, to ascribe one's own brave deeds to his renown, is the height of loyalty. The chief fights for victory; his vassals fight for their chief. If their native state sinks into the sloth of prolonged peace and repose, many of its noble youths voluntarily seek those tribes which are waging some war, both because inaction is odious to their race, and because they win renown more readily in the midst of peril, and cannot maintain a numerous following except by violence and war. Indeed, men look to the liberality of their chief for their war-horse and their blood-stained and victorious lance. Feasts and entertainments, which, though inelegant, are plentifully furnished, are their only pay. The means of this bounty come from war and rapine. Nor are they as easily persuaded to plough the earth and to wait for the year's produce as to challenge an enemy and earn the honour of wounds. Nay, they actually think it tame and stupid to acquire by the sweat of toil what they might win by their blood.

15.   Whenever they are not fighting, they pass much of their time in the chase, and still more in idleness, giving themselves up to sleep and to feasting, the bravest and the most warlike doing nothing, and surrendering the management of the household, of the home, and of the land, to the women, the old men, and all the weakest members of the family. They themselves lie buried in sloth, a strange combination in their nature that the same men should be so fond of idleness, so averse to peace. It is the custom of the states to bestow by voluntary and individual contribution on the chiefs a present of cattle or of grain, which, while accepted as a compliment, supplies their wants. They are particularly delighted by gifts from neighbouring tribes, which are sent not only by individuals but also by the state, such as choice steeds, heavy armour, trappings, and neck-chains. We have now taught them to accept money also.

16.   It is well known that the nations of Germany have no cities, and that they do not even tolerate closely contiguous dwellings. They live scattered and apart, just as a spring, a meadow, or a wood has attracted them. Their villages they do not arrange in our fashion, with the buildings connected and joined together, but every person surrounds his dwelling with an open space, either as a precaution against the disasters of fire, or because they do not know how to build. No use is made by them of stone or tile; they employ timber for all purposes, rude masses without ornament or attractiveness. Some parts of their buildings they stain more carefully with a clay so clear and bright that it resembles painting, or a coloured design. They are wont also to dig out subterranean caves, and pile on them great heaps of dung, as a shelter from winter and as a receptacle for the year's produce, for by such places they mitigate the rigour of the cold. And should an enemy approach, he lays waste the open country, while what is hidden and buried is either not known to exist, or else escapes him from the very fact that it has to be searched for.

17.   They all wrap themselves in a cloak which is fastened with a clasp, or, if this is not forthcoming, with a thorn, leaving the rest of their persons bare. They pass whole days on the hearth by the fire. The wealthiest are distinguished by a dress which is not flowing, like that of the Sarmatæ and Parthi, but is tight, and exhibits each limb. They also wear the skins of wild beasts; the tribes on the Rhine and Danube in a careless fashion, those of the interior with more elegance, as not obtaining other clothing by commerce. These select certain animals, the hides of which they strip off and vary them with the spotted skins of beasts, the produce of the outer ocean, and of seas unknown to us. The women have the same dress as the men, except that they generally wrap themselves in linen garments, which they embroider with purple, and do not lengthen out the upper part of their clothing into sleeves. The upper and lower arm is thus bare, and the nearest part of the bosom is also exposed.

18.   Their marriage code, however, is strict, and indeed no part of their manners is more praiseworthy. Almost alone among barbarians they are content with one wife, except a very few among them, and these not from sensuality, but because their noble birth procures for them many offers of alliance. The wife does not bring a dower to the husband,

but the husband to the wife. The parents and relatives are present, and pass judgment on the marriage-gifts, gifts not meant to suit a woman's taste, nor such as a bride would deck herself with, but oxen, a caparisoned steed, a shield, a lance, and a sword. With these presents the wife is espoused, and she herself in her turn brings her husband a gift of arms. This they count their strongest bond of union, these their sacred mysteries, these their gods of marriage. Lest the woman should think herself to stand apart from aspirations after noble deeds and from the perils of war, she is reminded by the ceremony which inaugurates marriage that she is her husband's partner in toil and danger, destined to suffer and to dare with him alike both in peace and in war. The yoked oxen, the harnessed steed, the gift of arms, proclaim this fact. She must live and die with the feeling that she is receiving what she must hand down to her children neither tarnished nor depreciated, what future daughters-in-law may receive, and may be so passed on to her grand-children.

19.   Thus with their virtue protected they live uncorrupted by the allurements of public shows or the stimulant of feastings. Clandestine correspondence is equally unknown to men and women. Very rare for so numerous a population is adultery, the punishment for which is prompt, and in the husband's power. Having cut off the hair of the adulteress and stripped her naked, he expels her from the house in the presence of her kinsfolk, and then flogs her through the whole village. The loss of chastity meets with no indulgence; neither beauty, youth, nor wealth will procure the culprit a husband. No one in Germany laughs at vice, nor do they call it the fashion to corrupt and to be corrupted. Still better is the condition of those states in which only maidens are given in marriage, and where the hopes and expectations of a bride are then finally terminated. They receive one husband, as having one body and one life, that they may have no thoughts beyond, no further-reaching desires, that they may love not so much the husband as the married state. To limit the number of their children or to destroy any of their subsequent offspring is accounted infamous, and good habits are here more effectual than good laws elsewhere.

20.   In every household the children, naked and filthy, grow up with those stout frames and limbs which we so much admire. Every mother suckles her own offspring, and never entrusts it to servants and nurses. The master is not distinguished from the slave by being brought up with greater delicacy. Both live amid the same flocks and lie on the same ground till the freeborn are distinguished by age and recognised by merit. The young men marry late, and their vigour is thus unimpaired. Nor are the maidens hurried into marriage; the same age and a similar stature is required; well-matched and vigorous they wed, and the offspring reproduce the strength of the parents. Sister's sons are held in as much esteem by their uncles as by their fathers; indeed, some regard the relation as even more sacred and binding, and prefer it in receiving hostages, thinking thus to secure a stronger hold on the affections and a wider bond for the family. But every man's own children are his heirs and successors, and there are no wills. Should there be no issue, the next in succession to the property are his brothers and his uncles on either side. The more relatives he has, the more numerous his connections, the more honoured is his old age; nor are there any advantages in childlessness.

21.   It is a duty among them to adopt the feuds as well as the friendships of a father or a kinsman. These feuds are not implacable; even homicide is expiated by the payment of a certain number of cattle and of sheep, and the satisfaction is accepted by the entire family, greatly to the advantage of the state, since feuds are dangerous in proportion to a people's freedom.

No nation indulges more profusely in entertainments and hospitality. To exclude any human being from their roof is thought impious; every German, according to his means, receives his guest with a well-furnished table. When his supplies are exhausted, he who was but now the host becomes the guide and companion to further hospitality, and without invitation they go to the next house. It matters not; they are entertained with like cordiality. No one distinguishes between an acquaintance and a stranger, as regards the rights of hospitality. It is usual to give the departing guest whatever he may ask for, and a present in return is asked with as little hesitation. They are greatly charmed with gifts, but they expect no return for what they give, nor feel any obligation for what they receive.

22. On waking from sleep, which they generally prolong to a late hour of the day, they take a bath, oftenest of warm water, which suits a country where winter is the longest of the seasons. After their bath they take their meal, each having a separate seat and table of his own. Then they go armed to business, or no less often to their festal meetings. To pass an entire day and night in drinking disgraces no one. Their quarrels, as might be expected with intoxicated people, are seldom fought out with mere abuse, but commonly with wounds and bloodshed. Yet it is at their feasts that they generally consult on the reconciliation of enemies, on the forming of matrimonial alliances, on the choice of chiefs, finally even on peace and war, for they think that at no time is the mind more open to simplicity of purpose or more warmed to noble aspirations. A race without either natural or acquired cunning, they disclose their hidden thoughts in the freedom of the festivity. Thus the sentiments of all having been discovered and laid bare, the discussion is renewed on the following day, and from each occasion its own peculiar advantage is derived. They deliberate when they have no power to dissemble; they resolve when error is impossible.

23. A liquor for drinking is made out of barley or other grain, and fermented into a certain resemblance to wine. The dwellers on the river-bank also buy wine. Their food is of a simple kind, consisting of wild-fruit, fresh game, and curdled milk. They satisfy their hunger without elaborate preparation and without delicacies. In quenching their thirst they are not equally moderate. If you indulge their love of drinking by supplying them with as much as they desire, they will be overcome by their own vices as easily as by the arms of an enemy.

24. One and the same kind of spectacle is always exhibited at every gathering. Naked youths who practise the sport bound in the dance amid swords and lances that threaten their lives. Experience gives them skill, and skill again gives grace; profit or pay are out of the question; however reckless their pastime, its reward is the pleasure of the spectators.

Strangely enough they make games of hazard a serious occupation even when sober, and so venturesome are they about gaining or losing, that, when every other resource has failed, on the last and final throw they stake the freedom of their own persons. The loser goes into voluntary slavery; though the younger and stronger, he suffers himself to be bound and sold. Such is their stubborn persistency in a bad practice; they themselves call it honour. Slaves of this kind the owners part with in the way of commerce, and also to relieve themselves from the scandal of such a victory.

25. The other slaves are not employed after our manner with distinct domestic duties assigned to them, but each one has the management of a house and home of his own. The master requires from the slave a certain quantity of grain, of cattle, and of clothing, as he would from a tenant, and this is the limit of subjection. All other household functions are discharged by the wife and children. To strike a slave or to punish him with bonds or with hard labour is a rare occurrence. They often kill them, not in enforcing strict discipline, but on the impulse of passion, as they would an enemy, only it is done with impunity. The freedmen do not rank much above slaves, and are seldom of any weight in the family, never in the state, with the exception of those tribes which are ruled by kings. There indeed they rise above the freeborn and the noble; elsewhere the inferiority of the freedman marks the freedom of the state.

26. Of lending money on interest and increasing it by compound interest they know nothing, – a more effectual safeguard than if it were prohibited.

Land proportioned to the number of inhabitants is occupied by the whole community in turn, and afterwards divided among them according to rank. A wide expanse of plains makes the partition easy. They till fresh fields every year, and they have still more land than enough; with the richness and extent of their soil, they do not laboriously exert themselves in planting orchards, inclosing meadows, and watering gardens. Corn is the only produce required from the earth; hence even the year itself is not divided by them into as many seasons as with us. Winter, spring, and summer have both a meaning and a name; the name and blessings of autumn are alike unknown.

27. In their funerals there is no pomp; they simply observe the custom of burning the bodies of illustrious men with certain kinds of wood. They do not heap garments or spices on the funeral pile. The arms of the dead man and in some cases his horse are consigned to the fire. A turf mound forms the tomb. Monuments with their lofty elaborate splendour they reject as oppressive to the dead. Tears and lamentations they soon dismiss; grief and sorrow but slowly. It is thought becoming for women to bewail, for men to remember, the dead.

Such on the whole is the account which I have received of the origin and manners of the entire German people.

Part II
The Middle Ages

Section II

(a) European Travelers

3

The Travels of Marco Polo

Marco Polo

Of the Wandering Life of the Tartars; of Their Domestic Manners; Their Food; and the Virtue and Useful Qualities of Their Women

The Tartars never remain fixed, but as the winter approaches remove to the plains of a warmer region, in order to find sufficient pasture for their cattle; and in summer they frequent cold situations in the mountains, where there is water and vegetation, and their cattle are free from the annoyance of horse-flies and other biting insects. During two or three months they progressively ascend higher ground, and seek fresh pasture, the grass not being adequate in any one place to feed the multitudes of which their herds and flocks consist.

Their huts or tents are formed of rods covered with felt, and being exactly round, and nicely put together, they can gather them into one bundle, and make them up as packages, which they carry along with them in their migrations, upon a sort of car with four wheels. When they have occasion to set them up again, they always make the entrance front to the south. Besides these cars they have a superior kind of vehicle upon two wheels, covered likewise with black felt, and so effectually as to protect those within it from wet, during a whole day of rain. These are drawn by oxen and camels, and serve to convey their wives and children, their utensils, and such provisions as they require. It is the women who attend to their trading concerns, who buy and sell, and provide everything necessary for their husbands and their families; the time of the men being entirely devoted to hunting, hawking, and matters that relate to the military life. They have the best falcons in the world, and also the best dogs.

They subsist entirely upon flesh and milk, eating the produce of their sport, and a certain small animal, not unlike a rabbit, which, during the summer season are found in great abundance in the plains. But they likewise eat flesh of every description, horses, camels, and even dogs, provided they are fat. They drink mares' milk, which they prepare in such a manner that it has the qualities and flavour of white wine.

Their women are not excelled in the world for chastity and decency of conduct, nor for love and duty to their husbands. Infidelity to the marriage bed is regarded by them as a vice not merely dishonourable, but of the most infamous nature. It is also admirable to observe the loyalty of the husbands towards their wives, amongst whom, although there are perhaps ten or twenty, there prevails a degree of quiet and union that is highly laudable. No

Marco Polo, *The Travels of Marco Polo [the Venetian]*, ed. Manuel Komroff, New York: Boni & Liveright, 1926, pp. 90–7, 159–61, 170–2, 174–6, 231–43.

offensive language is ever heard, their attention being fully occupied with their own affairs and their several domestic employments, such as the provision of necessary food for the family, the management of the servants, and the care of the children, which are amongst them a common concern.

The men are allowed the indulgence of taking as many wives as they choose. Their expense to the husband is not great, and on the other hand the benefit he derives from their training and from the occupations in which they are constantly engaged, is considerable. On this account he makes payment to the mother. The wife who is the first espoused has the privilege of superior attention, and is held to be the most legitimate, which extends also to the children borne by her. In consequence of this unlimited number of wives, the offspring is more numerous than amongst any other people. Upon the death of the father, the son may take to himself the wives he leaves behind, with the exception of his own mother. They cannot take their sisters to wife, but upon the death of their brothers they can marry their sisters-in-law. Every marriage is solemnized with great ceremony.

Of the God of the Tartars; and of Their Modes of Worship; of their Dress

The doctrine and faith of the Tartars are these: They believe in a deity whose nature is Sublime and Heavenly. To him they burn incense, and offer up prayers only for the enjoyment of intellectual and bodily health.

They worship another likewise, named Natigay, whose image, covered with felt or other cloth, every individual preserves in his house. To this deity they associate a wife and children, placing the former on his left side, and the latter before him. Him they consider as the divinity who presides over the Earth, protects their children, and guards their cattle and their grain. They show him great respect, and at their meals they never omit to take a fat morsel of the flesh, and with it to grease the mouth of the idol, and at the same time the mouths of its wife and children. They then throw out of the door some of the liquor in which the meat has been dressed, as an offering to the other spirits. This being done, they consider that their deity and his family have had their proper share, and proceed to eat and drink without further ceremony.

The wealthy Tartars dress in cloth of gold and silks, with skins of the sable, the ermine, and other animals, all in the richest fashion.

Concerning the Tartar Customs of War; of Their Arms and Obedience to Their Leaders

Their arms are bows, iron maces, and in some instances, spears; but the first is the weapon at which they are the most expert, being accustomed, from children, to employ it in their sports. They wear defensive armour made from buffalo and hides of other beasts, dried by the fire, and thus rendered extremely hard and strong. They are brave in battle, almost to desperation, setting little value upon their lives, and exposing themselves without hesitation to all manner of danger. Their disposition is cruel.

They are capable of supporting every kind of privation, and when there is a necessity for it, can live for a month on the milk of their mares, and upon such wild animals as they may chance to catch. Their horses are fed upon grass alone, and do not require barley or other grain. The men are trained to remain on horseback during two days and two nights, without dismounting; sleeping in that situation whilst their horses graze. No people upon earth can surpass them in fortitude under difficulties, nor show greater patience under wants of every kind. They are most obedient to their chiefs, and are maintained at small expense. From these qualities, so essential to the formation of soldiers, it is, that they are fitted to subdue the world, as in fact they have done in regard to a considerable portion of it.

When one of the great Tartar chiefs proceeds on an expedition, he puts himself at the head of an army of an hundred thousand horse, and organizes them in the following manner.

He appoints an officer to the command of every ten men, and others to command an hundred, a thousand, and ten thousand men, respectively. Thus ten of the officers commanding ten men take their orders from him who commands a hundred; of these, each ten, from him who commands a thousand; and each ten of these latter, from him who commands ten thousand.

By this arrangement each officer has only to attend to the management of ten men or ten bodies of men. Every company of a hundred men is denominated a *Tuc*, and ten of these constitute a *Toman*. When the army proceeds on service, a body of two hundred men is sent two days' march in advance, and parties are stationed upon each flank and in the rear, in order to prevent its being attacked by surprise.

When the service is distant they carry but little with them, and that, chiefly what is requisite for their encampment, and utensils for cooking. They subsist for the most part upon milk, as has been said. They are provided with small tents made of felt, under which they shelter themselves against rain. Should circumstances render it necessary, in the execution of a duty that requires despatch, they can march for ten days without lighting a fire or taking a meal. During this time they subsist upon the blood drawn from their horses, each man opening a vein, and drinking from his own cattle.

They make provision also of milk, thickened and dried to the state of a paste, which is prepared in the following manner. They boil the milk, and skimming off the rich or creamy part as it rises to the top, put it into a separate vessel as butter; for so long as that remains in the milk, it will not become hard. The latter is then exposed to the sun until it dries. Upon going on service they carry with them about ten pounds for each man, and of this, half a pound is put, every morning, into a leathern bottle, with as much water as is thought necessary. By their motion in riding the contents are violently shaken, and a thin porridge is produced, upon which they make their dinner.

When these Tartars come to engage in battle, they never mix with the enemy, but keep hovering about him, discharging their arrows first from one side and then from the other, occasionally pretending to fly, and during their flight shooting arrows backwards at their pursuers,

killing men and horses, as if they were combating face to face. In this sort of warfare the adversary imagines he has gained a victory, when in fact he has lost the battle; for the Tartars, observing the mischief they have done him, wheel about, and renewing the fight, overpower his remaining troops, and make them prisoners in spite of their utmost exertions. Their horses are so well broken-in to quick changes of movement, that upon the signal given, they instantly turn in any direction; and by these rapid manœuvres many victories have been obtained.

All that has been here related is spoken of the original manners of the Tartar chiefs; but at the present day they are much degenerated. Those who dwell in Cathay, forsaking their own laws, have adopted the customs of the people who worship idols, and those who inhabit the eastern provinces have adopted the manners of the Saracens.

Of the Rules of Justice; and of an Imaginary Kind of Marriage Between the Deceased Children of Different Families

Justice is administered by them in the following manner. When a person is convicted of a robbery not meriting the punishment of death, he is condemned to receive a certain number of strokes with a cane, – seven, seventeen, twenty-seven, thirty-seven, forty-seven, or as far as one hundred and seven, according to the value of the article stolen and circumstances of the theft. Many die under this chastisement. When for stealing a horse or other article that subjects the offender to capital punishment, he is condemned to suffer death, the sentence is executed by cutting his body in two with a sword. But if the thief has the means of paying nine times the value of the property stolen, he escapes all further punishment.

It is usual for every Chief of a tribe or other person possessing cattle, such as horses, mares, camels, oxen, or cows, to distinguish them by his mark, and then to suffer them to graze at large, in any part of the plains or mountains, without employing herdsmen to look after them. If any of them should happen to mix with the cattle of other proprietors, they are restored to the person whose mark they bear. Sheep and goats, on the contrary, have people to attend them. Their cattle of every kind are well-sized, fat, and exceedingly handsome.

When one man has had a son, and another man a daughter, although both may have been dead for some years, they have a practice of contracting a marriage between their deceased children, and of bestowing the girl upon the youth. They at the same time paint upon pieces of paper human figures to represent attendants with horses and other animals, dresses of all kinds, money, and every article of furniture; and all these, together with the marriage contract, which is regularly drawn up, they commit to the flames, in order that these things may be conveyed to their children in the other world, and that they may become husband and wife in due form. After this ceremony, the fathers and mothers consider themselves as mutually related, in the same manner as if a real connexion had taken place between their living children.

[...]

Of the Kind of Paper Money Issued by the Great Khan; and Made to Pass Current Throughout His Dominions

In this city of Kanbalu is the mint of the Great Khan, who may truly be said to possess the secret of the alchemists, as he has the art of producing money by the following process.

He causes the bark to be stripped from those mulberry-trees the leaves of which are used for feeding silk-worms, and takes from it that thin inner rind which lies between the coarser bark and the wood of the tree. This being steeped, and afterwards pounded in a mortar, until reduced to a pulp, is made into paper, resembling, in substance, that which is manufactured from cotton, but quite black. When ready for use, he has it cut into pieces of money of different sizes, nearly square, but somewhat longer than they are wide. Of these, the smallest pass for a half tournois; the next size for a Venetian silver groat; others for two, five, and ten groats;

others for one, two, three, and as far as ten bezants of gold. The coinage of this paper money is authenticated with as much form and ceremony as if it were actually of pure gold or silver; for to each note a number of officers, specially appointed, not only subscribe their names, but affix their seals also. When this has been regularly done by the whole of them, the principal officer, appointed by his Majesty, having dipped into vermilion the royal seal committed to his custody, stamps with it the piece of paper, so that the form of the seal tinged with the vermilion remains impressed upon it. In this way it receives full authenticity as current money, and the act of counterfeiting it is punished as a capital offence.

When thus coined in large quantities, this paper currency is circulated in every part of the Great Khan's dominions; nor dares any person, at the peril of his life, refuse to accept it in payment. All his subjects receive it without hesitation, because, wherever their business may call them, they can dispose of it again in the purchase of merchandise they may require; such as pearls, jewels, gold, or silver. With it, in short, every article may be procured.

Several times in the course of the year, large caravans of merchants arrive with such articles as have just been mentioned, together with gold tissues, which they lay before the Great Khan. He thereupon calls together twelve experienced and skilful persons, selected for this purpose, whom he commands to examine the articles with great care, and to fix the value at which they should be purchased. Upon the sum at which they have been thus conscientiously appraised he allows a reasonable profit, and immediately pays for them with this paper. To this the owners can have no objection, because, as has been observed, it answers the purpose of their own disbursements; and even though they should be inhabitants of a country where this kind of money is not current, they invest the amount in other articles of merchandise suited to their own markets.

When any persons happen to be possessed of paper money which from long use has become damaged, they carry it to the mint, where, upon the payment of only three per cent, they receive fresh notes in exchange. Should any be desirous of procuring gold or silver for the purposes of manufacture, such as of drinking-cups, girdles, or other articles wrought of these metals, they in like manner apply to the mint, and for their paper obtain the bullion they require.

All his Majesty's armies are paid with this currency, which is to them of the same value as if it were gold or silver. Upon these grounds, it may certainly be affirmed that the Great Khan has a more extensive command of treasure than any other sovereign in the universe.

[...]

Concerning the Black Stones Dug in Cathay Used for Fuel

Throughout this province there is found a sort of black stone, which they dig out of the mountains, where it runs in veins. When lighted, it burns like charcoal, and retains the fire much better than wood; insomuch that it may be preserved during the night, and in the morning be found still burning. These stones do not flame, excepting a little when first lighted, but during their ignition give out a considerable heat.

It is true there is no scarcity of wood in the country, but the multitude of inhabitants is so immense, and their stoves and baths, which they are continually heating, so numerous, that the quantity could not supply the demand. There is no person who does not frequent a warm bath at least three times in the week, and during the winter daily, if it is in their power. Every man of rank or wealth has one in his house for his own use; and the stock of wood must soon prove inadequate to such consumption; whereas these stones may be had in the greatest abundance, and at a cheap rate.

Of the Great and Admirable Liberality Exercised by the Great Khan Towards the Poor

It has been already stated that the Emperor distributes large quantities of grain to his subjects. We shall now speak of his great charity to and provident care of the poor in the city of Kanbalu. Upon his being informed of any respectable family, that had once lived in easy circumstances and by misfortunes reduced to poverty, or who, in consequence of infirmities, are unable to work for their living or to raise a supply of any kind of grain: to a family in that situation he gives what is necessary for their year's consumption. At the customary period they present themselves before the officers who manage this department of his Majesty's expenses and who reside in a palace where that business is transacted. Here they deliver a statement in writing of the quantity furnished to them in the preceding year, according to which they receive also for the present.

In a similar way the Emperor-provides clothing for his poor, which he has the means of doing from his tenths of wool, silk, and hemp. These materials he has woven into the different sorts of cloth, in a house erected for that purpose, where every artisan is obliged to work one day in the week for his Majesty's service. Garments made of stuffs thus manufactured he orders to be given to the poor families above described, as they are needed for their winter and their summer dresses. He also has clothing prepared for his armies, and in every city has a quantity of woollen cloth woven, which is paid for from the amount of the tenths levied at the place.

Of the Many Persons Who Apply for Relief at the Emperor's Court

It should be known that the Tartars, when they followed their original customs, and had not yet adopted the religion of the idolaters, were not in the practice of bestowing alms, and when a poor man applied to them, they drove him away saying, "Begone with your complaint of a bad season which God has sent you; had He loved you, as He loves me, He would have provided for you."

But since the wise men of the idolaters, and especially the Bacsis, already mentioned, have represented to his Majesty that providing for the poor is a good work and highly acceptable to their deities, he has relieved their wants in the manner stated, and at his court none are denied food who come to ask it. Not a day passes in which there are not distributed, by the regular officers, twenty thousand vessels of rice, millet, and panicum. By reason of this admirable and astonishing liberality which the Great Khan exercises towards the poor, the people all adore him.

[…]

Of the Religion of the Tartars; of the Opinions They Hold as to the Soul; and of Some of Their Customs

As has already been observed, these people are idolaters, and for deities, each person has a tablet fixed up against a high part of the wall of his chamber, upon which is written a name, that serves to denote the high, celestial, and sublime God. To this they pay daily adoration, with incense burning. Lifting up their hands and then striking their faces against the floor three times, they implore from Him the blessings of sound intellect and health of body; but of Him they ask nothing else. Below this, on the floor, they have a statue which they name Natigay, which they consider as the God of all terrestrial things or whatever is produced from the earth. They give him a wife and children, and worship him in a similar manner, burning incense, raising their hands, and bending to the floor. To him they pray for seasonable weather, abundant crops, increase of family, and the like.

They believe the soul to be immortal, after this fashion. Immediately upon the death of a man, it enters into another body, and that accordingly as he has acted virtuously or wickedly during his life, his future state will become, progressively, better or worse. If he be a poor man, and has conducted himself worthily and decently, he will be re-born, in the first instance, from the womb of a gentlewoman, and become, himself, a gentleman; next, from the womb of a lady of rank, and become a nobleman; thus continually ascending in the scale of existence until he be united to the divinity. But if, on the contrary, being the son of a gentleman, he has behaved unworthily, he will, in his next state,

be a clown, and at length a dog, continually descending and going down lower and lower.

Their style of conversation is courteous; they salute each other politely and with cheerful countenance, have an air of good breeding, and eat their food with particular cleanliness. To their parents they show the utmost reverence. Should it happen that a child acts disrespectfully or neglects to assist his parents when necessary, there is a public tribunal, whose especial duty it is to punish with severity this crime of filial ingratitude.

Malefactors guilty of various crimes, who are apprehended and thrown into prison, are executed by strangling. But such as remain for three years, being the time appointed by his Majesty for a general prison release, and are then liberated, have a mark branded upon one of their cheeks, that they may be recognized.

The present Great Khan has prohibited all species of gambling and other modes of cheating, to which the people of this country are addicted more than any others upon earth. As an argument for deterring them from this practice, he said: "I subdued you by the power of my sword, and consequently whatever you possess belongs of right to me: if you gamble, therefore, you are sporting with my property." He does not, however, take anything arbitrarily in virtue of this right.

The order and regularity observed by all ranks of people, when they present themselves before his Majesty, ought not to pass unnoticed. When they approach within half a mile of the place where he happens to be, they show their respect for his exalted character by assuming a humble, placid, and quiet demeanour, insomuch that not the least noise, nor the voice of any person calling out, or even speaking aloud, is heard. Every man of rank carries with him a small vessel, into which he spits, so long as he continues in the hall of audience, no one daring to spit on the floor; and this being done, he replaces the cover, and makes a salutation. They are accustomed likewise to take with them handsome buskins made of white leather, and when they reach the court, but before they enter the hall they put on these white buskins, and give those in which they had walked to the care of the servants. This practice is observed that they may not soil the beautiful carpets,

Figure 3.1 *The city of Kin-Sai*

which are curiously wrought with silk and gold, and exhibit a variety of colours.

[...]

Of the Noble and Magnificent City of Kin-Sai

Upon leaving Va-giu you pass, in the course of three days' journey, many towns, castles, and villages, all of them well inhabited and opulent. The people have abundance of provisions. At the end of three days you reach the noble and magnificent city of Kin-sai [= capital; Hang-chau], a name that signifies "The Celestial City," and which it merits from its pre-eminence to all others in the world, in point of grandeur and beauty, as well as from its abundant delights, which might lead an inhabitant to imagine himself in paradise.

This city was frequently visited by Marco Polo, who carefully and diligently observed and inquired into every circumstance respecting it, all of which he recorded in his notes, from whence the following particulars are briefly stated. According to common estimation, this city is an hundred miles in circuit. Its streets and canals are extensive, and there are squares, or market-places, which being necessarily proportioned in size to the prodigious concourse of people by whom they are frequented, are exceedingly spacious. It is situated between a lake of fresh and very clear water on the one side, and a river of great magnitude on the other, the waters of which, by a number of canals, large and small, are made to run through every quarter of the city, carrying with them all the filth into the lake, and ultimately to the sea. This furnishes a communication by water, in addition to that by land, to all parts of the town. The canals and the streets being of sufficient width to allow of boats on the one, and carriages in the other, to pass easily with articles necessary for the inhabitants.

It is commonly said that the number of bridges, of all sizes, amounts to twelve thousand. Those which are thrown over the principal canals and are connected with the main streets, have arches so high, and built with so much skill, that vessels with their masts can pass under them. At the same time, carts and horses can pass over, so well is the slope from the street graded to the height of the arch. If they were not so numerous, there would be no way of crossing from one place to another.

Beyond the city, and enclosing it on that side, there is a ditch about forty miles in length, very wide, and full of water that comes from the river before mentioned. This was excavated by the ancient kings of the province, in order that when the river should overflow its banks, the superfluous water might be diverted into this channel. This serves at the same time as a measure of defence. The earth dug out from thence was thrown to the inner side, and has the appearance of many hillocks, surrounding the place.

There are within the city ten principal squares or marketplaces, besides innumerable shops along the streets. Each side of these squares is half a mile in length, and in front of them is the main street, forty paces in width, and running in a direct line from one extremity of the city to the other. It is crossed by many low and convenient bridges. These market-squares are at the distance of four miles from each other. In a direction parallel to that of the main street, but on the opposite side of the squares, runs a very large canal, on the nearer bank of which capacious warehouses are built of stone, for the accommodation of the merchants who arrive from India and other parts with their goods and effects. They are thus conveniently situated with respect to the market-places. In each of these, upon three days in every week, there is an assemblage of from forty to fifty thousand persons, who attend the markets and supply them with every article of provision that can be desired.

There is an abundant quantity of game of all kinds, such as roebucks, stags, fallow deer, hares, and rabbits, together with partridges, pheasants, francolins, quails, common fowls, capons, and such numbers of ducks and geese as can scarcely be expressed; for so easily are they bred and reared on the lake, that, for the value of a Venetian silver groat, you may purchase a couple of geese and two couple of ducks.

There, also, are the shambles, where they slaughter cattle for food, such as oxen, calves, kids, and lambs, to furnish the tables of rich persons and of the great magistrates. As to the people of the lower classes, they eat every kind of meat, without any discrimination.

At all seasons there is in the markets a great variety of herbs and fruits, and especially pears of an extraordinary size, weighing ten pounds each, that are white in the inside, like paste, and have a very fragrant smell. There are peaches also, in their season, both of the yellow and white kind, and of a delicious flavour. Grapes are not produced there, but are brought in a dried state, and very good, from other parts. This applies also to wine, which the natives do not hold in estimation, being accustomed to their own liquor prepared from rice and spices. From the sea, which is fifteen miles distant, there is daily brought up the river, to the city, a vast quantity of fish; and in the lake also there is abundance, which gives employment at all times to persons whose sole occupation it is to catch them. The sorts are various according to the season of the year. At the sight of such an importation of fish, you would think it impossible that it could be sold; and yet, in the course of a few hours, it is all taken off, so great is the number of inhabitants, even of those classes which can afford to indulge in such luxuries, for fish and flesh are eaten at the same meal.

Each of the ten market-squares is surrounded with high dwelling-houses, in the lower part of which are shops, where every kind of manufacture is carried on, and every article of trade is sold; such, amongst others, as spices, drugs, trinkets, and pearls. In certain shops nothing is vended but the wine of the country, which they are continually brewing, and serve out fresh to their customers at a moderate price. The streets connected with the market-squares are numerous, and in some of them are many cold baths, attended by servants of both sexes. The men and women who frequent them, have from their childhood been accustomed at all times to wash in cold water, which they reckon highly conducive to health. At these bathing places, however, they have apartments provided with warm water, for the use of strangers, who cannot bear the shock of the cold. All are in the daily practice of washing their persons, and especially before their meals.

In other streets are the quarters of the courtesans who are here in such numbers as

I dare not venture to report. Not only near the squares, which is the situation usually appropriated for their residence, but in every part of the city they are to be found, adorned with much finery, highly perfumed, occupying well-furnished houses, and attended by many female domestics. These women are accomplished, and are perfect in the arts of caressing and fondling which they accompany with expressions adapted to every description of person. Strangers who have once tasted of their charms, remain in a state of fascination, and become so enchanted by their wanton arts, that they can never forget the impression. Thus intoxicated with sensual pleasures, when they return to their homes they report that they have been in Kin-sai, or The Celestial City, and look forward to the time when they may be enabled to revisit this paradise.

In other streets are the dwellings of the physicians and the astrologers, who also give instructions in reading and writing, as well as in many other arts. They have apartments also amongst those which surround the market-squares. On opposite sides of each of these squares there are two large edifices, where officers appointed by the Great Khan are stationed, to take immediate notice of any differences that may happen to arise between the foreign merchants, or amongst the inhabitants of the place. It is their duty likewise to see that the guards upon the several bridges in their respective vicinities are duly placed, and in cases of neglect, to punish the offenders at their discretion.

On each side of the principal street, already mentioned as extending from one end of the city to the other, there are houses and mansions of great size, with their gardens, and near to these, the dwellings of the artisans, who work in shops, at their several trades; and at all hours you see such multitudes of people passing and repassing, on their various avocations, that the providing food in sufficiency for their maintenance might be deemed an impossibility. It is observed, however, that on every market-day, the squares are crowded with tradespeople, who cover the whole space with the articles brought by carts and boats, for all of which they find sale. From the single article of pepper, some notion may be formed of the whole quantity of provisions, meat, wine, groceries, and the like, required for the consumption of the inhabitants of Kin-sai. Marco Polo learned from an officer employed in the Great Khan's customs, the daily amount of pepper bought was forty-three loads, each load being two hundred and forty-three pounds.

The inhabitants of the city are idolaters, and they use paper money as currency. The men as well as the women have fair complexions, and are handsome. The greater part of them are always clothed in silk, in consequence of the vast quantity of that material produced in the territory of Kin-sai, exclusively of what the merchants import from other provinces.

Amongst the handicraft trades exercised in the place, there are twelve considered to be superior to the rest, as being more generally useful. There are a thousand workshops for each craft, and each shop furnishes employment for ten, fifteen, or twenty workmen, and in a few instances as many as forty, under their respective masters. The opulent masters in these shops do not labour with their own hands, but, on the contrary, assume airs of gentility and affect parade. Their wives equally abstain from work. They have much beauty, as has been remarked, and are brought up with delicate and languid habits. The costliness of their dresses, in silks and jewelry, can scarcely be imagined. Although the laws of their ancient kings ordained that each citizen should exercise the profession of his father, yet they were allowed, when they acquired wealth, to avoid manual labour, provided they kept up the establishment, and employ persons to work at their paternal trades.

Their houses are well built and richly adorned with carved work. So much do they delight in ornaments of this kind, in paintings, and fancy buildings, that the sums they lavish on such objects are enormous.

The natural disposition of the native inhabitants of Kin-sai is peaceful, and by the example of their former kings, who were themselves unwarlike, they have been accustomed to habits of tranquillity. The management of arms is unknown to them, nor do they keep any in their houses. They conduct their mercantile and manufacturing concerns with perfect candour and honesty. They are friendly towards each other, and persons who inhabit the same street, both men and women, from the mere circumstance of neighbourhood, appear like one family.

In their domestic manners they are free from jealousy or suspicion of their wives, to whom great respect is shown, and any man would be accounted infamous who should presume to use indecent expressions to a married woman. To strangers also, who visit their city in the way of commerce, they give proofs of cordiality, inviting them freely to their houses, showing them friendly attention, and furnishing them with the best advice and assistance in their mercantile transactions. On the other hand, they dislike the sight of soldiery, not excepting the guards of the Great Khan, for they remind them that they were deprived of the government of their native kings and rulers.

On the borders of the lake are many handsome and spacious edifices belonging to men of rank and great magistrates. There are likewise many idol temples, with their monasteries, occupied by a number of monks, who perform the service of the idols. Near the central part are two islands, upon each of which stands a superb building, with an incredible number of apartments and separate pavilions. When the inhabitants of the city have occasion to celebrate a wedding, or to give a sumptuous entertainment, they resort to one of these islands, where they find ready for their purpose every article that can be required, such as vessels, napkins, table linen, and the like, which are provided and kept there at the common expense of the citizens, by whom also the buildings were erected. It may happen that at one time there are a hundred parties assembled there, at wedding or other feasts, all of whom, notwithstanding, are accommodated with separate rooms or pavilions, so judiciously arranged that they do not interfere with each other.

In addition to this, there are upon the lake a great number of pleasure vessels or barges, calculated for holding ten, fifteen, to twenty persons, being from fifteen to twenty paces in length, with a wide and flat flooring, and not liable to heel to either side in passing through the water. Such persons as take delight in the amusement, and mean to enjoy it, either in the company of their women or that of their male companions, engage one of these barges, which are always kept in the nicest order, with proper seats and tables, together with every other kind of furniture necessary for giving an entertainment. The cabins have a flat roof or upper deck, where the boatmen take their place, and by means of long poles, which they thrust to the bottom of the lake, which is not more than one or two fathoms in depth, they shove the barges along, until they reach the desired spot. These cabins are painted inside with various colours and with a variety of figures; all parts of the vessel are likewise adorned with painting. There are windows on each side, which may either be kept shut, or opened, to give an opportunity to the company, as they sit at table, of looking out in every direction and feasting their eyes on the variety and beauty of the scenes as they pass them. And truly the gratification afforded in this manner, upon the water, exceeds any that can be derived from the amusements on the land; for as the lake extends the whole length of the city, on one side, you have a view, as you stand in the boat, at a certain distance from the shore, of all its grandeur and beauty, its palaces, temples, convents, and gardens, with trees of the largest size growing down to the water's edge, whilst at the same time you enjoy the sight of other boats of the same description, continually passing you, filled in like manner with parties in pursuit of amusement. In fact, the inhabitants of this place, as soon as the labours of the day have ceased, or their mercantile transactions are closed, think of nothing else than of passing the remaining hours in parties of pleasure, with their wives or their mistresses, either in these barges, or about the city in carriages, of which it will here be proper to give some account, as constituting one of the amusements of these people.

Further Particulars Concerning the Great City of Kin-Sai

It must be observed, in the first place, that the streets of Kin-sai are all paved with stone and bricks, and so likewise are all the principal roads extending from thence through the province of Manji, by means of which passengers can travel to every part without soiling their feet. But as the couriers of his Majesty, who go on horseback with great speed, cannot make use of the pavement, a part of the road, on one side, is on their account left unpaved.

The main street of the city is paved with stone and brick to the width of ten paces on each side, the intermediate part being filled up with small gravel, and provided with arched drains for carrying off the rain-water that falls, into the neighbouring canals, so that it remains always dry. On this gravel carriages continually pass and repass. They are of a long shape, covered at top, have curtains and cushions of silk, and are capable of holding six persons. Both men and women who feel disposed to take their pleasure, are in the daily practice of hiring them for that purpose, and accordingly at every hour you may see vast numbers of them driven along the middle part of the street. Some of them proceed to visit certain gardens, where the company are introduced, by those who have the management of the place, to shady recesses contrived by the gardeners for that purpose. Here the men indulge themselves all day in the society of their women, returning home, when it becomes late, in the manner they came.

It is the custom of the people of Kin-sai, upon the birth of a child, for the parents to make a note, immediately, of the day, hour, and minute at which the delivery took place. They then inquire of an astrologer under what sign or aspect of the heavens the child was born; and his answer is likewise committed carefully to writing. When therefore he is grown up, and is about to engage in any mercantile adventure, voyage, or treaty of marriage, this document is carried to the astrologer, who, having examined it, and weighed all the circumstances, pronounces certain oracular words, in which these people, who sometimes find them justified by the event, place great confidence. Of these astrologers, or rather magicians, great numbers are to be met with in every market-place, and no marriage is ever celebrated until an opinion has been pronounced upon it by one of that profession.

It is also their custom, upon the death of any great and rich personage, to observe the following ceremonies. The relations, male and female, clothe themselves in coarse dresses, and accompany the body to the place appointed for burning it. The procession is likewise attended by performers on various musical instruments, which are sounded as it moves along, and prayers to their idols are chanted in a loud voice. When arrived at the spot, they throw into the flame many pieces of cotton-paper, upon which are painted representations of male and female servants, horses, camels, silk wrought with gold, as well as of gold and silver money. This is done, in the belief that the deceased will possess in the other world all these conveniences, in their natural state of flesh and bones, together with the money and the silks. As soon as the pile has been consumed, they sound all the instruments of music at the same time, producing a loud and long-continued noise. They imagine that by these ceremonies their idols are induced to receive the soul of the man whose corpse has been reduced to ashes.

In every street of this city there are stone buildings or towers. In case of a fire breaking out in any quarter, an accident by no means unusual, as the houses are mostly constructed of wood, the inhabitants may remove their effects to these towers for security.

By a regulation which his Majesty has established, there is a guard of ten watchmen stationed, under cover, upon all the principal bridges, of whom five do duty by day and five by night. Each of these guards is provided with a sonorous wooden instrument as well as one of metal, together with a water device, by means of which the hours of the day and night are ascertained. As soon as the first hour of the night is expired, one of the watchmen gives a single stroke upon the wooden instrument, and also upon the metal gong, which announces to the people of the neighbouring streets that it is the first hour. At the expiration of the second, two strokes are given; and so on progressively, increasing the number of strokes as the hours advance. The guard is not allowed to sleep, and must be always on the alert. In the morning, as soon as the sun begins to appear, a single stroke is again struck, as in the evening, and so onwards from hour to hour.

Some of these watchmen patrol the streets, to observe whether any person has a light or fire burning after the hour appointed for extinguishing them. Upon making the discovery, they affix a mark to the door, and in the morning the owner of the house is taken before the magistrates, by whom, if he cannot assign a legitimate excuse for his offence, he is punished. Should they find any person abroad at an unseasonable hour, they arrest and confine him, and in the morning he is carried before the same tribunal. If they notice any person who from lameness or other infirmity is unable to work, they place him in one of the hospitals, of which there are several in every part of the city, founded by the ancient kings, and liberally endowed. When cured, he is obliged to work at some trade.

Immediately upon the appearance of fire breaking out in a house, they give the alarm by beating on the wooden machine, when the watchmen from all the bridges within a certain distance assemble to extinguish it, as well as to save the effects of the merchants and others, by removing them to the stone towers that have been mentioned. The goods are also sometimes put into boats, and conveyed to the islands in the lake. Even on such occasions the inhabitants dare not stir out of their houses, when the fire happens in the night, and only those can be present whose goods are actually being removed, together with the guard collected to assist, which seldom amounts to a smaller number than from one to two thousand men.

In cases also of tumult or insurrection amongst the citizens, the services of this police guard are necessary; but, independently of them, his Majesty always keeps on foot a large body of troops, both infantry and cavalry, in the city and its vicinity, the command of which he gives to his ablest officers.

For the purposes of nightly watch, there are mounds of earth thrown up, at the distance of above a mile from each other, on the top of which a wooden frame is constructed, with a sounding board, which being struck with a mallet by the guard stationed there, the noise is heard to a great distance. If precautions of this nature were not taken upon occasions of fire, there would be danger of half the city being consumed; and their use is obvious also in the event of popular commotion, as, upon the signal being given, the guards at the several bridges arm themselves, and repair to the spot where their presence is required.

4

The Travels of Sir John Mandeville

John Mandeville

Of the Customs of the Saracens and of Their Law; How the Sultan Talked with the Author of This Book; and of the Beginning of Muhammad, etc.

Now, because I have talked of the Saracens and their lands, I will tell you something of their laws and their creed, as it is contained in the book of their law, the Koran. Some call it *Messaph* [Arabic *mashaf*, 'holy'] and some *Harme* [*horme*, 'holy'] according to the language of different countries. Muhammad gave them this book. Amongst other things in that book is contained the statement, and I have often read and seen it there, that good men, when they are dead, will go to Paradise, and the wicked shall go to the pains of Hell. All Saracens believe this firmly. And if they are asked what paradise they are talking about, they say it is a place of delights, where a man shall find all kinds of fruit at all seasons of the year, and rivers running with wine, and milk, and honey, and clear water; they say they will have beautiful palaces and fine great mansions, according to their deserts, and that those palaces and mansions are made of precious stones, gold and silver. Every man shall have four score wives, who will be beautiful damsels, and he shall lie with them whenever he wishes, and he will

always find them virgins. They all believe they will have all this in Paradise, and this is against our creed. The Saracens accept the Incarnation, and they will willingly speak of the Virgin Mary; they say that she was taught by an angel, and that the angel Gabriel told her that she had been chosen by God before the world's beginning to conceive Jesus Christ and bear Him; they say she bore Him and yet was a virgin afterwards as she was before. And the Koran agrees with this. They also say that Christ spoke as soon as He was born, and that He was (and is) a holy and a true prophet in word and deed, and merciful and just to all, and without sin. They also affirm that when the angel saluted Our Lady and told her of the Incarnation, she was greatly ashamed and astonished at his words; they say this was principally because there was at that time in the district an evil man, called Takyna, who dabbled in sorcery, through his enchantments pretending to be an angel and deceiving young maidens often to seduce them. Therefore Mary was afraid, and conjured the angel to say whether or not he was Takyna. And the angel answered her and told her to have no fear, for he was God's true messenger. Their book, the Koran, also says that when Mary was delivered of her Child, in the shade of a palm tree, she was greatly ashamed and wept, saying she wished she was dead. And immediately the Child spoke and comforted

John Mandeville, *The Travels of Sir John Mandeville*, trans. C. W. R. D. Moseley, London: Penguin Books, 1983, pp. 104–10, 141–4, 178–9.

her, saying, 'Be not afraid, for in you has God made His covenant for the salvation of the world.' And their Koran witnesses in many other places that Jesus Christ spoke as soon as He was born. That book says that Christ was sent by God Almighty into the world as an example and mirror for all men. It also speaks of the Day of Judgement, how God will come and judge all men; the good He will draw to His side and give them everlasting joy and glory, and the wicked He will damn to the unending torments of Hell. They say that Christ is the best among all the prophets, the most worthy, the nearest to God, and that He made the Gospels, in which are healthy doctrine, truth, and exhortation for those who believe in God; they say he was greater than a prophet, in that he lived without sin, gave sight to the blind, healed lepers and raised men to life again from the dead – and went to Heaven in His body. When they can get hold of written copies of the Gospels, they honour them greatly, especially the gospel of *Missus est*; that gospel those who are literate kiss with great devotion, and say it often in their prayers. Each year they fast for a whole month, eating only in the evening, and they keep them from their wives all that month. Those who are sick, though, are not obliged to perform this fast. The book, the Koran, also speaks of the Jews, saying they are wicked and accursed, because they will not believe that Jesus was sent from God; it also says they lie about Mary and her Son Jesus Christ, when they say they crucified Him. The Koran says they did not crucify Jesus, for God took Him up to Himself without death and transferred the form and appearance of His body to Judas Iscariot, and it was him the Jews crucified, thinking it was Jesus. But Jesus, they say, was taken all alive into Heaven, and in His flesh will He come to judge the world. This Christians do not believe, and therefore they say that they do not believe correctly when Christians maintain Christ was killed on the Cross. All their chief ideas are in the Koran. The Saracens also say that if Jesus had been crucified, God would have acted contrary to His justice in allowing such a guiltless innocent to die; they say we are wrong about this. But it is they who are wrong. They freely admit that all the deeds of Christ, His sayings, His teaching and His gospels are good, and true; and His miracles also are true. They freely confess that the Virgin Mary was a good and holy maiden, pure and unspotted, both before and after the birth of Christ; and that those who believe perfectly in God shall be saved. And because they come so near to our faith in these points – and many others – it seems to me that they could be much more quickly and easily converted to our creed by the preaching and instruction of Christian men. They say they well know from their prophecies that the law of Muhammad shall fail as the law of the Jews failed, and that the Christian law shall endure to the end of the world. If a man ask them what their creed is, they answer, 'We believe in God, who made Heaven and every-thing else from nothing, and nothing was made except by Him. We believe the Day of Judgement will come, when each man will be rewarded according to his deserts. We also truly believe that all that God spoke through His holy proph-ets while they were on earth is the truth.' They also say that Muhammad in the Koran ordained that every man should have three or four wives. But now they take more, for some of them have nine; and each man takes as many concubines as he can maintain on his wealth. If any of their wives should sin against her husband and let another man sleep with her, it is then lawful for her husband to divorce her and take another wife in her stead; but he has to give her a por-tion of his property. When men speak of the Trinity to them they say that there are three Persons, but not one God. For their Koran does not talk of the Trinity. Nevertheless they grant that God has a Word, for otherwise He would be dumb; and a Spirit, or else He would be without life. When men speak to them of Christ's Incarnation, of how by the word of the angel God sent wisdom to earth and [shrouded Himself] in the Virgin Mary, they say all this is true and they believe it, and that God's Word has great power, and the man who does not know God's Word does not know God. They also say that Christ was God's Word; so says the Koran, where it says that the angel spoke to Mary saying, 'Mary, God shall send to thee the Word of His mouth, and His name shall be called Jesus Christ.' Also they say that Abraham was God's friend, Moses God's spokesman, and Jesus Christ the Word and Spirit of God, and that Muhammad was the true messenger of God; of all these four Jesus was the worthiest and most excellent. Thus it seems that the Saracens have many articles of our faith, if not perfectly; so it would be the easier to convert them and bring them to our truth – especially those who are literate and know the Scriptures. For among them they have the Gospels and the Prophets and all the Bible, written in the Saracen language. But they do not understand Holy Writ spiritually, but according to the letter, as do the Jews; and so Saint Paul says, *Litera occidit, spiritus autem uiuificat*, which is to say, 'The letter kills, but the spirit giveth life.' Therefore some Saracens say that the Jews are wicked men, and cursed, because they have broken the Law that God gave them through Moses; and they say Christian men are wicked and evil because they do not keep the Commandment of the Gospel, which Jesus Christ ordained for them.

Now I shall tell you what the Sultan told me one day in his chamber. He made everyone else leave his chamber, lords as well as others who were there, for he wanted to have a private talk between ourselves alone. And when they had all gone out, he asked me how Christians governed themselves in our countries. And I said, 'Lord, well enough – thanks be to God.' And he answered and said, 'Truly, no. It is not so. For your priests do not serve God properly by righteous living, as they should do. For they ought to give less learned men an example of how to live well, and they do the very opposite, giving examples of all manner of wickedness. And as a result, on holy days, when people should go to church to serve God, they go to the tavern and spend all the day – and perhaps all the night – in drinking and gluttony, like beasts without reason which do not know when they have had enough. And afterwards through drunkenness they fall to proud speeches, fighting and quarrelling, till someone kills somebody. Christian men commonly deceive one another, and swear the most important oaths falsely. And they are, moreover, so swollen with pride and vainglory that they never know how to dress themselves – sometimes they wear short fashions of clothing, sometimes long, sometimes cut full, sometimes figure-fitting. You ought to be simple,

meek and truthful, and ready to give charity and alms, as Christ was, in whom you say you believe. But it is quite otherwise. For Christians are so proud, so envious, such great gluttons, so lecherous, and moreover so full of covetousness, that for a little silver they will sell their daughters, their sisters, even their own wives to men who want to lie with them. And everyone takes another's wife, and no one keeps his faith to another: and you so wickedly and evilly despise and break the Law that Christ gave you. Certainly it is because of your sinfulness that you have lost all this land which we hold and keep. Because of your evil living and your sin and not because of our strength God has given it into our hands. And we well know that when you serve your God properly and well, and serve Him with good works, no man shall be able to stand against you. We know too by our prophecies that the Christians shall recover this land again in the time to come, when you serve your God well and devoutly. But as long as you live as you do in wickedness and sin, we have no fear of you; for your God will not help you.' When I had heard the Sultan speak these words – and many more which I will not repeat now – I asked him, with great respect, how he came by so full a knowledge of the state of Christendom. And then he had all the great lords and worthies that he had previously sent out called in; and he detailed four of them – great lords – to talk to me. These described to me all the manners of my country, and of other countries in Christendom as fully and as truly as if they had always lived in them. These lords and the Sultan spoke French wonderfully well, and I was astonished by that. Finally I understood that the Sultan sends some of his lords to different kingdoms and lands in the guise of merchants – some with precious stones, some with cloths of gold, some with other jewels – and that these visit all realms in order to size up the manners of us Christian men and spot our weaknesses. It seemed to me then a cause for great shame that Saracens, who have neither a correct faith nor a perfect law, should in this way reprove us for our failings, keeping their false law better than we do that of Jesus Christ; and those who ought by our good example to be turned to the faith and Law of Jesus Christ are driven away by our wicked ways of living. And so it is no wonder that they call us sinful and wicked, for it is true. But they are very devout and honest in their law, keeping well the commandments of the Koran, which God sent them by His messenger Muhammad, to whom, so they say, the angel Gabriel spoke often, telling him the will of God.

You ought to know that Muhammad was born in Arabia, and at first was a poor fellow, looking after horses and camels and travelling with merchants to Egypt, which at that time was inhabited by Christians. In the deserts of Arabia, on the highroad to Egypt, there was a chapel, and a hermit living in it. And Muhammad went into this chapel to speak with the hermit. And when he entered the chapel, the doorway, which was very low, suddenly grew as tall as the gate of a great palace. This, as they say, was the first miracle he did, when he was young. After that Muhammad began to be wise, and rich, and a great astronomer. The prince of the land of Corodan [Khorasan] made him ruler and governor of his land; and he governed it wisely and graciously, so that, when the prince was dead, he married the princess, who was called Cadrige [Khadíja]. This Muhammad had epilepsy, and often fell through the violence of that illness; and the lady sorrowed much that she had married him. But he made her believe that each time he fell the angel Gabriel appeared and spoke to him, and that he fell down because of the dazzling brightness of the angel. And therefore the Saracens say that the angel Gabriel often spoke to him. This Muhammad reigned in Arabia in the year of Our Lord 620; he was of the race of Ishmael, who was Abraham's son, whom he begot on Agar [Hagar] his handmaiden. And for this reason some Saracens are called Ishmaelites, some Agarrenes after Hagar, and some Ammonites after two sons of Loth [Lot], which he begot on his two daughters. Some, quite properly, are called Saracens, after the city of Sarras [Shiraz?]. Also Muhammad once well loved a good hermit who lived in the wilderness a mile from Mount Sinai on the road as one goes from Arabia to Chaldea and India – a day's journey from the sea, where Venetian merchants often come to buy merchandise. And Muhammad went so often to this hermit

to hear him preach that his servants grew angry and disgruntled about it. For he went thither so often, and so eagerly listened to this hermit preaching that many a time he made his men stay awake all night long; and it seemed that his men dearly wished that this hermit were dead. So it happened one night that Muhammad was drunk with wine, and fell asleep; and while he slept, his men drew his own sword from its sheath and slew the hermit with it; when they had done this, they sheathed the sword again, all bloody. In the morning, when Muhammad woke and found the hermit dead, he was very angry and would have slain all his men, for he said they had murdered him among themselves. But with one accord and one voice they all said that he himself had slain him in his sleep, when he was drunk, and they showed him the sword all bloody; and then he believed that they were telling the truth. Then he cursed wine and all those who drink it; and therefore devout Saracens will not touch it. But they do have another kind of drink which is good and delicious and very fortifying, which is made of different spices; especially calamus, of which good sugar is made. Nevertheless some Saracens will gladly drink wine in private, but not publicly – for if they drink wine openly they will be censured for it. It sometimes happens that Christian men become Saracens, out of poverty, or foolishness, or through wickedness; and the man who is chief master and judge of their law, when he receives them into their faith, says *La elles ella sila Machomet rores alla hec*, which means, 'There is no God but one, and Muhammad his messenger.'

[…]

Of the Great Khan of Cathay; of the Royalty of His Palace, and How He Sits at Meat; and of the Great Number of Servants Who Serve Him

The land of Cathay is a great country, beautiful, rich, fertile, full of good merchandise. Every year merchants come there to get spices and other sorts of merchandise – they go there more frequently than they do elsewhere. You should understand that the merchants who come from Venice or Genoa or other places in Lombardy or the Greek Empire travel by land and sea for eleven or twelve months before they get to Cathay, the chief realm of the Great Khan. In the east there is an old city, near which the Tartarenes have built another, called Gaydon [the great court of the Mongols, near Peking]. This city has twelve gates, and each gate is a mile from the next, so the circuit of the city is twenty-four miles [*sic*]. This city is the seat of the Great Khan; his throne is in a very fair palace, the boundary wall of which is two miles and more long. Within that wall there are other fine palaces too. In the garden of the great palace is a hill on which is another beautiful and rich palace – there is not another like it in all the world. And all round the palace and the hill are many trees, bearing many different sorts of fruit; beyond, there are deep broad dykes; beyond those again, there are many fishponds and pools, whereon there are many water fowl, like swans, cranes, herons, bitterns, mallards and others. Outside those again are all kinds of wild game – harts and hinds, bucks and does, and roe deer, and others. And whenever the Great Khan wants to have sport hawking or hunting, he can kill wildfowl with hawks and kill deer with his hounds or other means without leaving his room. This palace, his seat, is wonderfully large and beautiful; and the hall of that palace is richly furnished. Within the hall are twenty-four pillars of gold; and all the walls are covered with the red skins of beasts, called *panters* [pandas?]. They are very fine animals, sweet smelling, and because of the good smell of the skins no harmful air can come therein. These skins are as red as any blood, and shine so in the sun that a man can hardly look at them because of their brightness. The folk of that country honour that beast, when they see it, on account of its good properties and the sweet smell that comes from it; they praise the skin of it as much as if it had been of fine gold. In the middle of the palace a dais has been made for the Great Khan, adorned with gold and precious stones. At its four corners there are four dragons made of gold. This dais has a canopy of silken cloth, barred across with gold and silver, and there are many large precious stones hanging on it. And below the dais are conduits full of drink, which the people of

the Emperor's court drink from; beside the conduits are set vessels of gold which men can drink from when they wish. This hall is nobly and gloriously set out in every way. First, up on the top of the high dais, in the very middle, the throne for the Emperor is positioned, high up from the pavement, where he sits and eats his food. The table he eats on is made of jewels set in fine gold, and is bordered with gold set full of gems. The steps up which he goes to his throne are all of precious stone set in gold. At the left side of his throne is the seat of his chief wife, one step lower than his; it is of jasper, with sides of fine gold set with precious stones, and her table is of jasper bordered with gem-inlaid gold. The seat of his second wife is a step lower than the other's; and her seat and table are adorned as magnificently as the other wife's. The table and seat of the third wife is a step lower still. For he always has three wives with him, wherever he goes far or near. Next to his third wife on the same side sit other ladies of the Emperor's kin, each one a step lower than another according to how near they are in blood-relationship to the Emperor. The women of that country who are married have on their heads something like a man's foot, made of gold and gems and peacock feathers, beautifully made and glinting in the light; this is a token that they are under the rule of a man. Those who are not wedded do not have such hats. On the right hand of the Emperor sits his eldest son, who will rule after him, a step lower than his father. His seat and table are in every way exactly like the Empress's. Then there sit other lords of the Emperor's family, everyone according to his degree, like the ladies on the other side. Each has a table to himself, like the ladies; they are either of jasper or crystal or amethyst or *lignum aloes*, which comes out of Paradise, or of ivory. And all the tables are bordered with gold set full of precious stones, so that there is not one that is not worth a great treasure. Under the Emperor's table, at his feet, sit four clerks, who write down all the words he says while he is eating, whether they be good or ill. For everything that he says really must be done, for his word must not be gainsaid for anything.

[...]

And great lords and barons stand before the Emperor's table to serve the Emperor; and none of them is so bold as to speak a word unless the Emperor speak first to them – except for minstrels who sing him songs, or tell him tales, or crack jokes or jests to please the Emperor. All the vessels which are used for serving in his hall or chamber, especially at his own table or at those where great lords sit, are of jasper or crystal or amethyst or fine gold. And all their cups are of emeralds or sapphires, of topazes or other precious stones. They make no vessels of silver, for they set no store by silver. They will neither eat nor drink of vessels made of it; they use it for steps, pillars, pavements for halls and chambers. In front of the hall door stand certain lords and other knights to ensure that none enters that door except those the Emperor wishes, unless he be of the household or a minstrel; no others dare come near.

You must know that I and my companions were living with the Great Khan for sixteen months as soldiers against the King of Manzi, for they were at war when we were there. The reason for our staying with him was that we greatly desired to see his great nobleness and the state and ceremonial of his court; also we wanted to see the extent of his riches, to know if what we had heard before was true. Truly, we found it more rich and noble than we had heard reported; and we should never have believed it if we had not seen it with our own eyes. There is no such court here in this land. For here kings and lords keep as few men in their courts as they can; but the Great Khan supports at his charge in his court each day folk without number. But you should know that food and drink are more pleasingly dressed in our country than there, and here men sit more decorously at meat than they do there. For all the common people of the court have their meat laid on their knees when they eat, without any cloth or towel, and for the most part they eat flesh, without bread, of all kinds of beasts. When they have finished eating, they wipe their hands on the skirts of their robe. They only eat once a day. This is the way the common folk in the Great Khan's court behave. But the stateliness of the Khan himself and of other lords who sit with him is noble and royal, surpassing that of all earthly men. For truly, under the firmament there is no lord so great nor so rich and powerful as the Great Khan of

Tartary. Not even Prester John, Emperor of Greater and Lesser India, nor the Sultan of Babylon, nor the Emperor of Persia, nor anyone else, can be compared to him. Truly, it is a great pity he is not a Christian; nevertheless he will gladly hear men speak of God and allow Christian men to live in his empire. For in his land no man is forbidden to believe in whatever religion it pleases him to believe. And if some men perhaps will not believe me about what I have said, and say it is all a fable, what I say about the nobleness and excellence and riches of the Great Khan and his court, and the multitude of men there that I told of, I do not really care. But let the man who will, believe it; and leave him alone who will not. I shall nevertheless say something of what I saw with my own eyes, of him and his people and the government of his court, whether they will believe it or not. Nevertheless I well know that if anyone had been there (or in the countries that border his land, if he had not been to his court), he would have heard so much of his nobility and excellence that he would easily believe what I myself have said. And so I am not going to stop myself telling you things that I know are true because of those who are ignorant of them or will not believe them.

[…]

Of the Goodness of the People in the Isle of Bragman; of King Alexander; and Why Prester John is So Called

Beyond this isle there is another, large, fertile, full of people. They are good folk, honest, and of good faith and good living according to the nature of their faith. And even if they are not Christian, nevertheless by natural instinct or law they live a commendable life, are folk of great virtue, flying away from all sins and vices and malice, and they keep the Ten Commandments well. For they are not proud nor covetous, they are not lecherous nor gluttonous. They do nothing to another man they would not have done to themselves. They set no store by the riches of this world, or by possession of earthly goods. They do not lie, nor swear oaths for no reason, but simply say a thing is, or is not; they say that he who swears is about to deceive his neighbour. This isle these people live in is called the Isle of Bragman [Brahmin]; and some men call it the Land of Faith. Through it runs a great river, which is called Thebe. Generally all the men of that isle and of other isles nearby are more trustworthy and more righteous than men in other countries. In this land are no thieves, no murderers, no prostitutes, no liars, no beggars; they are men as pure in conversation and as clean living as if they were men of religion. And since they are such true and good folk, in their country there is never thunder or lightning, hail nor snow, nor any other storms and bad weather; there is no hunger, no pestilence, no war, nor any other common tribulations among them, as there are among us because of our sins. And therefore it seems that God loves them well and is well pleased by their manner of life and their faith. They believe in God who made all things, and worship Him with all their power; all earthly things they set at nought. They live so temperately and soberly in meat and drink that they are the longest-lived people in the world; and many of them die simply of age, when their vital force runs out.

When Alexander the conqueror reigned, and conquered all the world, he came to that land and sent letters to them who lived there, saying he would come and destroy their land unless they would be subject to him as other lands were. And they wrote letters back to him of this tenor: 'What thing could satisfy that man to whom all the world is not enough? You will find nothing here with us that would be a reason for making war on us; we have no worldly riches, nor do we desire to have any. All the places of our land and all our goods, movable and immovable, are common to every man. All our riches are our meat and drink wherewith we sustain our bodies; our treasure is peace and concord and the love that is between us. Instead of elaborate dress, we use a cheap cloth to cover our worthless carrion. Our wives, too, are not proudly and richly arrayed to please our eyes, for we consider such adornment a great folly, applying to the wretched body more beauty than God has naturally given it; our wives desire no more beauty than nature has given them. Our land serves us for two things: our livelihood while we live and for burial when we are dead. And up to this time we have always been at peace, of which you would now despoil and disinherit us. A King we have among us, not to right any man's wrongs – for among us no man does another wrong – but simply to teach us to be obedient. We need to have no judges among us, for none of us does to another except what he would have done to himself. Therefore you can take from us nothing but our peace, which up to this time has always been amongst us.' And when King Alexander had seen their letters and read them, it seemed to him in his heart that it would be a great pity and great unmanliness to hurt or trouble such folk; and he granted them a guarantee of peace, and bade them to continue with their good living and follow their good customs without having any fear of him, for he would not harm them.

Section II

(b) The Muslim World

5

Travels in Asia and Africa, 1325–1354

Ibn Battuta

When we reached this river called Panj Áb, which is the frontier of the territories of the sultan of India and Sind, the officials of the intelligence service came to us and sent a report about us to the governor of the city of Multán. From Sind to the city of Dihlí [Delhi], the sultan's capital, it is fifty days' march, but when the intelligence officers write to the sultan from Sind the letter reaches him in five days by the postal service. In India the postal service is of two kinds. The mounted couriers travel on horses belonging to the sultan with relays every four miles. The service of couriers on foot is organized in the following manner. At every third of a mile there is an inhabited village, outside which there are three pavilions. In these sit men girded up ready to move off, each of whom has a rod a yard and a half long with brass bells at the top. When a courier leaves the town he takes the letter in the fingers of one hand and the rod with the bells in the other, and runs with all his might. The men in the pavilions, on hearing the sound of the bells, prepare to meet him, and when he reaches them one of them takes the letter in his hand and passes on, running with all his might and shaking his rod until he reaches the next station, and so the letter is passed on till it reaches its destination. This post is quicker than the mounted post. It is sometimes used to transport fruits from Khurásán which are highly valued in India; they are put on plates and carried with great speed to the sultan. In the same way they transport the principal criminals; they are each placed on a stretcher and the couriers run carrying the stretcher on their heads. The sultan's drinking water is brought to him by the same means, when he resides at Dawlat Ábád, from the river Kank (Ganges), to which the Hindus go on pilgrimage and which is at a distance of forty days' journey from there.

When the intelligence officials write to the sultan informing him of those who arrive in his country, he studies the report very minutely. They take the utmost care in this matter, telling him that a certain man has arrived of such-and-such an appearance and dress, and noting the number of his party, slaves and servants and beasts, his behaviour both in action and at rest, and all his doings, omitting no details. When the new arrival reaches the town of Multán, which is the capital of Sind, he stays there until an order is received from the sultan regarding his entry and the degree of hospitality to be extended to him. A man is honoured in that country according to what may be seen of his actions, conduct, and zeal, since no one knows anything of his family or lineage. The king of India, Sultan Muhammad Sháh, makes a practice of honouring strangers and distinguishing them by governorships or high dignities of

Ibn Battuta, *Travels in Asia and Africa, 1325–1354*, trans. H. A. R. Gibb, London: Routledge and Kegan Paul, 1929, pp. 183–6, 188–97, 202–4, 206–7, 212–13, 282–8, 292–5, 297–300.

State. The majority of his courtiers, palace officials, ministers of state, judges, and relatives by marriage are foreigners, and he has issued a decree that foreigners are to be given in his country the title of 'Azíz [Honourable], so that this has become a proper name for them.

Every person proceeding to the court of this king must needs have a gift ready to present to him, in order to gain his favour. The sultan requites him for it by a gift many times its value. When his subjects grew accustomed to this practice, the merchants in Sind and India began to furnish each newcomer with thousands of dinars as a loan, and to supply him with whatever he might desire to offer as a gift or to use on his own behalf, such as riding animals, camels, and goods. They place both their money and their persons at his service, and stand before him like attendants. When he reaches the sultan, he receives a magnificent gift from him and pays off his debt to them. This trade of theirs is a flourishing one and brings in vast profits. On reaching Sind I followed this practice and bought horses, camels, white slaves and other goods from the merchants. I had already bought from an 'Iráqí merchant in Ghazna about thirty horses and a camel with a load of arrows, for this is one of the things presented to the sultan. This merchant went off to Khurásán and on returning to India received his money from me. He made an enormous profit through me and became one of the principal merchants. I met him many years later, at Aleppo, when the infidels had robbed me of everything I possessed, but he gave me no assistance.

After crossing the river of Sind called Panj Áb, our way led through a forest of reeds, in which I saw a rhinoceros for the first time. After two days' march we reached Janání, a large and fine town on the bank of the river of Sind. Its people are a people called the Sámira, whose ancestors established themselves there on the conquest of Sind in the time of al-Hajjáj [712 A.D.]. These people never eat with anyone, nor may anyone observe them while they are eating, and they never marry outside their clan. From Janání we travelled to Síwasitán [Sehwan], a large town, outside which is a sandy desert, treeless except for acacias. Nothing is grown on the river here except

pumpkins, and the food of the inhabitants consists of sorghum and peas, of which they make bread. There is a plentiful supply of fish and buffalo milk, and they eat also a kind of small lizard stuffed with curcuma. When I saw this small animal and them eating it, I took a loathing at it and would not eat it. We entered Síwasitán during the hottest period of the summer. The heat was intense, and my companions used to sit naked except for a cloth round the waist and another soaked with water on their shoulders; this dried in a very short time and they had to keep constantly wetting it again.

[...]

On the road to Multán and ten miles distant from it is the river called Khusraw Ábád, a large river that cannot be crossed except by boat. At this point the goods and baggage of all who pass are subjected to a rigorous examination. Their custom at the time of our arrival was to take a quarter of everything brought in by the merchants, and exact a duty of seven dinars for every horse. The idea of having my baggage searched was very disagreeable to me, for there was nothing valuable in it, though it seemed a great deal in the eyes of the people. By the grace of God there arrived on the scene one of the principal officers from the governor of Multán, who gave orders that I should not be subjected to examination or search. We spent that night on the bank of the river and next morning were visited by the postmaster, who is the person who keeps the sultan informed of affairs in that town and district and of all that happens in it and all who come to it. I was introduced to him and went in his company to visit the governor of Multán, Qutb al-Mulk.

When I entered his presence, he rose to greet me, shook my hand, and bade me sit beside him. I presented him with a white slave, a horse, and some raisins and almonds. These are among the greatest gifts that can be made to them, since they do not grow in their land and are imported from Khurásán. The governor sat on a large carpeted dais, with the army commanders on his right and left and armed men standing at his back. The troops are passed in review before him and a number of bows are kept there. When anyone comes desiring to be enrolled in the army as an archer, he is given one of the bows to draw. They differ in stiffness, and his pay is graduated according to the strength he shows in drawing them. Anyone desiring to be enrolled as a trooper sets off his horse at a canter or gallop and tries to hit a target set up there with his lance. There is a ring there too, suspended to a low wall; the candidate sets off his horse at a canter until he comes level with the ring, and if he lifts it off with his lance he is accounted by them a good horseman. For those wishing to be enrolled as mounted archers there is a ball placed on the ground, and their pay is proportioned to their accuracy in hitting it with an arrow while going at a canter or gallop.

Two months after we reached Multán one of the sultan's household officers and the chief of police arrived to arrange for the journey of the new arrivals [to Delhi]. They came to me together and asked me why I had come to India. I replied that I had come to enter the service of the *Khúnd Álam* ["Master of the World"], as the sultan is called in his dominions. He had given orders that no one coming from Khurásán should be allowed to enter India unless he came with the intention of staying there. When I had given my answer they called the qádí and notaries and drew up a document witnessing to my undertaking and those of my company who wished to remain in India, but some of them refused to engage themselves. We then prepared for the journey to the capital, which is forty days' march from Multán through a continuous stretch of inhabited country. The principal member of our party was Khudháwand Zádah, qádí of Tirmidh, who had come with his wife and children. The chamberlain made special arrangements for his journey and took twenty cooks with him from Multán, himself going ahead with them every night to prepare his meals, etc.

[...]

Two days later we reached Ajúdahan [Pakpattan], a small town belonging to the pious Shaykh Faríd ad-Dín. As I returned to the camp after visiting this personage, I saw the people hurrying out, and some of our party along with them. I asked them what was happening and they told me that one of the Hindu infidels had died, that a fire had been kindled to burn him, and his wife would burn herself along with him. After the burning my companions came back and told me that she had

embraced the dead man until she herself was burned with him. Later on I used often to see a Hindu woman, richly dressed, riding on horseback, followed by both Muslims and infidels and preceded by drums and trumpets; she was accompanied by Brahmans, who are the chiefs of the Hindus. In the sultan's dominions they ask his permission to burn her, which he accords them. The burning of the wife after her husband's death is regarded by them as a commendable act, but is not compulsory; only when a widow burns herself her family acquire a certain prestige by it and gain a reputation for fidelity. A widow who does not burn herself dresses in coarse garments and lives with her own people in misery, despised for her lack of fidelity, but she is not forced to burn herself. Once in the town of Amjarí [Amjhera, near Dhar] I saw three women whose husbands had been killed in battle and who had agreed to burn themselves. Each one had a horse brought to her and mounted it, richly dressed and perfumed. In her right hand she held a coconut, with which she played, and in her left a mirror, in which she looked at her face. They were surrounded by Brahmans and their own relatives, and were preceded by drums, trumpets and bugles. Everyone of the infidels said to them "Take greetings from me to my father, or brother or mother, or friend" and they would say "Yes" and smile at them. I rode out with my companions to see the way in which the burning was carried out. After three miles we came to a dark place with much water and shady trees, amongst which there were four pavilions, each containing a stone idol. Between the pavilions there was a basin of water over which a dense shade was cast by trees so thickly set that the sun could not penetrate them. The place looked like a spot in hell – God preserve us from it! On reaching these pavilions they descended to the pool, plunged into it and divested themselves of their clothes and ornaments, which they distributed as alms. Each one was then given an unsewn garment of coarse cotton and tied part of it round her waist and part over her head and shoulders. The fires had been lit near this basin in a low lying spot, and oil of sesame poured over them, so that the flames were increased. There were about fifteen men there with faggots of thin wood and about ten others with heavy pieces of wood, and the drummers and trumpeters were standing by waiting for the woman's coming. The fire was screened off by a blanket held by some men, so that she should not be frightened by the sight of it. I saw one of them, on coming to the blanket, pull it violently out of the men's hands, saying to them with a smile "Do you frighten me with the fire? I know that it is a fire, so let me alone." Thereupon she joined her hands above her head in salutation to the fire and cast herself into it. At the same moment the drums, trumpets and bugles were sounded, the men threw their firewood on her and the others put the heavy wood on top of her to prevent her moving, cries were raised and there was a loud clamour. When I saw this I had all but fallen off my horse, if my companions had not quickly brought water to me and laved my face, after which I withdrew.

The Indians have a similar practice of drowning themselves and many of them do so in the river Ganges, the river to which they go on pilgrimage, and into which the ashes of those who are burned are cast. They say that it is a river of Paradise. When one of them comes to drown himself he says to those present with him, "Do not think that I drown myself for any worldly reason or through penury; my purpose is solely to seek approach to Kusáy," Kusáy being the name of God in their language. He then drowns himself, and when he is dead they take him out and burn him and cast his ashes into this river.

[...]

The city of Delhi is made up now of four neighbouring and contiguous towns. One of them is Delhi proper, the old city built by the infidels and captured in the year 1188. The second is called Sírí, known also as the Abode of the Caliphate; this was the town given by the sultan to Ghiyáth ad-Dín, the grandson of the 'Abbásid Caliph Mustansir, when he came to his court. The third is called Tughlaq Ábád, after its founder, the Sultan Tughlaq, the father of the sultan of India to whose court we came. The reason why he built it was that one day he said to a former sultan "O master of the world, it were fitting that a city should be built here." The sultan replied to him in jest "When you are sultan, build it." It came about by the decree of God that he became sultan, so he built it and called it by his own name. The fourth is called Jahán Panáh, and is set apart for the residence of the reigning sultan, Muhammad Sháh. He was the founder of it, and it was his intention to unite these four towns within a single wall, but after building part of it he gave up the rest because of the expense required for its construction.

The cathedral mosque occupies a large area; its walls, roof, and paving are all constructed of white stones, admirably squared and firmly cemented with lead. There is no wood in it at all. It has thirteen domes of stone, its pulpit also is made of stone, and it has four courts. In the centre of the mosque is an awe-inspiring column, and nobody knows of what metal it is constructed. One of their learned men told me that it is called *Haft Júsh*, which means "seven metals," and that it is constructed from these seven. A part of this column, of a finger's breadth, has been polished, and gives out a brilliant gleam. Iron makes no impression on it. It is thirty cubits high, and we rolled a turban round it, and the portion which encircled it measured eight cubits. At the eastern gate there are two enormous idols of brass prostrate on the ground and held by stones, and everyone entering or leaving the mosque treads on them. The site was formerly occupied by an idol temple, and was converted into a mosque on the conquest of the city. In the northern court is the minaret, which has no parallel in the lands of Islám. It is built of red stone, unlike the rest of the edifice, ornamented with sculptures, and of great height. The ball on the top is of glistening white marble and its "apples" [small balls surmounting a minaret] are of pure gold. The passage is so wide that elephants could go up by it. A person in whom I have confidence told me that when it was built he saw an elephant climbing with stones to the top. The Sultan Qutb ad-Dín wished to build one in the western court even larger, but was cut off by death when only a third of it had been completed. This minaret is one of the wonders of the world for size, and the width of its passage is such that three elephants could mount it abreast. The third of it built equals in height the whole of the other minaret we have mentioned in the northern court, though to one looking at it from below it does not seem so high because of its bulk.

[...]

Among the learned and pious inhabitants of Delhi is the devout and humble imám Kamál ad-Dín, called "The Cave Man" from the cave in which he lives outside the city. I had a slave-boy who ran away from me, and whom I found in the possession of a certain Turk. I proposed to take him back from him, but the shaykh said to me "This boy is no good to you. Don't take him." The Turk wished to come to an arrangement, so he paid me a hundred dinars and kept the boy. Six months later the boy killed his master and was taken before the sultan, who ordered him to he handed over to his master's sons, and they put him to death. When I saw this miracle on the part of the shaykh I attached myself to him, withdrawing from the world and giving all that I possessed to the poor and needy. I stayed with him for some time, and I used to see him fast for ten and twenty days on end and remain standing most of the night. I continued with him until the sultan sent for me and I became entangled in the world once again – may God give me a good ending!

This king is of all men the fondest of making gifts and of shedding blood. His gate is never without some poor man enriched or some living man executed, and stories are current amongst the people of his generosity and courage and of his cruelty and violence towards criminals. For all that, he is of all men the most humble and the readiest to show equity and justice. The ceremonies of religion are strictly complied with at his court, and he is severe in the matter of attendance at prayer and in punishing those who neglect it. He is one of those kings whose felicity is unimpaired and surpassing all ordinary experience, but his dominant quality is generosity. We shall relate some stories of this that are marvellous beyond anything ever heard before, and I call God and his Angels and His Prophets to witness that all that I tell of his extraordinary generosity is absolute truth. I know that some of the instances I shall relate will be unacceptable to the minds of many, and that they will regard them as quite impossible, but in a matter which I have seen with my own eyes and of which I know the

accuracy and have had a large share, I cannot do otherwise than speak the truth.

[...]

One of the Indian nobles claimed that the sultan had put his brother to death without cause, and cited him before the qádí. The sultan walked on foot and unarmed to the qádí's tribunal, saluted him and made obeisance, having previously commanded the qádí not to rise before him or move when he entered his court, and remained standing before him. The qádí gave judgment against the sultan, to the effect that he must give satisfaction to his adversary for the blood of his brother, and he did so. At another time a certain Muslim claimed that the sultan owed him a sum of money. They carried the matter before the qádí, who gave judgment against the sultan for the payment of the debt, and he paid it.

When a famine broke out in India and Sind, and prices became so high that a maund of wheat rose to six dinars, the sultan ordered that every person in Delhi should be given six months' provisions from the granary, at the rate of a pound and a half per person per day, small or great, freeman or slave. The doctors and qádís set about compiling registers of the population of each quarter and brought the people, each of whom received six months' provisions.

In spite of all we have said of his humility, justice, compassion for the needy, and extraordinary generosity, the sultan was far too ready to shed blood. He punished small faults and great, without respect of persons, whether men of learning, piety, or high station. Every day hundreds of people, chained, pinioned, and fettered, are brought to his hall, and those who are for execution are executed, those for torture tortured, and those for beating beaten. It is his custom that every day all persons who are in his prison are brought to the hall, except only on Fridays; this is a day of respite for them, on which they clean themselves and remain at ease – may God deliver us from misfortune! The sultan had a half-brother named Mas'úd Khán, whose mother was the daughter of Sultan 'Alá ad-Dín, and who was one of the most beautiful men I have ever seen on earth. He suspected him of wishing to revolt, and questioned him on the matter. Mas'úd confessed through fear of torture, for anyone who denies an accusation of this sort which the sultan formulates against him is put to the torture, and the people consider death a lighter affliction than torture. The sultan gave orders that he should be beheaded in the market place, and his body lay there for three days according to their custom.

[...]

On the 4th of Shawwal [8th June 1334] the sultan returned to the castle of Tilbat, seven miles from the capital, and the wazír ordered us to go out to him. We set out, each man with his present of horses, camels, fruits, swords, etc., and assembled at the gate of the castle. The newcomers were introduced in order of precedence and were given robes of linen, embroidered in gold. When my turn came I entered and found the sultan seated on a chair. At first I took him to be one of the chamberlains. When I had twice made obeisance the "king" of the Sultan's intimate courtiers said "*Bismillah*, Mawláná Badr ad-Dín," for in India they used to call me Badr ad-Dín, and *Mawláná* ["Our Master"] is a title given to all scholars. I approached the sultan, who took my hand and shook it, and continuing to hold it addressed me most affably in Persian, saying "Your arrival is blessed; be at ease, I shall be compassionate to you and give you such favours that your fellow-countrymen will hear of it and come to join you." Then he asked me where I came from and I answered him, and every time he said any encouraging word to me I kissed his hand, until I had kissed it seven times. All the new arrivals then assembled and a meal was served to them.

Afterwards the sultan used to summon us to eat in his presence and would enquire how we fared and address us most affably. He assigned us pensions, giving me twelve thousand dinars a year, and added two villages to the three he had already commanded for me. One day he sent the wazír and the governor of Sind to us to say, "The Master of the World says 'Whoever amongst you is capable of undertaking the function of wazír or secretary or commander or judge or professor or shaykh, I shall appoint to that office.'" Everyone was silent at first, for what they were wanting was to gain riches and return to their countries.

After some of the others had spoken the wazír said to me in Arabic "What do *you* say?" I replied "Wazírships and secretaryships are not my business, but as to qádís and shaykhs, that is my occupation, and the occupation of my fathers before me." The sultan was pleased with what I had said, and I was summoned to the palace to do homage on appointment as qádí of the Málikite rite at Delhi.

[...]

Some time later I withdrew from the sultan's service and attached myself to the learned and pious imám Kamál ad-Dín "The Cave Man," as I have already related. The sultan was in Sind at the time, and at hearing of my retreat from the world summoned me. I entered his presence dressed as a mendicant, and he spoke to me very kindly, desiring me to return to his service. I refused and asked him for permission to travel to Mecca, which he granted. This was at the end of second Jumádá 742 [early December 1341].

Forty days later the sultan sent me saddled horses, slave girls and boys, robes and a sum of money, so I put on the robes and went to him. I had a tunic of blue cotton which I wore during my retreat, and as I put it off and dressed in the sultan's robes I upbraided myself. Ever after when I looked at that tunic I felt a light within me, and it remained in my possession until the infidels despoiled me of it on the sea. When I presented myself before the sultan, he showed me greater favour than before, and said to me "I have sent for you to go as my ambassador to the king of China, for I know your love of travel." He then provided me with everything I required and appointed certain other persons to accompany me, as I shall relate presently.

The land of China is of vast extent, and abounding in produce, fruits, grain, gold and silver. In this respect there is no country in the world that can rival it. It is traversed by the river called the "Water of Life," which rises in some mountains, called the "Mountain of Apes," near the city of Khán-Báliq [Peking] and flows through the centre of China for the space of six months' journey, until finally it reaches Sín as-Sín [Canton]. It is bordered by villages, fields, fruit gardens, and bazaars, just like the Egyptian Nile, only that [the country through which runs] this river is even more richly cultivated and populous, and there are many waterwheels on it. In the land of China there is abundant sugar-cane, equal, nay superior, in quality to that of Egypt, as well as grapes and plums. I used to think that the 'Othmání plums of Damascus had no equal, until I saw the plums in China. It has wonderful melons too, like those of Khwárizm and Isfahán. All the fruits which we have in our country are to be found there, either much the same or of better quality. Wheat is very abundant in China, indeed better wheat I have never seen, and the same may be said of their lentils and chick-peas.

The Chinese pottery [porcelain] is manufactured only in the towns of Zaytún and Sín-kalán. It is made of the soil of some mountains in that district, which takes fire like charcoal, as we shall relate subsequently. They mix this with some stones which they have, burn the whole for three days, then pour water over it. This gives a kind of clay which they cause to ferment. The best quality of [porcelain is made from] clay that has fermented for a complete month, but no more, the poorer quality [from clay] that has fermented for ten days. The price of this porcelain there is the same as, or even less than, that of ordinary pottery in our country. It is exported to India and other countries, even reaching as far as our own lands in the West, and it is the finest of all makes of pottery.

The hens and cocks in China are very big indeed, bigger than geese in our country, and hens' eggs there are bigger than our goose eggs. On the other hand their geese are not at all large. We bought a hen once and set about cooking it, but it was too big for one pot, so we put it in two. Cocks over there are about the size of ostriches; often a cock will shed its feathers and [nothing but] a great red body remains. The first time I saw a Chinese cock was in the city of Kawlam. I took it for an ostrich and was amazed at it, but its owner told me that in China there were some even bigger than that, and when I got to China I saw for myself the truth of what he had told me about them.

The Chinese themselves are infidels, who worship idols and burn their dead like the Hindus. The king of China is a Tatar, one of

the descendants of Tinkiz [Chingiz] Khán. In every Chinese city there is a quarter for Muslims in which they live by themselves, and in which they have mosques both for the Friday services and for other religious purposes. The Muslims are honoured and respected. The Chinese infidels eat the flesh of swine and dogs, and sell it in their markets. They are wealthy folk and well-to-do, but they make no display either in their food or their clothes. You will see one of their principal merchants, a man so rich that his wealth cannot be counted, wearing a coarse cotton tunic. But there is one thing that the Chinese take a pride in, that is, gold and silver plate. Every one of them carries a stick, on which they lean in walking, and which they call "the third leg." Silk is very plentiful among them, because the silk-worm attaches itself to fruits and feeds on them without requiring much care. For that reason it is so common to be worn by even the very poorest there. Were it not for the merchants it would have no value at all, for a single piece of cotton cloth is sold in their country for the price of many pieces of silk. It is customary amongst them for a merchant to cast what gold and silver he has into ingots, each weighing a hundredweight or more or less, and to put those ingots above the door of his house.

The Chinese use neither [gold] dinars nor [silver] dirhams in their commerce. All the gold and silver that comes into their country is cast by them into ingots, as we have described. Their buying and selling is carried on exclusively by means of pieces of paper, each of the size of the palm of the hand, and stamped with the sultan's seal. Twenty-five of these pieces of paper are called a *bálisht*, which takes the place of the dinar with us [as the unit of currency]. When these notes become torn by handling, one takes them to an office corresponding to our mint, and receives their equivalent in new notes on delivering up the old ones. This transaction is made without charge and involves no expense, for those who have the duty of making the notes receive regular salaries from the sultan. Indeed the direction of that office is given to one of their principal amírs. If anyone goes to the bazaar with a silver dirham or a dinar, intending to buy something, no one will accept it from him or pay any attention to him until he changes if for *bálisht*, and with that he may buy what he will.

All the inhabitants of China and of Cathay use in place of charcoal a kind of lumpy earth found in their country. It resembles our fuller's earth, and its colour too is the colour of fuller's earth. Elephants [are used to] carry loads of it. They break it up into pieces about the size of pieces of charcoal with us, and set it on fire and it burns like charcoal, only giving out more heat than a charcoal fire. When it is reduced to cinders, they knead it with water, dry it, and use it again for cooking, and so on over and over again until it is entirely consumed. It is from this clay that they make the Chinese porcelain ware, after adding to it some other stones, as we have related.

The Chinese are of all peoples the most skilful in the arts and possessed of the greatest mastery of them. This characteristic of theirs is well known, and has frequently been described at length in the works of various writers. In regard to portraiture there is none, whether Greek or any other, who can match them in precision, for in this art they show a marvellous talent. I myself saw an extraordinary example of this gift of theirs. I never returned to any of their cities after I had visited it a first time without finding my portrait and the portraits of my companions drawn on the walls and on sheets of paper exhibited in the bazaars. When I visited the sultan's city I passed with my companions through the painters bazaar on my way to the sultan's palace. We were dressed after the 'Iráqí fashion. On returning from the palace in the evening, I passed through the same bazaar, and saw my portrait and those of my companions drawn on a sheet of paper which they had affixed to the wall. Each of us set to examining the other's portrait [and found that] the likeness was perfect in every respect. I was told that the sultan had ordered them to do this, and that they had come to the palace while we were there and had been observing us and drawing our portraits without our noticing it. This is a custom of theirs, I mean making portraits of all who pass through their country. In fact they have brought this to such perfection that if a stranger commits any offence that obliges him to flee from China, they send his portrait far and wide. A search is

then made for him and wheresoever the [person bearing a] resemblance to that portrait is found he is arrested.

[...]

China is the safest and best regulated of countries for a traveller. A man may go by himself a nine months' journey, carrying with him large sums of money, without any fear on that account. The system by which they ensure his safety is as follows. At every post-station in their country they have a hostelry controlled by an officer, who is stationed there with a company of horsemen and footsoldiers. After sunset or later in the evening the officer visits the hostelry with his clerk, registers the names of all travellers staying there for the night, seals up the list, and locks them into the hostelry. After sunrise he returns with his clerk, calls each person by name, and writes a detailed description of them on the list. He then sends a man with them to conduct them to the next post-station and bring back a clearance certificate from the controller there to the effect that all these persons have arrived at that station. If the guide does not produce this document, he is held responsible for them. This is the practice at every station in their country from Sín as-Sín to Khán-Báliq. In these hostelries there is everything that the traveller requires in the way of provisions, especially fowls and geese. Sheep on the other hand, are scarce with them.

To return to the account of our journey. The first city which we reached after our sea voyage was the city of Zaytún. [Now although *zaytún* means "olives"] there are no olives in this city, nor indeed in all the lands of the Chinese nor in India; it is simply a name which has been given to the place. Zaytún is an immense city. In it are woven the damask silk and satin fabrics which go by its name, and which are superior to the fabrics of Khansá and Khán-Báliq. The port of Zaytún is one of the largest in the world, or perhaps the very largest. I saw in it about a hundred large junks; as for small junks, they could not be counted for multitude. It is formed by a large inlet of the sea which penetrates the land to the point where it unites with the great river. In this city, as in all Chinese towns, a man will have a fruit-garden and a field with his house set in the middle of it, just as in the town of Sijilmása in our own country. For this reason their towns are extensive. The Muslims live in a town apart from the others.

On the day that I reached Zaytún I saw there the amír who had come to India as an envoy with the present [to the sultan], and who afterwards travelled with our party and was shipwrecked on the junk. He greeted me, and introduced me to the controller of the *douane* and saw that I was given good apartments [there]. I received visits from the qádí of the Muslims, the shaykh al-Islám, and the principal merchants. Amongst the latter was Sharaf ad-Dín of Tabríz, one of the merchants from whom I had borrowed at the time of my arrival in India, and the one who had treated me most fairly. He knew the Koran by heart and used to recite it constantly. These merchants, living as they do in a land of infidels, are overjoyed when a Muslim comes to them. They say "He has come from the land of Islám," and they make *him* the recipient of the tithes on their properties, so that he becomes as rich as themselves. There was living at Zaytún, amongst other eminent shaykhs, Burhán ad-Dín of Kázarún, who has a hermitage outside the town, and it is to him that the merchants pay the sums they vow to Shaykh Abú Isháq of Kázarún.

[...]

The land of China, in spite of all that is agreeable in it, did not attract me. On the contrary I was sorely grieved that heathendom had so strong a hold over it. Whenever I went out of my house I used to see any number of revolting things, and that distressed me so much that I used to keep indoors and go out only in case of necessity. When I met Muslims in China I always felt just as though I were meeting my own faith and kin. So great was the kindness of this doctor al-Bushrí that when I left Qanjanfú he accompanied me for four days, until I reached the town of Baywam Qutlú. This is a small town, inhabited by Chinese, a proportion of them being troops, the rest common people. The Muslim community there consists of four houses only, the inhabitants of which are agents of my learned friend. We put up at the house of one of them, and stayed with him for three days, after which I bade the doctor adieu and set out again.

I sailed up the river with the usual routine, stopping for dinner at one village, and for supper at another. After seventeen days of this, we reached the city of Khansá [Hang-chow], which is the biggest city I have ever seen on the face of the earth. It is so long that it takes three days to traverse in the ordinary routine of marches and halts. It is built after the Chinese fashion already described, each person, that is, having his own house and garden. It is divided into six cities, as we shall describe later. On our arrival a party came out to meet us, consisting of the qádí and the Shaykh al-Islám of the city, and the family of 'Othmán ibn Affán of Egypt, who are the principal Muslim residents there, accompanied by a white flag, drums, bugles, and trumpets. The governor of the city also came out [to meet us] with his escort, and so we entered the town.

Khansá consists of six cities, each with its own wall, and an outer wall surrounding the whole. In the first city are the quarters of the city guards and their commander; I was told by the qádí and others that they mustered twelve thousand men on the register of troops. We passed the first night after our entry in the house of their commander. On the second day we entered the second city through a gate called the Jews' Gate. In this city live the Jews, Christians, and sun-worshipping Turks, a large number in all; its governor is a Chinese and we passed the second night in his house. On the third day we entered the third city, and this is inhabited by the Muslims. Theirs is a fine city, and their bazaars are arranged just as they are in Islamic countries; they have mosques in it and muezzins – we heard them calling to the noon prayers as we entered. We stayed here in the mansion of the family of 'Othmán ibn 'Affán of Egypt. He was a wealthy merchant, who conceived a liking for this city and made his home in it, so that it came to be called 'Othmáníya after him, and he transmitted to his posterity the influence and respect which he enjoyed there. It was he who built the cathedral mosque of Khansá, and endowed it with large benefactions. The number of Muslims in this city is very large, and our stay with them lasted fifteen days. Every day and night we were the guests at a new entertainment, and they continuously provided the most sumptuous meats, and went out with us every day on pleasure rides into different quarters of the city.

One day they rode out with me and we entered the fourth city, which is the seat of government, and in which the chief governor Qurtay resides. When we entered the gate leading to it, my companions were separated from me, and I was found by the wazír, who conducted me to the palace of the chief governor Qurtay. It was on this occasion that he took from me the mantle which the saint Jalál ad-Dín of Shíráz had given me, as I have already related. No one resides in this city, which is the most beautiful of the six, except the sultan's slaves and servants. It is traversed by three streams, one of them being a canal taken off from the great river, which is used by small boats bringing provisions and coal to the town, and there are pleasure boats on it as well. The citadel lies in the centre of this city. It is of enormous size, and the government house stands in the middle of it, surrounded by [the court of] the citadel on all sides. Within it there are arcades, in which sit workmen making rich garments and weapons. The amír Qurtay told me that there were sixteen hundred master-workmen there, each with three or four apprentices working under him. They are all without exception the slaves of the Qán; they have chains on their feet, and they live outside the fortress. They are permitted to go out to the bazaars in the city, but may not go beyond its gate. They are passed in review before the governor every day, a hundred at a time, and if any one of them is missing, his commander is held responsible for him. Their custom is that when one of them has served for ten years, he is freed from his chains and given the choice between staying in service, without chains, or going wherever he will within the Qán's dominions, but not outside them. When he reaches the age of fifty he is exempted from work and maintained [by the state]. In the same way anyone else who has attained this age or thereabouts is maintained. Anyone who reaches the age of sixty is regarded by them as a child, and legal penalties cease to be applicable to him. Old men in China are greatly respected, and each one of them is called Atá, which means "Father."

The amír Qurtay is the principal amír in China. He entertained us in his palace, and prepared a banquet (their name for it is *towa*), which was attended by the principal men of the city. He had Muslim cooks brought, who slaughtered the animals [in accordance with Muslim ritual, so that the food should be ceremonially clean] and cooked the food. This amír, in spite of his exalted rank, presented the dishes to us with his own hand, and with his own hand carved the meat. We stayed with him as his guests for three days.

[…]

On the following day we entered the fifth and largest city, which is inhabited by the common folk. Its bazaars are good and contain very skilful artificers; it is there that the fabrics which take their name from this town are woven. We passed a night in this city as the guests of its governor, and on the morrow entered the sixth city through a gate called Boatmen's gate. This sixth city, which lies on the banks of the great river, is inhabited by seamen, fishermen, caulkers, and carpenters, along with archers and footsoldiers, all of them being slaves of the sultan. No other persons live [in this town] with them, and their numbers are very great. We spent a night there as the guests of its governor. The amír Qurtay equipped a vessel for us with all that was needed in the way of provisions, etc., and sent his suite with us to arrange for our hospitable reception [on the journey]. So we left this city, which is the last of the provinces of China [proper], and entered the land of Khítá [Cathay].

Cathay is the best cultivated country in the world. There is not a spot in the whole extent of it that is not brought under cultivation. The reason is that if any part is left uncultivated its inhabitants or their neighbours are assessed for the land-tax due thereon. Fruit-gardens, villages, and fields extend along both banks of this river without interruption from the city of Khansá to the city of Khán-Báliq [Peking], which is a space of sixty-four days' journey. There are no Muslims to be found in these districts, except casual travellers, since the country is not suitable for [their] permanent residence, and there is no large city in it, only villages and wide spaces, covered with corn, fruit-trees, and sugarcane. I have never seen anything in the world like it, except a space of four days' journey between Anbár and 'Ána [in 'Iráq; see p. 303].

We used to disembark every night and stay in the villages in order to receive our provisions as guests of the sultan.

[...]

When we reached the capital Khán-Báliq, we found that the Qán was absent from it at that time, as he had gone out to fight his cousin Fírúz, who had rebelled against him in the district of Qaráqorum and Bish-Báligh in Cathay. The distance between these places and the capital is a three months' journey through cultivated districts. After his departure the majority of his amírs threw off their allegiance to him and agreed to depose him because he had departed from the precepts of the *Yasáq*, that is, the precepts which were laid down by their ancestor Tinkíz [Chingiz] Khán, who laid waste the lands of Islám. They went over to his rebel nephew and wrote to the Qán to the effect that he should abdicate and retain the city of Khansá as an appanage. He refused to do so, fought them, and was defeated and killed.

It was a few days after our arrival at his capital that the news of this was received. The city was decorated; trumpets, bugles and drums were played, and games and entertainments held for the space of a month. Thereafter the slain Qán was brought, with about a hundred other slain, his cousins, relatives, and intimates. A great *ná'ús*, that is, a subterranean chamber, was dug for him and richly furnished. The Qán was laid in it with his weapons, and all the gold and silver plate from his palace was deposited in it with him. With him also were put four slavegirls and six of the principal mamlúks, who carried drinking vessels, then the door of the chamber was built up and the whole thing covered over with earth until it reached the size of a large mound. After that they brought four horses and drove them about the Qán's grave until they stopped [from exhaustion], then they set up a wooden erection over the grave and suspended the horses on it, having first driven a piece of wood through each horse from tail to mouth. The above-mentioned relatives of the Qán were also placed in subterranean chambers along with their weapons and house utensils, and they impaled over the tombs of the principal members, of whom there were ten, three horses each, and over the tombs of the rest one horse each.

This day was observed as a solemn holiday, and not one person was absent from the ceremony, men or women, Muslim or heathen. They were all dressed in mourning robes, which are white capes in the case of the infidels and [long] white garments in the case of the Muslims. The Qán's khátúns and courtiers lived in tents near his grave for forty days, some even more than that, up to a year; and a bazaar was established there to supply the food and other things which they required. Such practices as these are observed, so far as I can record, by no other people in these days. The heathen Indians and Chinese, on the other hand, burn their dead; other people do indeed bury the dead man, but they do not put anyone in with him. However, I have been told by trustworthy persons in the Negrolands that the heathen there, when their king died, used to make a *ná'ús* for him and put in with him some of his courtiers and servants, along with thirty of the sons and daughters of their principal families, first breaking their hands and feet, and they put in drinking vessels along with them.

When the Qán was slain, as we have related, and his nephew Fírúz obtained the sovereign power, he chose to make his capital at the city of Qaráqorum, on account of its proximity to the territories of his cousins, the kings of Turkistán and Transoxania. Afterwards several of the amírs who were not present when the Qán was killed revolted against him and intercepted communications and the disorders grew to serious proportions.

6

The Muqaddimah

Ibn Khaldun

Bedouin Civilization, Savage Nations and Tribes and Their Conditions of Life, Including Several Basic and Explanatory Statements

1   Both Bedouins and sedentary people are natural groups

It should be known that differences of condition among people are the result of the different ways in which they make their living. Social organization enables them to co-operate toward that end and to start with the simple necessities of life, before they get to conveniences and luxuries.

Some people live by agriculture, the cultivation of vegetables and grains; others by animal husbandry, the use of sheep, cattle, goats, bees, and silkworms, for breeding and for their products. Those who live by agriculture or animal husbandry cannot avoid the call of the desert, because it alone offers the wide fields, pastures for animals, and other things that the settled areas do not offer. It is therefore necessary for them to restrict themselves to the desert. Their social organization and co-operation for the needs of life and civilization, such as food, shelter, and warmth, do not take them beyond the bare subsistence level, because of their inability

(to provide) for anything beyond those (things). Subsequent improvement of their conditions and acquisition of more wealth and comfort than they need, cause them to rest and take it easy. Then, they co-operate for things beyond the bare necessities. They use more food and clothes, and take pride in them. They build large houses, and lay out towns and cities for protection. This is followed by an increase in comfort and ease, which leads to formation of the most developed luxury customs. They take the greatest pride in the preparation of food and a fine cuisine, in the use of varied splendid clothes of silk and brocade and other (fine materials), in the construction of ever higher buildings and towers, in elaborate furnishings for the buildings, and the most intensive cultivation of crafts in actuality. They build castles and mansions, provide them with running water, build their towers higher and higher, and compete in furnishing them (most elaborately). They differ in the quality of the clothes, the beds, the vessels, and the utensils they employ for their purposes. 'Sedentary people' means the inhabitants of cities and countries, some of whom adopt the crafts as their way of making a living, while others adopt commerce. They earn more and live more comfortably than Bedouins, because they live on a level beyond the level of bare necessity, and their way of making a living corresponds to their wealth.

Ibn Khaldun, *The Muqaddimah*, ed. N. J. Dawood, trans. Franz Rosenthal, Princeton, NJ: Princeton University Press, 1967, pp. 91–9, 123–5, 136–8.

It has thus become clear that Bedouins and sedentary people are natural groups which exist by necessity, as we have stated.

2 The Bedouins are a natural group in the world

We have mentioned in the previous section that the inhabitants of the desert adopt the natural manner of making a living, namely, agriculture and animal husbandry. They restrict themselves to the necessary in food, clothing, and mode of dwelling, and to the other necessary conditions and customs. They do not possess conveniences and luxuries. They use tents of hair and wool, or houses of wood, or of clay and stone, which are not furnished (elaborately). The purpose is to have shade and shelter, and nothing beyond that. They also take shelter in caverns and caves. The food they take is either little prepared or not prepared at all, save that it may have been touched by fire.

For those who make their living through the cultivation of grain and through agriculture, it is better to be stationary than to travel around. Such, therefore, are the inhabitants of small communities, villages, and mountain regions. These people make up the large mass of the Berbers and non-Bedouins.

Those who make their living from animals requiring pasturage, such as sheep and cattle, usually travel around in order to find pasture and water for their animals, since it is better for them to move around in the land. They are called 'sheepmen', that is, men who live on sheep and cattle. They do not go deep into the desert, because they would not find good pastures there. Such people include the Berbers, the Turks, the Turkomans and the Slavs, for instance.

Those who make their living by raising camels move around more. They wander deeper into the desert, because the hilly pastures with their plants and shrubs do not furnish enough subsistence for camels. They must feed on the desert shrubs and drink the salty desert water. They must move around the desert regions during the winter, in flight from the harmful cold to the warm desert air. In the desert sands, camels can find places to give birth to their young ones. Of all animals, camels have the hardest delivery and the greatest need for warmth in connection with it. (Camel nomads) are therefore forced to make excursions deep (into the desert). Frequently, too, they are driven from the hills by the militia, and they penetrate farther into the desert, because they do not want the militia to mete out justice to them or to punish them for their hostile acts. As a result, they are the most savage human beings that exist. Compared with sedentary people, they are on a level with wild, untamable animals and dumb beasts of prey. Such people are the Bedouins. In the West, the nomadic Berbers and the Zanâtah are their counter-parts, and in the East, the Kurds, the Turkomans, and the Turks. The Bedouins, however, make deeper excursions into the desert and are more rooted in desert life because they live exclusively on camels, while the other groups live on sheep and cattle, as well as camels.

It has thus become clear that the Bedouins are a natural group which by necessity exists in civilization.

3 Bedouins are prior to sedentary people. The desert is the basis and reservoir of civilization and cities

We have mentioned that the Bedouins restrict themselves to the bare necessities in their way of life and are unable to go beyond them, while sedentary people concern themselves with conveniences and luxuries in their conditions and customs. The bare necessities are no doubt prior to the conveniences and luxuries. Bare necessities, in a way, are basic, and luxuries secondary. Bedouins, thus, are the basis of, and prior to, cities and sedentary people. Man seeks first the bare necessities. Only after he has obtained the bare necessities does he get to comforts and luxuries. The toughness of desert life precedes the softness of sedentary life. Therefore, urbanization is found to be the goal to which the Bedouin aspires. Through his own efforts, he achieves what he proposes to achieve in this respect. When he has obtained enough to be ready for the conditions and customs of luxury, he enters upon a life of ease and submits himself to the yoke of the city.

This is the case with all Bedouin tribes. Sedentary people, on the other hand, have no desire for desert conditions, unless they are motivated by some urgent necessity or they cannot keep up with their fellow city dwellers.

Evidence for the fact that Bedouins are the basis of, and prior to, sedentary people is furnished by investigating the inhabitants of any given city. We shall find that most of its inhabitants originated among Bedouins dwelling in the country and villages of the vicinity. Such Bedouins became wealthy, settled in the city, and adopted a life of ease and luxury, such as exists in the sedentary environment.

All Bedouins and sedentary people differ also among themselves in their conditions of life. Many a clan is greater than another, many a tribe greater than another, many a city larger than another, and many a town more populous than another. ...

4   Bedouins are closer to being good than sedentary people

The reason for this is that the soul in its first natural state of creation is ready to accept whatever good or evil may arrive and leave an imprint upon it. Muhammad said: 'Every infant is born in the natural state. It is his parents who make him a Jew or a Christian or a heathen.' To the degree the soul is first affected by one of the two qualities, it moves away from the other and finds it difficult to acquire it. When customs proper to goodness have been first to enter the soul of a good person, and his (soul) has thus acquired the habit of (goodness, that person) moves away from evil and finds it difficult to do anything evil. The same applies to the evil person.

Sedentary people are much concerned with all kinds of pleasures. They are accustomed to luxury and success in worldly occupations and to indulgence in worldly desires. Therefore, their souls are coloured with all kinds of blameworthy and evil qualities. The more of them they possess, the more remote do the ways and means of goodness become to them. Eventually they lose all sense of restraint. Many of them are found to use improper language in their gatherings as well as in the presence of their superiors and womenfolk. They are not deterred by any sense of restraint, because the bad custom of behaving openly in an improper manner in both words and deeds has taken hold of them. Bedouins may be as concerned with worldly affairs as (sedentary people are). However, such concern would touch only the necessities of life and not luxuries or anything causing, or calling for, desires and pleasures. The customs they follow in their mutual dealings are, therefore, appropriate. As compared with those of sedentary people, their evil ways and blameworthy qualities are much less numerous. They are closer to the first natural state and more remote from the evil habits that have been impressed upon the souls (of sedentary people) through numerous and ugly, blameworthy customs. Thus, they can more easily be cured than sedentary people. This is obvious. It will later on become clear that sedentary life constitutes the last stage of civilization and the point where it begins to decay. It also constitutes the last stage of evil and of remoteness from goodness. Clearly, the Bedouins are closer to being good than sedentary people. ...

5   Bedouins are more disposed to courage than sedentary people

The reason for this is that sedentary people have become used to laziness and ease. They are sunk in well-being and luxury. They have entrusted the defence of their property and their lives to the governor and ruler who rules them, and to the militia which has the task of guarding them. They find full assurance of safety in the walls that surround them, and the fortifications that protect them. No noise disturbs them, and no hunting occupies their time. They are carefree and trusting, and have ceased to carry weapons. Successive generations have grown up in this way of life. They have become like women and children, who depend upon the master of the house. Eventually, this has come to be a quality of character that replaces natural disposition.

The Bedouins, on the other hand, live apart from the community. They are alone in the country and remote from militias. They have no walls or gates. Therefore, they provide their own defence and do not entrust it to, or rely upon others for it. They always carry weapons. They watch carefully all sides of the road. They take hurried naps only when they are together in company or when they are in the saddle. They pay attention to the most distant barking or noise. They go alone into the desert, guided by their fortitude, putting their trust in themselves. Fortitude has become a character quality of theirs, and courage their nature. They use it whenever they are called upon or roused by an alarm. When sedentary people mix with them in the desert or associate with them on a journey, they depend on them. They cannot do anything for themselves without them. This is an observed fact. (Their dependence extends) even to knowledge of the country, the directions, watering places, and crossroads. Man is a child of the customs and the things he has become used to. He is not the product of his natural disposition and temperament. The conditions to which he has become accustomed, until they have become for him a quality of character and matters of habit and custom, have replaced his natural disposition. If one studies this in human beings, one will find much of it, and it will be found to be a correct observation.

6 The reliance of sedentary people upon laws destroys their fortitude and power of resistance

Not everyone is master of his own affairs. Chiefs and leaders who are masters of the affairs of men are few in comparison with the rest. As a rule, man must by necessity be dominated by someone else. If the domination is kind and just and the people under it are not oppressed by its laws and restrictions, they are guided by the courage or cowardice that they possess in themselves. They are satisfied with the absence of any restraining power. Self-reliance eventually becomes a quality natural to them. They would not know anything else. If, however, the domination with its laws is one of brute force and intimidation, it breaks their fortitude and deprives them of their power of resistance as a result of the inertness

that develops in the souls of the oppressed, as we shall explain.

When laws are (enforced) by means of punishment, they completely destroy fortitude, because the use of punishment against someone who cannot defend himself generates in that person a feeling of humiliation that, no doubt, must break his fortitude.

When laws are (intended to serve the purposes of) education and instruction and are applied from childhood on, they have to some degree the same effect, because people then grow up in fear and docility and consequently do not rely on their own fortitude.

Thus, greater fortitude is found among the savage Arab Bedouins than among people who are subject to laws. Furthermore, those who rely on laws and are dominated by them from the very beginning of their education and instruction in the crafts, sciences, and religious matters, are thereby deprived of much of their own fortitude. They can scarcely defend themselves at all against hostile acts. This is the case with students, whose occupation it is to study and to learn from teachers and religious leaders, and who constantly apply themselves to instruction and education in very dignified gatherings. This situation and the fact that it destroys the power of resistance and fortitude must be understood.

It is no argument that the men around Muḥammad observed the religious laws, and yet did not experience any diminution of their fortitude, but possessed the greatest possible fortitude. When the Muslims got their religion from Muḥammad, the restraining influence came from themselves, as a result of the encouragement and discouragement he gave them in the Qur'ân. It was not a result of technical instruction or scientific education. The laws were the laws and precepts of the religion that they received orally and which their firmly rooted belief in the truth of the articles of faith caused them to observe. Their fortitude remained unabated, and it was not corroded by education or authority. 'Umar said, 'Those who are not (disciplined) by the religious law are not educated by God.' 'Umar's desire was that everyone should have his restraining influence in himself. His certainty was that Muḥammad knew best what is good for mankind.

(The influence of) religion, then, decreased among men, and they came to use restraining laws. The religious law became a branch of learning and a craft to be acquired through instruction and education. People turned to sedentary life and assumed the character trait of submissiveness to law. This led to a decrease in their fortitude.

Clearly, then, governmental and educational laws destroy fortitude, because their restraining influence is something that comes from outside. The religious laws, on the other hand, do not destroy fortitude, because their restraining influence is something inherent. Therefore, govermental and educational laws influence sedentary people, in that they weaken their souls and diminish their stamina, because they have to suffer them both as children and as adults. The bedouins, on the other hand, are not in the same position, because they live far away from the laws of government, instruction, and education. ...

7   Only tribes held together by group feeling can live in the desert

It should be known that God put good and evil into the nature of man. Thus, He says in the Qur'ân: 'We led him along the two paths.' He further says: 'And inspired the soul with wickedness as well as fear of God.'

Evil is the quality that is closest to man when he fails to improve his customs and when religion is not used as the model to improve him. The great mass of mankind is in that condition, with the exception of those to whom God gives success. Evil qualities in man are injustice and mutual aggression. He who casts his eye upon the property of his brother will lay his hand upon it to take it, unless there is a restraining influence to hold him back. The poet thus says:

Injustice is a human trait. If you find
A moral man, there is some reason why he is
*   not unjust*

Mutual aggression of people in towns and cities is averted by the authorities and the government, which hold back the masses under their control from attacks and aggression upon each other. They are thus prevented by the influence of force and governmental authority from mutual injustice, save such injustice as comes from the ruler himself.

Aggression against a city from outside may be averted by walls, in the event of unpreparedness, a surprise attack at night, or inability (of the inhabitants) to withstand the enemy during the day. Or it may be averted with the help of government auxiliary troops, if (the inhabitants are) prepared and ready to offer resistance.

The restraining influence among Bedouin tribes comes from their *shaykhs* and leaders. It results from the great respect and veneration they generally enjoy among the people. The hamlets of the Bedouins are defended against outside enemies by a tribal militia composed of noble youths of the tribe who are known for their courage. Their defence and protection are successful only if they are a closely knit group of common descent. This strengthens their stamina and makes them feared, since everybody's affection for his family and his group is more important (than anything else). Compassion and affection for one's blood relations and relatives exist in human nature as something God put into the hearts of men. It makes for mutual support and aid, and increases the fear felt by the enemy.

Those who have no one of their own lineage (to care for) rarely feel affection for their fellows. If danger is in the air on the day of battle, such a man slinks away and seeks to save himself, because he is afraid of being left without support. Such people, therefore, cannot live in the desert, because they would fall prey to any nation that might want to swallow them up.

If this is true with regard to the place where one lives, which is in constant need of defence and military protection, it is equally true with regard to every other human activity, such as prophecy, the establishment of royal authority, or propaganda. Nothing can be achieved in these matters without fighting for it, since man has the natural urge to offer resistance. And for fighting one cannot do without group feeling, as we mentioned at the beginning.

8 Group feeling results only from blood relationship or something corresponding to it

(Respect for) blood ties is something natural among men, with the rarest exceptions. It leads to affection for one's relations and blood relatives, (the feeling that) no harm ought to befall them nor any destruction come upon them. One feels shame when one's relatives are treated unjustly or attacked, and one wishes to intervene between them and whatever peril or destruction threatens them. This is a natural urge in man, for as long as there have been human beings. If the direct relationship between persons who help each other is very close, so that it leads to close contact and unity, the ties are obvious and clearly require the (existence of a feeling of solidarity) without any outside (prodding). If, however, the relationship is somewhat distant, it is often forgotten in part. However, some knowledge of it remains and this causes a person to help his relatives for the known motive, in order to escape the shame he would feel in his soul were a person to whom he is somehow related treated unjustly.

Clients and allies belong in the same category. The affection everybody has for his clients and allies results from the feeling of shame that comes to a person when one of his neighbours, relatives, or a blood relation in any degree is humiliated. The reason for it is that a client (-master) relationship leads to close contact exactly, or approximately in the same way, as does common descent. It is in that sense that one must understand Muḥammad's remark, 'Learn as much of your pedigrees as is necessary to establish your ties of kindred.' It means that pedigrees are useful only in so far as they imply the close contact that is a consequence of blood ties and that eventually leads to mutual help and affection. Anything beyond that is superfluous. For a pedigree is something imaginary and devoid of reality. Its usefulness consists only in the resulting connection and close contact. If the fact of (common descent) is obvious and clear, it evokes in man a natural affection, as we have said. If, however, its existence is known only from remote history, it moves the imagination but faintly. Its usefulness is gone, and preoccupation with it becomes gratuitous, a kind of

game, and as such is not permissible. In this sense, one must understand the remark, 'Genealogy is something which is of no use to know and which it does no harm not to know.' This means that when common descent is no longer clear and has become a matter of scientific knowledge, it can no longer move the imagination and is denied the affection caused by group feeling. It has become useless.

[...]

On Dynasties, Royal Authority, the Caliphate, Government Ranks, and All That Goes with These Things. The Chapter Contains Basic and Supplementary Propositions

[...]

2 When a dynasty is firmly established, it can dispense with group feeling

The reason for this is that people find it difficult to submit to general dynastic (power) at the beginning, unless they are forced into submission by strong superiority. The new government is something strange. People are not familiar with, or used to, its rule. But once leadership is firmly vested in the members of the family qualified to exercise royal authority in the dynasty, and once (royal authority) has been passed on by inheritance over many generations and through successive dynasties, the beginnings are forgotten, and the members of that family are clearly marked as leaders. It has become a firmly established article of faith that one must be subservient and submissive to them. People will fight with them in their behalf, as they would fight for the articles of faith. By this time, (the rulers) will not need much group (feeling to maintain) their power. It is as if obedience to the government were a divinely revealed book that cannot be changed or opposed.

(The rulers) maintain their hold over the government and their own dynasty with the help, then, either of clients and followers who grew up in the shadow and power of group feeling, or of tribal groups of a different descent who have become their clients.

Something of the sort happened to the 'Abbâsids. The group feeling of the Arabs had been destroyed by the time of the reign of al-Mu'tasim and his son, al-Wâthiq. They tried to maintain their hold over the government thereafter with the help of Persian, Turkish, Daylam, Saljûq, and other clients. Then, the (non-Arabs) and their clients gained power over the provinces (of the realm). The influence of the dynasty grew smaller, and no longer extended beyond the environs of Baghdad. Eventually, the Daylam closed in upon and took possession of (that area). The caliphs were ruled by them. Then (the Daylam), in turn, lost control. The Saljûqs seized power after the Daylam, and the (caliphs) were ruled by them. Then (the Saljûqs), in turn, lost control. Finally, the Tatars closed in. They killed the caliph and wiped out every vestige of the dynasty.

The same happened to the Umayyad dynasty in Spain. When its Arab group feeling was destroyed, small princes seized power and divided the territory among themselves. In competition with each other, they distributed among themselves the realm of the Umayyad dynasty. Each one of them seized the territory under his control and aggrandized himself. (These rulers) learned of the relations that existed between the non-Arabs (in the East) and the 'Abbâsids. (Imitating them), they adopted royal surnames and used royal trappings. There was no danger that anyone would take (the prerogatives they claimed) away from them or alter (the situation in this respect), because Spain was no longer the home of groups and tribes.

They tried to maintain their power with the help of clients and followers and with that of the Zanâtah and other Berber tribes which infiltrated Spain from the (African) shore. They imitated the way the Umayyad dynasty in its last stages had tried to maintain its power with their help. (These newcomers) founded large states. Each one of them had control over a section of Spain. They also had a large share of royal authority, corresponding to (that of) the dynasty they had divided up. They thus remained in power until the Almoravids, who shared in the strong Lamtûnah group feeling,

crossed the sea. The latter came and replaced and dislodged them from their centres. They obliterated all traces of (the small princes) who were unable to defend themselves because they had no (longer any) group feeling. ...

[...]

12   Dynasties have a natural life span like individuals

In the opinion of physicians and astrologers, the natural life span of individuals is one hundred and twenty years, that is, the period astrologers call the great lunar year. Within the same generation, the duration of life differs according to the conjunctions. It may be either more or less than one hundred and twenty years. The life span of persons who are under some particular conjunction will be a full hundred years. Of others, it will be fifty, or eighty, or seventy years, accordingly as the indications of conjunctions noted by these observers may require. The life of a Muslim lasts between sixty and seventy years. The natural life span of one hundred and twenty years is surpassed only on the occasion of rare configurations and extraordinary positions on the firmament. Such was the case with Noah and with a few among the peoples of 'Âd and Thamûd.

The same applies to the life span of dynasties. Their duration may differ according to the conjunctions. However, as a rule no dynasty lasts beyond the life span of three generations. A generation is identical with the average duration of the life of a single individual, namely, forty years, the time required for growth to be completed and maturity reached.

Our statement is confirmed by the significance of the (forty-year) sojourn of the children of Israel in the desert. Those forty years were intended to bring about the disappearance of the generation then alive and the growth of another generation, one that had not witnessed and felt the humiliation in Egypt. This is proof of the assumption that forty years, which is identical with the (average) life of a single individual, must be considered the duration of a generation.

We have stated that the life of a dynasty does not as a rule extend beyond three generations. The first generation retains the desert qualities, desert toughness, and desert savagery. (Its members are used to) privation and to sharing their glory (with each other); they are brave and rapacious. Therefore, the strength of group feeling continues to be preserved among them. They are sharp and greatly feared. People submit to them.

Under the influence of royal authority and a life of ease, the second generation changes from the desert attitude to sedentary culture, from privation to luxury and plenty, from a state in which everybody shared in the glory to one in which one man claims all the glory for himself while the others are too lazy to strive for glory, and from proud superiority to humble subservience. Thus, the vigour of group feeling is broken to some extent. People become used to lowliness and obedience. But many of the old virtues remain in them, because they had had direct personal contact with the first generation and its conditions, and had observed with their own eyes its prowess and striving for glory and its intention to protect and defend (itself). They cannot give all of it up at once, although a good deal of it may go. They live in hope that the conditions that existed in the first generation may come back, or they live under the illusion that those conditions still exist.

The third generation, then, has (completely) forgotten the period of desert life and toughness, as if it had never existed. They have lost (the taste for) the sweetness of fame and for group feeling, because they are dominated by force. Luxury reaches its peak among them, because they are so much given to a life of prosperity and ease. They become dependent on the dynasty and are like women and children who need to be defended. Group feeling disappears completely. People forget to protect and defend themselves and to press their claims. With their emblems, apparel, horseback-riding, and (fighting) skill, they deceive people and give them the wrong impression. For the most part, they are more cowardly than women upon their backs. When someone comes and demands something from them, they cannot repel him. The ruler, then, has need of other, brave people to support him. He takes many clients and followers. They help the dynasty to some degree, until God permits it to be destroyed, and it goes with everything it stands for.

As one can see, we have there three generations. In the course of these three generations, the dynasty grows senile and is worn out. Therefore, it is in the fourth generation that (ancestral) prestige is destroyed.

Three generations last one hundred and twenty years, as stated before. As a rule, dynasties do not last longer than that many years, a few more or a few less, save when, by chance, no one appears to attack them. When senility becomes preponderant, there may be no claimant (for dynastic power, and then nothing will happen), but if there should be one, he will encounter no one capable of repelling him. If the time is up, (the end of the dynasty) cannot be put off for a single hour, nor can it be advanced.

In this way, the life span of a dynasty corresponds to the life span of an individual; it grows up and passes into an age of stagnation and thence into retrogression. Therefore, people commonly say that the life span of a dynasty is one hundred years. ...

Part III
The Renaissance

History of a Voyage to the Land of Brazil, otherwise Called America

Jean de Léry

Of the Big Roots and the Millet of Which the Savages Make Flour That They Eat Instead of Bread; and of Their Drink, Which They Call *Caouin*

Since we have heard in the preceding chapter how our savages are outwardly adorned and equipped, to relate things in order it seems to me appropriate to treat next their common and ordinary sources of food. In the first place, one must note that although they do not have, and therefore do not sow or plant, wheat or vines in their country, nevertheless, as I have seen and experienced, they dine and feast well without bread or wine.

In their country our Americans have two kinds of root, which they call *aypi* and *maniot*, which in three or four months grow as big around as a man's thigh, and about a foot and a half long. Once they have pulled them up, the women – for the men don't concern themselves with this – dry these roots over a fire on the *boucan* (which I shall describe later), or else sometimes take them green, and grate them on a flat piece of wood in which certain little pointed stones have been set, just as we grate cheese and nutmeg; thus they reduce them to a flour as white as snow. This raw flour, like the white juice that comes out of it (of which I shall speak in a moment) has the fragrance of starch made of pure wheat soaked a long time in water, when it is still fresh and liquid. After I came back over here, whenever I happened to be in a place where starch was being made, the scent of it made me remember the odor one usually picks up in the savages' houses when they are making root flour.

To prepare it, the Brazilian women then take big earthen pots that hold more than a bushel each, which they themselves make very skillfully for this use, and put them on the fire, with a quantity of flour in them; while it cooks, they stir it continually with split gourds, which they use as we use dishes. As it cooks this way the flour forms something like little hailstones, or apothecary's pills.

Now they prepare this two different ways: some, which the savages call *ouy-entan*, is cooked hard, and this they take with them when they go to war, because it keeps better, and some, called *ouy-pou*, is less cooked and more tender, and it is so much better than the first that when you eat it fresh you would say that it is the center of a loaf of warm white bread. For either method, as the flour is cooked, its taste changes and becomes more agreeable and delicate.

Jean de Léry, *History of a Voyage to the Land of Brazil, otherwise Called America*, trans. Janet Whatley, Berkeley. CA: University of California Press, 1990, pp. 69–77, 158–69.

Although these flours taste good, and are nourishing and easy to digest, especially when they are fresh, nonetheless, as I discovered, they are by no means suitable for making bread. It is true that one can make with it a kind of dough, which, rising like that made of wheat flour with leavening, is as fine and white as if it were, indeed, wheat bread; but as it cooks, the crust and all the top dries out and burns, and when it comes to cutting or breaking the bread, you find that the inside is all dry and has turned back into flour. For that reason I think that he who first reported that the Indians who live at twenty-two or twenty-three degrees south of the Equator – who must be our Tupinamba – lived on bread made from wood shavings, had probably heard of the roots I am speaking of, but failing to observe what I have recounted, made a mistake.

Both kinds of flour are good for making a porridge which the savages call *mingant*. This is especially good when they soak it in some fat broth, for then it becomes lumpy like rice, and has a very good flavor. But for all that, our Tupinamba – men, women, and children – are accustomed from their youth upward to eating it dry instead of bread, and are so adept in their style of eating it that when they take it with four fingers from their earthen pot or some other vessel, they can toss it from a considerable distance, and it lands so neatly in their mouths that they don't spill a bit of it. We Frenchmen, wanting to imitate them, tried to eat it that way; but not being adept at the method, instead of throwing it into our mouths, we spread it all over our cheeks and covered our entire faces with flour. So unless we wanted to be got up like clowns – especially those of us who wore beards – we were compelled to eat it with spoons.

After these *aypi* and *maniot* roots are grated green, in the way I have described to you, the women will sometimes make big balls of the fresh, damp flour that comes from them; squeezing them and pressing them hard between their hands, they will extract from them a juice almost as white and clear as milk. This they catch in earthen plates and dishes and put it out to warm in the sun, which makes it clot and congeal like curds. When they want to eat it they pour it into other

earthen pans, and in those they cook it over the fire as we do omelettes; it is very good prepared in that way.

The *aypi* root is good not only for its flour, but also when cooked whole on the ashes or in front of the fire; when it gets tender and splits and becomes floury, you can eat it like a chestnut roasted on hot coals, which is what it tastes like. However, it is not the same with the *maniot* root, for that is only good as a well-cooked flour, and it is poisonous if it is eaten any other way.

The plants or stems of both, which are only slightly different from each other in form, grow to the height of small juniper trees, and have leaves rather like the peony. But what is to be noticed and admired in these *aypi* and *maniot* roots of our land of Brazil is the way they multiply. The branches are almost as tender and easy to break as hemp; nevertheless, however many you can break and stick as deep as you can into the earth, then without any other cultivation, that many big roots you will have at the end of two or three months.

The women make holes in the earth with a pointed stick, and by this means also plant two kinds of coarse millet, red and black, which is popularly known in France as "Saracen wheat" (the savages call it *avati*). From this they also make a flour, which is cooked and eaten in the same way as that made from roots. And I think now (contrary to what I said in the first edition of this history, where I made a distinction between two things that, now that I have thought about it, I believe are the same) that this *avati* of our Americans is what the historian of the Indies calls *maize*, which he says also serves as wheat for the Indians of Peru. For here is the description he gives of it.

"The maize stalk," he says, "grows to the height of a man, and more; it is rather thick, and puts forth leaves like those of marsh reeds. The ear is like a wild pine cone; the grain is coarse, and is neither round nor square, nor as long as our grain. It ripens in three or four months, and in countries that are irrigated by streams, in a month and a half. For one seed it yields one, two, three, four, five hundred, and it has been found that some have multiplied to six hundred: which also shows the fertility of this land now owned by the Spaniards."

Another has written that in some places in East India the soil is so good that, by the report of those who have seen it, wheat, barley, and millet grow more then twenty feet high.

And that is all I have seen of the customs concerning what is used for all kinds of breads in the country of the savages in the land of Brazil, called "America."

[...]

So as better to distinguish the matters that I have undertaken to treat, before I speak of the flesh, fish, fruits, and other foodstuffs utterly unlike those of our Europe with which our savages nourish themselves, I must speak of their drink, and the way it is made.

In the first place, it must be noted that just as their men have no hand in the making of the flour, but rather leave that whole task to their women (as you have already heard), they do likewise concerning their drink, and are even more scrupulous in their refusal to meddle in the making of it. These roots, *aypi* and *maniot*, serve as their chief nourishment, prepared in the way that I have just described; now here is how they handle them to make their customary drink.

After the women have cut up the roots as fine as we cut turnips for stewing, they let the pieces boil in water in great earthen vessels; when they see them getting tender and soft, they remove the pots from the fire and let them cool a little. When that is done, several of the women, crouched around these great vessels, take from them these little round pieces of softened root. First they chew them and twist them around in their mouths, without swallowing them; then they take the pieces in their hands, one after the other, and put them into other earthen vessels which are already on the fire, and in which they boil the pieces again. They constantly stir this concoction with a stick until they see that it is done, and then, removing it from the fire a second time, without straining it, they pour it all into other bigger earthen jars, each having the capacity of about an eleven-gallon Burgundy wine-measure. After it has clarified and fermented, they cover the vessels and leave the beverage until people want to drink it, in the manner that I will shortly describe. To give you a better picture of all this, these last big vessels that I have just

mentioned are made almost like the big earthen vats that I have seen used for laundry in some parts of the Bourbonnais and the Auvergne, except that they are narrower at the mouth and in the upper part.

Our American women likewise boil and then chew the coarse millet they call *avati*, and make a brew like that made from the roots I have mentioned. I repeat expressly that it is the women who perform this task: for although I have seen no distinction made between the young girls and the married women in this respect, the men nevertheless hold the firm opinion that if they were to chew the roots or the millet to make this beverage, it would be no good. They even consider it as unseemly for their sex to deal with it as people over here find it strange (rightly, I think) to see those great clumsy peasant men of Bresse take the distaff to spin. The savages call this beverage *caouin*. It is cloudy and thick like wine lees, and has almost the taste of sour milk; they have it both red and white, just as we do our wine.

Since these roots and the coarse millet that I have spoken of grow in their country the year round, they make this beverage in all seasons, and sometimes in such quantity that I have seen more than thirty of these big vessels (which, as I have told you, hold more than fifty quarts each) set out in a row in the middle of their houses, where they remain covered until it is time to have a *caouin* celebration.

But before we get to that point, I beg permission to offer (without any implied approval of this vice) a prologue: Yield, you Germans, Flemings, Lansquenets, Swiss, and all you over here who profess to drink and carouse, for after you have heard how our Americans acquit themselves in this domain, you will confess that compared to them you know nothing about it, and you will have to abandon the field to them.

When they set to it, and especially when they formally execute a prisoner of war to eat him in the ceremonies that we will see later, their custom (quite the contrary of ours concerning wine, which we like cool and clear) being to drink this *caouin* warm, the first thing that the women do is to make a little fire around the earthen vessels, where it will be heated lukewarm. That done, they begin by uncovering the first vessel at one end, and stir up the beverage; they dip it out with big gourd-halves, each holding about three pints. The men dance past the women, one after the other, and the women, serving as cupbearers, present to each man one of these big cupfuls – not forgetting to quaff it themselves; and neither one nor the other ever fails to toss it off in one gulp. But do you know how many times? Until the vessels – even if there were a hundred – are all empty, and there is not a single drop of *caouin* remaining. And in fact I have seen them go three days and three nights without ceasing to drink, and even after they were so sated and drunk that they could take no more – since to abandon the game would have been to be reputed womanish, and more than *schelm* among the Germans – , when they had vomited they went at it again, more valiantly than before.

Now what is still stranger and more remarkable among our Tupinamba is that, just as they eat nothing during their drinking bouts, so, too, when they eat they drink nothing during their meal; therefore when they saw us mingle the two, they found our custom very strange. If someone says at this point, "So they do as horses do?" the answer given by a joker in our company was that at least you don't have to bridle them or bring them to the river to drink, and there is no danger of their breaking their cruppers.

One must note, however, that while on the one hand they do not observe particular hours for dinner, supper, or light repasts, as we do over here, and do not hesitate if they are hungry to eat as readily at midnight as at noon, on the other hand, since they never eat when they are not hungry, you could say that they are as sober in their eating as they are excessive in their drinking. Some of them have the cleanly habit of washing their hands and their mouths before and after meals; however, I think they do this because otherwise their mouths would always be pasty from those root and millet flours, which, as I have said, they customarily use instead of bread. While they are eating they preserve a marvellous silence, so that if they have something to say, they save it until they have finished. When

they heard us prating and chattering during our meals, as is the custom of Frenchmen, they made great fun of us.

As long as this *caouinage* lasts, our American rakehells and carousers heat their brains hotter and hotter, singing, whistling, egging each other on, and exhorting each other to behave valiantly, and to take many prisoners when they go to war; lined up like cranes, they dance unceasingly, going back and forth through the house where they are assembled, until it is all over: that is, they never leave as long as they think there is anything left in the vessels. As proof of what I have said – that they are first and supreme in drunkenness – I believe there are some of them who on a single one of these occasions drink more than twenty pots each of *caouin*. Throughout all this they are covered with feathers, as I described them in the preceding chapter, and in this costume they kill and eat a prisoner of war; drunk as priests, they are enacting the Bacchanales of the ancient pagans, and it is a sight to see them roll their eyes. It does sometimes happen that neighbors with neighbors, seated in their cotton beds hung in the air, will drink in a more modest fashion; but their custom being such that all the men of a village, or several villages, usually assemble to drink (which they do not do for eating), these private drinking parties rarely take place.

Whether they drink a little or a lot, in addition to what I have said – that they never breed melancholy, but rather assemble every day to dance and make merry in their villages – the young marriageable men have this particular custom: each of them dons one of those feather clusters called *araroye* that are tied on the hips, sometimes with the *maraca* in hand, and those little dried fruits – the ones I mentioned, that rattle like snailshells – tied around their legs. They do almost nothing else every night but come and go in this get-up, leaping and dancing from house to house; seeing them and hearing them so often at this business, I was reminded of those over here whom we call "morris dancers," who, during the festivals of the patron saints of each parish, go about in fools' garb, scepter in hand and bells on their legs, dallying and dancing the morris in among the houses and town squares.

But it must be noted that in all savages' dances, whether they line up one after another, or (as I shall describe when I speak of their religion) arrange themselves in a circle, neither the women nor the girls ever join the men, and if they want to dance, they do it separately.

[…]

As for us, when we were first in that country, we thought that we could avoid the spitting that, as I have mentioned, the savage women use in the composition of their *caouin*. So we pounded *aypi* and *maniot* roots with millet, which we boiled together, thinking to prepare this beverage in a more seemly fashion. But to tell the truth, experience showed us that, made thus, it wasn't any good; so little by little, we accustomed ourselves to drinking the other as it was. We didn't usually resort to it, however, because we had all the sugarcane we could want. We would leave it to soak for several days in water that we had cooled a little, because of the warm climate; we drank the sugared water with great pleasure. Because of the temperature of that country, the beautiful, clear freshwater springs and rivers are so good (in fact, I will say, incomparably more healthful than those over here) that you can drink from them all you like, without suffering any ill effect; we usually drank the water pure, without adding anything to it. The savages call fresh water *uh-ete*, and salt water *uh-een*. They pronounce these words with the throat, as the Hebrews do with the letters that they call guttural (these were the most troublesome to pronounce of all the words in their language).

To conclude: I have no doubt that some of those who have heard what I have said concerning the chewing and twisting around of the roots and millet in the mouths of the savage women when they concoct their *caouin*, will have been nauseated, and will have spit. To allay this disgust, I entreat them to remember what we do when we make wine over here. Let them consider merely this: in the very places where the good wines grow, at the time of grape-harvest the wine-makers get into the tubs and vats, and with their bare feet and sometimes with their shoes, they tread the grapes; as I have seen, they crush them again the same way on the winepresses. Many things go on which are hardly more pleasing than this

custom of chewing among the American women. If thereupon someone says, "Yes, but as it ferments in the vats the wine expels all that filth," I reply that our *caouin* is purged the same way, and that therefore on this point the one custom is as good as the other.

What One May Call Laws and Civil Order Among the Savages: How Humanely They Treat and Receive Friends Who Visit Them; and of the Tears and Joyous Speeches That the Women Make to Welcome Them

As for the civil order of our savages, it is an incredible thing – a thing that cannot be said without shame to those who have both divine and human laws – how a people guided solely by their nature, even corrupted as it is, can live and deal with each other in such peace and tranquillity. (I mean, however, each nation within itself, or among allied nations: as for enemies, you have seen in another chapter how harshly they are treated.) Nevertheless, if it happens that some of them quarrel (which occurs so rarely that during almost a year I was with them I only saw them fight with each other twice), by no means do the others try to separate them or make peace; on the contrary, even when the adversaries are on the point of putting each others' eyes out, they let them go ahead without saying a word to prevent them. However, if anyone is wounded by his neighbor, and if he who struck the blow is apprehended, he will receive a similar blow in the same part of his body by the kinsmen of the one injured. If the wounds of the latter prove to be mortal, or if he is killed on the spot, the relatives of the dead man will take the life of the killer in the same way. In short, it is a life for a life, an eye for an eye, a tooth for a tooth, and so forth; but as I have said, this is very rarely seen among them.

The real property of this people consists of houses and of many more excellent pieces of land than they need for their subsistence. In a given village of five or six hundred people, while several families may live in the same house, nevertheless each has its own place, and the husband keeps his wife and children separate; however, there is nothing to keep you from seeing down the full length of these buildings, which are usually more than sixty feet long.

It is a curious fact worth noting that the Brazilians, who usually stay only five or six months in a place, carry with them the big pieces of wood and tall *pindo* plants, with which their houses are made and covered; thus they often move their very villages from place to place. These, however, still retain their former names, so that we have sometimes found villages at a quarter- or half-league's distance from the location where we had visited them before. Their dwellings being so easily transported, you can imagine that they have no great palaces (such as those attributed to the Peruvian Indians, whose wooden houses are so well built that there are rooms one hundred fifty feet long and eighty feet wide); and no one of the Tupinamba nation ever begins a dwelling or any other building that he will not see built and rebuilt twenty times in his life, if he lives to the age of manhood. If you ask them why they move their household so often, they simply answer that the change of air keeps them healthier, and that if they did other than what their grandfathers did, they would die immediately.

With regard to fields and trees, each head of a family will have several acres of his own, in a place that suits him, where he makes his garden and plants his root crops. As for the rest, all the to-do about dividing inheritances, or going to court to place boundaries and separate property – they leave all that to the miserly landowners and wrangling pettifoggers over here.

As for their furnishings, I have already mentioned in several places in this account what they consist of. Still, to omit nothing of what I know about the domestic economy of our savages, I will first speak of the women's method of spinning cotton, which they use to make cord and other things as well, and especially to make the beds, the style of which I will also explain. Here is how they work with it. After they have pulled it from the boll (which I have described in the chapter treating the plant that bears it), they spread it out a little with their fingers, without carding it further, and heap it beside them, either on the ground or on some other object, for they use no distaff as the women do over here. Their spindle is a round stick, no bigger than a finger and about a foot long, which passes through the middle of a little board, round like a wooden trencher and of about that thickness. They attach the cotton to the longer end of this lengthwise stick, spinning it on their knees and releasing it with the hand as spinners do their spindles: with this roller twirling like a top in the midst of their houses or elsewhere, they make the great nets for their beds. I later brought to France some of the finer cord, so well spun and tightly twisted by these same women that when I had a white cloth doublet stitched with it, everyone who saw it thought it was fine purled silk.

As for those cotton beds, which the savages call *inis*, their women make them on wooden looms, which are not laid flat like those of our weavers, nor equipped with so many devices, but are simply raised in front of them at their height. When they have laid the warp in their style, beginning the plaiting from the bottom, they make some of the beds with fishnet, and others more densely like heavy canvas. These beds are for the most part four, five or six feet long and about five feet wide; they have loops at each end also made of cotton, to which the cords are tied for hanging them in the air by attaching them to wooden beams set crosswise in their houses expressly for the purpose.

When they go to war, or sleep in the woods during a hunt, or by the seashore, or by their fishing streams, they hang them between two trees. When these cotton beds are soiled, whether from sweat, or from the smoke of the fires that are burning continually in the houses where they hang, or in some other way, the American women gather from the woods a wild fruit, in form like a flat pumpkin, but much bigger, so that it is all you can do to carry one in your hand. They cut it in pieces, soak it in water in a big earthen vessel, and beating it with wooden sticks, they work up great billows of foam. They use this as soap, and the beds come out as white as snow or as fuller's sheets.

[...]

To sum up the other furnishings of our Americans: the women, who among themselves have all the housework to do, make a great many receptacles and earthen vessels to prepare and store the beverage called *caouin*, as well as cooking pots, both round and oval, and pans of medium and small sizes; although the earthenware is not smooth and even on the outside, it is so polished and sealed on the inside by a certain white liquid that hardens, that our potters over here could do no finer work. These women even dilute certain grayish pigments for their task, and with their brushes they paint a thousand pretty little designs of interlaced curves, tendrils, and other delightful patterns on the inside of these earthen vessels, especially in those that hold flour and other foodstuffs. So you are served quite properly – indeed, more properly than by those over here who serve out of wooden vessels.

It is true that these American painters lack one thing: once they have created with their brushes whatever their fancy has dictated, if you ask them to do the same for you again, they will not be able to imitate the first piece of work, because they have no other plan, model, or sketch than the quintessence of a nimble brain; so you will never see the same design twice.

Our savages also have gourds and other big fruits, split and hollowed out, from which they make their drinking cups, called *coui*, as well as other little containers for other purposes. They also have boxes and baskets, big and small, very neatly woven, some of reeds and some of yellow grasses or straw, called *panacons*; they store flour in them or whatever else they please. I have already described their weapons, feather garments, the device they call a *maraca*, and other utensils, so I will discuss them no further.

With the houses of our savages built and furnished, it is time to go visit them.

Now to take up this subject in a general way: although the Tupinamba receive very humanely the friendly strangers who go to visit them, nevertheless the Frenchmen and others from over here who do not understand their language find themselves at first marvelously disconcerted in their midst. The first time that

I myself frequented them was three weeks after we arrived at Villegagnon's island, when an interpreter took me along to four or five villages on the mainland. The first one – called *Yabouraci* in the native language and "Pepin" by the French (because of a ship that loaded there once, whose master had that name) – was only two leagues from our fort. When we arrived there, I immediately found myself surrounded by savages, who were asking me "*Marapé-derere, marapé derere?*" meaning "What is your name? What is your name?" (which at that time I understood no better than High German). One of them took my hat, which he put on his head; another my sword and my belt, which he put around his naked body; yet another my tunic, which he donned. Deafening me with their yells, they ran through the village with my clothing. Not only did I think that I had lost everything, but I didn't know what would become of me. As experience has shown me several times since, that was only from ignorance of their way of doing things; for they do the same thing to everyone who visits them, and especially those they haven't seen before. After they have played around a little with one's belongings, they carry them all back and return them to their owners.

The interpreter had warned me that they wanted above all to know my name; but if I had said to them Pierre, Guillaume, or Jean, they would have been able neither to retain it nor to pronounce it (in fact, instead of saying "Jean," they would say "Nian"). So I had to accommodate by naming something that was known to them. Since by a lucky chance my surname, "Léry," means "oyster" in their language, I told them that my name was "*Léryoussou*," that is, a big oyster. This pleased them greatly; with their "*Teh!*" of admiration, they began to laugh, and said, "That is a fine name; we have not yet seen any *Mair* (that is, a Frenchman) of that name." And indeed, I can say with assurance that never did Circe metamorphose a man into such a fine oyster, nor into one who could converse so well with Ulysses, as since then I have been able to do with our savages.

One must note that their memory is so good that as soon as someone has told them his name, if they were to go a hundred years (so to speak) without seeing him, they will never forget it. Presently I will tell about the other ceremonies they observe when they receive friends who go to see them.

But for the moment I will continue to recount some of the noteworthy things that happened to me during my first journey among the Tupinamba. That same day the interpreter and I were going on to spend the night in another village called *Euramiri* (the French call it "Goset," because of an interpreter of that name who stayed there). Arriving at sunset, we found the savages dancing and finishing up the *caouin* of a prisoner whom they had killed only six hours earlier, the pieces of whom we saw on the *boucan*. Do not ask whether, with this beginning, I was astonished to see such a tragedy; however, as you will hear, that was nothing compared to the fright that I had soon after.

We had entered one of the village houses, where each of us sat, according to custom, in a cotton bed hung in the air. After the women had wept (in a manner that I will describe in a moment) and the old man, the master of the house, had made his speech of welcome, the interpreter – who was not new to the customs of the savages, and who, moreover, liked to drink and *caouiner* as much as they did – without saying a single word to me, nor warning me of anything, went over to the big crowd of dancers and left me there with some of the savages. So after eating a little root flour and other food they had offered us, I, weary and asking only for rest, lay down in the cotton bed I had been sitting on.

Not only was I kept awake by the noise that the savages made, dancing and whistling all night while eating their prisoner; but, what is more, one of them approached me with the victim's foot in hand, cooked and *boucané*, asking me (as I learned later, for I didn't understand at the time) if I wanted to eat some of it. His countenance filled me with such terror that you need hardly ask if I lost all desire to sleep. Indeed, I thought that by brandishing the human flesh he was eating, he was threatening me and wanted to make me understand that I was about to be similarly dealt with. As one doubt begets another, I suspected straight away that the interpreter, deliberately betraying me,

had abandoned me and delivered me into the hands of these barbarians. If I had seen some exit through which to flee, I would not have hesitated. But seeing myself surrounded on all sides by those whose intentions I failed to understand (for as you will hear, they had not the slightest thought of doing me harm), I firmly expected shortly to be eaten, and all that night I called on God in my heart. I will leave it to those who understand what I am saying, and who put themselves in my place, to consider whether that night seemed long.

At daybreak my interpreter (who had been off carousing with those rascals of savages all night long in other village houses) came to find me. Seeing me, as he said, not only ashen-faced and haggard but also feverish, he asked me whether I was sick, or if I hadn't rested well. Distraught, I answered wrathfully that they had well and truly kept me from sleeping, and that he was a scoundrel to have left me among these people whom I couldn't understand at all; still as anxious as ever, I urged that we get ourselves out of there with all possible speed. Thereupon he told me that I should have no fear, and that it wasn't us they were after. When he recounted the whole business to the savages – who, rejoicing at my coming, and thinking to show me affection, had not budged from my side all night – they said that they had sensed that I had been somewhat frightened of them, for which they were very sorry. My one consolation was the hoot of laughter they sent up – for they are great jokers – at having (without meaning to) given me such a scare.

The interpreter and I went from there to several other villages, but I will content myself with what I have just recounted as a sample of what happened to me during my first journey among the savages, and go on to generalities.

Let me now set forth the ceremonies that the Tupinamba observe when they receive friends who go to visit them. In the first place, as soon as the visitor has arrived in the house of the *moussacat* whom he has chosen for his host (the *moussacat* being the head of a household, who offers food to people passing through the village, and whom one must visit first in each village before going anywhere else if one is not to offend him), he is seated on a cotton bed suspended in the air, and remains there for a short while without saying a word. Then the women come and surround the bed, crouching with their buttocks against the ground and with both hands over their eyes; in this manner, weeping their welcome to the visitor, they will say a thousand things in his praise. For example: "You have gone to so much trouble to come to see us; you are good; you are valiant." And if it is a Frenchman, or some other stranger from over here, they will add: "You have brought us so many fine things that we do not have in this country." Spouting big tears, they will string out this kind of applause and flattery. If the newly arrived guest who is seated in the bed wants in turn to please them, he must assume the appropriate expression, and if he doesn't quite get to the point of tears (I have seen some of our nation, who, upon hearing the bleating of these women next to them, were such babies as to be reduced to tears themselves), at least when he answers them he must heave a few sighs and pretend to weep.

This first salutation having been graciously performed by the American women, the *moussacat*, busy making an arrow or some other object (as you see in the illustration), will meanwhile have spent a quarter of an hour or so pretending not to see you – a blandishment quite contrary to our embraces, hugs, kisses, and handclasps upon the arrival of our friends. Then, approaching you, he will first use this style of speaking: "*Ere-joubé?*" that is, "Have you come?" and then "How are you? What would you like?" and so forth; to which you must respond according to the forms of conversation in their language which you will see hereafter. Then he will ask you if you want to eat; if you reply "Yes," he will immediately have prepared and brought to you, in fine earthen vessels, the flour that they eat instead of bread, as well as meat, poultry, fish, and other food; but since they have no tables, benches, or stools, the service will be right on the ground in front of your feet. As for drink, if you want a *caouin*, he will give you some if he has any. After the women have wept beside the visitor, they will bring him fruit or some other small gift from their region, to obtain him combs, mirrors, or the little glass beads that they put around their arms.

Figure 7.1

If, moreover, you want to sleep in that village, the old man will not only stretch out for you a fine white bed, but also, even though it does not get cold in their country, he will place around the bed, against the night's humidity, four or five small fires, which will often be relit in the course of the night, along with some little screens that they call *tatapecoua*, made like the masks that the ladies over here hold in front of them when they are next to the fire, to keep it from spoiling their faces.

[...]

After the guests have drunk and eaten, in the way I have described, and rested or slept in their houses, if they are courteous, they ordinarily present knives to men, or scissors, or tweezers for plucking out beards; to the women, combs and mirrors; and to the little boys, fishhooks. If beyond that there are dealings about food supplies or other things that they have, you ask what they want for it, and upon giving them whatever is agreed upon, you can carry it off and go on your way.

Since, as I have said elsewhere, there are no horses, donkeys, or other beasts of burden in their country, they simply travel on their own two feet. If the foreign visitors are weary, they have only to present a knife or some other object to the savages; the latter, prompt as they are to please their friends, will offer to carry them. In fact, while I was over there, there were those who put us on their shoulders, with their heads between our thighs and our legs hanging against their bellies, and carried us that way more than a league without resting. Sometimes, to give them some relief, we told them to stop; laughing at us, they would say in their language: "What? Do you think we are women, or so slack and weak of heart that we might faint under the burden?" "I would carry you a whole day without stopping for rest," said one of them who had me around his neck. We, for our part, would roar with laughter at these two-footed mounts, applauding them and cheering them on, and saying, "Well then! Let's keep going!"

As for their natural fellow-feeling, every day they distribute and present each to each the venison, fish, fruit, and the other good things of their country, and not only would a savage die of shame (so to speak) if he saw his neighbor lacking what he has in his power to give, but also, as I have experienced it, they practice the same liberality toward foreigners who are their allies. As an example of this I will recount the time when … two Frenchmen and I had lost our way in the woods – when we thought we were going to be eaten by a huge and terrifying lizard – , and moreover, during the space of two days and a night that we were lost, suffered greatly from hunger. When we finally found ourselves in a village called *Pauo*, where we had been on other occasions, we could not have received a better welcome than we had from the savages of that place. To begin with, when they heard us recount the troubles we had endured, and the danger we had been in – not only of being devoured by cruel beasts, but also of being seized and eaten by the Margaia, our enemy and theirs, whose land we had unintentionally approached – and when

they saw the state we were in, all scratched up by the thorns that we had gone through in the wilderness, they took such pity on us that I can't help saying that the hypocritical welcomes of those over here who use only slippery speech for consolation of the afflicted is a far cry from the humanity of these people, whom nonetheless we call "barbarians."

They had begun (and here they reminded me of the manner of the ancients) by sending for fine clear water and washing the feet and legs of us three Frenchmen, who were seated each on a separate bed. Upon our arrival the old men had given orders to prepare food for us, and had even ordered the women to prepare quickly some soft flour (which I would as soon eat as good hot white bread); seeing us somewhat refreshed, they immediately had us served, in their style, with many good foods such as venison, poultry, fish, and exquisite fruit, which they are never without.

When evening fell, the elder who was our host had the children taken away from us so that we might rest more comfortably. In the morning when we awoke he said to us, "Well, *Atour-assats* (that is, perfect allies) did you sleep well last night?" We replied that we had, indeed, and he said to us: "Rest some more, my children, because I could tell last night that you were very weary." In short, it is hard for me to express the hospitality that was offered us by those savages, who in truth acted toward us just as, according to Saint Luke in the Acts of the Apostles, the barbarians of the Isle of Malta treated Saint Paul and those who were with him after they had escaped the shipwreck. Now since we never travelled without each having a leather sack full of small merchandise that served us as money in our dealings with this people, at our departure we could give as we pleased: that is (as is the custom) knives, scissors, and tweezers to the elders; combs, mirrors, bracelets, and glass buttons to the women; and fishhooks to the little boys.

So that you may better understand the great store they set by these things, I will recount the following. One day when I was in a village, my *moussacat* (he who had received me into his house) entreated me to show him everything I had in my *caramemo*, that is, in my leather sack. He had brought to me a fine big earthen vessel in which I arranged all my effects. Marveling at the sight, he immediately called the other savages and said to them: "I pray you, my friends, consider what a personage I have in my house for since he has so many riches, must he not be a great lord?" And yet, as I said, laughing with a companion of mine who was there with me, what this savage held in such high esteem was in sum five or six knives with different kinds of handles, and as many combs, mirrors, and other small objects that would not have been worth two testoons in Paris. As I have said elsewhere, they love above all those who show liberality; since I wanted to exalt myself even more than he had done, I gave him freely and publicly, in front of everyone, the biggest and handsomest of my knives, which he set as much store by as might someone in our France who had just received a golden chain worth a hundred crowns.

Now you may want to know whether we felt safe among the savages of America. Just as they hate their enemies so mortally (as you have already heard) that when they have captured them, without any discussion of terms, they slay and eat them, so, on the contrary, they love so dearly their friends and confederates (as we were to the Tupinamba nation) that to keep them safe and spare them any hardship they would have had themselves cut into a hundred thousand pieces. Having had experience of them, I would entrust myself to them, and in fact felt myself safer among this people we call savage, than I would now in some parts of our France, among disloyal and degenerate Frenchmen. (I speak only of those who are such: as for worthy people, of whom by the grace of God the kingdom is not yet empty, I would be very sorry to taint their honor.)

8

Of Cannibals

Michel de Montaigne

When King Pyrrhus invaded Italy, after he had surveyed the army that the Romans had sent out against him, drawn up in battle array, "I know not," he said "what barbarians these are" (for the Greeks so called all foreign nations), "but the disposition of this army that I see is in no wise barbarian." The Greeks said the same of the army that Flaminius led into their country; and Philip, when he saw from a little hill the order and arrangement of the Roman camp in his kingdom under Publius Sulpicius Galba. Thus we see how we should beware of adhering to common opinions, and that we must weigh them by the test of reason, not by common report.

I had with me for a long time a man who had lived ten or twelve years in that other world which has been discovered in our time in the region where Villegaignon made land, and which he christened Antarctic France. This discovery of a boundless country seems to be worth consideration. I do not know whether I can be assured that some other may not hereafter be found, so many greater personages having been deceived about this one. I fear that our eyes may be greater than our stomachs, and that we have more curiosity than capacity. We grasp at every thing, but clutch nothing but wind. Plato speaks of Solon narrating that he learned from the priests of the city of Sais in Egypt that in times past, and before the Deluge, there was a large island called Atlantidis, just at the mouth of the Strait of Gibraltar, which was of greater extent than Africa and Asia together, and that the kings of that country – who not only possessed that island, but had extended their dominion so far on the continent that they held the breadth of Africa as far as Egypt, and the length of Europe as far as Tuscany – undertook to stride into Asia and to subdue all the nations on the shores of the Mediterranean as far as the Euxine; and to this end they traversed all Spain, Gaul, and Italy, even to Greece, where the Athenians resisted them; but, some time later, the Athenians and they and their island were swallowed up by the Deluge. It is very probable that that immense inundation made strange changes in the inhabited places of the earth, as it is thought that the sea cut off Sicily from Italy, –

> They say that these lands were once torn violently asunder in a great convulsion; till then the two lands had been but one, –

Cyprus from Syria, and the island of Negropont from the mainland of Bœotia; and elsewhere joined lands that were formerly separate, filling with mud and sand the channels between them, –

> Long a sterile fen, fit for the oar, it now feeds the neighbouring towns and feels the weight of the plough.

Michel de Montaigne, "Of Cannibals," in *The Essays of Michel de Montaigne*, trans. George B. Ives, New York: The Heritage Press, 1946, pp. 271–88.

But there is no great likelihood that this new world that we have just discovered is that island; for it almost touched Spain, and it would be an incredible effect of the inundation to have moved it away, as it is, more than twelve hundred leagues; besides which, the explorations of modern navigators have almost made sure that this is not an island, but mainland, connected with the East Indies on one side, and elsewhere with the countries that lie under the two poles; or, if divided from them, it is by so narrow a passage that it is not thereby entitled to be called an island. It seems as if there may be motions in those great bodies as in our own, some natural, others irregular. When I see the encroachment that my river Dordogne is making on its right bank, in my own day, and how much it has gained in twenty years, and has undermined the foundations of several buildings, I see clearly that it is an unusual disturbance; for if the river had always so done, or if it were always so to do, the face of the world would be subverted. But they are subject to changes: sometimes they overflow on one side, sometimes on the other; sometimes they keep within their banks. I am not speaking of sudden inundations, of which we can lay our hand on the causes. In Medoc, along the seacoast, my brother, Sieur d'Arsac, saw an estate of his buried under the sand which the sea threw upon it; the roofs of some buildings are still visible; his revenues and domain are transformed into very poor pastures. The people of the place say that for some time past the sea pushes on so effectually toward them, that they have lost four leagues of land. These sands are her harbingers; and we see great moving sand dunes that march half a league before her and steadily advance.

The other assertion of ancient times with which it is attempted to connect this discovery, is in Aristotle – that is, if that little treatise of *Unheard-of Wonders* be his. He there relates that certain Carthaginians, having started across the Atlantic Sea from the Strait of Gibraltar, and having sailed a long while, finally discovered a large, fertile island, well covered with forests, and watered by broad and deep rivers, far distant from any mainland; and that they, and others after them, attracted by the bounty and fertility of the soil, went thither with their wives and children, and set up their habitation there. The lords of Carthage, seeing that their country was being gradually depopulated, expressly forbade, upon pain of death, that any more of their people should go thither, and expelled these new settlers, fearing, so it is said, that, as time passed, they might so multiply that they would supplant themselves, and ruin their state. This narrative of Aristotle's agrees no better with our newly-discovered territories.

This man that I had was a simple, plain fellow, which is a nature likely to give true testimony; for intelligent persons notice more things and scrutinise them more carefully; but they comment on them; and to make their interpretation of value and win belief for it, they can not refrain from altering the facts a little. They never represent things to you just as they are: they shape them and disguise them according to the aspect which they have seen them bear; and to win faith in their judgement and incline you to trust it, they readily help out the matter on one side, lengthen it, and amplify it. It needs a man either very truthful or so ignorant that he has no material wherewith to construct and give verisimilitude to false conceptions, and one who is wedded to nothing. My man was such a one; and, besides, he on diverse occasions brought to me several sailors and traders whom he had known on his travels. So I am content with this information, without enquiring what the cosmographers say about it. We need topographers who would give us a detailed description of the places where they have been. But when they have the advantage over us of having seen Palestine, they desire to enjoy the privilege of telling us news about all the rest of the world. I could wish that every one would write what he knows and as much as he knows, not about one subject alone, but about all others; for one may have some special knowledge or experience as to the nature of a river or a fountain, who about other things knows only what every one knows. He will undertake, however, in order to give currency to that little scrap of knowledge, to write on the whole science of physics. From this fault spring many grave disadvantages.

Now, to return to what I was talking of, I think that there is nothing barbaric or uncivilised in that nation, according to what I have been told, except that every one calls "barbarism" whatever he is not accustomed to. As, indeed, it seems that we have no other criterion of truth and of what is reasonable than the example and type of the opinions and customs of the country to which we belong: therein [to us] always is the perfect religion, the perfect political system, the perfect and achieved usage in all things. They are wild men, just as we call those fruits wild which Nature has produced unaided and in her usual course; whereas, in truth, it is those that we have altered by our skill and removed from the common kind which we ought rather to call wild. In the former the real and most useful and natural virtues are alive and vigorous – we have vitiated them in the latter, adapting them to the gratification of our corrupt taste; and yet nevertheless the special savour and delicacy of diverse uncultivated fruits of those regions seems excellent even to our taste in comparison with our own. It is not reasonable that art should gain the preeminence over our great and puissant mother Nature. We have so overloaded the beauty and richness of her works by our contrivances that we have altogether smothered her. Still, truly, whenever she shines forth unveiled, she wonderfully shames our vain and trivial undertakings.

The ivy grows best when wild, and the arbutus springs most beautifully in some lovely cave; birds sing most sweetly without teaching.

All our efforts can not so much as reproduce the nest of the tiniest birdling, its contexture, its beauty, and its usefulness; nay, nor the web of the little spider. All things, said Plato, are produced either by nature, or by chance, or by art; the greatest and most beautiful by one or other of the first two, the least and most imperfect by the last.

These nations seem to me, then, wild in this sense, that they have received in very slight degree the external forms of human intelligence, and are still very near to their primitive simplicity. The laws of nature still govern them, very

little corrupted by ours; even in such pureness that it sometimes grieves me that the knowledge of this did not come earlier, in the days when there were men who would have known better than we how to judge it. I am sorry that Lycurgus and Plato had not this knowledge; for it seems to me that what we see in intercourse with those nations surpasses not only all the paintings wherewith poetry has embellished the golden age, and all its conceptions in representing a happy condition of mankind, but also the idea and aspiration, even, of philosophy. They could not conceive so pure and simple an artlessness as we by experience know it to be; nor could they believe that human society could be carried on with so little artificiality and human unitedness. It is a nation, I will say to Plato, in which there is no sort of traffic, no acquaintance with letters, no knowledge of numbers, no title of magistrate or of political eminence, no custom of service, of wealth, or of poverty, no contracts, no successions, no dividings of property, no occupations except leisurely ones, no respect for any kinship save in common, no clothing, no agriculture, no metals, no use of wine or grain. The very words that signify falsehood, treachery, dissimulation, avarice, envy, slander, forgiveness, are unheard of. How far from such perfection would he find the Republic he imagined: *men recently from the hands of the gods.*

These are the first laws that nature gave.

For the rest, they live in a country with a most agreeable and pleasant climate; consequently, according to what my witnesses have told me, it is a rare thing to see a sick man there; and they have assured me that any one palsied, or blear-eyed, or toothless, or bent with old age is never to be seen. These people are settled on the sea-shore, and are shut in, landward, by a chain of high mountains, leaving a strip a hundred leagues or thereabouts in width. They have a great abundance of fish and meats, which bear no resemblance to ours, and they eat them without other elaboration than cooking. The first man who rode a horse there, although he had been with them on several other voyages, so terrified them in that guise that they shot him to death with arrows before they could recognise him.

Their buildings are very long and can hold two or three hundred souls; they are built of the bark of large trees, fastened to the earth at one end and resting against and supporting one another at the ridge-pole, after the fashion of some of our barns, the roofing whereof falls to the ground and serves for side and end walls. They have wood so hard that they cut with it and make swords of it, and gridirons for cooking their meat. Their beds are a cotton web, hung from the roof like those in our ships, each person having his own, for the women lie apart from their husbands. They rise with the sun and eat immediately after rising, for the whole day's need; for they have no other meal than this. They do not drink then, as Suidas says of certain Oriental nations who drank when not eating; they drink many times during the day, and a great deal. Their beverage is made of some root, and is of the colour of our light wines; they drink it only luke-warm. This beverage will keep only two or three days; it is rather sharp in taste, not at all intoxicating, good for the stomach, and laxative for those who are not accustomed to it; it is a very pleasant drink for those wonted to it. Instead of bread they use a certain substance like preserved coriander. I have tasted it; its flavour is sweetish and rather insipid. The whole day is passed in dancing. The young men go hunting wild animals with bows. A part of the women employ themselves meanwhile in warming their drink, which is their chief duty. Some one of the old men, in the morning, before they begin to eat, counsels the whole collected household walking from end to end of the building and repeating the same phrase many times, until he has completed the turn (for the buildings are fully a hundred paces in length). He enjoins upon them only two things – valour against the enemy and friendship for their wives. And they never fail, by way of response, to note the obligation that it is their wives who keep their drink warm and well-seasoned for them. There can be seen in many places, and, among others, in my house, the fashion of their beds, of their twisted ropes, of their wooden swords and the wooden armlets with which they protect their wrists in battle, and of the long staves, open at one end, by the sound of which they mark time in their dancing. They are clean-shaven, and they shave much more closely than we do, with no other razor than one of wood or stone.

They believe their souls to be immortal, and that they who have deserved well of the gods have their abode in that quarter of the heavens where the sun rises; the accursed, in the Occident. They have I know not what kinds of priests and prophets, who very rarely come among the people, having their abode in the mountains. On their arrival a great festival and solemn assemblage of several villages takes place. (Each building such as I have described is a village, and they are about a French league distant one from another.) The prophet speaks to them in public, inciting them to virtue and to their duty; but their whole moral teaching contains only these two articles: resoluteness in war and affection for their wives. He prophesies things to come and the results they may hope for from their undertakings; shows them the way toward war, or dissuades them from it; but all this is under the condition that, when he fails to prophesy truly, and if it chances them otherwise than he predicted to them, he is chopped into a thousand pieces if they catch him, and condemned as a false prophet. For this reason, he who has once erred is never seen again. Divination is a gift of God; that is why the misuse of it should be a punishable imposture. Among the Scythians, when the soothsayers failed in their venture, they were laid, loaded with chains, in carts filled with brushwood and drawn by oxen, in which they were burned alive. Those who manage things subject to the guidance of human knowledge are excusable if they do with them what they can; but these others, who come cheating us with assurances of an extra-ordinary power which is beyond our ken – must not they be punished, both because they do not carry out the fact of their promise, and for the foolhardiness of their imposture?

They wage wars against the tribes that live on the other side of their mountains, farther inland, to which they go entirely naked, with no other weapons than bows, or wooden swords pointed at the end like the heads of our boar spears. The obstinacy of their combats is wonderful, and they never end save with slaughter and bloodshed; for as to routs and panic, they do not know what those are. Every man brings back as his trophy the head of the foe he has killed, and fastens it at the entrance of his abode. After they have for a long while treated their prisoners well and supplied them with all the comforts they can think of, the head man summons a great assemblage of his acquaintances. He ties a rope to one of the prisoner's arms, by the end of which he holds him at a distance of some paces, for fear of being injured by him; the other arm he gives to his dearest friend to hold in the same way; and they two, before the assembly, kill him with their swords. That done, they roast him, and all eat him in common and send portions to those of their friends who are absent. This is not, as some think, for sustenance, as the Scythians of old did, but to indicate an uttermost vengeance. And therefore, having observed that the Portuguese, who had allied themselves with their adversaries, made use, when they captured them, of another sort of death for them, which was to bury them to the waist and cast many darts at the rest of their bodies, and hang them afterward, they thought that these people from the other part of the world, who had spread the knowledge of many villainies among their neighbours, and who were much more expert than they in all sorts of evil-doing, would not choose that sort of vengeance without good reason, and that it must be more painful than theirs; and they began to lay aside their old fashion and to follow this one.

I am not sorry that we note the savage horribleness there is in such an action; but indeed I am sorry that, while rightly judging their misdeeds, we are very blind to our own. I think there is more barbarism in eating a living man than a dead one, in rending by torture and racking a body still quick to feel, in slowly roasting it, in giving it to dogs and swine to be torn and eaten (as we have not only read but seen in recent days, not among long-time foes, but among neighbours and fellow citizens, and, what is worse, in the guise of piety and religion), than in roasting it and eating it after it is dead. Chrysippus and Zeno, heads of the Stoic school, did indeed think that there was no harm in using a dead body for any thing demanded by our need, and in deriving suste-

nance from it; like our ancestors, who, being besieged by Cæsar in the town of Alexia, determined to relieve hunger during the siege by the bodies of old men, women, and other persons useless for fighting.

The Gascons, it is said, prolonged life by the use of such food.

And physicians do not fear to make use of it in every sort of way for our health, whether to be applied internally or externally; but there was never found an opinion so unreasonable as to excuse treachery, disloyalty, tyranny, and cruelty, which are our common faults.

We can, then, rightly call them barbarians with respect to the rules of reason, but not with respect to ourselves, who surpass them in every sort of barbarism. Their warfare is wholly noble and honourable, and has as much excuse and beauty as that malady of mankind can have. With them it has no other motive than simply eagerness of prowess. They are not at strife for the conquest of new territories, for they still enjoy that natural fertility which supplies them, without labour and without trouble, with all things necessary, in such abundance that they have no reason to enlarge their boundaries. They are still at that fortunate point of desiring only so much as is ordained by their natural needs: every thing beyond that is superfluous for them. They generally call those of the same age brothers, those younger, children; and the old men are fathers to all the others. They leave to their heirs in common the undivided full possession of property, without other title than that flawless one which Nature gives to her creatures on bringing them into the world.

If their neighbours come from beyond the mountains to attack them and win the victory over them, the victor's gain is glory, and the advantage of having proved the superior in valour and prowess; for no otherwise do they give heed to the property of the vanquished; and they turn back to their own country, where they lack nothing that is necessary, nor do they lack that great gift of knowing how to enjoy their condition happily and to be content with it. When the turn of the others comes, they do the same; they ask no other ransom of their prisoners than the admission and acknowledgement that they are conquered; but there is not one found in a whole age who does not prefer death rather than to abate, either by manner or by word, a single jot of the grandeur of an invincible courage; not one is seen who does not prefer to be killed rather than merely to ask not to be. They give them every liberty, so that life may be all the dearer to them; and they entertain them usually with threats of their future death, of the torments they will have to suffer, of the preparations that are being made to that end, of the lopping off of their limbs, and of the feast there will be at their expense. All this is done for the sole purpose of extorting from their lips some faltering or downcast word, or of making them long for flight, in order to obtain this advantage of having frightened them and of having shaken their firmness. For, if rightly understood, true victory consists in this single point: –

That only is victory which forces the foe in his own mind to acknowledge himself conquered.

The Hungarians, very valorous fighters, did not formerly carry their point beyond reducing their enemy to their mercy; for, having extorted this admission from him, they let him go without injury and without ransom, save, at the most, forcing him to promise not henceforth to take arms against them.

We obtain many advantages over our enemies, which are borrowed advantages, not our own. It is the quality of a porter, not of merit, to have stouter arms and legs; it is a lifeless and corporeal faculty to be always ready; it is a stroke of fortune to make our enemy stumble, and to dazzle his eyes by the glare of the sun; it is a trick of art and knowledge – which may fall to a dastardly and worthless person – to be skilled in fencing. A man's estimation and value depend upon his heart and his will; that is where his true honour lies; valour is strength, not of arms and legs, but of the mind and the soul; it does not depend upon the worth of our horse or of our armour, but upon our own. He who falls persistent in his will, *if be fall, be fights kneeling.* He who abates no whit of his

firmness and confidence for any danger from death not far away; he who, while yielding up his soul, still gazes at his foe with an unshrinking and disdainful eye – he is beaten, not by us, but by fortune; he is killed, not conquered. The most valiant are sometimes the most unfortunate. So too there are defeats no less triumphant than victories. Nor did those four sister victories, the most splendid that the eyes of the sun can ever have seen, – of Salamis, Platæa, Mycale, and Sicily, – ever venture to compare all their combined glory to the glory of the defeat of King Leonidas and his men at Thermopylæ.

Who ever rushed with a more praiseworthy and more ambitious longing to the winning of a battle than did Captain Ischolas to the loss of one? Who ever more skilfully and carefully assured himself of safety than he of his destruction? He was appointed to defend a certain pass in the Peloponnesus against the Arcadians; finding himself wholly unable to do this because of the nature of the place and the inequality of the forces, and making up his mind that all who should meet the enemy would by necessity remain on the field; on the other hand, deeming it unworthy, both of his own valour and nobleness of spirit and of the Lacedæmonian name, to fail in his commission, he took a middle course between those two extremes, in this way: the youngest and most active of his force he preserved for the protection and service of their country, and sent them back to it; and with those who would be less missed, he decided to hold the pass, and by their deaths to make the enemy purchase the entrance thereto as dearly as possible. And so it fell out: for, being presently surrounded on all sides by the Arcadians, after he and his had made a great slaughter of them, they were all killed. Is there any trophy assigned to victors, which would not be more justly due to these vanquished? The real surmounting has for its part strife, not safety; and the honour of courage consists in fighting, not in winning.

To return to our narrative, these prisoners, despite all that is done to them, are so far from yielding that, on the contrary, during the two or three months that they are kept in captivity, they bear themselves cheerfully; they urge their masters to make haste to put them to that test;

they defy them, insult them, upbraid them with their cowardice and with the number of battles they have lost in mutual combat. I have a ballad written by a prisoner wherein is this taunt: Let them come boldly every one, and gather together to dine upon him; for they will at the same time eat their own fathers and grandfathers, who have served as food and nourishment for his body; "these muscles," he says, "this flesh, and these veins are your own, poor fools that you are; you do not recognise that the substance of your ancestors' limbs still clings to them. Taste them carefully, and you will find in them the flavour of your own flesh" – a conceit which has no smack of barbarism. Those who depict them when dying, and who describe the act of putting them to death, depict the prisoner as spitting in the faces of those who kill him and making mouths at them. Verily, in comparison with ourselves these men are savages indeed; for it must be that they are so, or else that we are so; there is a wonderful distance between their behaviour and ours.

The men have several wives, and they have the larger number in proportion to their reputation for valour. A notably beautiful thing in their marriages is that the same eagerness that our wives have to keep us from the friendship and good-will of other women, theirs have to an equal degree to obtain this for their husbands. Being more solicitous for their husband's honour than for any other thing, they seek, and make it their care to have, as many companions as they can, forasmuch as it is a testimony to the husband's valour. Our wives will cry out on this as a miracle: it is not so; it is a properly matrimonial virtue, but of the highest type. And in the Bible, Leah, Rachel, Sarah, and the wives of Jacob gave their beautiful maidservants to their husbands; and Livia seconded the appetites of Augustus, to her own detriment; and the wife of King Dejotarus, Stratonica, not only lent to her husband for his use a very beautiful young maid in her service, but carefully brought up their children and gave them a helping hand toward the succession to their father's estates. And, to the end that it may not be thought that all this is done from simple and slavish compliance with usage, and by the influence

of the authority of their ancient customs, without reflection and without judgement, and because their wits are so dull that they can not take any other course, some examples of their ability should be brought forward. Besides what I have just quoted from one of their warlike songs, I have another, an amorous one, which begins in this way: "Adder, stay thee; stay thee, adder, to the end that my sister may make, after the pattern of thy markings, the fashion and workmanship of a rich girdle, which I may give to my love; so shall thy beauty and thy grace be for all time more highly esteemed than all other serpents." Now I have enough knowledge of poetry to form this judgement, that not only is there nothing barbaric in this conception, but that it is quite Anacreontic. Their language, moreover, has a soft and pleasant sound, and much resembles the Greek in its terminations.

Three of this people – not knowing how dear the knowledge of the corruption of this country will some day cost their peace of mind and their happiness, and that from this intercourse will be born their ruin, which conjecture may be already in process of confirmation; most miserable in having allowed themselves to be tricked by the desire for things unknown, and in having left the sweetness of their own skies, to come to gaze at ours – were at Rouen at the time that the late King Charles the Ninth was there. The king talked with them a long while; they were shown our modes of life, our magnificence, and the outward appearance of a beautiful city. Thereafter some one asked them what they thought of all this, and wished to learn from them what had seemed to them most worthy of admiration. They mentioned in reply three things, of which I have forgotten the third, and am very sorry for it; but I remember two. They said that, in the first place, they thought it very strange that so many tall, bearded men, strong and well armed, who were about the king (they probably referred to the Swiss of the Guard), should humble themselves to obey a child, and that they did not rather choose some one of themselves to command them. Secondly (they have a fashion of speech of calling men halves of one another), they had perceived that there were among us some men gorged to the full with all sorts of possessions, and that their other halves were beggars at their doors, gaunt with hunger and destitution; and they thought it strange that these poverty-stricken halves could suffer such injustice, and that they did not take the others by the throat or set fire to their houses. I talked with one of them a very long while; but I had an interpreter who followed me so badly, and who was so hindered by his stupidity from grasping my ideas, that I could not have any pleasure in it. When I asked what advantage he derived from his superior position among his people (for he was a captain and our seamen called him king), he said that it was the privilege of marching at their head in war. By how many men he was followed. He indicated a certain extent of ground, as if to signify that it was by as many men as that space would hold – perhaps four or five thousand. Whether, when there was no war, all his authority was at an end. He said that he still retained the right, when he visited the villages that were in his dependence, to have paths made for him through the thickets of their forests.

All this does not seem too much amiss; but then, they do not wear breeches!

9

Method for the Easy Comprehension of History

Jean Bodin

... The same heat brings about a counteraction – they drink rather often. They call thirst the appetite for wet and cold. This form of carousing, which the Germans, especially the Saxons, use, as well as the dwellers near the Baltic Sea, can never be changed at any time or by any laws. "To devote day and night to drink," says Tacitus, "is a disgrace to no man; numerous brawls are usual between the intoxicated." But Athenaeus, charging the Scythians with "drinking of unmixed wine," from the old proverb, said that the Laconians "whenever they wish to drink a stronger mixture, call it drinking Scythian fashion. Chamaeleon of Heracleia, in the book about drunkenness, said, 'Right it were to celebrate in Scythian fashion.'" ...

They likewise overflow with humor. From this, hunger is created by the desire for hot and dry; yet they are pleased less by food than by drink, since they have more heat themselves. This is the reason why Hippocrates thought that it was impossible for the same man to take both food and drink copiously. When Tacitus noticed this fact among the Germans, he did not understand the cause. "Fasting and cold they bear," says he, "inured to the nature of the sky and the soil," because the climate is cold and the soil sterile. Nay, rather the internal heat resists more vigorously the surrounding cold. Energizing humor wards off hunger.

An abundance of humor is evidenced in the growth by which marine animals, on account of excess of water, excel the remaining animal life. From this also comes a gruff and severe voice, although among the Spanish, Carthaginians, and Ethiopians it is unusually thin and clear. In the three latter this proves cold and dryness; in the Germans, dampness and heat. Too much moisture produces in lead and green wood a heavy sound. Heat also opens the interior passages [of the body], while cold closes them. Hence women, by nature colder, speak in a higher tone than men. In a moderate temperature the voice becomes sweet and melodious, as in the Asiatics, the Italians, and the French. Excessive dampness causes the northerners to dissolve in perspiration when they make their way to the south or wage wars in the warm regions.

"The Germans," said Tacitus, "have a curious inconsistency of nature, since the same men love doing nothing, and hate quiet. Either they wage wars, or when they abstain from wars, they abandon themselves to sleep and to food." The inner warmth drives them to action, as may be seen in boys, whom heat does not permit to rest, but moisture brings softness and goes out in sweat. So Plutarch confirmed these things in the life of Marius, where he wrote that the damp bodies of the Cimbri are usually softened by heat and sweat. Wherefore the Spanish and

Jean Bodin, *Method for the Easy Comprehension of History*, trans. Beatrice Reynolds. New York: Columbia University Press, 1945, pp. 94–102, 109–17, 242–3.

the Italians, if they sustain the first attacks of the French and the Germans, easily break them, as Polybius first noticed and Marius and Caesar then established in famous victories. About the French Caesar said that at the beginning of the fight they were more than men – afterwards weaker than women. Tacitus made the same comment about the Germans: "Great bodies have the Germans, and powerful only for the first attack. Impatient at the same time of work and of drudgery, they do not endure thirst and heat at all. Cold, on the other hand, they bear easily." As Pomponius Mela wrote, up to the age of puberty they go about naked. Galen, however, marveled at the story that they are plunged into cold water by their parents as soon as they are born. But Julian Augustus explained this in his "Discourse at Antioch, The Beardhater." He said that the bastard children of the Germans are drowned in the Rhine; the legitimate swim. He wrote this extravagantly, however, and without authority.

The Africans, with dry, cold, and very hard bodies, bear work and heat patiently, as Aphrodisaeus wrote in *Questions*. Yet they cannot bear the cold, since they have no internal heat, unlike the Scythians, who endure external heat with difficulty, since they are abundantly supplied within. In the same way horses, by their very nature warm and wet, live with difficulty in Ethiopia, but more easily in Scythia. On the other hand, asses, dry and cold, are lively in Africa, tired in Europe, nonexistent in Scythia.

Those who occupy the middle region are impatient of both cold and heat, since the mean contends with each extreme; both, however, they endure equally well. I do not call the mean between the pole and the equator the middle region, but that space halfway between the tropic and the pole, because heat is not violent under the equator, as we have made plain, although it is under the tropic. So the most temperate region will not be that which runs from the thirtieth parallel to the fortieth, but that from the fortieth to the fiftieth; and the more moderate, the more it slopes to the east. In this tract lie Further Spain, France, Italy, Upper Germany to the Main, both Pannonias, Illyricum, both Mysias, Dacia, Moldavia, Macedonia, Thrace, and the best part of Asia

Minor, Armenia, Parthia, Sogdiana, and a large part of Greater Asia. The nearer to the east the regions lie, however, the more temperate they are, although they seem to incline more to the south, as Lydia, Cilicia, Asia, and Media. However, we shall speak of the east in its proper place. The southerners nearer to us, then, are the Spanish, Sicilians, Peloponnesians, Cretans, Syrians, Arabs, Persians, Susians, Gedrosians, Indians, Egyptians, Cyrenaeians, Phoenicians, Numidians, Libyans, Moors, and the Americans who inhabit Florida, but they are such that those who dwell in the same latitude further west are of a colder temperament. The northerners, in turn, are those who inhabit the land from the fiftieth parallel to the sixtieth. They are, however, more temperate than their neighbors who have their homes near the seventieth. In the former tract are Britain, Ireland, Denmark, part of Gothland, Lower Germany from the Main and the Bug River even to farthest Scythia and Tartary, which cover a good part of Europe and Greater Asia.

[...]

The chief discussion is about the peoples who dwell from the thirtieth parallel to the sixtieth, because we know their history, about which we must form an opinion. We have almost no material for other peoples, but by this illustration we shall learn what must be believed about all. The Mediterranean peoples, then, as far as concerns the form of the body, are cold, dry, hard, bald, weak, swarthy, small in body, crisp of hair, black-eyed, and clear-voiced. The Baltic peoples, on the other hand, are warm, wet, hairy, robust, white, large-bodied, soft-fleshed, with scanty beards, bluish grey eyes, and deep voices. Those who live between the two show moderation in all respects. But this one thing is open to question: that the southerners, weak by the consent of all, are yet hard; the northerners, indeed, are robust, but soft. In opposition to this, Hippocrates and almost all the other writers said that Scythians and mountaineers who resemble the type of the Scythians were hard, wild, and born to endure labor. Among these conflicting opinions of historians and philosophers, however, we shall judge correctly about history, as well as reconcile with Hippocrates and Alexander, Livy, Tacitus, Polybius,

Plutarch, and Caesar, who reported that the French and the Germans were impatient of work, if we grant that the northerners in a cold region patiently bear labor, but in a warm region dissolve in sweat and languish. With this the account of Agathias about the Germans and of Krantz about the Scandinavians agree – that they wage war willingly in the winter, but rarely in the summer.

In contrast, the southerners easily endure heat suited to their nature, although they become more energetic in a cold region, languid in a warm one. And so, as I hear, in their language the Spanish women usually call the Germans "soft fish." But the Celts and the Belgae, when they come into Italy or Provence, are tortured by the mosquitoes and vermin to an unusual extent because of the softness of their skin. The natives, due to their toughness, are not annoyed so much.

We have given enough about the form of body from which the habits of mind are inferred and a correct judgment of history is developed. Since the body and the mind are swayed in opposite directions, the more strength the latter has, the less has the former; and the more effective a man is intellectually, the less strength of body he has, provided the senses are functioning. It is plain, therefore, that the southerners excel in intellect, the Scythians in body. Aristotle intimates this in Book VII of the *Politics;* robust and spirited men have less talent, and their public affairs are not properly directed. Africans, however, have more than enough wisdom, but not enough strength. Yet this is necessary, both for repelling enemies and also for protecting the citizens.

The third class is composed of men who possess the fine arts of obeying and commanding, who can blunt the cunning of the southerners with their strength and withstand the attack of the Scythians through their wisdom. From this type Vitruvius thought that soldiers should be selected, since they excel no less in sagacity than in strength. How rightly, I leave to the opinion of others. The historical problem is left for solution – why Goths, Huns, Heruli, and Vandals invaded Europe, Asia, and Africa, but, lacking wisdom, could not hold it. Those who adopted

the plans of wise men have founded nations suited to civil society and have held flourishing empires for a long time; the poets do not inappropriately depict Pallas armed or Achilles protected by her. Since Scythians almost always dislike letters, and southerners arms, they could not found a great empire. In both respects the Romans achieved success with the greatest felicity and sagely combined gymnastics with music, as Plato wished. It is true that they received laws and letters, that is, civil discipline, from the Greeks, just as they received the Palladium; they acquired naval science from the Phoenicians and Sicilians. On the other hand, they obtained military experience through constant warfare: whereas formerly they learned from the custom of the Scythians to strike only with the edge of the sword, afterwards they learned from the Spanish to pierce with the point as well, as is stated in Polybius. So it ought not to seem remarkable that they excelled all peoples in the fame of their deeds, when they joined to discipline the highest gifts of nature. But it came about by a certain divine goodness – or shall I say wisdom? – that the Africans have more wit and the Scythians a more powerful physique, lest, if He had given a foxlike cunning to men wild as bulls or great strength and endurance to Carthaginians keen as foxes, they might use His gifts for destruction. Nothing is more cruel, said Aristotle, than armed injustice. Moreover, he believed that those to whom He allotted moderate strength excelled the remainder in humanity and justice, a trait which in *Questions* he attributed to a temperate climate. "Why," said he, "are people who suffer from too great cold or heat uncivilized?" Is it because the best climate makes the best customs? In that case why do all historians praise so highly the innocence and the justice of the Scythians and execrate the customs of the southerners?

Here I seek a decision in history, in order that we may not have disagreement between philosophers and historians. The matter is not without complexity, for fat men are not at all evil, as Caesar decided rightly about Antony and Dolabella, but Brutus and Cassius, lean men, must be feared. The northerners, however, are heavy, the southerners lean. What Tacitus said of the Germans is therefore true: "The race is not astute or cunning; for the freedom of revelry opens the secrets of the heart, and the frank opinion of all is reconsidered the next day. Due weight is given to both periods." Moreover, this is one reason why kings and tyrants formerly sought for their bodyguard, and in these days also always seek, Thracians, Scythians, Germans, Circassians, and Helvetians at large salaries; not that they distrust the strength of their own men, as many stupidly think, but that they understand that in the vast bodies of the Thracians there lies concealed the minimum of cunning and malice and that they are more pleased with the office of soldier than with that of ruler. In what respect, then, are they called cruel and uncivilized? The reason is obvious, for the farther one is from human culture, that is, from the nature of men, the nearer he approaches to the likeness of beasts, which, since they are lacking in reason, are unable to restrain their wrath and appetites. So it happens that the northerners are carried by impulse into acts of cruelty. Hence Thucydides called the Thracians, when they feared nothing, "The most ruthless race." Tacitus also said about the Germans, "They are accustomed to kill without strict discipline, but on a wrathful impulse, like an enemy." In this way the Hungarians, when they had killed Gritti, dyed their military cloaks and spears in his blood, according to national custom. The Britons, in a civil war, killed twelve out of forty kings, as well as innumerable princes, indeed a hundred in thirty years, after they had a little respite from external wars. If the chronicles of the Poles and Jovius are true, the Transylvanians drove their soldiers into a frenzy of cruelty by a three-day fast. This was done so that the men might use great severity in their treatment of George, the leader of the rioters (he had transfixed on stakes some Hungarian magnates). As a result the soldiers tore apart with their teeth the limbs of the still-breathing leader and swallowed them; then, cutting the disemboweled man into bits, they served them cooked on spits to the captives. I pass over the savagery of Dracula, the prince of Transylvania, universally conceded to be excessive. I omit also the formerly unheard-of cruelties of the Goths and the Huns,

practiced not only against men but also against animals, towns, fortresses, gravestones, and sepulchers of the Romans, which they overturned from their foundations. They could not restrain their wrath any more than their other appetites. Tacitus said about the Germans: "When sober they play dice in the midst of serious things; so great is their recklessness of gain or of loss that when all else fails, they will stake personal liberty on the last throw." Hence comes that lust of possession among the Germans and the French, reproached by Procopius, which is so great that they abandon life for gold and war for money.

The southerners are not so avaricious as they are parsimonious and stingy; the Scythians, on the other hand, are extravagant and rapacious. Since they know that they are at a disadvantage, they are unusually suspicious. This trait our men formerly knew well enough. Holster related to me the additional fact that spies and listeners in Gothland hide in public inns, for suspicion arises from want of knowledge. They do not have intercourse with southerners unless they are sober, and when they feel themselves deceived, they draw back, or often anticipate by deceiving the strangers, or as a last resort use force. Whereby it happens that by universal consent they are supposed to be as perfidious as the southerners. (Of this fact the old historians were entirely ignorant, because they had no intercourse with the Scythians.) Later, when they left their homes, they revealed their character. Since the Franks came from Germany into France (for the Germans boast that the French are of Teutonic origin), it is in keeping that Procopius, in speaking of the Franks, commented: "This race is the most likely of all to betray their faith." And Vopiscus said: "It is customary for the Franks to break their faith laughingly." Hence, Alciati wrote that a scorpion's tail was tossed at the Germans. This proverb we retain in France in the vulgar tongue – with due apologies, may it be said, lest our discourse should seem to harm the name of any race. I am not discussing this particular characteristic, but the inborn nature of each race. In this trait, however, the Germans are exceeded to a considerable degree by the Danes and the Norwegians, from whom they differ widely. Certainly greater perfidy or cruelty of people toward princes or of princes among themselves was never engendered than between Christian and Gustavus, between Danes and Swedes. From these races originate also the Normans, who, the common people believe, are unreliable.

But if from want of reasoning and wisdom the northerners cannot control their appetites and furthermore are regarded as intemperate, suspicious, perfidious, and cruel why are the southerners much more cruel and perfidious even than these? Here again I seek the decision in history. It is evident that by nature the southerners have the greatest gifts of ability; thus Columella, in Book i, chapter iii, declared: "It is well known that the Carthaginians, a very acute race, said 'the field must be weaker than the plowman.'" Concerning the Egyptians who fought against Caesar, Hirtius said: "These very clever men shrewdly constructed the things they saw made by us, so that our men seemed to imitate their work." A little later the same author added, "The race of Egyptians is much given to treachery." Moreover, who does not know how artfully and how long the Carthaginians eluded the power of the Romans? Nevertheless, they always practiced incredible cruelty against the enemy, as may be seen in the Punic War and also in that combat which the Spendii and the Carthaginians, both Phoenicians, waged against each other. As Polybius said, "It far exceeded all wars of which we have heard in cruelty and all kinds of crimes." Yet the things related by Polybius about the cruelty of the Carthaginians would seem ludicrous if anyone compared them with the history of Leo the African, or even with the unheard-of cruelty of Muley-Hasan and his sons, which not so long ago they practiced against the citizens and then against each other. For Muley-Hasan, driven from the kingdom whence he had driven his father, came as a suppliant to Emperor Charles, suffering from the loss of his eyes, which had been burnt out through the brutal violence of his brother.

Thus from the Carthaginians, we can trace the gouging of eyes, tearing of limbs, skinning, cutting, slow burning, and impaling. But the breaking of the whole body on a wheel originated with the Germans, as may be seen in Munster's description of Cologne. From these punishments Italians, French, Spanish, Greeks, and Asiatics have always turned in horror or unwillingly have learned them from others. Before the Portian Law (which even then forbade rods on the body of citizens) for capital punishment the Romans executed criminals with an axe or by breaking their necks; later the method was starvation; at length exile was permitted. Among the Greeks the use of hemlock was customary. This the Chiians even tempered with water, as Theophrastus said, so that they might invite death without distress. They judged that in death itself more than enough bitterness lay, unless, indeed, a man were guilty of some new and horrible crime. Lest anyone should believe that such cruelty spreads from vicious training, as Polybius maintains, let him consider the nature of the South Americans, who plunge boys into the blood of slain enemies, then suck the blood, and feast on the broken limbs.

The cruelty of the southerners and of the Scythians is therefore very different, because the latter are driven to wrath by impulse alone and to revenge by a certain magnanimous valor of the soul; after they have been irritated, they can easily be mollified. The southerners are not easily angered, but when once angry they can with difficulty be softened: they attack the enemy with a foxlike cunning, not with open violence, and they inflict horribly painful torture upon the conquered. This savagery comes partly from that despotism which a vicious system of training and undisciplined appetites have created in a man, but much more from a lack of proportion in the mixing of humors. This, in its turn, comes from elements affected unequally by external forces. The elements are disturbed by the power of the celestial bodies, while the human body is encompassed in the elements, the blood in the body, the spirit in the blood, the soul in the spirit, the mind in the soul. Although this last is free from all materiality, yet it is very much influenced by the closeness of the association. So it happens that those who are in the furthest regions are more inclined to vices. As black bile is removed from the blood [with difficulty], in the same way as dregs from wine, so disturbances of the intellect which proceed from black bile are difficult to eradicate.

[...]

Now, since the mind does excel the body and greater force of genius exists in the south than in the north, there is no doubt that the more able part of the world extends to the south and that greater virtues are in the southerners than among the Scythians. The greater vices likewise are found wherever the former migrate. Hence we shall easily understand a judgment from the history of Livy. After he had commemorated the virtues of Hannibal, he said, "The many great virtues of the man were equaled by monstrous vices: inhuman cruelty, perfidy more than Punic, no truthfulness, no respect for holiness, no fear of the gods, no regard for oaths, no reverence." What Machiavelli wrote is false – that men at the last cannot be extremely wicked, quoting the example of Paul Baglioni, the tyrant of Perugia, who although he could easily have killed Pope Julius along with his escort, preferred to lose control rather than perpetrate such a crime. Hannibal would not have acted in this way. The same Machiavelli called the Italians, the Spanish, and the French the wickedest of all races. In one passage he extolled the justice and sagacity of the Germans in a most remarkable way. Elsewhere he attacked their perfidy, avarice, and haughtiness. These contradictions have developed from ignorance of the customs and nature of each people. Stupid and uncouth men cannot be really infamous, but, as Plato said, in great talents great virtues or vices are usually present; as the fecund earth produces a large supply of noxious weeds unless it is cultivated and when worked in a proper manner becomes really fruitful. But sterile earth, on the other hand, produces neither healthful nor noxious weeds, nor anything at all except with the greatest effort. So also I judge to be the case with the talents of the southerners and of the Scythians. For this reason it is not remarkable that almost all historians and poets – from Aeschylus to the present – praise the great integrity of the Scythians and attack the cunning of the southerners. "The good customs among the Germans," said Tacitus, "have more force than good laws elsewhere." In those days, however, the Germans lacked any kind of training, so they did not differ much from beasts, as they themselves confess. Since

they lived in the utmost ignorance, I do not see why their integrity is worthy of so much encomium, for they could not really be either very good or very evil. On the other hand, the man who when he has the chance to be unjust advisedly cultivates virtues whose value he has appreciated is worthy of the highest praise, either because there is only one approach to virtue, like a straight line, around which, here and there, are many oblique lines, or because men, even if they have been shown the extremes of good and of evil, are inclined more to wickedness, from which they cannot be deterred by cruel punishments alone or by the threat of eternal death. Not even the reward of immortality impels them to justice, so that many think that men would live in the highest integrity and be much happier if they had never tasted the fruits of evil (without which, however, the nature of good cannot be understood), but, like other animate beings, had lived in accordance with their own nature. We have seen, indeed, that the Scythians and the mountaineers, trained by no discipline, approach more nearly to this type.

Out of this difficulty remains the question, what judgment must be formed of the historians who attack the superstition, impiety, magic, infamous lusts, and cruelties of the Greeks, Egyptians, Arabs, and Chaldeans, yet omit the qualities which are praiseworthy? From these people letters, useful arts, virtues, training, philosophy, religion, and lastly *humanitas* itself flowed upon earth as from a fountain. The Scythians, however, do not lack industry, nor do those who hold the middle region, but the southerners attained the most outstanding gifts from immortal God, which cannot be understood better or be judged more certainly for historical purposes than if we use the analogy of the human body, or the well-constituted state, or the world and the celestial constellations.

For the sake of theory let us imagine, therefore, that certain planets preside over these three peoples set up in that order in which we have given them; let us attribute Saturn to the southerners, Jupiter to the next group, and Mars to the northerners. Returning the round again, Venus to the southerners (the sun like a fountain of light, will be common to all), Mercury to the next, and the moon to the northerners. From this distribution, as it were, of three peoples, we shall understand more plainly the precise power of all nature. For the Chaldeans say that the power of Saturn controls the understanding, that of Jupiter guides action, that of Mars directs production. This, moreover, is understood by the best Hebrew expounders of nature. They called Saturn quiet, than which nothing can be of greater importance for contemplation. Jupiter they called just. The Greeks took this idea, as they did all good things, from the Hebrews. They imagined that justice was sitting on the side of Jupiter. But Mars they called strong and brave. On this account the Chaldeans and the Greeks thought he ruled over war. Saturn, of course, is said to be cold, Mars warm, Jupiter more moderate than either. The first presides over knowledge and those things which find their realization in solitary contemplation of the truth; the second wisdom, which is embodied in action, embracing all virtues; the third, arts and fabrication, which depend upon skill and strength. The first pertains to the mind, the second to reason, the last to imagination. For the southern people, through continued zeal for contemplation, befitting black bile, have been promoters and leaders of the highest learning. They have revealed the secrets of nature; they have discovered the mathematical disciplines; finally, they first observed the nature and the power of religion and the celestial bodies. Because the Scythians are less suited to contemplation, on account of the supply of blood and humor (by which the mind is so weighed down that it hardly ever emerges), they voluntarily began to take an interest in those things which fall under the senses, that is, in the exercise of the arts and fabrication. Hence from the northerners come those objects called "mechanical" – engines of war, the art of founding, printing, and whatever belongs to the working of metals, which George Agricola, a German, has discussed so exhaustively that Aristotle and Pliny in this respect appear to have understood nothing. It should not seem remarkable that Italians and Spanish are accustomed to seek aid from Germans and Britons because by some celestial gift they know how to find the hidden veins of earth, and, when found, to open them.

Likewise the same sons of Mars in former times always cultivated military discipline, and still do with incredible enthusiasm. They practice arms, level mountains, draw off waters, and usually devote themselves to hunting, farming, cattle raising, or to the arts of construction, so that their talent seems to be placed in their hands. This fact is made clear enough by every kind of household utensil and implement, which is made so skillfully and ingeniously by these men that other peoples marvel at the products, but cannot reproduce them. This is, perhaps, what Plato meant when he said that Mars and Vulcan had discovered the arts. If, then, we are to have faith in the astrologers, those who have Mars in the ascendant at their birth will be either soldiers or skilled workers.

On the other hand, men of the middle region are not designed for the secret sciences as are the southerners or dedicated to manual crafts like the northerners, but are the best fitted for managing affairs. If anyone reads all the writings of the historians he will judge that from men of this type institutions, laws, and customs first came, and the best method of directing the state; then, also, commerce, government, rhetoric, dialectic, and finally the training of a general. Moreover, the masters of these disciplines are said to be Jupiter and Mercury; whoever has Jupiter or Mercury or both in the ascendant at his inception is said to be suited by his very nature to such pursuits. Indeed, it is evident from the reading of histories that great empires have always flourished in Asia, Greece, Assyria, Italy, Gaul, and Upper Germany, which lie between the pole and the equator from the fortieth to the fiftieth degree; and from those regions the greatest rulers, the best legislators, the most equitable judges, the sagest jurisconsults, the most versatile orators, the cleverest merchants, finally, the most famous players and dramatic actors have had their origin. No jurisconsults come from Africa, much less from Scythia; no orators, few poets, fewer historians, very few who ply an abundant and profitable commerce, such as Italians, Greeks, Spanish, and Asiatics. Let us then compare these facts with history, that we may judge more correctly concerning the entire matter.

Galen complained that no philosopher ever came from Scythia except Anacharsis, although many were from Greece. Where he discussed the Gauls, whose nature he had, of course, discovered and known through continued contacts, the Emperor Julian wrote, "The Celts bestowed no pains on philosophy or on mathematical discipline; but they are interested in dialectics and rhetoric." Hence Juvenal's "Eloquent France taught the British lawyers." Indeed, the very religion which they used makes this plain. "The Gauls worship especially the god Mercury," said Caesar. "There are many images of him; they consider him inventor of the arts; they think that he has great power in seeking riches and pursuing trade." A lasting experience has approved these historical passages. For nowhere in the world are there more advocates, nowhere is civil law cultivated with greater zeal. Occult knowledge and mathematical discipline are, however, really neglected.

On the contrary, the southerners, since the innate humor of black bile causes prolonged meditation, betake themselves voluntarily from the conduct of affairs and seek the desert solitudes. The power of contemplation and meditation (which is called by the Hebrews and Academicians a precious death) consists, in fact, in this: it sharpens the wits and divides man from man. When he has attained this, he not only sees the secrets of natural things but also, with a purified mind, is borne to the heavens on swift pinions, and is filled with the knowledge of things divine. Afterwards, through the assistance of immortal God, he reveals difficult and wonderful matters to unlearned men. For this reason it should not seem strange to those who have read history that the ablest philosophers, mathematicians, prophets, and finally all religions in the world have poured forth from those regions as from the most plenteous spring. Not that the divine mind is unwilling to breathe upon man elsewhere its heavenly spirit. That would be wicked to say, since God flourishes everywhere, like the splendor of the sun. Yet as that same splendor shows itself more in very limpid water than in turbid, so also the divinity shines more clearly in a purified mind than in one looking downward, influenced by contact with the

body and disturbed by warring perturbations within itself. Those who have a greater abundance of blood and humor with more difficulty separate themselves from these earthly dregs, so that not without justice did Heraclitus call wise men "dry souls." What Jerome Cardan said is absurd and not at all worthy of a philosopher – that a man is very wise because he is very wet and warm, for we see that those beasts which are the colder are the more sagacious, as Aristotle wrote in Book II *De partibus animalium*. Let us take as illustration the very wise elephant, whose blood, Pliny recounted, was the coldest of all.

Since these things are so, it is easy to judge the truth of what the historians report about the religion of the southerners. In particular, Leo the African said with reference to the foundations of the temples, "There are in the city of Fez seven hundred temples. The greatest has a circuit of one thousand paces and thirty-one doors; nine hundred torches are burning day and night." We may also believe what Alvarez reported in the history of the Abyssinians about the unheard-of size of the temples, about the infinite number of monks, who walk around, not only in isolated areas but also in the countryside, in crowds, in the market place, and in the camps; from them even the armies are conscripted, since the princes themselves follow this way of life. Moreover, the king, who is called Negus and Jochan Belul, that is, very precious jewel, acts like a priest, proceeds like a priest in vestment and ornament, with priests leading and bearing religious symbols before him. In addition, he told of fasts of the whole people that are plainly incredible if anyone compares them with ours. If, however, you should exercise historical judgment, you will pronounce them really credible. Many sustain life without bread on raw lentils or vegetables cooked in plain water and, of course, tasteless. Others wear an iron band like a belt on their bare flesh. In the time of fasts, that is, a third of the year, many pass the nights without rest. Some of them sleep in water up to the neck. There are some who stand for twenty-four hours and gaze into the heavens. On stated days all flagellate themselves repeatedly with rods and whips. Those who sin against the faith only a little or refuse to kiss a wooden cross (as some do) are burned in avenging flames. They think that fortunate as well as unfortunate experiences flow equally from the will of one all-powerful God, a belief very useful for the protection of the state and for a happy life. Yet how stupid they are in managing affairs and governing the country is made plain by the fact that they do not cease lashing a man who has committed a fault before the victim has paid the fine stipulated by the person who is beating. Moreover, a chief justice, who like the chancellor directs the most important affairs, often is flogged to death by order of the king. A murderer is delivered for crucifixion to the relatives of the dead. All judgments, however, are handed down without any documents or writing. Debtors, unless they can make payment, are given into servitude to their creditors. No wages are paid to the soldier, no leaves given, but each one is required to carry barley or some similar thing. There are no towns, no camps, no fortresses. The people roam about the country hither and thither, the leader lives in tents, although he has valuable household goods and considerable wealth. They do not use paper, but entrust the public accounts to vellum. Such proceedings prove that men of this type are little suited to manage affairs.

Even less adapted are the Scythians, who accomplish everything by force of arms like slaves and in the way of wild beasts. As Tacitus wrote about the ancient Germans, "The official does nothing either public or private without arms." To this Boemus, a German, and Munster also agree today in these words: "Injuries suffered they rarely avenge by law, but by sword and pillage; nor are they ashamed to plunder." Moreover, what is more iniquitous or more barbarous than what customarily happens at Clagenfurt? If anyone is suspected of theft, he is killed. Then they hold a trial. This custom, they say, is taken from the Huns and the Goths. From them also the laws of dueling are taken. Of all kinds of injustice, none can be greater or more base than that a weak and helpless man, when he has been insulted, should be scornfully treated unless he tries the issue at arms and exposes his life to perils, no matter how strong the adversary may be. By this system even the Scythians

would be justly scorned if they were matched with beasts which outdo them in strength. In general it has been so arranged by nature that Scythians, who have less reason, but more strength, should place the height of all virtues in military glory; southerners in piety and reverence; but those of the middle region in wisdom. Although all defend the state by every means, nevertheless some habitually use force, some awe of the divine; the rest more often rely upon law and legal decisions.

So it should not seem strange that the majesty of the caliphs, or priests of the Ismaelite faith, was so great that they had ultimate control not only of laws and of religions but also of empire and arms and all possessions, then of liberty and servitude, finally the right of life and death over everyone. But the Turks, the progeny of the Scythians, and the Mamelukes, by race Circassians, first broke away from their domination and drove them out from their ancient holdings.

Perhaps this is why we are told by the poets that Saturn was driven from power by Jupiter, which means that in early times wise and pious men were created kings for the sake of dispensing justice. Although men thought that through the performance of duty alone they could continue in office, nevertheless they could not succeed in this way, since of course very many were influenced neither by awe of the divine nor by any other scruple. So the more sagacious, taking over power, began to rule the state, while the religious and philosophic gave attention to sacrifices and contemplation, and the plebs took up military training, farming, and manual arts. From this it happens that wise men maintain the state with prayers and warnings; the prudent by rule and command; the strong by power and activity. By these three divisions – principles, ordinances, and actions – I say, the state is supported.

Priests and wise men give warning; officials issue orders; agents carry them out. Thus Anaxagoras influenced Pericles; Plato, Dion; Isocrates, Nicocles; Plutarch, Trajan; Polybius, Scipio. And constantly, with sensible precepts of wisdom or some religious teaching, the Magi advised the Persians; the Brahmins, the Indians; the seers, the Greeks; and the pontiffs, the Romans. Yet they were incapable of managing affairs, a fact which Plato, although a very wise man, exemplified when he took over the state committed to his care. In the same way Aristotle wrote that Anaxagoras, a very learned man, lacked prudence because he suffered himself to die of hunger and want through neglecting his finances, a thing which happened also to Theodore Gaza in extreme old age. So Philo commended Moses with high praise, because alone among all mortals he was at the same time a very brave general, a prudent legislator, and a most holy prophet.

It remains, then, to apply to the republic of the world the same analysis that has been made about one state, so that when the functions of the various peoples have been meted out wisdom may in a way belong to the southerners, strength to the Scythians, and prudence to the intervening races. This idea may be seen even in the parts of the soul. For the mind itself warns, reason commands, and then the senses, like agents, are employed for carrying out orders, and in the threefold power of the soul – animal, vital, and natural – the first, of course, brings motion and sensation from the brain, the second the vital spirit from the heart, the third quickening power from the liver. I think that there is no better way of understanding the inborn nature of each people or of obtaining a truer and more definite opinion about the history of each than if this microcosm be compared with the great man, that is, with the world. Therefore, what Plato did in his *Republic* we shall do for the republic of the world, but a trifle differently. He wished control to be in the possession of guardians, whom he placed in the mind, like Pallas in the citadel. In this he seemed to wish to restore the reign of Saturn; hence that sentence of his praised by all – yet understood by few – "Either kings should be philosophers, or philosophers should reign." Philosophy, however, the perpetual contemplation of the most beautiful things, as all Academicians would have it, has nothing in common with military or civil affairs. Furthermore, he armed soldiers and stationed them in the heart, because there is placed the seat of anger. Finally he assigned farmers and manual workers to the liver, so that they might supply food and necessaries

for the state. Nevertheless, these arrangements could not be carried through without great disturbance.

[...]

In the first place, Philip Melanchthon says that a monarchy seems to him that sovereign power of a state which can subjugate the riches and resources of others. In that case we should use the word "empire," since "monarchy" cannot be applied to the popular form of government of the Romans. Yet if we should weigh the matter without considering the technicalities of terms, surely the Germans do not relevantly claim the monarchy of the Romans, since they hold beneath their sway hardly the hundredth part of the world, and the king of Spain has an empire greater than that of the Germans, in both number of people and extent of domain – omitting the American regions (over which in great part he rules), three times greater than Europe. But the Germans are not even equal to the king of Portugal, if we define empire by the magnitude of the area. He seized almost the entire shore of Africa by force, and by means of the strongest defense works frequently he has driven off the attacks of barbarians. At this point someone will say, we must take into consideration, not the number of men or the extent of territory, but power and endurance, and of course I agree with them in this. Yet I do not see in what way Germany could have resisted the legions of Spain and Italy under the leadership of Charles V, who, if he had not been restrained by the valor of the French, would have reduced that empire to the form of a province, as the Germans in famous and still extant documents have testified. They render equal thanks to us.

... what has Germany to oppose to the sultan of the Turks? Or which state can more aptly be called a monarchy? This fact is obvious to everyone – if there is anywhere in the world any majesty of empire and of true monarchy, it must radiate from the sultan. He owns the richest parts of Asia, Africa, and Europe, and he rules far and wide over the entire Mediterranean and all but a few of its islands. Moreover, in armed forces and strength he is such that he alone is the equal of almost all the princes, since he drove the armies of the Persians and the Muscovites far beyond the boundaries of the empire. But he seized provinces of the Christians and the empire of the Greeks by force of arms, and even devastated the lands of the Germans. I shall not discuss the prince of Ethiopia, called by his people Jochan Bellul, that is, precious gem, whose empire is little less than all Europe. What of the emperor of the Tartars, who rules tribes barbarous in their savagery, countless in number, unconquered in strength? If you compare Germany with these, you compare a fly to an elephant.

10

Letter to Joseph Scaliger

Henri Lancelot Voisin de la Popelinière

Sir,

In your last letters, where you supported my critique of the Sybils, you advised me to draw general conclusions from particular history, especially for the most noteworthy phenomena, whether natural or human. If the capacity for judgment is the most noble and necessary quality of mankind, nothing can make it more solid in my opinion than travel and the careful observation of foreign lands, in order to perfect the study of history. So far, the deeds of the peoples of the islands and coasts of Africa and America have hardly aided me in my researches to better know and judge the source, form, nourishment, progress, and variable effects of all the good and bad inclinations of men. This is what the Greek and Roman philosophers, historians, and jurists have written, but only in general terms, concerning natural law, the law of persons, or the civil laws of each nation. The most remarkable actions of all men are drawn from these three sets of customs or institutions, but it seems to me that we have only noticed those of civilized peoples or those whom we quite incorrectly call savages. We have little knowledge of those who are really savage. From what I can gather, based on our discoveries and on authors who have left us some accounts, we can judge the difference between savages and civilized nations. It still remains for us to take into account the various deeds of

the oldest and most notable among civilized peoples, the Asians, especially the Orientals. These, some have suggested, were the first civilized nations; at least, given that they are the first to be heated by the rays of that great torch [the sun, which rises in the east], they have received, if not the first, at least the liveliest, clearest and most continuous effects of those celestial bodies, making them fittest to create so many beautiful human institutions. It is astonishing that for so many centuries until now people have lacked the desire or the courage, the means or the good fortune to travel to see them. For the past hundred years, now that routes by land and by sea have been discovered, it would seem that the dangers have discouraged travelers, with the exception of Paul the Venetian [Marco Polo], Ludovico di Varthema,[1] Amerigo Vespucci, and Columbus of Genoa and a few others who hoisted the flag to show the way. But not a single one of them managed his journey in a way that could live up to such a praiseworthy project, in order to discover principles which benefit all mankind, showing how savages and (as some have claimed) isolated peoples have been little by little socialized and united by various human institutions. The simple curiosity to witness strange things seems to have motivated the first two [travelers], just as profit and honor motivated the others. Thus, in their accounts, they

Henri Lancelot Voisin de la Popelinière, "Letter to Joseph Scaliger," French text reprinted in George Huppert, *The Idea of Perfect History*, trans. Robert Launay, Urbana, IL: University of Illinois Press, 1970.

have only left us unsubstantial things with little relation to our particular situation, not a single trait worthy of being cited as an example for any of our [European] states.

We should thus aim for the complete and accurate knowledge of men, either here or abroad: of every state and form of government, as determined by the land which nourishes them; the sea by which commodities (but also threats) arrive; and even the air and the sky which, aside from the influences touted by astrologers, provide occasion and advantages for their voyages and other projects which they formulate.

You know only too well that the most famous of the Greeks, Solon, Democritus, Empedocles, Pythagoras (if he was indeed Greek), Lycurgus, Plato and others hardly traveled further than Babylon, the Euphrates, or Egypt, from which they nonetheless brought home the majority of what they recorded in their writings, either because the Orient was not open to Greeks before Alexander's conquests, or that they lacked the courage or the means – unless it is we who have lost these records of antiquity. I am persuaded that a judicious man could record noteworthy and beautiful things if he had the means to provide for the journey, to make purchases, to write, to paint and to engrave a record of it and to prepare for his return. Democritus, rich as he was at first, spent all his wealth in this way, and was mocked for it on his return by his neighbors and kinsmen; Aristotle claims all the seven sages were similarly mocked. Solon did better, bringing with him fruits and merchandise from his own land which he sold and bartered to defray the expenses of his trip and his return to Greece. This Greek prince needs to be imitated. This is why, disturbed that no one in our own time has undertaken such an important project, I am proposing to you to that I go and undertake it, in any way you see fit. That is to say, provided there is some way that I accommodate myself to your fellow Dutchmen, who they say travel there from year to year. Aside from the fact that I cannot believe that you don't have a firm acquaintance with them, and less still that you wouldn't write letters to your

friends on my behalf and moreover that the gentlemen of Leyden would not do as you wish, petitioning the Estates General to accept a man of honor who could render them good service if only they would employ him. My aim is certainly not to impede their trade or even to share in their profits, but just to satisfy my mind. Moreover, they seem to me so wedded to their profits, so loaded with mad ambitions and lost in vain youthful curiosity, that it seems high time that by now they would not be so ill disposed to recognize true worth and honor.

You will tell me that one must be satisfied with one's lot, to tailor one's ambitions to one's own size and not attempt to undertake something too grand. I admit it and have done so for more than forty years, but my project does not seem too ambitious for a gentleman, given that it is easy, profitable, and sufficient for a simple merchant. If I accomplish it, I will be the first to trumpet the glory of those who assisted me. If not, I will console myself with entertaining such a noble desire and a praiseworthy attempt to do what no one else has undertaken. I would be content to serve as a witness to posterity that this century, however ignoble, is not as void of men of honor and courage as some foreigners (and even our own nephews) might imagine. At least one would see it better furnished with tools and instruments to make beautiful things than with artisans worth of conceiving them and taking them to perfection.

I nevertheless await your opinion beforehand, which will determine my resolution. In expectation of this, Sir, I pray that God maintain you in his good graces and me in yours, as enthusiastically as I wish to remain forever your very humble and loving servant.

POPELINIERE
From Paris, this 4th of January 1604

NOTE

1   An early sixteenth-century Italian traveler to Arabia, India, and Indonesia.

Part IV

The Seventeenth Century

Section IV

(a) Jesuits and the Comparative Perspective

11

Natural and Moral History of the Indies

José de Acosta

How There is Some Knowledge of God Among the Indians

First, although the gross darkness of unbelief has obscured the minds of those nations, in many ways the light of truth and reason works in them to some small degree; and so most of them acknowledge and confess a supreme Lord and Maker of all, whom the Peruvians called Viracocha, adding a very excellent name such as Pachacamac or Pachayachachic, which means the creator of heaven and earth, and Usapu, which means admirable, and other similar names. They worshiped him, and he was the chief god that they venerated, gazing heavenward. And the same belief exists, after their fashion, in the Mexicans and the Chinese today and in other heathen peoples. This is very similar to what is told in the Book of Acts of the Apostles, when Saint Paul was in Athens and saw an altar with the inscription "Ignoto Deo," to the unknown God, from which the Apostle took the subject of his preaching, telling them, "What therefore you worship without knowing it, that I preach to you." And so, similarly, all those who preach the Gospel to the Indians today have little difficulty in persuading them that there is a supreme God and

Lord of all, and that he is the God of the Christians and the true God. Yet it has greatly astonished me that even though they do have the knowledge that I mention, they have no word of their own with which to name God. For, if we try to find in the Indian languages any word corresponding to this one, *God*, as it is *Deus* in Latin and *Theos* in Greek, and *El* in Hebrew and in Arabic *Allah*, it cannot be found in the language of Cuzco, nor in the Mexican tongue. And so those who preach or write for the Indians use our Spanish word *Dios*, adjusting its pronunciation and accent to the properties of the Indian languages, which are very diverse. This shows what a weak and incomplete knowledge they have of God, for they do not even know how to name him except by using our word. But indeed they did have a sort of knowledge, and so they built a very splendid temple for him in Peru, calling it Pachacamac, which was the chief sanctuary of that realm. And as I have said, *Pachacamac* means the same as *Creator*, although they also performed their idolatries in this temple, worshiping the devil and representations of him; and they also made sacrifices and offerings to Viracocha, and that temple held supreme place among the temples that the Inca kings possessed...

José de Acosta, *Natural and Moral History of the Indies*, ed. Jane E. Mangan, trans. Frances M. López-Morillas, Durham, NC: Duke University Press, 2002, pp. 256–61, 264–9, 276–82, 329–33, 339–47.

Of the First Sort of Idolatry, that of Natural and Universal Things

After the Viracocha, or supreme god, the sun was and is the entity that the heathen chiefly venerate and worship, and after the sun those other things prominent in celestial or elemental nature, such as moon, morning star, sea, and earth. After Viracocha and the sun, the Inca lords of Peru placed thunder in the third *huaca*, or temple, and gave it three names: Chuquiilla, Catuilla, and Intiillapa. They imagine that it is a man in the sky with a sling and a club and that he has power over rain and sleet and thunder and everything else pertaining to the region of the air, where clouds are formed. This *huaca* (for that is what they call their temples), was common to all the Indians of Peru, and they offered different sacrifices to this god. And in Cuzco, which was the court and capital, children were also sacrificed to him, just as they were to the sun. They adored these three that I have named, Viracocha, Sun, and Thunder, in a different way from all the other gods, as Polo writes that he has ascertained, placing a gauntlet or glove on their hands when they raised them to worship these gods. They also worshiped Earth, which they called Pachamama, just as the ancients celebrated the goddess Tellus, and the sea, which they called Mamacocha, just as the ancients called it Thetis or Neptune. They also worshiped the rainbow, and it was the arms or insignia of the Inca, with two serpents stretched along its sides. Among the stars that all of them commonly worshiped was the group they called Collca, which we call the Pleiades. They attributed different functions to different stars, and worshiped those whose favor they needed, just as the shepherds adored and sacrificed to a star that they called Urcuchillay, which they say is a sheep of many colors that is skilled in the preservation of their flocks and is apparently the one the astronomers call Lyra. And the same Indians adore two other stars near it, which they call Catuchillay and Urcuchillay, which they fancy to be a ewe with a lamb. Others worshiped a star that they call Machacuay, which has

charge of serpents and snakes, to prevent their harming them, just as another star called Chuquichinchay, which means tiger, is responsible for tigers, bears, and lions. And generally speaking they believed that for each of the animals and birds on earth there was a similar one in the heavens, responsible for that animal's procreation and increase; and so they assigned meanings to certain stars, like the one they call Chacana, and Topatorca and Mamana, and Mirco and Miquiquiray, and others, to the point that in some sense they approached the tenets of Plato's ideas.

In almost the same way, after the supreme god the Mexicans worshiped the sun, and so they called Hernán Cortés (as he states in a letter to the Emperor Charles V) son of the sun because of the speed and energy with which he encompassed the land. But they offered their greatest worship to the idol called Huitzilopochtli, whom that whole nation called the Almighty and lord of creation; and as such the Mexicans built him the largest and loftiest temple, and the most beautiful and sumptuous building, whose position and massive strength can be guessed from the ruins of it that remain in the center of the City of Mexico. But in this respect the idolatry of the Mexicans was more grievously in error and more pernicious than that of the Incas, as will become clear later; for the greater part of their worship and idolatry was given to idols and not to natural phenomena in themselves, although they attributed these natural effects such as rain and flocks and war and procreation to the idols, just as the Greeks and Romans also set up idols to Phoebus and Mercury and Jupiter and Minerva and Mars, etcetera.

Finally, whoever looks carefully at all this will discover that the devil's method of deceiving the Indians is the same as that with which he deceived the Greeks and Romans and other ancient unbelievers, by making them believe that these noble creations – sun, moon, stars, elements – had power and authority of their own to do good or evil to men. And, although God has created these things for the service of man, man has been so unsuccessful in ruling and governing them that on the one hand he has tried to raise himself to be God and on the other has recognized and subjected himself to creatures lower than he, by worshiping and invoking these works and ceasing to worship and invoke the Creator, as the sage so well expresses it in these words: "But all men are vain, in whom there is not the knowledge of God: and who by these good things that are seen could not understand him that is, neither by attending to the works have acknowledged who was the workman. But have imagined, either the fire, or the wind, or the swift air, or the circle of the stars, or the great water, or the sun and moon, to be the gods that rule the world. With whose beauty, if they, being delighted, took them to be gods: let them know how much the Lord of them is more beautiful than they. For the first author of beauty made all those things. Or if they admired their power and their effects, let them understand by them, that he that made them is mightier than they. For by the greatness of the beauty, and of the creature, the creator of them may be seen, so as to be known thereby." Thus far the words of the Book of Wisdom, from which very wonderful and effective arguments can be taken to convince the idolatrous heathen of their great error, for they would rather serve and revere the creature than the Creator, as the Apostle so rightly argues. But because this does not fall within my present intent, and is sufficiently expressed in the sermons that have been written against the Indians' errors, for the moment it will suffice to say that the Indians worshiped the supreme God in the same way that they worshiped those vain and lying gods. For the way of praying to Viracocha and to the sun, and to the stars and the other *huacas* or idols, was to open their hands and make a certain sound with their lips like someone kissing, and to request what each one wanted, and to offer sacrifice to the god. There was, however, a difference in the words when they spoke to the great Ticciviracocha, to whom they chiefly attributed the power to rule over all things, and to the others as gods or private lords, each one in his house, who were intercessors with the great Ticciviracocha. This way of worshiping by opening the hands and making a kissing gesture is in some sense like the one that the holy Job abominates as proper to

idolaters, saying, "If I beheld the sun when it shone, and the moon going in brightness: and my heart in secret hath rejoiced, and I have kissed my hand with my mouth (which is a very great iniquity, and a denial against the most high God)."

[...]

Of Another Kind of Idolatry with the Dead

Another kind of idolatry, very different from those I have described, is the kind that the heathen have employed with the dead whom they loved and respected. ...

... [T]hey reached the pinnacle of their idolatries by the same process that is described in Scripture. First, they tried to preserve the bodies of their kings and great lords, and they were kept whole, without smelling or corrupting, for more than two hundred years. This was the way the Inca kings of Cuzco were kept, each in his chapel and temple. The viceroy, Marqués de Cañete, in order to extirpate idolatry, had three or four of them removed and brought to Ciudad de los Reyes, and it caused great astonishment to see human bodies so many years old with such a beautiful appearance and completely whole. Each of these Inca kings left all his treasures and assets and revenues to support his temple, where his body was placed along with those of many of his ministers and all his family dedicated to his cult. No subsequent king usurped the treasures and precious vessels of his predecessor but instead gathered new treasures for himself and his palace. They were not content with this idolatrous worship of dead bodies but also made statues of them; and each king during his lifetime had a stone idol or statue of himself made, which was called *guaoiqui*, meaning "brother," for both in life and death the same veneration had to be paid to that statue as to the Inca himself. These statues were taken to war and carried in procession to pray for rain and good growing seasons, and different feasts and sacrifices were made to them. There were a great many of these idols in Cuzco and its district, but it is believed that the superstitious practice of worshiping these stones has entirely or almost entirely ceased since they were discovered by the efforts of Licentiate Polo, and the first of them was that of Inca Roca, chief of the tribe of Hanan Cuzco. Other tribes likewise have great respect for the bodies of their ancestors, together with their statues, which they worship and venerate.

Of the Superstitions that were Employed with the Dead

Among the Indians of Peru there was a widespread belief that their souls lived on after this life, and that the good received glory and the bad punishment, and so there is little difficulty in persuading them of these articles of faith. But they did not grasp the idea that bodies would arise along with souls, and so they expended a great deal of effort, as has been said, in preserving bodies and honoring them after death. To this end their descendants clothed them and made sacrifices; the Inca kings especially, in their burials, had to be accompanied by a large number of servants and women for their service in the other life. And so on the day they died their favorite women and servants and officials were killed so that they might go to serve them in the other life. On the death of Huayna Capac, the father of Atahualpa, during whose reign the Spaniards came into Peru, more than a thousand persons of all ages and conditions were put to death for his service and company in the other life. They were killed after much singing and excessive drinking and considered themselves fortunate; many things were sacrificed to the dead, especially children, and with their blood they drew a line from ear to ear on the dead man's face. This same superstition and inhumane practice, of killing men and women for the company and service of the dead in the other life, has been used and is still used by other barbarian nations. And according to Polo it has been almost universal in the Indies, and the Venerable Bede even says that the Angles, before they were converted to the Gospel, had the same custom of killing people to accompany and serve the dead. The story is told of a Portuguese who, when he was a captive among savages, received an arrow wound from which he lost an eye. When they wanted to sacrifice him to accompany a dead chief, he replied that those who dwelt in the other life would have a poor opinion of the dead man if his people gave him a one-eyed man for a companion and that it was better to give him one with two eyes; and as this reasoning seemed good to the savages they let him go.

Apart from this superstition of sacrificing men to the dead, which is done only with very important chiefs, there is another that is much more common and widespread all over the Indies, that of placing food and drink for the dead on their tombs and in their caves and believing that they feed themselves with it, which according to Saint Augustine was also an error of the ancients. And even today many heathen Indians secretly disinter their dead from churches and cemeteries and bury them on hills or in ravines, or in their own houses, in order to give them food and drink. They also used to put silver in their mouths, in their hands, and in their bosoms, and dress them in new and usable clothing, folded under the shroud. They believe that the souls of their dead wander about and feel cold and thirst and hunger and travail, and that is why they celebrate their anniversaries by bringing them food and drink and clothing. For this reason the prelates in their synods rightly insist upon the priests making the Indians understand that the offerings placed on tombs in the church are food and drink not for souls but for the poor, or ministers of the Church, and that it is God alone who nourishes souls in the other life, for they do not eat or drink any corporeal thing. And it is very important for them to learn this thoroughly, so as not to change holy usage into heathen superstition, as many of them do.

Of the Funeral Rites that the Mexicans and Other Nations Used

Having recounted what many of the nations of Peru did with their dead, in this respect I must now make special mention of the Mexicans, whose funeral rites were extremely solemn and full of absurdities. It was the office of the priests and other religious in Mexico (who had very strange customs, as will be described later) to bury the dead and perform their obsequies. And the places where they buried them were in fields and in the court-yards of their own houses. Others were carried to the places of sacrifice in the hills, and others were burned and their ashes buried in the tem-ples; and all of them were buried with all the clothing and jewels and precious stones they possessed. And when bodies were burned they put the ashes into jars and placed in the jars their jewels and gems and ornaments, no mat-ter how rich. They chanted the funeral offices like responses and lifted the bodies of the dead many times, performing elaborate ceremonies. They ate and drank during these funerals, and if the dead were persons of quality clothing was given to all those who had come to the burial. When someone died they laid him in a room until all his friends and acquaintances arrived from all around, and these brought the dead man gifts and greeted him as though he were alive; and if he was a king or the lord of some town they offered slaves to be killed so as to serve him in the other world. They also killed his priest or chaplain, for all the nobles had a priest to perform ceremonies within the house, and they killed him so that he could minister to the dead man. They killed the chamberlain, the butler, the dwarfs and hunch-backs (for they made great use of such per-sons), and those among his brothers who had served him most, for it was a mark of greatness among the nobles to be served by their broth-ers and the others I have mentioned. Last, they killed everyone in his household so that they could go and establish one in the other world. And, lest they suffer poverty there, they buried great wealth in gold, silver, precious stones, richly embroidered curtains, gold bracelets, and other rich pieces; and if the dead man was burned they did the same with all the people and ornaments that were given to him for the other world. They took all those ashes and buried them with great solemnity; the ceremo-nies lasted for ten days, during which plaintive and mournful chants were sung.

The priests dispatched the dead with dif-ferent ceremonies, as they themselves had requested, and these were so numerous that they can hardly be counted. Captains and nobles had their insignias and trophies placed upon them, according to their exploits and the valor they had demonstrated in war and gov-ernance, for they had their special devices and weapons for this purpose. All of these objects and tokens were carried before the corpse to the place where it was to be buried or burned, accompanied by a procession in which the priests and temple dignitaries walked with dif-ferent tokens, some swinging censers and oth-ers singing, and still others playing on woeful flutes and drums, which greatly increased the weeping of vassals and relatives. The priest who was conducting the office was arrayed in the insignias of the idol whom the dead man had represented, for all the nobles represented idols and enjoyed their reputations, which caused them to be greatly esteemed and hon-ored. These insignias that I mention were usu-ally carried by members of the orders of chivalry; and, if the body was to be burned, after they had taken it to the place where the ashes were to be produced, they surrounded it and everything pertaining to it with candle-wood, as I have said, and set fire to it, con-stantly feeding the flame with resinous woods until all had been reduced to ashes. Then a priest came out dressed in the accoutrements of the devil, with mouths painted on all the joints and many eyes made of mirrors. He car-ried a large stick with which he stirred all those ashes very vigorously and boldly, presenting such a savage spectacle that it struck horror into all present. And sometimes this same priest wore other different costumes, accord-ing to the dead man's rank. ...

Of the Temples that Have Been Found in the Indies

Let us begin, therefore, with temples: just as the Supreme God decreed that a dwelling be dedicated to him, in which his holy name would be celebrated with special devotion, so the devil for his purposes persuaded the hea-then to make him splendid temples and spe-cial places of worship and sanctuaries. In each province of Peru there was one chief *huaca*, or house of worship, and in addition to this there were several universal ones that served for all the realms of the Incas. Two were preeminent among them all. One was called Pachacama, which is four leagues from Lima, and even today the ruins of a very old and immense building can be seen, from which Francisco Pizarro and his men took that vast store of gold and silver vessels and pitchers that were brought them when they held the Inca Atahualpa prisoner. There are reliable accounts that in this temple the devil spoke visibly and gave replies through his oracle and that sometimes a spotted snake was seen; and this speaking and responding by the devil in these false temples, and deceiving the wretched people, is a very common and proven thing in the Indies. However, in places where the Gospel has entered and raised the sign of the holy cross, the father of lies has fallen notably silent, as Plutarch wrote in his era, *Curcessaverit Pythias fundere oracula.* And Saint Justin Martyr deals at length with the silence that Christ imposed on the devils who spoke through idols, as was prophesied much earlier in Holy Writ. The method used by the heathen sorcerers and priests to consult the gods was in the manner that the devil had taught them: usually it was at night, and they entered turned away from the idol, walking backward. And, bending low and bowing their heads, they assumed an ugly posture and thus consulted with him. Usually the reply was a sort of horrible whistle, or a scream, which struck them with horror, and everything that they were told and commanded was intended for their deception and perdition. Thanks to God's mercy and the great power of Jesus Christ, little of this is found today. There was another even more important temple and place of worship in Peru, which was in the city of Cuzco, where the monastery of Santo Domingo is now, and from the building's blocks and stones that remain to this day it is easy to see that it was a very important place. This temple was like the Roman Pantheon in that it was the house and dwelling place of all the gods. For the Inca kings placed in it the gods of all the provinces and peoples that they conquered, and each idol was in its special place and the people of its

province came to worship and venerate it, with enormous expenditure of things that they brought to minister to it; and thus the Incas believed that the conquered provinces were safe because their gods were being held hostage, as it were. The Punchao was there, which was an idol of the sun, made of very fine gold and with a great abundance of precious stones, set facing the east so cleverly that when the sun came up it struck the idol; and as it was very fine metal, it returned the sun's rays with such brilliance that it seemed another sun. The Incas worshiped this idol as their god, and also as Pachayachachic, who is the maker of the heavens. They say that among the spoils of this rich temple a soldier received that beautiful gold plaque of the sun and that he gambled it away one night in the course of a protracted game; hence the origin of the proverb that circulates in Peru about great gamblers, saying, "he gambles away the sun before it rises."

Of the Splendid Temples of Mexico

But the Mexicans' superstition was incomparably greater, in their ceremonies as well as the great size of their temples, which the Spaniards used to call *cu*; and this must have been a word taken from the islanders of Santo Domingo or Cuba, like many others in use that are not words from Spain or any other language employed in the Indies today, such as *maíz, chicha, vaquiano, chapetón,* and other similar words. There was, then, in Mexico the *cu*, the famous temple of Huitzilopochtli, whose very large enclosure formed a beautiful courtyard inside; it was all built of great hewn stones carved to resemble snakes, each joined to another, and that is why this enclosure had the name of *coatepantli*, which means "precinct of snakes." Above the chambers and chapels where the idols were there was a very handsome parapet made of small stones as black as jet, carefully and harmoniously arranged, and with the whole area plastered in red and white, which looked very fine from below. Above this parapet were handsome battlements made in spiral shape; the buttresses were finished off with two stone Indians in a sitting position, with candelabra in their hands, and from these emerged something like the hangings of a cross, with rich yellow and green feathers at their ends and long pennons of the same. Within the precinct of this courtyard were many apartments for religious, and others higher up for priests and *papas*, which was what they called the high priests who served the idol. This courtyard was so large and spacious that, although it seems incredible, eight or ten thousand men could assemble there to dance in a circle, as was the custom in that realm. It had four gates or entrances, east and west, north and south; each of these entrances marked the beginning of a very beautiful causeway two or three leagues long; and hence, in the middle of the lake, where the city of Mexico was founded, there were four very broad causeways in the form of a cross, which made the city very attractive. In these entrances were four gods or idols, each with its face turned toward one of the causeways. Opposite the door of this temple of Huitzilopochtli were thirty steps 180 feet long, divided by a street that ran between them and the courtyard wall. At the top of the steps was a broad walk 30 feet wide, all whitewashed; in the middle of this walk was a carefully constructed palisade made from tall trees placed in a row and 6 feet apart. These trunks were very thick and were all bored with small holes. From bottom to top, completely filling the palisade, were thin wands placed through the holes in the timbers, on which many human skulls were strung by the temples; each wand bore twenty heads. These rows of skulls reached from the bottom to the top of the tree trunks and filled the palisade from end to end, and so many and so densely packed were the skulls that they caused amazement and horror. These were the skulls of the men they had sacrificed, for after they had killed and eaten them they would bring the skulls and deliver them to the priests of the temple, and they would string them up there until they fell to pieces; and they took care to replace with others those that fell. At the summit of the temple were two chambers resembling chapels, and in them the two aforesaid idols, Huitzilopochtli

and Tlaloc. These chapels were made with carved figures, and they were so lofty that a staircase of 120 stone steps led up to them. Before these apartments was a courtyard 40 feet square, in the middle of which was a green stone shaped like a sharp-pointed pyramid five handbreadths high, which was placed there for the human sacrifices that they performed; for when a man was thrown onto it face up his body was made to bend backward, and then they opened him and tore out his heart, as will be described later.

In the City of Mexico there were eight or nine other temples like this one I have described, adjoining each other within a large enclosure, with their own staircases and their courtyards with apartments and sleeping rooms. Some of them had their entrances on the west, others on the east, others on the south, others on the north, all very well built and possessing towers with different kinds of battlements and paintings and many stone figures and reinforced with large and broad buttresses. These were dedicated to different gods, but second to the temple of Huitzilopochtli was that of the idol Tezcatlipoca, who was the god of penitence and punishment, and it was very tall and beautifully built. There were 80 steps leading up to it, at the top of which was an open space 120 feet wide and next to it a room completely hung with curtains of different colors and workmanship; the door was low and broad and always covered with a veil, and only the priests could enter it. The whole temple was decorated very elaborately, with a number of effigies and carvings, for these two temples were like cathedral churches, and the rest in comparison to them were like parish churches and hermitages. And they were so spacious, and had so many chambers, that there were ministers in them, and colleges and schools and priests' houses...

Of the Priests and the Offices they Performed

In every nation of the world men can be found who are specially dedicated to the cult of a god, either true or false, and these serve for the sacrifices and to declare to the people what their gods command. In Mexico there was very great emphasis upon this, and the devil, mimicking the usages of the Church of God, also established his order of lesser and greater and supreme priests and others resembling acolytes and others like the Levites of old. And the most astonishing thing for me is that apparently the devil tried to usurp the cult of Christ even in name, for the highest priests, and as it were the supreme pontiffs, were called *papas* by the Mexicans in their ancient tongue, as is proved today by their histories and accounts. The priests of Huitzilopochtli succeeded by inheritance from certain districts assigned for this purpose. The priests of other idols succeeded by election or by being offered to the temple from childhood. The constant duty of the priests was to cense the idols, which they did four times on every ordinary day: the first time at dawn, the second at noon, the third at sunset, and the fourth at midnight. At this hour all the dignitaries of the temple arose, and instead of bells they blew on large trumpets and conch shells, and others played a mournful tune on little flutes for a long while. And after they had played the priest whose office it was came out dressed in a white garment like a dalmatic, with his censer in his hand full of coals, which he took from the brazier or stove that perpetually burned before the altar. In the other hand he had a bag full of incense, which he placed in the censer, and going in to the idol he censed it very reverently. Then he took a cloth and with it cleaned the altar and the curtains. This done, all went together to a room and there did a sort of very severe and cruel penance, cutting themselves and drawing blood in a way that will be described when dealing with the penance that the devil taught to his adherents. They never failed to perform these matins at midnight. No others could take part in the sacrifices, only the priests according to the rank and dignity of each. They also preached to the people during certain festivities, as we will recount when we deal with these; they had their revenues and were also given ample offerings. The annointing with which they consecrated priests will also be described. In Peru they lived off the lands reserved for their gods, called *chácaras* there, which were numerous and very rich.

[...]

How the Opinion of Those Who Believe that the Indians Lack Understanding is False

Having dealt with matters pertaining to the religion practiced by the Indians, in this book I intend to write of their customs and polity and government, with two aims in mind. One is to refute the false opinion that is commonly held about them, that they are brutes and bestial folk and lacking in understanding or with so little that it scarcely merits the name. Many and very notable abuses have been committed upon them as a consequence of this false belief, treating them as little better than animals and considering them unworthy of any sort of respect. Those who have lived among them with some degree of zeal and consideration, and have seen and known their secrets and their counsels, well know that it is a common and harmful delusion. In addition, little attention is paid to all Indians by those who think they know a great deal about them and who are usually the most ignorant and presumptuous of men. I see no better way of refuting this pernicious opinion than to describe their order and behavior when they lived under their own law. In it, although they had many barbaric traits and baseless beliefs, there were many others worthy of admiration; these clearly give us to understand that they have a natural capacity to receive good instruction and that they even surpass in large measure many of our own republics. And it is no wonder that there were gross errors among them, for these are found even in the gravest legislators and philosophers, not excepting Lycurgus and Plato. In the wisest republics, such as those of the Romans and Athenians, we see signs of ignorance deserving of laughter; and, certainly, if the republics of the Mexicans and Incas had been described in the times of the Romans or Greeks, their laws and government would be respected. But if, knowing nothing of this, we enter by the sword and neither hear nor understand them, we do not believe that the Indians' affairs deserve repute but treat them like game hunted in the hills and brought to us for our service and whim.

The most diligent and learned men who have penetrated and attained their secrets, their ancient style, and their government judge them in a very different way, amazed that there could have been so much order and reason among them. One of these authors is Polo Ondegardo, whom I chiefly follow in things pertaining to Peru, and in matters of Mexico Juan de Tovar, a former prebendary of the Church in Mexico and now a religious in our Society of Jesus; on the orders of the viceroy Don Martín Enríquez, he made a diligent and lengthy study of that nation's old histories. And I do not mention other weighty authors who have informed me very fully, either in writing or orally, of everything I am going to recount. The other aim that can be achieved with knowledge of the laws and customs and polity of the Indians is to help them and rule them by those very laws, for in whatever does not contradict the law of Christ and his Holy Church, they ought to be governed according to their statutes, which are as it were their municipal laws. Through ignorance of these, errors of no little importance have been committed, for those who judge and rule them have not known how to judge and rule their subjects. This, in addition to being an offense and an unreasonable thing done to them, causes great harm, for it makes us Spaniards abhorred as men who are and always have been their enemies in both good and evil.

Of the Method of Calculating Time and the Calendar that the Mexicans Used

Beginning, therefore, with the divisions of time and the calculations that the Indians used, which is one of the most remarkable proofs of their cleverness and skill, I will first state how the Mexicans reckoned and distributed their year and will tell of their months and calendar and their reckoning of centuries or ages. They divided the year into eighteen months and assigned twenty days to each month, making a total of three hundred and sixty days; the other five that remained to fill out the rest of the year were not assigned to any month but were counted separately, and these were called days of idleness, during which the people did nothing, nor did they go to the temple. They spent them only in visiting one another and wasting time, and the temple priests ceased to sacrifice. When those days were over they again began the calculation of their year, whose beginning and first month was March, when the leaves begin to turn green again, although they took three days from February, for the first day of their new year was the twenty-sixth of February, as is evident in their calendar. Our own calendar has been incorporated into it with remarkably accurate reckoning and skill, done by the early Indians first encountered by the Spaniards. I have seen this calendar and still have it in my possession, and it is worthy of study in order to understand the reasoning power and skill of these Mexican Indians. Each of the eighteen months to which I referred has its special name and its own picture and sign, and this was commonly taken from the chief festival that took place in that month or from the differences in appearance that the year causes. And they had certain days marked on their calendar for all their festivals. They counted weeks by thirteen days and marked each day with a zero or small round dot, multiplying the zeroes up to thirteen, and then began to count again: one, two, and so on. They also divided the years by using four signs, giving a sign to each year. These signs were four figures: one was a house, another a rabbit, the third a piece of cane, the fourth a flint; and they pictured them thus and used them to name the current year, saying, "In such and such houses or such and such flints of such and such a wheel, such a thing happened," for it must be understood that their wheel, which is like a century, contained four weeks of years, each week consisting of thirteen years, so that the sum of them all was fifty-two years. They painted a sun in the center, and then four arms or lines came out from it to the circumference of the wheel in the shape of a cross, thus dividing the circumference into four parts, each of them with its line of the same color, of which there were four different ones: green, blue, red, and yellow. And each of these had its thirteen compartments with its sign of house, rabbit, cane, or flint, each representing its year, and at one side they painted what had happened in that year. And so I saw in the calendar of which I have spoken an indication of the year when the Spaniards entered Mexico, with a picture of a man dressed in our style of clothing, painted in red, for that was the dress of the first Spaniard that Hernán Cortés sent.

At the end of the fifty-two years that closed the wheel they employed an amusing ceremony, and it was that on the last night they broke all the vessels they possessed and extinguished all the fires, saying that in one of the wheels the world was sure to come to an end and that perchance it was the one in which they were living, and that since the world was going to end there was no need to cook or eat, and for what did they need vessels or fire; and they would stay like this all night, saying that perhaps dawn would never come again, all of them watching very closely to see if the sun would rise. When they observed that dawn was coming they played on many drums and horns and flutes and other instruments of rejoicing and merriment, saying that God was granting them another century, which was fifty-two years, and then they began another wheel. On the day on which dawn ushered in another century they lit new fires and bought new dishes, pots, and everything necessary for cooking, and all went for new fire to the place where the high priest had lighted it, with a most solemn procession going before as a sign of thanks-giving because the dawn had come and granted them another century. This was their method of counting years and months and weeks and centuries.

[…]

Of the Kinds of Letters and Writing that the Mexicans Used

Among the nations of New Spain there is great knowledge and memory of their ancient customs. And when I desired to learn how the Indians could preserve their histories in so much detail I realized that, although they did not possess the care and refinement of the Chinese and Japanese, still they did not lack some kinds of letters and books, with which they preserved after their fashion the deeds of their ancestors. In the province of Yucatan, seat of the bishopric known as that of Honduras, there were some books with leaves in the Indian style, either bound or folded, in which the wisest Indians kept the distribution of time, and knowledge of plants and animals and other things pertaining to nature, as well as their ancient customs, and it was the result of great zeal and diligence. A missionary there thought that all of it must be witches' spells and magic art and insisted that they be burned, and indeed those books were burned, which was regretted afterward not only by the Indians but by curious Spaniards who desired to know the secrets of that land. The same fate has befallen other things, which, because our people thought that all of it was superstition, meant the loss of many memories of ancient and hidden things that might have been of no little use. This happens out of unhealthy zeal on the part of those who, without knowing or wanting to know anything about the Indians, indiscriminately dub everything witchcraft, and say that the Indians are all drunkards, and ask what they can know or understand.

Those who have tried to investigate these matters in the proper way have found many things worthy of consideration. One of the members of our Society of Jesus, a very sensible and clever man, brought together in the province of Mexico the old men of Texcoco and Tula and Mexico and conferred with them at length, and they showed him their collections of books and their histories and calendars, a sight very much worth seeing. For they had their pictures and hieroglyphs with which they represented things in the following way: things that had shapes were painted in their own image, and for things that did not have actual shapes they had characters signifying this, and hence were able to express whatever they wanted. And for a reminder of the time when each thing happened they had those painted wheels, each containing a century, which as I said before was of fifty-two years; and they painted these things beside those wheels, corresponding to the year in which memorable events occurred, using the pictures and characters I have described. For instance, by placing a picture of a man with a red hat and jacket in the sign of the cane, which was the century at the time, they marked the year when the Spaniards came into their land; and they did the same with other events. But because their figures and characters were not as adequate as those of our writing and letters, this meant that they could not make the words conform exactly but could only express the essential part of ideas. ...

And I say this because some persons who read such long and elegant speeches in Mexican history will easily believe that they were invented by the Spaniards and not really composed by the Indians; but once they understand the truth they will not fail to give proper credit to the Indians' histories. The Indians also wrote down these same speeches after their own fashion, with pictures and characters; and, to satisfy my mind about this, I have seen the prayers of Our Father and Ave Maria, the Creed, and the general confession written in the Indian way I have described; and surely everyone who sees it will be astonished, because to signify the phrase "I, a sinner, do confess" they paint an Indian kneeling at the feet of a religious, as if confessing; and then for the expression "Omnipotent God" they paint three faces with crowns to represent the Trinity; and for the glorious Virgin Mary they paint the face of Our Lady and a bust of her with a child; and for Saint Peter and Saint Paul two heads with crowns, and keys and a sword, and in this way the whole confession is written in pictures. And where there are no pictures they put characters, such as in "wherein I have sinned"; from this the keenness of the Indians' minds can be inferred, for the Spaniards never taught them this way of writing our prayers and matters of faith, nor could they have thought of it had they not had a very clear idea of what they were being taught. I also saw written in Peru, in the same style of pictures and characters, the confession of all his sins that an Indian brought when he came to confession, painting each of the Ten Commandments in a particular way and then making certain signs like ciphers, which were the sins that he had committed against each commandment. I have no doubt that, if many of the most complacent Spaniards were given the task of memorizing such things

by the use of pictures and signs, they would not succeed in committing them to memory in a whole year or perhaps even in ten.

Of the Memory Aids and Reckonings Used by the Indians of Peru

Before the Spaniards came the Indians of Peru had no kind of writing at all, either by letters or characters or ciphers or pictures, like those of China or Mexico; but this did not prevent them from preserving the memory of ancient times, nor did they fail to keep a reckoning for all their affairs whether of peace, war, or government. For they were very diligent in passing tradition from one generation to another, and the young men received and preserved what their elders told them as a sacred trust and taught it to their successors with the same care. Apart from this task, they compensated in part for the lack of writing and letters with pictures like those of Mexico, (although those of Peru were very coarse and rough), and in part, indeed principally, with *quipus*. *Quipus* are memory aids or registers made up of cords on which different knots and different colors signify different things. What they achieved in this way is incredible, for whatever books can tell of histories and laws and ceremonies and accounts of business all is supplied by the *quipus* so accurately that the result is astonishing. Appointed to possess these *quipus*, or memorials, were officials who today are called *quipucamayos*, and these men were obliged to render an account of each thing, like public notaries here in Spain, and hence they had to be believed absolutely. There were different *quipus*, or strands, for different subjects, such as war, government, taxes, ceremonies, and lands. And in each bunch of these were many knots and smaller knots and little strings tied to them, some red, others green, others blue, others white: in short, just as we extract an infinite number of differences out of twenty-four letters by arranging them in different ways and making innumerable words, they were able to elicit any number of meanings from their knots and colors. This is true to the extent that nowadays in Peru every two or three years, when a Spanish governor is subjected to a trial of residency, the Indians come forward with their small proven reckonings, saying that in a certain town they gave him six eggs and he did not pay for them, and in such and such a house a hen, and in another place two bundles of hay for his horses, and that he paid only so and so many tomines and still owes so and so many; and all of this is accurately proved with a quantity of knots and bundles of strands, which they consider to be witnesses and authentic writing. I saw a bundle of these strings on which an Indian woman had brought a written general confession of her whole life and used it to confess just as I would have done with words written on paper; and I even asked about some little threads that looked different to me, and they were certain circumstances under which the sin required to be fully confessed.

[...]

Of the Government and Monarchs that They Had

It is a proven fact that barbarian peoples show their barbarity most clearly in their government and manner of ruling, for the more closely men approach to reason the more humane and less arrogant is their government, and those who are kings and nobles conform and accommodate themselves to their vassals, acknowledging that they are equal by nature and inferior only in the sense that they have less obligation to care for the public good. But among barbarians the case is the opposite, for their government is tyrannical and they treat their subjects like beasts while they themselves desire to be treated like gods. Therefore, many tribes and Indian peoples do not allow kings or absolute lords but live in free communities; and only for certain things, chiefly war, do they raise up captains and princes, who are obeyed while that occasion lasts and then return to their previous estate. This is the way most of this New World is governed, where there are no organized kingdoms nor established republics, nor hereditary and recognized princes or kings; however, there are some lords and principal men who are like knights, of higher status than the common herd. This is the case in almost the whole land of Chile, where the Araucanos, and those of Tucapel and others, have resisted the Spaniards for so many years. It was the situation in all the New Realm of Granada, and in Guatemala and the islands, and all of Florida and Brazil and Luzón, and other very extensive territories, except that in many of them their barbarity is even greater, for they scarcely recognize any head and all command and govern together. In those places everything is governed by whim and violence and unreason and disorder, and the most powerful man prevails and commands. In the East Indies there are extensive and well-organized kingdoms, like those of Siam and Bisnaga and others, which can put a hundred thousand and two hundred thousand men into the field whenever they wish; and superior to all the others is the greatness and power of the kingdom of China, whose monarchs have lasted for more than two thousand years according to them, thanks to their splendid form of government. In the West Indies only two established kingdoms or empires have been discovered, that of the Mexicans in New Spain and that of the Incas in Peru, and I could not easily say which of these has been a more powerful realm. For in buildings and the splendor of his court Moctezuma surpassed the rulers of Peru, but in treasures and wealth and extension of territory the Incas were greater than the Mexicans. In point of antiquity the realm of the Incas was older, though not by much, and I think they were equal in feats of arms and victories. One thing is certain, that these two realms greatly surpassed all the other Indian dominions that have been discovered in the New World as to good order and degree of civic organization as well as power and wealth, and exceeded them much more in superstition and the cult of their idols, for they were very similar in many ways. In one thing they were very different, for among the Mexicans the succession of the kingdom was by election, as in the Roman Empire, and among those of Peru it was by inheritance and blood, as in the kingdoms of Spain and France. ...

12

Relation of What Occurred in New France, in the Year 1634

Paul Le Jeune

On the Good Things Which are Found Among the Savages

If we begin with physical advantages, I will say that they possess these in abundance. They are tall, erect, strong, well proportioned, agile; and there is nothing effeminate in their appearance. Those little Fops that are seen elsewhere are only caricatures of men, compared with our Savages. I almost believed, heretofore, that the Pictures of the Roman Emperors represented the ideal of the painters rather than men who had ever existed, so strong and powerful are their heads; but I see here upon the shoulders of these people the heads of Julius Cæsar, of Pompey, of Augustus, of Otho, and of others, that I have seen in France, drawn upon [101] paper, or in relief on medallions.

As to the mind of the Savage, it is of good quality. I believe that souls are all made from the same stock, and that they do not materially differ; hence, these barbarians having well formed bodies, and organs well regulated and well arranged, their minds ought to work with ease. Education and instruction alone are lacking. Their soul is a soil which is naturally good, but loaded down with all the evils that a land abandoned since the birth of the world can produce. I naturally compare our Savages with certain villagers, because both are usually without education, though our Peasants are superior in this regard; and yet I have not seen any one thus far, of those who have come to this country, who does not confess and frankly admit that the Savages are more intelligent than our ordinary peasants.

Moreover, if it is a great blessing to be free from a great evil, our Savages are happy; for the two tyrants who provide hell and torture for many of our Europeans, do not reign [102] in their great forests, – I mean ambition and avarice. As they have neither political organization, nor offices, nor dignities, nor any authority, for they only obey their Chief through good will toward him, therefore they never kill each other to acquire these honors. Also, as they are contented with a mere living, not one of them gives himself to the Devil to acquire wealth.

They make a pretence of never getting angry, not because of the beauty of this virtue, for which they have not even a name, but for their own contentment and happiness, I mean, to avoid the bitterness caused by anger. The Sorcerer said to me one day, speaking of one of our Frenchmen, "He has no sense, he gets angry; as for me, nothing can disturb me; let hunger oppress me, let my nearest relation pass to the other life, let the Hiroquois, our enemies, massacre our people, I never get angry." What he says is not an article of faith; for, as he

Paul Le Jeune, "Relation of what occurred in New France, in the year 1634," in *Jesuit Relations and Allied Documents*, vol. 6, ed. Reuben Thwaites, Cleveland, OH: Burrows Brothers, 1901, pp. 229–69 (rectos only).

is more haughty than any other Savage, so I have seen him oftener out of humor than any of them; it is true also that he often restrains and governs himself by force, especially [103] when I expose his foolishness. I have only heard one Savage pronounce this word, *Ninichcatihin*, "I am angry," and he only said it once. But I noticed that they kept their eyes on him, for when these Barbarians are angry, they are dangerous and unrestrained.

Whoever professes not to get angry, ought also to make a profession of patience; the Savages surpass us to such an extent, in this respect, that we ought to be ashamed. I saw them, in their hardships and in their labors, suffer with cheerfulness. My host, wondering at the great number of people who I told him were in France, asked me if the men were good, if they did not become angry, if they were patient. I have never seen such patience as is shown by a sick Savage. You may yell, storm, jump, dance, and he will scarcely ever complain. I found myself, with them, threatened with great suffering; they said to me, "We shall be sometimes two days, sometimes three, without eating, for lack of food; take courage, *Chihiné*, let thy soul be strong to endure suffering and hardship; keep thyself from being sad, otherwise thou wilt be sick; see how we do not cease to laugh, [104] although we have little to eat." One thing alone casts them down, – it is when they see death, for they fear this beyond measure; take away this apprehension from the Savages, and they will endure all kinds of degradation and discomfort, and all kinds of trials and suffering very patiently. Later, I shall give several examples of this, which I am reserving for the end of these chapters.

They are very much attached to each other, and agree admirably. You do not see any disputes, quarrels, enmities, or reproaches among them. Men leave the arrangement of the household to the women, without interfering with them; they cut, and decide, and give away as they please, without making the husband angry. I have never seen my host ask a giddy young woman that he had with him what became of the provisions, although they were disappearing very fast. I have never heard the women complain because they were not invited to the feasts, because the men ate the good

pieces, or because they had to work continually, – going in search of the wood for the fire, making the Houses, dressing the skins, and busying themselves in [105] other very laborious work. Each one does her own little tasks, gently and peacefully, without any disputes. It is true, however, that they have neither gentleness nor courtesy in their utterance; and a Frenchman could not assume the accent, the tone, and the sharpness of their voices without becoming angry, yet they do not.

They are not vindictive among themselves, although they are toward their enemies. I will here give an example that ought to confound many Christians. In the stress of our famine, a young Savage from another quarter came to see us, who was as hungry as we were. The day on which he came was a day of fasting for him and for us, for there was nothing to eat. The next day, our hunters having taken a few Beavers, a feast was made, at which he was well treated; he was told besides that the trail of a Moose had been seen, and that they were going to hunt for it the next day; he was invited to remain and to have his share of it; he answered that he could stay no longer, and, having inquired about the place where the animal was, he went away. Our Hunters, having found and killed this Elk the [106] next day, buried it in the snow, according to their custom, to send for it on the following day. Now, during the night, my young Savage searched so well, that he found the dead beast, and took away a good part of it without saying a word. When the theft became known to our people, they did not get into a rage and utter maledictions against the thief, – all their anger consisted in sneering at him; and yet this was almost taking away our life, this stealing our food when we were unable to obtain any more. Some time afterward, this thief came to see us; I wanted to represent to him the seriousness of his offence, but my host imposed silence; and when this poor man attributed his theft to the dogs, he was not only excused, but even received to live with us in the same Cabin. Then he went for his wife, whom he carried upon his back, for her legs are paralyzed; a young female relative who lives with him brought his little son; and all four took their places in our little hut, without ever being reproached for this theft; on the contrary they were received very kindly, and were treated as if [107] belonging to the family. Tell a Savage that another Savage has slandered him, and he will bow the head and not say a word; if they meet each other afterward, they will pretend not to know anything about it, acting as if nothing had been said. They treat each other as brothers; they harbor no spite against those of their own nation.

They are very generous among themselves and even make a show of not loving anything, of not being attached to the riches of the earth, so that they may not grieve if they lose them. Not long ago a dog tore a beautiful Beaver robe belonging to one of the Savages, and he was the first one to laugh about it. One of the greatest insults that can be offered to them, is to say, "That man likes everything, he is stingy." If you refuse them anything, here is their reproach, as I remarked last year: *Khisakhitan Sakhita*, "Thou lovest that, love it as much as thou wilt." They do not open the hand half-way when they give, – I mean among themselves, for they are as ungrateful as possible toward strangers. You will see them take care of their kindred, the children of their friends, widows, orphans, and old men, never reproaching them in the least, giving them abundantly, [108] sometimes whole Moose. This is truly the sign of a good heart and of a generous soul.

As there are many orphans among these people, – for they die in great numbers since they are addicted to drinking wine and brandy, – these poor children are scattered among the Cabins of their uncles, aunts, or other relatives. Do not suppose that they are snubbed and reproached because they eat the food of the household. Nothing of the kind, they are treated the same as the children of the father of the family, or at least almost the same, and are dressed as well as possible.

They are not fastidious in their food, beds, and clothes, but are very slovenly. They never complain of what is given them; if it be cold, if it be warm, it does not matter. When the food is cooked, it is divided without waiting for any one, not even the master of the house; a share is reserved for him, which is given to him cold. I have never heard my host complain because

they did not wait for him, if he were only a few steps from the Cabin. They often sleep upon the ground, at the sign of the [109] stars. They will pass one, two, and three days without eating, not ceasing to row, hunt, and fatigue themselves as much as they can. It will be seen in the course of this relation, that all I have said in this chapter is very true; and yet I would not dare to assert that I have seen one act of real moral virtue in a Savage. They have nothing but their own pleasure and satisfaction in view. Add to this the fear of being blamed, and the glory of seeming to be good hunters, and you have all that actuates them in their transactions.

On Their Vices and Their Imperfections

The Savages, being filled with errors, are also haughty and proud. Humility is born of truth, vanity of error and falsehood. They are void of the knowledge of truth, and are in consequence, mainly occupied with thought of themselves. They imagine that they ought by right of birth, to enjoy the liberty of Wild ass colts, rendering no homage to any one whomsoever, except when they like. They have reproached me a hundred times because we [110] fear our Captains, while they laugh at and make sport of theirs. All the authority of their chief is in his tongue's end; for he is powerful in so far as he is eloquent; and, even if he kills himself talking and haranguing, he will not be obeyed unless he pleases the Savages.

I do not believe that there is a nation under heaven more given to sneering and bantering than that of the Montagnais. Their life is passed in eating, laughing, and making sport of each other, and of all the people they know. There is nothing serious about them, except occasionally, when they make a pretense among us of being grave and dignified; but among themselves they are real buffoons and genuine children, who ask only to laugh. Sometimes I annoyed them a little, especially the Sorcerer, by calling them children, and showing them that I never could place any reliance upon all their answers; because, if I questioned them about one thing, they told me about something else, only to get something to laugh and jest about; and consequently I could not know when they were speaking seriously, or when they were jesting. The usual conclusion of their discourses and conversations is: "Really, we did make [111] a great deal of sport of such and such a one."

I have shown in my former letters how vindictive the Savages are toward their enemies, with what fury and cruelty they treat them, eating them after they have made them suffer all that an incarnate fiend could invent. This fury is common to the women as well as to the men, and they even surpass the latter in this respect. I have said that they eat the lice they find upon themselves, not that they like the taste of them, but because they want to bite those that bite them.

These people are very little moved by compassion. When any one is sick in their Cabins, they ordinarily do not cease to cry and storm, and make as much noise as if everybody were in good health. They do not know what it is to take care of a poor invalid, and to give him the food which is good for him; if he asks for something to drink, it is given to him, if he asks for something to eat, it is given to him, but otherwise he is neglected; to coax him with love and gentleness, is a language which they do not understand. As long as a patient can eat, they will carry [112] or drag him with them; if he stops eating, they believe that it is all over with him and kill him, as much to free him from the sufferings that he is enduring, as to relieve themselves of the trouble of taking him with them when they go to some other place. I have both admired and pitied the patience of the invalids whom I have seen among them.

The Savages are slanderous beyond all belief; I say, also among themselves, for they do not even spare their nearest relations, and with it all they are deceitful. For, if one speaks ill of another, they all jeer with loud laughter; if the other appears upon the scene, the first one will show him as much affection and treat him with as much love, as if he had elevated him to the third heaven by his praise. The reason of this is, it seems to me, that their slanders and derision do not come from malicious

hearts or from infected mouths, but from a mind which says what it thinks in order to give itself free scope, and which seeks gratification from everything, even from slander and mockery. Hence they are not troubled even if they are told that others are making sport of [113] them, or have injured their reputation. All they usually answer to such talk is, *mama irinisiou*, "He has no sense, he does not know what he is talking about;" and at the first opportunity they will pay their slanderer in the same coin, returning him the like.

Lying is as natural to Savages as talking, not among themselves, but to strangers. Hence it can be said that fear and hope, in one word, interest, is the measure of their fidelity. I would not be willing to trust them, except as they would fear to be punished if they failed in their duty, or hoped to be rewarded if they were faithful to it. They do not know what it is to keep a secret, to keep their word, and to love with constancy, – especially those who are not of their nation, for they are harmonious among themselves, and their slanders and raillery do not disturb their peace and friendly intercourse.

I will say in passing that the Montagnais Savages are not thieves. The doors of the French are open to them, because their hands can be trusted; [114] but, as to the Hurons, if a person had as many eyes as they have fingers on their hands, he could not prevent them from stealing, for they steal with their feet. They make a profession of this art, and expect to be beaten if they are discovered. For, as I have already remarked, they will endure the blows which you give them, patiently, not as an acknowledgment of their fault, but as a punishment for their stupidity in allowing themselves to be detected in their theft. I will leave the description of them to our Fathers who are going there, whose lot I would envy, were it not that he who assigns us our departments is always worthy of love and always adorable, whatever part or portion he may give us.

Eating among the Savages is like drinking among the drunkards of Europe. Those dry and ever-thirsty souls would willingly end their lives in a tub of malmsey, and the Savages in a pot full of meat; those over there, talk only of drinking, and these here only of eating. It is giving a sort of insult to a Savage to refuse the pieces which he offers you. A certain one, seeing that I had declined what my host [115] offered me to eat, said to me, "Thou dost not love him, since thou refusest him." I told him that it was not our custom to eat at all hours; but, nevertheless, I would take what he would give me, if he did not give it to me quite so often. They all began to laugh; and an old woman said to me that, if I wished to be loved by their tribe, I must eat a great deal. When you treat them well, they show their satisfaction with your feast in these words, *tapoué nimitison*, "I am really eating," as if their highest content were in this action; and at the end of the banquet, they will say as an act of thanks, *tapoué nikhispoun*, "I am really full;" meaning, "Thou hast treated me well; I am full to bursting." It seems to me that I have spoken of this before. They believe that it is foolish and stupid to refuse; the greatest satisfaction that they can have in their Paradise is in the stomach. I do not hesitate to exclaim: Oh, how just is the judgment of God, that these people, who place their ultimate happiness in eating, are always hungry, and are only fed like dogs; for their most splendid feastings are, [116] so to speak, only the bones and the leavings of the tables of Europe! Their first act, upon awakening in the morning, is to stretch out their arms toward their bark dish full of meat, and then to eat. When I first began to stay with them, I tried to introduce the custom of praying to God before eating, and in fact I pronounced a blessing when they wanted it done. But the Apostate said to me, "If you want to pray as many times as they will eat in your Cabin, prepare to say your *Benedicite* more than twenty times before night." They end the day as they begin it, always with a morsel in their mouths, or with their pipes to smoke when they lay their heads on the pillow to rest.

The Savages have always been gluttons, but since the coming of the Europeans they have become such drunkards, that, – although they see clearly that these new drinks, the wine and brandy, which are brought to them, are depopulating their country, of which they themselves complain, – they cannot abstain from drinking, taking pride in getting drunk and in making others drunk. It is true that they die in great

[117] numbers; but I am astonished that they can resist it as long as they do. For, give two Savages two or three bottles of brandy, they will sit down and, without eating, will drink, one after the other, until they have emptied them. The company of these Gentlemen is remarkably praiseworthy in forbidding the traffic in these liquors. Monsieur de Champlain very wisely takes care that these restrictions are observed, and I have heard that Monsieur the General du Plessis has had them enforced at Tadoussac. I have been told that the Savages are tolerably chaste. I shall not speak of all, not having been among them all; but those whom I have met are very lewd, both men and women. God! what blindness! How great is the happiness of Christian people! How great the chastisement of these Barbarians! In place of saying, as we do very often, through wonder, "JESUS! what is that? My God! who has done that?" these vile and infamous people pronounce the names of the private parts of man and woman. Their lips are constantly foul with these obscenities; and it is the same with the little children. So I said to them, at one time, that if [118] hogs and dogs knew how to talk, they would adopt their language. Indeed, if the shameless Sorcerer had not come into the Cabin where I was, I should have gained thus much from my people, that not one of them would dare to speak of impure things in my presence; but this impertinent fellow ruled the others. The older women go almost naked, the girls and young women are very modestly clad; but, among themselves, their language has the foul odor of the sewers. It must be admitted, however, that if liberty to gorge oneself in such filth existed among some Christians, as it does among these people, one would see very different exhibitions of excess from what are seen here; for, even despite the laws, both Divine and human, dissoluteness strides more openly there than here. For here the eyes are not offended. The Sorcerer alone has been guilty of any brutal action in my presence; the others only offended my ears, but, perceiving that I heard them, they were ashamed.

Now, as these people are well aware of this corruption, they prefer to take [119] the children of their sisters as heirs, rather than their own, or than those of their brothers, calling in question the fidelity of their wives, and being unable to doubt that these nephews come from their own blood. Also among the Hurons, – who are more licentious than our Montagnais, because they are better fed, – it is not the child of a Captain but his sister's son, who succeeds the father.

The Sorcerer told me one day that the women were fond of him, for, as the Savages say, it is his demon that makes the sex love him. I told him that it was not honorable for a woman to love any one else except her husband; and that, this evil being among them, he himself was not sure that his son, who was there present, was his son. He replied, "Thou hast no sense. You French people love only your own children; but we all love all the children of our tribe." I began to laugh, seeing that he philosophized in horse and mule fashion.

With all these fine qualities, the Savages have another, more annoying than those of which we have spoken, but not so wicked; it is [120] their importunity toward strangers. I have a habit of calling these countries, "the land of importunity toward strangers," because the flies, which are the symbol and visible representation of it, do not let you rest day or night. During certain Summer months, they attack us with such fury, and so continually, that no skin is proof against their sting, and every one pays his blood as tribute. I have seen persons so swollen after being stung by them, that one would think they would lose their eyes, which can scarcely be seen; now all that is nothing, for this annoyance can be dispelled by means of smoke, which the flies cannot stand, but this remedy attracts the Savages, – if they know our dinner hour, they come purposely to get something to eat. They ask continually, and with such incessant urgency, that you would say that they are always holding you by the throat. If you show them anything whatever, however little it may be adapted to their use, they will say, "Dost thou love it? Give it to me."

A certain man said to me one day, that in his [121] country they did not know how to conjugate the verb *do*, in the present, and still less in the past. The Savages are so ignorant of this conjugation, that they would not give you the value of an obole, if they did not expect, so to speak, to get back a pistole; for they are ungrateful in the highest degree.

We have kept here and fed for a long time our sick Savage, who came and threw himself into our arms in order to die a Christian, as I have stated above. All his fellow-savages were astonished at the good treatment we gave him; on his account, his children brought a little Elk meat, and they were asked what they wished in exchange, for the presents of the Savages are always bargains. They asked some wine and Gunpowder, and were told that we could not give them these things; but that, if they wished something else that we had, we would give it to them very gladly. A good meal was given them, and finally they carried back their meat, since we did not give them what they asked for, threatening that they would come after their father, which they did; but the good man did not wish [122] to leave us. From this sample, judge of the whole piece.

Now do not think that they act thus among themselves; on the contrary, they are very grateful, very liberal, and not in the least importunate toward those of their own nation. If they conduct themselves thus toward our French, and toward other foreigners, it is because, it seems to me, that we do not wish to ally ourselves with them as brothers, which they would very much desire. But this would ruin us in three days; for they would want us to go with them, and eat their food as long as they had any, and then they would come and eat ours as long as it lasted; and, when there was none left, we would all set to work to find more. For that is the kind of life they live, feasting as long as they have something; but, as we know nothing about their mode of hunting, and as this way of doing is not praiseworthy, we do not heed them. Hence, as we do not regard ourselves as belonging to their nation, they treat us in the way I have described. If any stranger, whoever he may be, unites with their party, they will treat him as one of their own nation. A young Hiroquois whose [123] life they had spared, was like a child of their own family. But if you carry on your affairs apart from them, despising their laws or their customs, they will drain from you, if they can, even your blood. There is not an insect, nor wasp, nor gadfly, so annoying as a Savage.

I am rather tired of talking about their irregularities; let us speak of their uncleanness, and then end this chapter.

They are dirty in their habits, in their postures, in their homes, and in their eating; yet there is no lack of propriety among them, for everything that gives satisfaction to the senses, passes as propriety.

I have said that they are dirty in their homes; the entrance to their Cabins is like a pig-pen. They never sweep their houses, they carpet them at first with branches of pine, but on the third day these branches are full of fur, feathers, hair, shavings, or whittlings of wood. Yet they have no other seats, nor beds upon which to sleep. From this it may be seen how full of dirt their clothes must be; it is true that this dirt [124] and filth does not show as much upon their clothes as upon ours.

The Sorcerer leaving our Cabin for a while, asked me for my cloak, because it was cold, he said, as if I more than he were exempt from the rigors of Winter. I lent it to him, and, after having used it more than a month, he returned it to me at last so nasty and dirty, that I was ashamed of it, for it was covered with phlegm and other filth which gave it a different color. Seeing it in this condition, I purposely unfolded it before him, that he might see it. Knowing very well what I meant, he quite aptly remarked to me, "Thou sayest that thou wouldst like to be a Montagnais and Savage, like us; if that is so, do not be troubled about wearing the cloak, for that is just the way our clothes look."

As to their postures, they follow their own sweet wills, and not the rules of good breeding. The Savages never prefer what is decent to what is agreeable. I have often seen the pretended magician lie down entirely naked, – except a miserable strip of cloth dirtier than a dish-cloth, and blacker than an ovenmop, – draw up one of his [125] legs against his thigh, place the other upon his raised knee, and harangue his people in this position, his audience being scarcely more graceful.

As to their food, it is very little, if any, cleaner than the swill given to animals, and not always even as clean. I say nothing in exaggeration, as I have tasted it and lived upon it for almost six months. We had three persons in our Cabin afflicted with scrofula, – the son of the Sorcerer, whose ear was very disgusting and horrid from this disease; his nephew, who had it in his neck; and a daughter, who had it under one arm. I do not know whether this is the real scrofula; whatever it is, this sore is full of pus, and covered with a horrible-looking crust. They are nearly all attacked by this disease, when young, both on account of their filthy habits, and because they eat and drink indiscriminately with the sick. I have seen them a hundred times paddle about in the kettle containing our common drink; wash their hands in it; drink from it, thrusting in their heads, like the animals; and throw into it their leavings; for this is the custom of the Savages, to thrust sticks into it that are half-burned and covered with ashes; to dip therein [126] their bark plates covered with grease, the fur of the Moose, and hair; and to dip water therefrom with kettles as black as the chimney; and after that, we all drank from this black broth, as if it were ambrosia. This is not all; they throw therein the bones that they have gnawed, then put water or snow in the kettle, let it boil, and behold their hippocras. One day some shoes, which had just been taken off, fell into our drink; they soaked there as long as they pleased, and were withdrawn without exciting any special attention, and then the water was drunk as if nothing whatever had happened. I am not very fastidious, but I was not very thirsty as long as this malmsey lasted.

They never wash their hands expressly before eating, still less their kettles, and the meat they cook, not at all, – although it is usually (I say this because I have seen it hundreds of times) all covered with the animal's hairs, and with those from their own heads. I have never drunk any broth among them, from which I did not have to throw out many of these hairs, and a variety of other rubbish, such as cinders, little [127] pieces of wood, and even sticks with which they have stirred the fire and frequently stirred up the contents of the kettle. I have occasionally seen them take a blazing brand and put it in the ashes to extinguish it, then, almost without shaking it, dip it into the kettle where our dinner was simmering.

When they are engaged in drying meat, they will throw down upon the ground a whole side of the Moose, beat it with stones, walk over it, trample upon it with their dirty feet; the hairs of men and of animals, the feathers of birds, if they have killed any, dirt and ashes, – all these are ground into the meat, which they make almost as hard as wood with the smoke. Then when they come to eat this dried meat, all goes together into the stomach, for they have not washed it. In fact, they think that we are very foolish to wash our meat, for some of the grease goes away with the water.

When the kettle begins to boil, they gather the scum very carefully and eat it as a delicacy. They gave some to me as a favor, and during our famine I found it good; but since [128] then, when I sometimes happened to decline this present, they called me fastidious and proud. They take delight in hunting rats and mice, the same as rabbits, and find them just as good.

The Savages do not eat as we French do, from a dish or other vessel, common to all those at the table; but one of them takes down the kettle from the fire and distributes to each one his share; sometimes presenting the meat at the end of a stick, but oftener without taking this trouble, he will throw you a piece of meat boiling hot, and full of grease, as we would throw a bone to a dog; saying, *Nakhimitchimi*, "Take it! this is thy share, here is thy food." If you are quick, you catch it in your hands; otherwise, look out that your gown does not catch it, or that the ashes do not serve as salt, for the Savages have no other.

I found myself very much embarrassed, in the beginning; for not daring to cut the meat they gave me in my bark dish, for fear of spoiling the dish, I did not know how to manage it, not having any plate. Finally I had to become all to all, and a Savage with the Savages. I [129] cast my eyes upon my companion, then I tried to be as brave a man as he was. He took his meat in his open hand, and cut from it morsel after morsel, as you would do with a piece of bread. But if the meat is a little tough, or if it slips away from the knife from being too soft, they hold one end of it with their teeth, and the other with the left hand, then the right hand plays upon it in violin fashion, the knife serving as a bow. And this is so common among the Savages, that they have a word to express this action, which we could only explain with several words and by circumlocution. If you were to lose your knife, as there are no cutlers in these great forests, you are compelled to take your share in your two hands, and to bite into the flesh and into the fat, as bravely but not so politely, as you would bite into a quarter of an apple. God knows how the hands, the mouth, and a part of the face shine after this operation. The trouble was, I did not know upon what to wipe them. To carry linen with you would require a mule, or a daily [130] washing; for, in less than no time, everything is converted into dish-cloths in their Cabins. As to them, they wipe their hands upon their hair, which they allow to grow very long, or else, upon their dogs. I saw a woman who taught me a secret; she wiped her hands upon her shoes, and I did the same. I also used Moose fur, pine branches, and, especially, powdered rotten wood. These are the hand-towels of the Savages. One does not use them as pleasantly as a piece of Holland linen, but perhaps more gaily and joyously. Enough has been said of their filth.

13

Memoirs and Remarks ... Made in Above Ten Years Travels through the Empire of China

Louis Le Comte

Amongst the several models and plans of government which the ancients framed, we shall perhaps meet with none so perfect and exact as is that of the Chinese monarchy. The ancient lawgivers of this potent empire formed it in their days very little different from what it is in ours. Other states, according to the common fate of the things of this world, are sensible of the weakness of infancy, are born mishapen and imperfect; and, like men, they owe their perfection and maturity to time. China seems more exempted from the common laws of nature; and, as though God himself had founded their empire, the plan of their government was not a whit less perfect in its cradle, than it is now after the experience and trial of four thousand years.

During all which time the Chinese had never so much as heard of the name of republick; and when lately, on the Hollanders arrival, they heard of it, it seemed so strange to them that they have scarcely yet done admiring at it. Nothing could make them understand how a state could regularly be governed without a king; they looked upon a republick to be a monster with many heads, formed by the ambition, headiness, and corrupt inclination of men in times of publick disorder and confusion.

As they bear an aversion to republican government, so are they yet more set against tyranny

and oppression, which they say proceeds not from the absoluteness of the prince's power, for they cannot be too much their subjects masters; but from the prince's own wildness, which neither the voice of nature, nor the laws of God can ever countenance. The Chinese are of opinion, that the obligation, which is laid on their kings not to abuse their power, is rather a means to confirm and establish them, than to occasion their ruin; and that this useful constraint, which they themselves lay on their passions, does no more diminish their power or authority here on earth, than the like constraint derogates from the majesty and power of the Almighty, who is not the less powerful because he cannot do evil.

An unbounded authority which the laws give the emperor, and a necessity which the same laws lay upon him to use that authority with moderation and discretion, are the two props which have for so many ages supported this great fabrick of the Chinese monarchy. The first principle thereof, that is instilled into the people, is to respect their prince with so high a veneration as almost to adore him. They stile him the Son of Heaven, and the only Master of the World. His commands are indisputable, his words carry no less authority with them, than if they were oracles; in short, every thing that comes from him is sacred. He is

Louis Le Comte, *Memoirs and Remarks, Geographical, Historical, ... and Ecclesiastical. Made in Above Ten Years Travels through the Empire of China*, London: Olive Payne, 1738, pp. 248–51, 258, 262–3, 270–84.

seldom seen, and never spoken to but on the knees. The grandees of the court, the princes of the blood; nay, his own brothers bow to the ground, not only when he is present, but even before his throne; and there are set days every week or month, in which the nobility assemble, who meet in one of the courts of the palace, to acknowledge the authority of their prince by their most submissive adorations, tho' he perhaps be not there in person.

When he is ill, especially if dangerously, the palace is full of Mandarines of every order, who spend night and day in a large court, in habits proper for the occasion, to express their own grief, and to ask of Heaven their prince's cure. Rain, snow, cold, or any other inconveniences excuse them not from the performance of this duty; and, as long as the emperor is in pain or in danger, any one that saw the people would think that they fear nothing but the loss of him.

Besides, interest is no small occasion of the great respect which is shewn him by his subjects; for, as soon as he is proclaimed emperor, the whole authority of the empire is in his hands, and the good or ill fortune of his subjects is owing wholly to him.

First, all places in the empire are in his disposal, he bestows them on whom he thinks fit; and, besides, he is to be looked upon as the disposer of them the more, because none of them are ever sold. Merit, that is, honesty, learning, long experience, and especially a grave and sober behaviour, is the only thing considered in the candidates, and no other considerations can lay any claim to favour. Neither is this all, that he hath the choice of all officers of state; but, if he dislikes their management when chosen, he dismisses or changes them without more ado. A peccadillo has heretofore been thought enough to render a Mandarine incapable of continuing in his place; and I am told that a governor of one of their cities was turned out, because on a day of audience his cloaths were thought too gay to become the gravity of his office; the emperor thinking a person of that humour not fit to fill such a place, or to act as a magistrate who represents his prince.

I myself saw at Pekin an example of this sovereign power, at which I was the more surprized because it was brought about with so little disturbance. It was discovered that three

Colaos (who are Mandarines as honourable for their places amongst the Chinese, as our ministers of state are amongst us) had taken money under-hand for some services done by them in the execution of their office. The emperor, who was informed of it, took away their salaries immediately, and ordered them without farther trouble to retire. What became of the two first, or how they were used, I cannot tell; but the other, who had a great while been a magistrate, and was as much esteemed for his understanding as he was respected for his age, was condemned to look after one of the palace gates amongst other common soldiers, in whose company he was listed.

I saw him myself one day in this mean condition; he was upon duty as a common centinel; when I passed by him, I bowed to him, as indeed every one else did; for the Chinese still respected in him the slender remains of that honour which he had just before possessed.

[...]

One would imagine that this unlimited power should often occasion very unfortunate events in the government, and indeed it sometimes hath, as nothing in this world is without its alloy of inconvenience. Yet so many are the provisions, and so wise the precautions which the laws have prescribed to prevent them, that a prince must be wholly insensible of his own reputation, and even interest, as well as of the publick good, who continues long in the abuse of his authority.

[...]

Interest, which has a far greater command over some tempers than the love of reputation, is as great a motive to the emperor to be guided by the ancient customs, and to adhere to the laws. They are so wholly made for his advantage, that he cannot violate them without doing some prejudice to his own authority; nor can he make new and unusual laws, without exposing his kingdom to the danger of change and confusion. Not that the grandees of his court, or his parliaments, how zealously soever they may seem to assert their ancient customs, are easily provoked to a revolt, or to make use of their prince's government, as an occasion to diminish his authority. Altho' there are some examples of this in history, yet they seldom occur, and, whenever they do, it is under such circumstances as seem to go a great way towards their justification.

But such is the temper of the Chinese, that when their emperor is full of violence and passion, or very negligent of his charge, the same spirit of perverseness possesses also his subjects. Every Mandarine thinks himself the sovereign of his province or city, when he does not perceive it taken care of by a superior power. The chief ministers sell places to those who are unfit to fill them. The viceroys become so many little tyrants. The governors observe no more the rules of justice. The people by these means oppressed and trampled under foot, and by consequence miserable, are easily stirred up to sedition. Rogues multiply and commit insolences in companies; and in a country, where the people are almost innumerable, numerous armies do in an instant get together, who wait for nothing but an opportunity, under specious pretences, to disturb the publick peace and quiet.

Such beginnings as these have occasioned fatal consequences, and have oftentimes put China under the command of new masters. So that the best and surest way for an emperor, to establish himself in his throne, is to give an exact regard and an intire obedience to those laws, whose goodness hath been confirmed by the experience of more than four thousand years.

[...]

You will think it doubtless an inconceivable thing, that a prince should have time to examine himself the affairs of so vast an empire as is that of China. But besides that wars and foreign negotiations never spend his time, which in Europe is almost the sole business of the councils; besides this, I say, their affairs are so well digested and ordered, that he can with half an eye see to which party he ought to incline in his sentence, and this because their laws are so plain, that, they leave no room for intricacy or dispute. So that two hours a day is time enough for that prince to govern himself an empire of that extent, that were there other laws, might find employment for thirty kings; so true it is, that the laws of China, are wise, plain, well understood, and exactly adequate to the particular genius and temper of that nation.

To give your eminence a general notion of this, I shall think it sufficient to remark to you three things, which are exceeding conducive to the publick peace, and are as it were the very soul of the government. ...

The first moral principle respects private families, and injoins children such a love, obedience, and respect for their parents, that neither the severity of their treatment, the impertinency of their old age, nor the meanness of their rank, when the children have met with preferment, can ever efface. One can't imagine to what a degree of perfection this first principle of nature is improved. There is no submission, no point of obedience which the parents can't command, or which the children can refuse. These children are obliged to comfort them when alive, and continually to bewail them when dead. They prostrate themselves a thousand times before their dead bodies, offer them provisions, as tho' they were yet alive, to signify that all their goods belong to them, and that from the bottom of their hearts they wish them in a capacity to enjoy them. They bury them with a pomp and expence which to us would seem extravagant, they pay constantly at their tombs a tribute of tears, which ceremonies they often perform even to their pictures, which they keep in their houses with all imaginable care, which they honour with offerings, and with as due a respect as they would their parents, were they yet alive. Their kings themselves are not excused this piece of duty, and the present emperor has been observant of it, not only to his predecessors of his own family, but even to those who were not. For one day, when in hunting he perceived afar off the magnificent monument which his father had; erected for Tcoumtchin, the last Chinese emperor, who lost his life and crown in a rebellion, he ran to the place, and fell on his knees before the tomb, and even wept, and in a great concern for his misfortune: *O prince!* says he, *O emperor worthy of a better fate! you know that your destruction is no ways owing to us; your death lies not at our door, your subjects brought it upon you. It was them that betrayed you. It is upon them, and not on my ancestors, that Heaven must send down vengeance for this act.* Afterwards he ordered flambeaux to be lit, and incense to be offered. During all which time he fixed his countenance on the ground, and arose not till all these ceremonies were over.

The ordinary term of mourning is three years, during which time the mourner can exercise no publick office; so that a Mandarine is obliged to forsake his employ, and a minister of state his office, to spend all that time in grief. If a father be honoured after his death as a god, to be sure he is obeyed in his family like a prince, over whom he exercises a despotick power; as absolute master not only of his estate, which he distributes to whom he pleases, but also of his concubines and children, of whom he disposes with that liberty and power, that he may sell them to strangers when their behaviour displeases him. If a father accuses his son of any crime before a Mandarine, there needs no proof of it; it's supposed to be true, that the son is in the fault if the father be displeased. This paternal power is of that extent, that there is no father, but may take his son's life away, if he will stick to his accusation. When we seemed amazed at this procedure, we were answered: Who understands the merit of the son better than the father, who has brought him up, educated him, and such a long time observed all his actions? And again, can any person have a greater love, or a more sincere affection for him? If therefore he who knows the case exactly, and loves him tenderly, condemns him, how can we pronounce him guiltless and innocent? And when we objected, that some persons have an inbred dislike of others, and that fathers who were men, as well as fathers, were capable of such antipathies against some of their children; they answered, that men were not more unnatural than savage beasts, the cruellest of which never destroyed their young ones for a frolick; but supposing there be such monsters among men, their children, by their modesty and sweetness of temper, must tame and soften them. But after all, say they, the love of their children is so deeply imprinted in the hearts of parents, that antipathy, or dislike, unless provoked and inflamed by the undutiful stubbornness and disorderly behaviour of their children, can never erase.

If it should happen that a son should be so insolent as to mock his parents, or arrive to that height of fury and madness as to lay violent hands on them; it is the whole empire's concern, and the province where this horrible violence is committed is alarmed. The emperor himself judges the criminal. All the Mandarines near the place are turned out, especially those of that town, who have been so negligent in their instructions. The neighbours are all reprimanded for neglecting, by former punishments, to stop the iniquity of this criminal before it came to this height; for they suppose that such a diabolical temper as this must needs have shewed itself on other occasions, since it is hardly possible to attain to such a pitch of iniquity at once. As for the criminal there is no punishment which they think too severe: They cut him into a thousand pieces, burn him, destroy his house to the ground, and even those houses which stand near it, and set up monuments and memorials of this so horrible an insolence.

Even the emperors themselves can't reject the authority of their parents, without running the risque of suffering for it; and history tells us a story which will always make the affection which the Chinese have to this duty appear admirable. One of the emperors had a mother who managed a private intrigue with one of the lords of the court; the notice, which was publickly taken of it, obliged the emperor to shew his resentment of it, both for his own honour and that of the empire; so that he banished her into a far distant province; and because he knew that this action would not be very acceptable to his princes and Mandarines, he forbad them all, under pain of death, giving him advice therein. They were all silent for some time, hoping that of himself he would condemn his own conduct in that affair; but, seeing that he did not, they resolved to appear in it, rather than suffer so pernicious a precedent.

The first, who had the courage to put up a request to the emperor in this matter, was put to death on the spot. His death put not a stop to the Mandarines proceedings; for a day or two after another made his appearance, and, to shew all the world that he was willing to sacrifice his life for the publick, he ordered his hearse to stand at the palace gate. The emperor minded not this generous action, but was the rather more provoked at it. He not only sentenced him to death, but, to terrify all others from following his example, he ordered him to be put to the torture. One would not think it prudence to hold out longer. The Chinese were of another mind, for they resolved to fall one after another rather than basely to pass over in silence so base an action.

There was therefore a third who devoted himself; he, like the second, ordered his coffin to be set at the palace gate, and protested to the emperor that he was not able any longer to see him still guilty of his crime. *What shall we lose by our death*, says he, *nothing but the sight of a prince, upon whom we can't look without amazement and horror. Since you will not hear us, we will go and seek out yours and the empress your mother's ancestors. They will hear our complaints, and perhaps in the dark and silence of the night you will hear ours and their ghosts reproach you with your injustice.*

The emperor being more enraged than ever at this insolence, as he called it, of his subjects, inflicted on this last the severest torments he could devise. Many others, encouraged by these examples, exposed themselves to torment, and did in effect die the martyrs of filial duty, which they stood up for with the last drop of their blood. At last this heroick constancy wearied out the emperor's cruelty; and whether he was afraid of more dangerous consequences, or was himself convinced of his own fault; he repented, as he was the father of his people, that he had so unworthily put to death his children; and as a son of the empress, he was troubled that he had so long misused his mother. He recalled her therefore, restored her to her former dignity, and after that, the more he honoured her, the more was he himself honoured of his subjects.

The second moral principle, which obtains among them, is to honour their Mandarines as they would the emperor himself, whose person the Mandarines represent. To retain this credit the Mandarines never appear in publick without a retinue, and face of grandeur that commands respect. They are always carried in a magnificent chair open; before them go all the officers of their courts, and round them are carried all the marks and badges of their dignity. The people, wherever they come, open to the right and left to let them pass thro'. When they administer justice in their palaces, no body

speaks to them but on their knees, be they of what quality they will, and since they can at any time command any persons to be whipped, no one comes near them without trembling.

Heretofore, when any Mandarine took a journey, all the inhabitants of the towns thro' which he passed ran in a crowd to meet him, and proffer their services; conducting him with all solemnity thro' their territory: now when he leaves his office which he has administer'd to the satisfaction of all men; they give him such marks of honour; as would engage the most stupid to the love of virtue and justice. When he is taking his leave in order to lay down his office, almost all the inhabitants go in the highways, and place themselves some here, some there, for almost fourteen or fifteen miles together; so that every where in the road one sees tables handsomely painted, with sattin table-cloths, covered with sweet-meats, tea, and other liquors.

Every one almost constrains him to stay, to sit down and eat or drink something. When he leaves one, another stops him, and thus he spends the whole day among the applauses and acclamations of his people: and, which is an odd thing, every one desires to have something which comes from off him. Some take his boots, others his cap, some his great coat; but they, who take any thing, give him another of the same sort, and, before he is quit of this multitude, it sometimes happens that he has had thirty different pairs of boots on.

Then he hears himself called publick benefactor, the preserver and father of his people. They bewail the loss of him with wet eyes; and a Mandarine must be very insensible indeed, if he does not in his turn shed a tear or two, when he sees such tender marks of affection: for the inhabitants are not obliged to shew him this respect, and, when they do not like the administration of a governor, they shew themselves as indifferent at his departure, as they do affectionate and sorry at the loss of a good one.

The extraordinary respect which children pay to their parents, and people to their governors, is the greatest means of preserving quietness in their families, and peace in their towns; I am persuaded that all the good order, in which we see so mighty a people, flows from these two springs.

The third principle of morality established among them is this, that it is very necessary that all people should observe towards each other the strictest rules of modesty and civility; that they should behave themselves so obligingly and complaisantly, that all their actions may have a mixture of sweetness and courtesy in them. This, say they, is that which makes the distinction between man and beast, or between the Chinese and other men; they pretend also that the disturbance of several kingdoms is owing to the rough and unpolished temper of their subjects. For those tempers, which fly out into rudeness and passion, perpetually embroiled in quarrels, which use neither respect nor complaisance towards any, are fitted to be incendiaries and disturbers of the publick peace. On the contrary, people who honour and respect each other, who can suffer an injury, and dissemble or stifle it; who religiously observe that difference which either age, quality, or merit have made; a people of this stamp are naturally lovers of order, and when they do amiss it is not without violence to their own inclinations.

The Chinese are so far from neglecting the practice of this maxim, that in several instances they carry it on too far. No sort of men are excused from it; tradesmen, servants, nay, even countrymen have their ways of expressing kindness and civility to one another; I have often been amazed to see footmen take their leave of each other on their knees, and farmers in their entertainments use more compliments and ceremonies than we do at our publick treats. Even the seamen, who from their manner of living, and from the air they breathe, naturally draw in roughness, do yet bear to each other a love like that of brothers, and pay that deference to one another, that one would think them united by the strictest bands of friendship.

The state, which has always, in policy, accounted this as most conducive to the quiet of the empire, has appointed forms of salutation, of visiting, of making entertainments, and of writing letters. The usual way of salutation is to lay your hand cross your breast, and bow your head a little. Where you would still shew a greater respect, you must join your hands together, and carry them almost to the ground, bowing your whole body; if you pass by a person of eminent quality, or receive such an one into your house, you must bend one knee, and remain in that posture till he whom you thus salute takes you up, which he always does immediately. But when a Mandarine appears in publick, it would be a criminal sauciness to salute him in any sort of fashion, unless you have occasion to speak to him: you must step aside a little, and holding your eyes on the ground, and your arms cross your sides, stay till he be gone past you.

Altho' very familiar acquaintance make visits without any ceremony, yet for those friends, who are not so, custom has prescribed a set form of visiting. The visitor sends his servant before with a piece of red paper, on which is wrote his own name, and a great many marks of respect to the person he visits, according as his dignity or quality is. When this message is received, the visitor comes in, and meets with a reception answerable to his merit. The person visited sometimes stays for the visitor in the hall, without going out to meet him, or if he be of a much superior quality, without rising from his seat; sometimes he meets the visitor at his door; sometimes he goes out into the courtyard, and sometimes even into the street to bring him in. When they come into view, they both run and make a low bow. They say but little, their compliments are in form, one knows what he must say, and the other how he must answer; they never beat their brains, like us, to find out new compliments and fine phrases. At every gate they make a halt where the ceremonies begin afresh, and the bows are renewed to make each go first; they use but two ways of speaking on this occasion, which are Tsin; that is, Pray be pleased to enter; and Poucan. It must not be. Each of them repeats his word four or five times, and then the stranger suffers himself to be persuaded, and goes on to the next door, where the same thing begins anew.

When they come to the room where they are to stay, they stand near the door on a row, and every one bows almost to the ground; then follow the ceremonies of kneeling, and going on this or that side to give the right hand, then the chairs are saluted (for they have their compliments paid them as well as the men, they rub them to take all dust away, and bow in a respectful manner to them) then follow the contentions about the first place; yet all this makes no confusion. Use has made it natural to the Chinese, they know before what themselves, and what others are to do; every one stays till the others have done in their order what is expected, so that there happens no confusion or disturbance.

It must be owned that this is a great piece of fatigue, and after so many motions and different postures, in which they spend a quarter of an hour before they are to sit down, it must be own'd they have need enough of rest. The chairs are set so that every body sits opposite to one another; when you are sat, you must fit straight, not lean back, your eyes must look downward, your hands must be stretched on your knees, your feet even, not across, with a grave and composed behaviour, not be over-forward to speak. The Chinese think that a visit consists not in mutual converse so much as in outward compliment and ceremony, and in China the visitor may truly and properly say he comes to pay his respects, for oftentimes there are more honours paid than words spoken.

A missionary did aver to me, that a Mandarine made him a visit, in which he spoke never a word to him. This is always certain, that they never overheat themselves with discoursing, for one may generally say of them, that they are statues or figures placed in a theatre for ornament, they have so little of discourse and so much of gravity.

Their speech is mightily submissive and humble, you will never hear them say, for example, *I am obliged to you for the favour you have done me*, but thus, *the favour which my lord, which my instructor has granted to me, who am little in his eyes*, or *who am his disciple, has extremely obliged me*. Again, they don't say, *I make bold to present you with a few curiosities of my country*; but *the servant takes the liberty to offer to his lord a few curiosities which came from his mean and vile country*. Again, not *Whatsoever comes from your kingdom or province is well worked*; but *whatsoever comes from the precious kingdom, the noble province of the lord, is extraordinary fine, and exceeding well wrought*. In like manner in all other cases, they never say I or you in the first or second person; but *me your servant*,

me your disciple, me your subject. And instead of saying *you*, they say, *the doctor said, the lord did, the emperor appointed*. It would be a great piece of clownishness to say otherwise, unless to our servants.

During the visit the tea goes round two or three times, where you must use a ceremony when you take the dish, when you carry it to your mouth, or when you return it to the servant. When you depart it is with the same ceremonies with which you came in, and you conclude the comedy with the same expence you began it. Strangers are very uncouth at playing their parts herein, and make great blunders. The reasonable part of the Chinese smile at them and excuse them; others take exceptions at it, and desire them to learn and practise before they venture in publick: for this reason they allow ambassadors forty days to prepare for their audience of the emperor; and, for fear they should miss any ceremony, they send them, during the time allowed, masters of the ceremonies, who teach them, and make them practise.

Their feasts are ceremonious even beyond what you can imagine, you would think they are not invited to eat, but to make grimaces. Not a mouthful of meat is eaten, or a drop of wine drank but it costs an hundred faces. They have, like our concerts of musick, an officer who beats time, that the guests may all together in concord take their meat on their plates, and put it into their mouths, and lift up their little instruments of wood, which serve instead of a fork, or put them again in their places in order. Every guest has a peculiar table, without tablecloth, napkin, knife, or spoon; for every thing is ready cut to their hands, and they never touch any thing but with two little wooden instruments tipp'd with silver, which the Chinese handle very dexterously, and which serve them for an universal instrument.

They begin their feasts with drinking wine, which is given to every guest at one and the same time in a small cup of China or silver, which cup all the guests take hold of with both hands: every one lifts his vessel as high as his head, presenting their service thereby to one another without speaking, and inviting each other to drink first. It is enough if you hold the cup to your mouth only without drinking during the time while the rest drink; for, if the outward ceremonies are observed and kept, it is all one to them whether you drink or not.

After the first cup, they set upon every table a great vessel of hash'd meat, or Ragoo. Then every one observes the motions of the master of the feast, who directs the actions of his guests. According as he gives the sign, they take their two little instruments, brandish them in the air, and, as it were, present them, and after exercising them after twenty fashions, which I can't express, they strike them into the dish, from whence they cleaverly bring up a piece of meat, which must be eaten neither too hastily nor too slowly, since it would be a rudeness either to eat before others, or to make them stay for you. Then again they exercise their little instruments, which at length they place on the table in that posture wherein they were at first. In all this, you must observe time, that all may begin and end at once.

A little after, comes the wine again, which is drank with all the ceremonies aforesaid. Then comes a second mess, which they dip into as into the first, and thus the feast is continued until the end, drinking between every mouthful, till there have been twenty or four and twenty different plates of meat at every table, which makes them drink off as many cups of wine; but, we must observe, that besides that, I have said, that they drink as much or as little as they will at a time, their wine cups are very little, and their wine is small.

When all the dishes are served, which are done with all imaginable order, no more wine is brought, and the guests may be a little more free with their meat, taking indifferently out of any of these dishes before them, which yet must be done when the rest of the guests take out of some of their dishes, for uniformity and order is always sacred. At this time they bring rice and bread, for, as yet, nothing but meat has been brought; they bring likewise fine broths, made of flesh or fish, in which the guests, if they think fit, may mingle their rice.

They sit at table serious, grave, and silent, for three or four hours together. When the master of the house sees they have all done eating, he gives the sign to rise, and they go aside for a quarter of an hour into the hall or garden to entertain and divert themselves. Then they come again to the table, which they find set out with all sorts of sweet-meats, and dry'd fruits, which they keep to drink with their tea.

These customs, so strictly enjoin'd, and so extremely troublesome, which must be performed from one end to the other of the feast, keeps all the guests from eating, who do not find themselves hungry till they arise from the table. Then they have a great mind to go and dine at home; but a company of strollers come and play over a comedy, which is so tedious, that it wearies one as much as that before at the table did. Nor is tediousness the only fault, for they are commonly very dull and very noisy; no rules are observed, sometimes they sing, sometimes bawl, and sometimes howl, for the Chinese have little skill in making declamations. Yet, you must not laugh at this folly, but all the while admire at the politeness of China, at its ceremonies, instituted, as they say, by the discretion of the ancients, and still kept up by the wisdom of the moderns.

The letters, which are wrote from one to another, are as remarkable for their civilities and ceremonies, which are as many, and as mysterious as the others. They don't write in the same manner as they speak; the bigness of the characters, the distance between the lines, the innumerable titles of honour given to the several qualities of persons, the shape of the paper, the number of red, white, or blue covers for the letter, according to the person's condition, and a hundred other formalities, puzzle sometimes the brain of the most understanding men amongst them, for there is scarce any one who is secretary enough to write and send one of their letters as it ought to be.

There are a thousand other rules practised by the better sort in ordinary conversation, which you must observe, unless you would be accounted a clown; and tho' in a thousand instances these things favour more of a ridiculous affectation than of real politeness, no one can deny nevertheless, but that these customs, which people observe so exactly, do inspire into them a sweetness of temper, and a love of order. These three moral principles, that is, the respect which children pay their parents, the veneration which all pay the emperor and his officers, and the mutual humility and courtesy of all people, work their effect the better, because, supported by a wife and well-understood policy.

14

Customs of the American Indians Compared with the Customs of Primitive Times

Joseph François Lafitau

Journeys

I took particular pleasure in reading Apollonius of Rhodes' poem on the expedition of the Argonauts, because of the perfect resemblance which I find in all the rest of the work between these famous heroes of antiquity, and the present day barbarians, in their voyages and military undertakings. Hercules and Jason, Castor and Pollux, Zetes and Calais, Orpheus and Mopsus, and all those other half-gods, who rendered themselves immortal, and to whom people have burned incense only too readily, are so well represented by a troop of rascals and miserable savages that I seem to see [pass] before my eyes those famous conquerors of the Golden Fleece, but this resemblance lowers the conception which I had formed of the glory [of these heroes], and I am ashamed for the greatest kings and princes in the world that they have thought themselves honoured to be compared to them.

The famous ship Argo which has for anchor a … stone tied to a laurel root cord, to which Hercules' weight alone served as ballast and which the Argonauts carried on their shoulders for twelve days and twelve nights in the Lybian fables, has nothing to distinguish it from a dugout or at most from a long-boat (chaloupe). This Hercules himself who chose

his place on the benches with the others and took an oar in his hand, who plunged into the woods to make an oar of a little fir tree after breaking his; who, every time that they selected land to camp, lay on the shore, in the open air, on a bed of leaves or branches, is a savage in all ways and is not superior to them [the Indians].

Initiation to the Mysteries

But all the truths of religion were expressed more clearly and in a more significant manner in the ceremonies and tests of the mysteries than [they were] in the symbols and in some isolated customs of which we have just spoken, for, although there were mingled in them abominations and shameful things, like the *phalli* and *ithyphalli* and the holy debauches to which people abandoned themselves, so it is said, during these nocturnal mysteries and feasts hidden in the silence of the night; we can clearly discover that these were abuses which had slipped in and were diametrically [266] opposed to their initial spirit which was a spirit of death to oneself, of penance and sanctification.

The inviolable secrecy enjoined upon the participants makes it impossible to give any details of what happened in the initiations.

Joseph François Lafitau, *Customs of the American Indians Compared with the Customs of Primitive Times*, vol. I, ed. and trans. William Fenton and Elizabeth Moore, Toronto: The Champlain Society, 1974, pp. 116–17, 180–1, 186–9, 217–19, 283, 287–8, 290–9.

Even the secular authors, when they have a natural occasion to speak of them in their histories, stop respectfully, limit themselves to a religious silence and make profession of being silent on all those religious matters on which our curiosity would wish to be better informed and is most keenly aroused. Without entering into a detailed description which would have exposed or brought to light the secret of these mysteries, there are certain matters of which they have not left us in ignorance. From what they say, we can conclude that the initiations took in rather a long period of time and a number of different actions which can be reduced to certain capital points which prove the system which I have just advanced.

The initiations had, as it were, two different states. The first was a state of expiation and the second a state of sanctification and perfection and, it is, perhaps, these two states which made the distinction between what were called the great and the little mysteries.

[267] In the state of expiation which was truly one of penance, they [the initiates] kept themselves in retreat and silence; they fasted rigorously, abstained from the allowed pleasures of matrimony, made a confession of their sins, passed through many purifications representing the state of a mystical death and regeneration; finally, they underwent penalties which appeared to be a penance and an atonement for past sins.

For initiations of this sort, it was necessary to withdraw from the worldly occupations which might have offered distraction from the single-minded devotion due the things of God. For that purpose, there were places of retreat set apart where there was no communication with the secular world. These asylums were probably either in consecrated woods or within temple confines in which only those destined to the service of the altars dwelt.

As it appears by the solemn response required of the initiates, fasting was a necessary requirement for the initiations of the mysteries: *jejunavi* [I have fasted]: these fasts were extremely [268] strict, and, although we do not know precisely in what they consisted, it seems, nevertheless, that, in certain places, they lasted a very long time: that they [the

participants] abstained not only from the flesh of all living things but also from many other foods which might have appealed, no matter how little, to a delicate taste. The ancients were convinced that fasting, disengaging the soul from the material, rendered it more fitted to communicate with the gods.

It was the same with continence in which it was necessary to have lived for a certain length of time. That was called *in casto esse* [to be in a condition of chastity] and the initiates were required to take solemn oath that they had passed through this test. Those for whom continence was difficult lessened the pricking of the flesh by drinking hemlock; others put under their mats certain plants which they believed had the virtue of conserving chastity. This law was more or less extensive according to the places and the different conditions of the initiates. Some were obliged to observe it only for the time of the initiation; others made a profession of it for all their lives, but the priests of Cybele were forced to stop being men.

[...]

The soul, regenerated to a new life, had to pass to the state of perfection signified by the word τελετή applied to these mysteries because of the perfection which they were thought to give or rather to which they bound [the initiates]. This perfection consisted in a perfect disengagement from all fleshly things which it was necessary to renounce willingly, a disengagement in retreat from the pleasures of society, from the goods of the earth by the adoption of voluntary poverty, by asking for alms and by living from the altar according to the profession which they [the initiates] seemed to make in the solemn words, *tympano manducavi*: finally, it was necessary to put the soul into such a state of indifference that nothing could touch it. Suidas says that no one could be initiated until he had passed successively through the test of many torments, and given authentic testimony that he had acquired the perfection of saintliness, an apathy and a perfect insensibility to all things. Saint Gregory of Naziance speaks of these tests by the sword, by fire, etc., that people underwent in the mysteries of Mithra and he compares with them a fine example of Christian constancy in the person of Mark of Arethusa, a venerable old man who let himself be dragged by horses, trampled under foot, thrown in sewers and suffered all sorts of indignities, as ignominious as painful, without showing the least sign of displeasure.

[...]

There were, as it were, different orders in the initiations. Such hard tests were not, it seems, demanded of everyone, but also the knowledge of the mysteries was not communicated to all equally. The diviners, pythonesses, priests, idols who were to have, by their profession, a more intimate communication with the gods, also bought their knowledge by difficult tests; their initiation lasted much longer; and, even when they were initiated, they were forced to a greater austerity of life because of the dignity and holiness of their ministry.

Yet all underwent initiation. In some places the children were initiated but the most suitable age seems to have been that of puberty. Those who did not undergo initiation at that age did so unfailingly at least before death. The uninitiated were regarded as unholy, excluded from the temple of Ceres. It was a capital crime for them to enter it.

[...]

Application to the Americans of What Has Been Said of the Initiations of the Ancients

If I had to show the conformity of these initiations and mysteries of the ancients with the religions of the East Indies, of Japan and China, or even with those of such highly organized American nations as the Mexicans and Peruvians, I should have a vast field to cover, for no similarity is more clearly marked than [theirs] with the doctrine of the Mexican and Peruvian priests, but especially than that of the Brahmans, Bonzes and the Talapoins whom I think are the successors of the Egyptian priests, disciples of Isis and Osiris, and who are certainly successors of the Gymnosophysts of India, depositaries of the orgies of Bacchus; nothing is clearer than the conformity between their doctrine of the purification of souls and the Platonic ideas; their belief in sin is also characteristic and the manner of expiating it

by lustrations and a kind of confession similar to that of the ancients, is also found among the Gaures in Persia, the Brahmans, Japanese, Siamese, and Peruvians; the conformity is found, likewise in the perfection to which they aspire by the profession of a penitent, austere life, passed in fasts, abstinence, chastity, poverty, mortification [of the flesh] and finally in the practice of the virtues, virtues of which they possess in truth only the external appearance, but, in this appearance, they find the claim of an entirely holy origin. We take pleasure in reading in the works of the authors who have written on the subject how the young people were initiated in the schools of the Bonzes. In Mexico, there were communities of men and women where the young girls on the one hand and the young men on the other, all of them, without exception, were instructed for an entire year and lived under a regime so strict and rigid that no noviciate of a religious order in Europe could compare his ordeals with theirs.

[...]

Initiations of the Primitive Peoples of North America

The Huron, Iroquois and Algonquian tribes also have their initiations which they still celebrate. All that I know about them is that they are begun at the age of puberty; that they [the initiates] retreat into the woods, the youths under an elder or a shaman's direction, the young girls under a matron's. During this time, they fast very strictly; and, as long as their fast lasts, they blacken their faces, the tops of their shoulders and their chests. In particular, they pay careful attention to their dreams and report them exactly to those in charge of them. The latter examine, with scrupulous care, their pupils' conduct and confer often with the ancients about what concerns them or happens to them, to determine what they should take for their *Oïaron* or *Manitou* on whom the future happiness of their [the young peoples'] life must depend. They also draw conclusions to determine for what these initiates ought to be fitted in the future, so that the test is a sort of vocational one.

I have no doubt at all that their initiations and tests were almost like those of the Virginian tribes of which we spoke at first but, whether they had already lost many of their customs when the Europeans began to visit them, or whether they carefully concealed their mysteries which require as inviolable a secrecy as those of the ancients, a secrecy without which they believe that their tests would be ineffective and useless, or, finally, whether the Europeans were not careful enough in questioning them or capable of penetrating adequately the spirit of the rites which they saw performed, we lack any detailed account of them in the old Relations, and there remain only hints and general information but these are, nevertheless, adequate for us to formulate probable enough conjectures.

Fathers le Jeune and Brébeuf mention their fasts and retreats. The former speaks as follows:

"Now and then they [the Montagnais] observe a very strict fast, not all of them, but some who want to live a long time. My host, noticing that I ate only once a day during Lent, told me that some of their people fasted in order to have a long life; but he added that they withdrew alone into a little cabin apart from the others and, while there, they neither drank nor ate, sometimes for a week and, at other times for ten days. Others have told me that they emerge from this cabin [looking] like skeletons and that sometimes they are carried out half dead. I have not seen any of these great fasters but I have seen great diners. In truth I have no difficulty in believing in these excesses for all the false religions are full of childnesses, excesses and uncleannesses."

"I have seen," says the same writer, "another devotional ceremony performed by the sorcerer which I believe belongs only to those of his profession. A little cabin is erected for him, distant a stone's throw or two from the others. He retires into it to remain there alone eight or ten days, or more or less. Now, day and night, he can be heard crying, howling and beating his drum; but he is not so solitary that others do not go to help him sing and that the women do not go to visit him. It is there that many licentious deeds are committed."

Father le Jeune, as he himself confesses, understood the Indian language only very imperfectly. He reports very well on what he himself saw but he had to guess at the answers to his questions. People who do that tell things rather as they conceive them than as they actually are.

The Indians may well use their retreats wrongfully to cover their abominations. The ancients did the same thing in their bacchanals but that was an abuse contrary to the spirit of their retreat itself, one of the most essential conditions of which was continence; for, besides what I have said of their vestals and hermits, it is certain that there was a certain time which was and still is consecrated to it.

They [the Indians] have a high opinion of virginity and, among all the Indian tribes, there is either in their customs or language, something to indicate the esteem in which they hold it. The term signifying virgin in Abenaki is *Coussihouskoue* which translated literally means "the respected female," from *Coussihan*, a term which designates not only a respect of inner esteem but also a respect outwardly shown in behaviour. The term *Gaouinnon* which, in the Iroquois language also means a virgin is so ancient that we no longer know the meaning of its root.

They attribute to virginity and chastity certain particular qualities and virtues and it is certain that, if continence appears to them an essential condition for gaining success, as their superstition suggests to them, they will guard it with scrupulous care and not dare to violate it the least bit in the world for fear that their fasts and everything that they could do besides would be rendered useless by this non-observance.

They are persuaded that the love of this virtue extends as far as the natural sentiments of plants so that there are [among them] those which have a feeling of modesty as if they were animate; and so that, to be effective in remedies or even when the diviners are not called upon, they expect to be employed and put to work by chaste hands, lest they lose efficacy. Several [Indians] have said to me often, speaking of their illnesses, that they knew very well secrets for curing them but that, being married, they could no longer make use of them.

Father Brébeuf speaks thus of their diviners. "Formerly these offices of *Arendiouann* (that is to say, diviners) were valued more highly than they are to-day. They are now obtained by means of feasts. There was a time when it was necessary to fast thirty whole days in a cabin apart, without anyone's approaching it except a servant who to be worthy of carrying wood to it, prepared himself by fasting."

This is tantamount to saying that, by Father Brébeuf's time, they had already lost very many of their usages, or else that Father Brébeuf himself did not comprehend everything that came under his observation. In reality all those feasts of which he speaks are not at all contrary to the fast of the one for whom they are made. He cites us also an example [of one] which he witnessed which resembles closely the custom in antiquity since it is a question of an Indian who had dreamed, so he said, that he would become *Arendiouann* [a major Shaman] if he had fasted thirty days and who kept the whole tribe in suspense for all that time. He fasted eighteen of them without eating anything but tobacco. Father Brébeuf thought him daft and that this [time of] fasting had finally driven him completely mad. Nevertheless, there were several feasts in his honour and, in the last one, a detailed account of which Father Brébeuf excused himself from giving for fear of being too long-winded, he adds that, for the present, it is sufficient to say in general "that never did frenzied Bacchantes of bygone times, do anything more furious in their orgies."

The Indians have lost still more of their customs since that time, a fact which they themselves recognize and regret for, in the misfortunes which have come upon them, they say that they ought not to complain and that they are being punished for having abandoned the practices of retreats and fasts.

[...]

Political Government

Different forms of government
Monarchical government

No less an injustice has been done the American Indians in the representation of them as barbarians without laws or police than in the statement that no traces of religion were to be found among them. Each tribe has its own form of government. In some of the tribes we see the monarchical state in its perfection with a great respect for the king and an absolute submission to all his wishes. In Mexico and Peru, the sovereigns were respected to the point of adoration. Today, some peoples of Louisiana seem to honour their chiefs with a religious and divine cult as images of the divinity and even as divinities. All of them, even the chiefs of the nomadic tribes of the Algonquian language family and the primitive peoples of South America affect a despotic authority of which they are so jealous that they would expose themselves to destruction rather than unite with one another for fear of losing part of their authority. Each one of these petty kings forms a state from one little river to the other. This river often bears the name of the chief and of his village. I imagine that a similar situation existed in ancient times and gave rise to the belief in the metamorphosis of these kings into rivers to which they gave the name of *Cornigeri*, as a mark of their sovereignty.

[...]

Government of the Iroquois and Huron

Whatever the origin of the Iroquois and Huron may be, they have kept this form of government in its first simplicity for, besides this gynocracy which is exactly the same as that of the Lycians, in which the care of affairs is in the men's hands only by way of procuration, all the villages govern themselves in the same way, by themselves, and as if they were independent of each other. We see also, in each, the same distribution of families, the same civil laws, the same order so that anyone who sees one, sees them all. When, however, affairs of interest to the whole of the tribe are to be discussed, they unite in a general council to which the deputies of each village go. This is done with so much equality and zeal for the common welfare that there results from it a harmony and an admirable unanimity which works for the safety of the tribe and which, for that reason, nothing can break asunder.

Of Families or Clans

That is only a general sketch of their government. To come now to a more fully detailed account, each village is divided into three families as I have said; namely, those of the Wolf, the Bear and the Turtle. Each family has its chiefs, Agoïanders, elders, warriors. United all together these comprise the [governing] body of the village and form the state in their republic.

These families are what the clans were formerly and we shall sometimes use this name to indicate them. The origin of these clans is very ancient and the term, in its original meaning, denotes the number of the divisions which existed, in the earliest times, among the greatest number of peoples; whether, by them, one meant to distinguish three different branches from the same stock [465] which could be traced back to Noah's three children whose posterity is intermingled in several places or whether they were, indeed, three different peoples, united, as were in the foundation of Rome, the Rhamnesians, Tatienses, and Lucerians whose chiefs were Romulus, Tatius and Lucumon.

[...]

In the course of years the name clan has been employed indifferently to signify all the branches of the same family in whatever number they may be, as names were made use of in cities no longer to mark the peoples' divisions but the different quarters of those same cities where the number of the people had multiplied considerably.

As for the Iroquois, they have always been few in number, and, as the necessity of transporting themselves elsewhere when their land is worn out, has forced them to divide into many villages rather than to starve because of the overpopulation in a single one, they have kept their former division and only the family of the Turtle has been subdivided into large and small.

Of the Chiefs

Each clan has its chief, as their kings were called, whether they are the Archagetes of the two families of the Heraclidae or the chiefs, Romulus, Tatius and Lucumon, of the three families in Rome. The names given these chiefs mark their preeminence over their clan. Besides the names which they, like other individuals, bear, they have still others, which are those indicating dignity and jurisdiction.

The first of these is *Roiander Gôa*, meaning "noble par excellence," from *gaïander*, the usual word meaning nobility. The second is that of the clans themselves, which they represent and which are, as it were, collected in their person. It is in this sense that they say the *Hoghouaho*, the *Hoskereouak*, the *Hannoouara*, that is, the [Great] Wolf, the [Great] Bear, the [Great] Turtle "has said," "has done," etc. By this form of speech, they signify equally and without equivocation, the chiefs, clans and lands dependent on them. These names will doubtless appear ridiculous to us, but, if we consider that, in antiquity, the peoples' names were, as we have said, the names of the divinity and that these were the names of the animals, which were his symbol, we shall doubtless have another impression. With the Mendesians, for example, who represented Pan under the figure of a he-goat, to say "Mendes has said," is a way of saying (the same thing as) "Pan has said," "God has said," and, it seems to me that nothing is better fitted to give us an idea of the royalty or authority of the peoples' chiefs than the idea and even the expressions used by the peoples in speaking of their chiefs as if they were talking of the divinity in his own name. The third name is that of *Roksten Gôa*, meaning "the Old Man," or the "Ancient par Excellence." This name is not always suitable to the age of the person designated, for he is often only an infant but it is appropriate to the character with which they endow the one whom they wish to conciliate with respect and veneration by [calling him by] a name which indicates maturity, wisdom and all the other qualities suitable to those who, by their rank and preeminence are, as it were, the fathers and pastors of the people, as Homer calls them. Finally they take the proper name of the land itself: thus, among the Onnontagués [Onondaga], Sagosendagété [Name-Bearers], and, among the Tsonnonontouans, [Big Hills People-Seneca], *Tsonnonkeritaoui* and *Te-Ionninnokaraouen*, [He holds open the door], are names proper to the country and some of its chiefs, particularly to village chiefs.

For, although the chiefs appear to have equal authority, and are extremely careful not to appear to take upon themselves [too many] duties and make themselves despotic, there are always, nevertheless, some of them preeminent over the others; and these are, as nearly as I can judge, either the one whose household [lineage] has founded the village, or the one whose clan is most numerous or the one who is ablest. I confess, however, that I cannot always (very well) decide which one it is.

The chief's dignity is perpetual and hereditary in his lodge [maternal household], passing always to his aunt's children or his sisters' or his nieces' on the maternal side. From the moment that the tree has fallen, it is necessary, they say, to raise it up again. The matriarch, after conferring with [the members of] her household, confers again with those of her clan to whom she makes acceptable the one chosen for the succession, a choice which she is free to make. She does not always consider the right of age and usually selects the one best fitted, by his good qualities, to hold this rank. When the choice has been made, the nomination is made in the village by wampum belts. The one chosen is exhibited there, and, as soon as he is shown, he is immediately proclaimed and recognized. He is proclaimed in the same way and exhibited in the other villages of the Iroquois Nation and all the other allied nations. This act is always accompanied by festivals and solemnities. The other tribes have almost the same manner of having a chief recognized.

After the tree is thus reerected, if the one elected is still young and incapable of directing affairs by himself, they add roots to the tree to sustain it and keep it from falling; that is, they give him what the Spartans used to call ΠΡΟΔΙΚΟΣ, a tutor or regent, just as we do today in monarchical states, during the heir's minority. This tutor is recognized and proclaimed everywhere at the same time as his pupil and is charged personally, in this pupil's name, with all that the latter would have to do for the public good if his age rendered him capable of it.

The chiefs' authority properly extends over the people of their clan whom they consider their children. They usually call them their nephews. They rarely use a term corresponding to that of subject. Although they have a real authority which some know how to use, they still affect to give so much respect to liberty that one would say, to see them, that they are all equal. While the petty chiefs of the monarchical states have themselves borne on their subjects' shoulders and have many duties paid them, they have neither distinctive mark, nor crown, nor sceptre, nor guards, nor consular axes to differentiate them from the common people. Their power does not appear to have any trace of absolutism. It seems that they have no means of coercion to command obedience in case of resistance. They are obeyed, however, and command with authority; their commands, given as requests, and the obedience paid them, appear entirely free. This freedom serves to hold the chiefs in check. It engages them to command nothing which might cause trouble and be followed by a refusal. It serves also to cause the inferiors to execute with good grace all orders given so that they can persuade themselves that they obey less because they are commanded to do so than because they are quite willing to obey orders. Good order is kept by this means; and, in the execution of things, there is found a mutual adaptation of chiefs and members of society and a hierarchy such as could be desired in the best regulated state.

Although the chiefs have no mark of distinction and superiority so that, except in a few individual cases, they cannot be distinguished from the crowd by the honours due to be paid them, people do not fail to show always a certain respect for them. It is especially in public affairs that their dignity is sustained. The councils assemble by their orders; they are held in their lodges unless there is a public lodge like a town hall, reserved only for councils; business is transacted in their names; they preside over all sorts of meetings; they play a considerable role in feasts and community distributions; they are often given presents; and, finally, they have certain other prerogatives resulting from their preeminent status, as also they have certain onerous duties which serve to counterbalance the slight advantages which they may have in other respects.

Of the Agoïanders

Lest the chiefs usurp too great authority and make themselves too absolute, they are checked, as it were, by being given deputies who share with them the sovereignty of the territory and are called also the *Agoïanders*. These Agoïanders are almost what the Ephori were at Sparta and the Cosmes on the Isle of Crete, in their origin, and before the latter had usurped an authority which blotted out that of the kings. The Agoïanders are subordinated to the chief one who is their leader and is called *Roïander Gôa* to denote his preeminence. In each clan, each individual and distinct matrilineage has one person who acts as representative for it. The women choose them and are often in this position themselves. Their duty is to watch more immediately over the nation's interest; to keep an eye on the funds or public treasury; to provide for its conservation and watch over the use which should be made of it. When they have been chosen, they are recognized in the councils but they are not shown before the allied nations as is the custom and practice for the chiefs.

The senate

After the Agoïanders comes the senate, composed of the Old Men or Old People, called, in their language, *Agokstennha*. The number of these senators is not fixed. Each person has the right to enter the Council to vote when he has reached the age of maturity which has (attributed to it) as a prerogative, wisdom and an understanding of affairs. There, as elsewhere, each one knows how to make himself esteemed according to his skill.

The warriors

The fourth and last body is that of the *Agoskenrhagete* or warriors, composed of young people in condition to bear arms. The chiefs of the tribes [clans] are usually the leaders when they have passed their tests of military exercises and are capable of command. But, beside that, there are also recognized as war chiefs those who deserve commendation and have given proofs of valour, good conduct and service.

[Number of offices]

In all states, offices had to be multiplied (whatever the form of government) as the people multiplied and became more difficult to govern because of their greater number. Then it became necessary to divide up the authority with the requisite subordination, putting part of it into different hands to hold the subjects to their duty. The Iroquois, always few in number, never needed that multitude of inferior magistrates who owe their origin only to the fact that there was indispensable need of them elsewhere. Their chiefs and senate have always been sufficient for them as they were for all peoples in their (first) beginnings. They can all take part in the government without being in the way; no one is excluded from the Senate from the moment that his age gives him entree to the Council. By this means, the people are protected from the too aggressive who attain posts through ambition and intrigue and make the people victims of their ambition.

Councils

The women are always the first to deliberate or who should deliberate, according to their principles on private or community matters. They hold their councils apart and, as a result of their decisions, advise the chiefs on matters on the mat, so that the latter may deliberate on them in their turn. The chiefs, on this advice, bring together the old people of their clan and, if the matter which they are treating concerns the common welfare, they all gather together in the general Council of the Nation.

The warriors also have their council apart for matters within their competence but all the individual councils are subordinate to that of the Old People which is the superior council, as it were.

[The Council of elders]

This Council has closed and open sessions. The former are held to deliberate on their different interests of whatever nature they may be, the latter to announce their decisions publicly or dispose of all other business of the nation which requires some ceremony, such as receiving ambassadors, replying to them, declaring (chanting) war, mourning for the dead [Condolence Council], holding festivals, etc.

Those who are to attend the Secret Council are individually notified. The council fire is always lighted, either in the public lodge or in those of the chiefs which, for that reason, usually have five or even seven fires, that is are four or six compartments longer than those having only one fire.

Although there is no regular time for holding those councils, people usually go to them at nightfall. The Senate has, certainly, none of the august majesty of that of the Roman Republic [in the days] immediately before [the time of] the Caesars but I believe that it is not at all inferior to that of Rome herself when she went to take the plough from the Serrans and Cincinnati to make them consuls and dictators. They are a troupe of dirty men seated on their backsides, hunched up like monkeys, with their knees up to their ears, or lying in different positions, either flat on their backs or with their stomachs in the air, who, all of them, pipes in their mouths, treat affairs of state with as much coolness and gravity as the Junta of Spain or the Council of the Sages [Council of the Ten] at Venice.

Council of the old people

Almost no one except the Ancients is present at these councils and has a deliberative voice in them. The chiefs and Agoïanders would be ashamed to open their mouths in them, if they did not have, joined to their dignity, the advantages of age. If they are present at them, it is rather to listen and inform themselves than to speak. The very chiefs who are most respected both because of their ability and age, defer so much, through respect, to the Senate's authority, that they do nothing except report themselves or through their people, the subject to be set forth. After this, they always conclude by saying, "Think it over yourselves, Ye Ancients, Ye are the masters: order."

The manner of deliberation is with slowly rising emphasis and great maturity of treatment. Each of the opposing sides first takes up the proposition in a few words and sets forth

all the reasons which have been alleged pro and con by those who first expressed their opinion. He then states his own opinion and concludes with these words: "That is my thought on the subject of this, our Council." To this, all the members of the assembly answer *hoo* or *etho*, that is to say "that is good" whether he has spoken well or badly.

After their deliberation on whatever subject it may be, there is almost no reason, for or against, which they have not seen or weighed and, when they want to take account of their decision, they make it so plausible that it is difficult not to interpret it in the way that they do. In general, we may say that they are more patient than we in examining all the consequences and results of a matter. They listen to one another more quietly, show more deference and courtesy than we toward people who express opinions opposed to theirs, not knowing what it is to cut a speaker off short, still less to dispute heatedly: they have more coolness, less passion, at least to all appearances, and bear themselves with more zeal for the public welfare. Also it has been by a most refined policy that they have gained the ascendancy over the other nations, that they have gained the advantage over the most warlike after dividing them, rendered themselves formidable to the most distant, and maintain themselves today in a state of tranquil neutrality between the French and English by which they have been able to make themselves both feared and sought after.

What I say of their zeal for the public good is still not so universal that many do not think of their private interests and that the chiefs principally do not bring into play many secret activities to gain success in their intrigues. There are some who play the game so skilfully and surely that they cause the council to deliberate many days in succession on a matter all decided between them and the principal heads before it was put on the mat. As the chiefs consider one another, however, and as none wishes to appear to arrogate to himself any superiority which might arouse jealousy, they manage themselves more than others in the councils; and, although they may be its guiding spirit (soul), political expediency obliges them to talk little and listen to others' opinions rather than express their own; but each one has at hand a man who is a kind of incendiary, as it were, and who, being without concern for his person, dares to say quite freely all that he thinks *à propos*, as he has agreed with the chief for whom he acts before entering the council session.

Orators

Usually the orators perform that role. The chiefs know how to gain ascendancy over their minds and take advantage of their facility in speaking and saying all that they wish.

But it is principally in the public councils and solemn transactions that the orators appear brilliant. They alone speak in them, their duty properly consisting in announcing all the business which has been discussed in the secret councils, in declaring the results of all deliberations and in bearing the news authoritatively in the name of the entire village and nation.

This role is not easy to sustain. It demands a great capacity, the knowledge of councils, a complete knowledge of all their ancestors' ways, wit, experience and eloquence. Not considered at all in the qualifications is whether they are of a ranking maternal household; their personal merits and talents are the only things considered. It is rare to find persons who fill this post worthily. Scarcely one or two in a village fulfil it even passably. Recourse must often be had to the people of other villages and nothing is neglected to attract outsiders capable of carrying on this work well who have gained some reputation in it.

These orators' discourses do not consist of long harangues, composed on the model of those of Demosthenes or Cicero. The Iroquois, like the Lacedaemonians with a quick and concise discourse. Their style is, however, full of figures of speech and quite metaphorical; it is varied according to the different nature of the business. On certain occasions, it gets away from ordinary language and resembles our courtly style; on others, it is sustained by a keener action than that of our actors on the stage. They have, withal, a capacity for mimicry; they speak with gestures as much as with

the voice and act out things so naturally as to make them seem to take place under their audience's eyes.

The orator has, near him, one or two persons to remind him of what he is to say, to refresh his memory on what decisions have been reached and to watch that he says things in the proper order. This is done, however, with courtesy and without interruptions.

But he himself, during his discourse, is careful to ask the assembly, from time to time, if he has announced things well, in the way in which they should be heard and have been decided. Several of the Council respond to him by an *etho* of approbation. He takes advantage also of pauses to consult his assistants. After his report follows the *nio-hen*, the general cry of consent. It is done in this way. One of the Old Men cries; "*nio-hen?*" All the others answer "*nio*." This is done three times in each clan's name. That is the kind of formula to ask whether everyone is satisfied but it is really done only as a form, for everyone always answers "yes." It seems, however, set up in such a way as to give opportunity to those who would judge it a proper time to make remonstrance or protest.

The women have their orators who speak for them in the public councils. Sometimes also they choose an orator among the men who speaks as if he were a woman and sustains that role but that is seldom done except in foreign affairs or meetings of the confederated tribes [Council of the League].

When the orators have wit and *savoir faire* they gain a great deal of credit and authority. The famous Garakontié who has served religion and the French colony so well was only an orator at Onnontagué [Onondaga]: and this man was so much respected by his people that he managed the Five Iroquois Nations as he wished. We read of the Lycians that they had similar orators equally well accredited when they were skilful enough to gain esteem. At the time of the war of the Triumvirate it was one of these orators named Nancrates who kept the Lycians from entering into an alliance with Brutus and Cassius who then forced them to defend their country's corridor by force of arms against the troops of Caesar's two famous murderers and, by doing this, brought about the ruin of the Xanthians of which we have already spoken.

Affairs of state

Men, being everywhere the same and born with the same good or bad qualities the affairs treated in the Council of the Indians are of almost the same nature as those which our jurisprudence and politics in Europe comprise. There are purely civil matters, regulatory and criminal, and other matters which are properly affairs of state, such as making war or peace, sending or receiving ambassadors, contracting new alliances or strengthening old ones.

Section IV

(b) Globetrotters

15

Travels in Persia, 1673–1677

John Chardin

Of the Temper, Manners, and Customs of the Persians

The *Persian* Blood is naturally thick; it may be seen by the *Guebres*, who are the remainder of the ancient *Persians*; they are homely, ill shap'd, dull, and have a rough Skin, and an Olive Complexion. The same Thing is observ'd also in the Provinces next the *Indus*, whereof the Inhabitants are little better shap'd than the *Guebres*, because they marry only amongst them: But in the other Parts of the Kingdom, the *Persian* Blood is now grown clearer, by the mixture of the *Georgian* and *Circassian* Blood, which is certainly the People of the World, which Nature favours most, both upon the Account of the Shape and Complexion, and of the *Boldness* and *Courage*; they are likewise *Sprightly*, *Courtly* and *Amorous*. There is scarce a Gentleman in *Persia*, whose Mother is not a *Georgian*, or a *Circassian* Woman; to begin with the King, who commonly is a *Georgian*, or a *Circassian* by the Mother's side; and whereas, that Mixture begun above a hundred Years ago, the Female kind is grown fairer, as well as the other, and the *Persian* Women are now very *handsome*, and very well *shap'd*, tho' they are still inferior to the *Georgians*: As to the Men, they are commonly *Tall*, *Straight*, *Ruddy*, *Vigorous*, have a good Air, and a pleasant Countenance. The Temperateness of their Climate, and the Temperance they are brought up in, do not a little contribute to their Shape and Beauty. Had it not been for the Alliance before mention'd, the Nobility of *Persia* had been the ugliest Men in the World; for they originally came from those Countries between *China* and the *Caspian* Sea, call'd *Tartary*; the Inhabitants whereof being the homeliest Men of *Asia*, are short and thick, have their Eyes and Nose like the *Chinese*, their Face flat and broad, and their Complexion yellow, mix'd with black.

As to the Natural Parts, the *Persians* have them as beautiful as their Bodies; their Fancy is lively, quick and fruitful; their Memory easy and copious; they have a ready disposition to Sciences, and to the *Liberal* and *Mechanick Arts*, and to *War* also; they love *Glory*, or rather *Vanity*, which is only the Shadow of it; they are of a tractable and complying Temper, of an easy and plodding Wit; they are *courtly*, *civil, complisant*, and *well-bred*; they have naturally an eager bent to *Voluptuousness, Luxury, Extravagancy*, and *Profuseness*; for which Reason, they are ignorant both of Frugality and Trade. In a Word, they are born with as good natural Parts as any other People, but few abuse them so much as they do.

They are true Philosophers on the account of Riches, and the Misfortunes of the World,

John Chardin, *Travels in Persia, 1673–1677*, New York: Dover Publications, 1988, pp. 183–97.

and on the Hope and Fear of a Future State; they are little guilty of Covetousness, and are only desirous of getting, that they may spend it; they love to enjoy the Present, and deny themselves nothing that they are able to procure, taking no Thought for the Morrow, and relying wholy on Providence, and their own Fate; they firmly believe it to be sure and unalterable, and carry themselves honestly in that respect; so when any Misfortune happens to them, they are not cast down, as most Men are, they only say quietly, *Mek toub est, i.e.* That is written, or, it is ordained, that that should happen.

Twenty Years ago, it was the Opinion of several People in *Europe*, and of the most Noted and most Understanding Men, that the *Persians* would embrace the fair Opportunity of the *Turks* great Defeat to recover *Babylon* from them; and that they would declare War with the *Sultan*, now they saw him so low, beaten every where, and losing such large Countries. And I always said on the contrary; That I was sure they would take no Notice of it, because 'tis the Humour of the *Persians*, above all things, to value Life, and to enjoy it. They have lay'd by their Warlike Temper, and have given themselves up to Wantonness, which they don't suppose can be found in a great Bustle, and in dubious and laborious Undertakings.

Those Men are the most lavish Men in the World, and the most careless of the Morrow, as I said just now. They cannot keep Money; and whatever Riches fall to them, they waste all in a very little time. Let, for Instance, the King give fifty or a hundred thousand Livres to any Man, he lays it out in less than a Fortnight, in buying Slaves of both Sexes; in hiring handsome Wives; in setting up a noble Equipage; in furnishing a House, or cloathing himself richly: And so spends the whole Sum so fast, without any regard to the Time to come, that unless some new Supplies intervene in two or three Months time, our Gentleman will be forced to sell again his whole Equipage by Piece-meal, beginning with his Horses; then his needless Servants; then his Concubines and Slaves; and lastly, even his own Cloaths. I have seen a thousand Instances of that Kind, one of them amongst the rest is very strange; An Eunuch who had been long Lord High Chamberlain, and for two Years the declared Favourite, the power of disposing of all Posts and Employments, and commanding as if himself had been King, and who consequently had frequent and favourable Opportunities of heaping up vast Riches, was turn'd out of Favour, but however not out of his Estate. Two Months were scarce elaps'd, but he was forc'd to borrow Money upon Pawns, his Credit was at an End, as well as his Money; not but that he had acquired vast Riches, but he wasted them as fast as he got them.

The most commendable Property of the Manners of the *Persians*, is their kindness to Strangers; the Reception and Protection they afford them, and their Universal Hospitality, and Toleration, in regard to Religion, except the Clergy of the Country, who, as in all other Places, hate to a furious Degree, all those that differ from their Opinions. The *Persians* are very civil, and very honest in Matters of Religion; so far that they allow those who have embraced theirs, to recant, and resume their former Opinion; whereof, the *Cedre*, or *Priest*, gives them an Authentick Certificate for Safety sake, in which he calls them by the Name of *Apostat*, which amongst them is the highest Affront. They believe that all Men's Prayers are good and prevalent; therefore, in their Illnesses, and in other Wants, they admit of, and even desire the Prayers of different Religions: I have seen it practis'd a thousand Times. This is not to be imputed to their Religious Principles, tho' it allows all sorts of Worship; but I impute it to the sweet Temper of that Nation, who are naturally averse to Contest and Cruelty.

The *Persians* having the Character of *Wanton* and *Profuse*; one may easily believe them to be *Lazy* also; those two Properties being inseparable. Their Aversion to Labour is the most common Occasion of their Poverty. The *Persians* call the Lazy, and Unactive Men, *Serguerdan*, i.e. turning the Head this Way, and that Way. Their Language is full of those Circumlocutions; as for Instance, to express a Man reduced to a Mendicant State, they say, *Gouch Negui Micoret*, he eats his Hunger.

The *Persians* never Fight; all their *Anger*, being not blustering and passionate, as in our

Country, goes off with ill Language; and what's very Praiseworthy, is, that, what Passion soever they be in, and among whatever profligate Wretches they may light, still they Reverence God's Name, and he is never blasphemed. That Nation cannot conceive how the *Europeans*, when they are in a Passion can disown God; tho' they themselves are very often guilty of taking his Name in vain, without any Need or Provocation; their usual Oaths are, *By the Name of God*; *By the Spirits of the Prophets*; *By the Spirits*, or the *Genius of the Dead*; as the *Romans* swore, *By the Genius of the Living*. The Gentlemen and Courtiers commonly swear, *By the King's Sacred Hand*, which is the most inviolable Oath. The common Affirmations are, *Upon my Head*, *Upon my Eyes*.

Two opposite Customs are commonly practis'd by the *Persians*; that of praising God continually, and talking of his Attributes, and that of uttering Curses, and obscene Talk. Whether you see them at Home, or meet them in the Streets, going about Business or a Walking; you still hear them uttering some Blessing or Prayer, such as, *O most great God*; *O God most praiseworthy*; *O merciful God*; *O nursing Father of Mankind*; *O God forgive me*, or, *help me*. The least Thing they set their Hand to do, they say, *In the Name of God*; and they never speak of doing any thing, without adding, *If it pleases God*. Lastly, they are the most devout, and most constant Worshippers of the God-head; and at the same time, come out of the same Men's Mouths a thousand obscene Expressions. All Ranks of Men are infected with this odious Vice. Their Bawdy talk is taken from Arse, and C—t, which Modesty forbids one to Name; and when they intend to abuse one another, they invent some nasty Trick of one another's Wives, tho' they never saw or heard of them; or wish they may commit some Nastiness. 'Tis so among the Women, and when they have spent their Stock of bawdy Names, they begin to call one another *Atheists*, *Idolaters*, *Jews*, *Christians*; and to say to one another, *The Christians Dogs are better than thou, may'st thou serve for an Offering to the Dogs of the Franks*.

Men of all Ranks, as is beforemention'd, are observ'd to use such filthy Expressions,

but not so common, and to that degree; for I must confess, that the Mobb is generally infected with it. The first time I waited on the Lord Steward of the King's Household, in the Year 1666, the *Persian* Court being in *Hircania*, a Man of Distinction came to him about some Business, the Lord Steward said to him, why don't you go to the first Minister, to whom I have already sent you back; the Man Answer'd very Modestly; *My Lord, I have been there, and he told me, that your Majesty* (they give that Title to the Nobles as well as to the King) *is to determine the Matter*; *Gaumicoret*, answer'd he, *I wonder'd to hear the Lord Steward speak in that Manner of the first Minister*; for the Word *Gau*, signifies a Turd, and *Micoret*, he eats: That's the usual Expression amongst them, to intimate a wrong or false Answer.

That's one of the least Faults of the *Persians*; they are besides, Dissemblers, Cheats, and the basest and most impudent Flatterers in the World. They understand Flattering very well; and tho' they do it with Modesty, yet they do it with Art, and Insinuation. You would say, that they intend as they speak, and would swear to it: Nevertheless, as soon as the Occasion is over, such as a Prospect of Interest, or a Regard of Compliance, you plainly see that all their Compliments were very far from being sincere. They take an Opportunity of praising Men, when they come out of a House, or pass by them, so that they may be heard; and they speak so seasonably, that the Praise seems to come naturally from them, and carries no Air of Flattery along with it. Besides those Vices which the *Persians* are generally adicted to, they are Lyers in the highest Degree; they speak, swear, and make false Depositions upon the least Consideration; they borrow and pay not; and if they can Cheat, they seldom lose the Opportunity; they are not to be trusted in Service, nor in all other Engagements; without Honesty in their Trading, wherein they overreach one so ingeniously, that one cannot help being bubbl'd; greedy of Riches, and of vain Glory, of Respect and Reputation, which they endeavour to gain by all Means possible. Being void of true Virtue, they affect the Shew of it, whether out of a Design to impose on themselves, or the better to attain the Ends of their vain *Glory*, their *Ambition*, and their *Wantonness*. Hypocrisy is the common Disguise they appear in; they would turn a League out of the Way, to avoid a Bodily Pollution; such as brushing as they go by a Man of a different Religion, and receiving one in their House in Rainy Weather, because the Wet of his Cloaths pollutes whatever touches them, whether Persons or Goods: They walk gravely, make their Prayers and Purgations at set Times, and with the greatest Shew of Devotion; they hold the Wisest and Godliest Conversation possible, discoursing constantly of God's Glory, and of his Greatness, in the Noblest Terms, and with all the outward Shew of the most fervent Faith. Altho' they be naturally dispos'd to good Nature, Hospitality, Pitty, Contempt of the World, and of its Riches, they affect them nevertheless, that they may appear to be possest of a larger Share of them than they really are. Whoever sees them only passing by, or in a Visit, will always give them the best Character in the World; but he that deals with them, and pries into their Affairs, will find that there is little Honesty in them; and that most of them are *Whited Sepulcres*, according to our Saviour's Expression, which I think the more proper here, because the *Persians* study particularly a strict Observation of the Law. That is the Character of the Generality of the *Persians*: But there is without doubt, an Exception to that general Depravity; for among some of the *Persians*, there is as much Justice, Sincerity, Virtue and Piety to be found, as among those who profess the best Religions. But the more one Converses with that Nation, the fewer one finds included in the Exception, the Number of Truly, Honest and Courteous *Persians* being very small.

After what I have been saying, one will hardly be persuaded, that the *Persians* are so careful of the Education of Youth as they really are; which is very true, notwithstanding. The Nobility, *i.e.* Men of Distinction, and substantial Housekeepers' Children, (for among the *Persians* there is no Nobility strictly so called) are very well brought up. They commonly take in Eunuchs to look after them, who are instead of Governors, and have them always in their Sight, keeping them very strictly, and carrying them out only to visit their Relations, or to see the Exercises performed, or the Solemnity of Feasts. And because they might not be spoiled at School, or at the College, they are not sent thither, but have Masters at Home. They are likewise very careful that they don't converse with the Servants, lest they should hear or see an immodest thing; and that the Servants carry themselves before them respectfully and Discreetly. The Common People bring up likewise their Children carefully; they don't suffer them to ramble about the Streets, to take ill Courses, to learn to Game, and to Quarrel, and learn rogueish Tricks. They are sent twice a Day to School, and when they come back, their Parents keep them by them, to initiate them in their Profession, and in the Business they are designed for: The Youth do not begin to come abroad into the World 'till they be past twenty, except they be marry'd before; for in that Case they are sooner set at Liberty, and left to themselves. By the word married, I mean joined to a Wife, or a Spouse by Contract; for at sixteen or seventeen, they give them a Bedfellow, if they be Amorous. They appear, at their entrance into the World, Wise, Well-bred, Obliging, Shame-fac'd, little Talkers, Grave, Mindful, and Chaste in their Life and Conversation: But most of them take to ill Courses soon, and give themselves up to Luxury; and for want of an Estate or Income to indulge their Inclinations, they fall to unlawful Practices, which offer themselves every Minute, and appear very plausible.

The *Persians* are the most Civiliz'd People of the *East*, and the greatest Complimenters in the World. The Polite Men amongst them, are upon a level with the Politest Men of *Europe*. Their Air, their Countenance, is very well composed, Lovely, Grave, Majestical, and as Fond as may be; they never fail complimenting one another about the Precedency, either going out or coming into a House, or when they meet, but 'tis over presently. They look upon two things in our Manners, as very ridiculous, *viz.* Contending so long, as we do, who shall go first; and covering our Head, to do Honour to any Man, which amongst them is a want of Respect, or a Liberty which no body takes but with his Inferiors or familiar Friends: They observe the right and the left Hand, but our Left is their Right, and so 'tis all over the *East*.

They say, that *Cyrus* began first to place Men on his left Hand, out of respect to them, because that side is the weaker part of the Body, and the most exposed to Danger.

They visit one another regularly on all occasions of Mirth and Sadness, and at solemn Feasts, the rich wait then for the Visits of inferior People, which they return afterwards. The Courtiers go and pay their Compliments Night and Morning to the Ministers, and wait upon them from their Palace to Court. They are led into large Halls, where they set Tobacco and Coffee before them, till the Lord, who is still on the Woman's side, comes out. As soon as they see him, every one rises, and stands up in his own Place; he goes by, bows his Head to the Company, and the Company to him again, but much lower; then he goes and sits down in his usual Place: He beckons to the Company to sit down; and when he is ready to go, he rises, goes out first, and every one follows him. The Rich receive also in that manner their Inferiors, but they use more Ceremony with their Equals, and their Superiors: They wish them well come before they sit down, and mind to sit down but after they are sat, and to rise after them when they go out. The Master of the House sits always at the upper end: And when he is willing to shew any Body some particular Respect, he beckons him to come and sit down by him; he does not offer him his Place, for the Person he offers it to, would look upon it as an Affront, but out of an extraordinary respect to him, and goes and sits down beside the Stranger below him.

When the Person visited is in his Hall, and is an Eminent Person, they behave themselves in this manner: The Visiter goes in softly, steps to the next empty Seat where he stands with his Feet close to one another, his Hands over one another in his Girdle, stooping a little with his Head, with his Eyes fix'd, and a grave and thoughtful Countenance, till the Master of the House beckons to him to sit down, which he never fails to do presently, either with his Hand, or with his Head. When a Man receives a Visit from his Superior, he rises as soon as he sees him come in, and offers to meet him half way. If he is visited by his Equal, he rises half way. If by an Inferior somewhat deserving, he only makes a motion of rising. Visiters seldom

rise if any Body comes into the Room, except the Master of the House doth it, or any body has some particular Reason of shewing that respect to him that comes in. There is beside much more Ceremony observed in *Persia* at sitting down. Before Men to whom Respect is due, a Man sits presently on his Heels, with his knees and Feet close to one another: Before his Equals, he sits easier, that is, he sits on his Breech, his Legs a-cross, and his Body upright. They call that Posture *Tehazanou*, *i.e.* sitting on four Knees, because the Knees and Ancles lie flat on the Ground: Friends and familiar Acquaintance say presently *Sit down easy*, i.e. cross your Legs as you please; but unless they have sat half a Day in the same Place, they don't shift their Situation. The *Eastern* People are not near so restless, and so uneasy as we; they sit gravely and soberly, make no motion with their Body, or very seldom, except it be to ease themselves, but they never make any to help their Discourse; our way upon that account surprizes them strangely; for they don't believe, that a Man that is in his Wits, can be so full of Action as we are. 'Tis also amongst them a great piece of Rudeness for a Man to shew his Toes when he sits, he must hide them under his Gown. That the Reader may the better understand how they sit in *Persia*, I have caused two [sic] Figures to be set on the other side, where the Posture is exactly represented. Their usual way of Saluting is with a Nod, or laying their Right-hand on their Mouth, which is the way among Friends after a long Absence. Lastly, they also Kiss one another, and give a short Embrace, after a return from a long Journey, and on extraordinary Occasions.

Those are the usual Manners relating to Action; those relating to Discourse are yet smoother, and more obliging. They receive their Visitors pleasantly with a *Koc-homedy*, *i.e.* you are come in good; *Safa a crudy*, you purge us with your Presence; *Giachuma calibut*; the Place you use to sit in at my House, has been empty; otherwise nobody has been here deserving the Honour, to supply your Absence, and such like Compliments; which are multiplied and repeated every foot, according to the Respect they have for the Visitors. I'll repeat it once more; The *Persians* are the most kind

Figure 15.1 *Persian in usual sitting position*

People in the World; they have the most moving and the most engaging Ways, the most complying Tempers, the smoothest and the most flattering Tongues, avoiding in their Conversation, Relations or Expressions which may occasion Melancholy Thoughts: And when the Discourse or Occasion obliges them to it, they use Circumlocutions to avoid at least the Tragical Terms; for Instance, if they would say that a Man is dead, they say, *Amrekodber chuma bakchid*, i.e. he has made you a Gift of the Share of Life which he had, otherwise, he might have liv'd still many Years; but out of the Love he has for you, he has joined them to those you have yet to run. I remember upon that Account, a short and ingenious Story of the General of the Musketiers, in the time of *Abas* the Second; That Prince, who was a Man of bright Parts, had given that General a White Bear to keep, which had been brought him from *Muscovy*, supposing that he would take more Care of it than they would in the Park of wild Beasts: However, the *Bear* did not live long, the King being acquainted with it some time after, desired to know what he died of, and asked the General, *What's become of my white Bear? Sir*, Answer'd he, *he has made you a Gift of the share of Life he had*. The King smiling said to him, *You are a Bear your self, for wishing that the Years of a Beast be added to mine*. They tell another Story pretty like that of the same General, which I insert here, with a Design to acquaint the Reader with the *Persian* Expressions. The King was Walking a short League off of *Ispahan*, along the Hill *Rousopha*, a thick Cloud lighting on the Point of a Rock, the King said to the General, *Look at that black Cloud, on the Point of that Rock, it is like the Hats of the Franks*. The *Eastern* Nations give that Name to the *European Christians. That's true, Sir*, answer'd the General, *and God grant you may Conquer them all; How is it possible*, Reply'd the King Smiling, *that I should Conquer them all, who are two thousand Leagues off me, when I can't Conquer the Turks, who are my nearest Neighbours?* They condole in these Terms, *Sercuma Salamet bachet*, i.e. *May your Head be safe and sound*; otherwise, *Your Life is so dear to me, that I care little who dies, so you do but live; or your Preservation is my only Concern.*

The Compliments observ'd in Letters, Memoires, and Petitions, are still longer and exacter than the Verbal ones, which are spoken in the Presence of Friends: But seeing I shall have an Occasion to discourse of them elsewhere, I shall only say here, that they have a Book on Purpose, containing the Titles to be given to all Orders of Men, from the King to the Cobler. That Book is call'd *Tenassour*, i.e. Method or Rule. Men of Business have it by Heart. I shall give no Abstracts of them, because the Stile of them may be seen in the Letters I have Inserted in my Journey from *Paris* to *Ispahan*, and in several Petitions, which one may read hereafter. One of their Politenesses in Discourse, is to speak always in the Third Person, both when they speak to others, and speak of themselves, much in the same Manner as the *Germans* do.

As civil as that Nation is, they never Act out of Generosity; 'tis a Property they are Strangers to in the East, their Bodies and Estates being Subject to a Despotick and Arbitrary Power, their Minds and Hearts are so likewise; They do nothing but out of a Principle of *Interest*, that is to say, out of *Hope* or *Fear*: And they cannot conceive that there should be such a Country where People will do their Duty from a Motive of *Virtue only*, without any other *Recompence*. It is quite the Contrary with them; they are paid for every thing, and before Hand too. One can ask nothing of 'em, but with a Present in one's Hand; and they have thereupon this Proverb, *That one comes back from a Judge, as one went to him*; As much as to say, that if one goes there with an empty Hand, one comes back without having any Justice done one. The poorest and most miserable People never appear before a Great Man, or one from whom they would ask some Favour, but at the same time they offer a Present, which is never refus'd, even by the greatest Lords of the Kingdom, such as *Fruit, Fouls, Lamb*, &c. Every one gives of that

which he is possest of most, and of the Profession which he is of, and those who have no Profession give Money. It is accounted an Honour to receive these sorts of Presents; they make 'em Publickly, and generally take that time when there is most Company. This is the general Custom throughout all the *East*; and it may be, one of the Ancientest in the World. As this seems very *Mean* and *Dishonest* with the *Europeans*, I shall not add, that it is neither perhaps the most *Reasonable*, and I shall not take upon me to defend it. I shall only say, that the *Persians* do the Service always for which they take the Present, and that they do it Instantly, or the first Opportunity that offers. They likewise make Presents to their Patrons and Benefactors, upon Festivals, and other such like solemn Occasions, without asking any particular Favour of them.

The *Persians* neither love walking Abroad, nor Travelling. As to that of walking Abroad, they look upon that Custom of ours to be very Absurd; and they look upon the walking in the Alley, as Actions only proper for a Madman. They ask very gravely for what one goes to the End of the Alley, and why one does not stand still, if one has Business to go there. This proceeds no doubt from their living in a Climate that is more even than ours. They are not so Sanguine as we are *Northward*, nor so Fiery. The most Spirituous part of their Blood perspiring more than it does with us, which is the Reason that they are not so subject to the Motions of the Body, which look so like Lightness and Disquietude, and which go often to Extravagence, and even to Madness. They don't know such a Remedy in *Persia*, as that which we call *Exercise*; they are much better sitting or learning, than walking. The *Women* and the *Eunuchs* generally Speaking, use no Exercise, and are always sitting or lying, without prejudicing the Health: For the Men, they ride on Horseback, but never walk, and their Exercises are only for Pleasure, and not for Health. The Climate of each People is always, as I believe, the principal Effect of the Inclinations and Customs of the Men, which are no more different among them, than that of the Temper of the Air is different from one Place to another. As for what relates to travelling, those Journeys that are made out of pure

Curiosity, are still more inconceivable to the *Persians*, than walking Abroad. They have no Taste of the Pleasure we enjoy in seeing different Manners from ours, and hearing of a Language which we do not Understand. When the *French* Company in the *East-Indies* sent Deputies to the King of *Persia*, the King of *France* sent two likewise, but without any Character, Nam'd *Lalain*, and *Boullaye*; and the Credential Letter imported, *That these Gentlemen having an Inclination to Travel, and joining with these French Merchants, who are the Deputies, in order to see the World; the King made use of this Opportunity to write to his* Persian *Majesty to recommend this Company of* French Merchants *to him*. I came to the Court of *Persia* when these Gentlemen were solliciting their Affairs, concerning which the Minister talk'd with me very often, and I found immediately, that this Letter was not at all pleasing to them upon many Accounts; as among others, because it was Occasionally sent. The Ministers ask'd me, if we had no more Regard for the Great Kings in our part of the World, than to send Letters to 'em by People not Deputed on Purpose: But they hung mightily upon those Words, *Gentlemen who have a mind to Travel*, which could not be put into their Language, without an Air of Absurdity, being a thing not practis'd, or even so much as known. They ask'd me if it was possible that there should be such People amongst us, who would travel two or three thousand Leagues with so much Danger, and Inconveniency, only to see *how they were made, and what they did in Persia, and upon no other Design*. These People are of Opinion, as I have observ'd, that one cannot better attain to Virtue, nor have a fuller Taste of Pleasure than by resting and dwelling at Home, and that it is not good to Travel, but to acquire Riches. They believe likewise, that every Stranger is a Spy if he be not a Merchant, or a Handicrafts-Man, and the People of Quality look upon it to be a Crime against the State to receive 'em among them, or to Visit them. It is from this Spirit of theirs no doubt, that the *Persians* are so grosly Ignorant of the present State of other Nations of the World, and that they do not so much as understand *Geography*, and have no Maps; which comes from this,

that having no Curiosity to see other Countries, they never mind the Distance, nor Roads, by which they might go thither. They have no such thing among 'em as Accounts of Foreign Countries, neither *Gazetts, News A-la-main*, nor *Offices of Intelligence*. This would seem very strange to People who pass their time in asking after News, and whose Health and Rest in a Manner, are Interested in it, as well as to those who apply themselves with so much care to the Study of the Maps and other Accounts; but this is however very true; and as I have represented the *Persians*, it is plain, that all that Knowledge is not requisite for the Pleasure and Tranquility of the Mind. The Ministers of State generally Speaking, know no more what passes in *Europe*, than in the World of the Moon. The greatest Part, even have but a confus'd Idea of *Europe*, which they look upon to be some little Island in the *North* Seas, where there is nothing to be found that is either Good or Handsome; *from whence it comes*, say they, *that the Europeans go all over the World, in search of fine Things, and of those which are Necessary, as being destitute of them.*

Yet notwithstanding what I have been saying, it is certainly true, that there is not that Country in the World, which is less dangerous to travel in from the Security of the Roads, for which they provide with a great deal of Care; neither is it less Expensive any where, by Reason of the great Number of publick Buildings, which they keep for Travellers, in all Parts of the Empire, as well in the Cities, as in the Country. They lodge in those Houses without being put to any Charge; besides which, there are Bridges and Causways, in all the Places where the Roads are too bad, which are made for the Sake of the Caravans, and of all those who travel from a motive of Gain.

The Custom of the *Persians* who Traffick, or are in Business, is, that when they have got a Sum of Money together, they employ it first of all in Purchasing a House, which they never buy quite built, but rebuild it to the Size which they would have it; making use of a Proverb, *That a House which a Man buy's quite built, is no more proper for his Family, than a Garment that he buy's ready made is fit for his Body.* There are few People in *Persia* who Rent

Houses. The poorest sort are generally the Owners of the Houses wherein they dwell. This proceeds from two Causes, *First*, That the *Persians* have not a Genius naturally bent upon Traffick. And the *Second* is, That their Religion forbids them taking any Interest for lending of Money, which is the Reason why every one avoids paying of Rent, but chooseth rather to buy a House, because he does not know how to employ his Money better. The next Purchase to this which the *Persians* make, is what they call *Bazarga*, or Market-place, which is a Gallery of Shops from one End to the other, most commonly Vaulted over, which they cause to be built near their House, or which they buy as Occasion offers. That generally is the first Land Estate which they buy. They afterwards purchase a Bath, then a *Caravanseray* or Inn. One might perhaps imagine that these Estates pay 'em a Yearly or Quarterly Rent, as they do with us; but one shall be surprized to find that they lett those Places by the Day, and oblige them to pay their Rents every Night, not so much as trusting 'em till next Morning; which is the Reason why those who acquire Estates and build upon 'em, cause the Buildings to be close to their Gates, that their Servants may the more commodiously receive their Rent. This however respects only the meaner sort of People, the others paying by the Week or the Month. But as they have no great Moveables in the *East*, that they neither make use of Tables, nor Chairs, nor Bedsteads, nor Cabinets, nor near so many Utensils for the Kitchin, a Lodger may much easier run away from them than with us. The richest among 'em, after having amass'd a great Estate for themselves and Children, set themselves about Publick Edifices, as Colleges, with Foundations for so many Students; after that, *Caravanseray's* or Inns upon the great Roads, for the reception of those who travel that way, without costing them any thing; then Bridges; and they end with Mosques, with a Revenue to entertain Priests, and something to distribute to Charities. The *Persians*, who call these Foundations *Sonab a caret*, as much as to say Merit for the future Life, say likewise, that these Beneficences are *kreir Jary*, as they speak it; that is to say, growing Goods; because, say they, the Prayers that are said in these Free Lodgings, and in these Temples, and when one

actually makes use of the other Accommodations, turn to the advantage of the Founders, and are attributed to them.

There are no other Carriages in *Persia* but Beasts for the Saddle, and great Tubs in the Nature of Cradles, cover'd and shut, wherein the Women of Quality Travel, two upon a Camel, of which I shall give a Description elsewhere. They have neither Coaches, Chariots, Litters, nor Chaises, whether because the Country is Mountainous, or that this is a Country broke off by Canals on every side, every body goes on Horseback, or upon a Mule, or upon those sort of Asses that Amble, and go nimble and easy. The Shop-keepers and Handy-crafts Men, have their Saddle-Beasts, and none but the poorest sort go on Foot. I leave it to the Reader, to make yet more Remarks on the Manners of the *Persians*, in the Series of my Relations, where I shall have occasion to speak of them.

The Names which the *Persians* bear, are given 'em, either at their coming into the World, or when they are Circumcis'd, as they are to all the other *Mahometans*: And these Names are taken either from Eminent Persons of their Religion, from the *Old-Testament*, from their Histories, or they are Names of Power; for every one takes or gives himself a Name, according to his Mind; but they have no particular Sir-Names, or Names of the Family and Line; for their Sir-Names they take to themselves by way of Honour, the Proper Name of their Father, and sometimes that of their Son, in saying, such a one, the Father of such a one, or such a one, the Son of such a one; as for Example, *Abraham*, the Son of *Jacob*, and *Mahammed*, the Father of *Aly*. This is the Custom, time out of Mind, of naming themselves in the *East*. You may see it likewise in the *Old-Testament*, where one finds, for Example, the Kings of *Assyria* call'd *Ben Adad*, as much as to say Sons of *Adad*, and those of *Palestine* call'd *Abimelec*, that is to say, Son of *Melec*, a Term that signifies King. It is likewise very common among 'em to have several Sir-names, the one taken from the Name of his Father, and the other from his Son; and even to bear the Name of several of his Children, as the *Calif Abrachid*, the fifteenth *Calif* of the Race of the *Abassides*, who is sometimes named *Abon*

Jafer, sometimes *Abon Mahammed*, which are the Names of his Sons. In short, it is very common with them to take for their Sir-name, the Calling that has been exercised, whether by the Father, or by his Ancestors, whether Liberal or Mechanick, by which they rais'd themselves in the World, *Mahammed Caian*, *Mahammed* the *Taylor*, *Soliman Atari*, *Soliman* the *Druggist*, *Jouacri*, the *Jeweller*, *Stanboni*, the *Constantinopolitan*, by Reason of his having got an Estate there; and what is Remarkable, as very Praiseworthy in my Opinion, that they are not ashamed of bearing these Sir-names after they become Rich, are raised to the highest Dignities, and are put into the greatest Employments. This is because they are rais'd by the Sciences, by their Employments, and especially by their Riches. There are but very few who are tied to it by Descent.

As for Titles, they are not at all affected in the *East*, whether from Birth or Office. Every one fastens to his Name as he pleases, without the haughty Titles of Duke, Prince, and King: There are those which they never put after the Name, as the Title of *Mirza*, which signifies the Son of a Prince. This is to distinguish the Royal Personages from the rest of the World, who place these Titles before and after their Names quite another way, and contrary to others. One very strange Thing, and which one would scarce believe, is, that the *Persians* Glory in bearing the Title of Slaves. I speak of the People rais'd at Court, and who were born or bred up to Employments; they call themselves, by way of Honour, *Slaves of the King*, or *Slaves of the Saints*; for Example, The Duke Slave of *Ibrahim*, or of *Mahammed*, or of the King. These sort of Names, denote generally a Man in Offices, or one who aspires to 'em.

When a Male Child is born into the World, it is the Custom for the Father to give every thing that he has upon him, to him who brings him the News. They come to him with their Turban off their Head, and say to him, *You have a Male Child born*; and he must strait make a Present for this good News, and as it were to buy his Clothes again, and what he has upon him.

16

A New Voyage Round the World

William Dampier

… *Monmouth* and *Grafton* Isles are very hilly, with many of those steep inhabited Precipices on them, that I shall describe particularly. The two small Islands are flat and even; only the *Bashee* Island hath one steep scraggy Hill, but *Goat*-Island is all flat and very even.

The Mold of these Islands in the Valley, is blackish in some places, but in most red. The Hills are very rocky: The Valleys are well watered with Brooks of fresh Water, which run into the Sea in many different places. The Soil is indifferent fruitful, especially in the Valleys; producing pretty great plenty of Trees (tho' not very big) and thick Grass. The sides of the Mountains have also short Grass, and some of the Mountains have Mines within them; for the Natives told us, that the yellow Metal they shewed us, (as I shall speak more particularly) came from these Mountains; for when they held it up, they would point towards them.

The Fruit of the Islands are a few Plantains, Bonanoes, Pine-apples, Pumkins, Sugar-canes, &c. and there might be more if the Natives would, for the Ground seems fertile enough. Here are great plenty of Potatoes, and Yams, which is the common Food for the Natives, for Bread-kind: For those few Plantains they have, are only used as Fruit. They have some Cotton growing here of the small Plants.

Here are plenty of Goats, and abundance of Hogs; but few Fowls, either wild or same. For this I have always observed in my Travels, both in the *East* and *West-Indies*, that in those Places where there is plenty of Grain, that is, of Rice in one, and Maiz in the other, there are also found great abundance of Fowls; but on the contrary, few Fowls in those Countries where the Inhabitants feed on Fruits and Roots only. The few wild Fowls that are here, are Parakites, and some other small Birds. Their same Fowl are only a few Cocks and Hens.

Monmouth and *Graston* Islands are very thick inhabited; and *Bashee* Island hath one Town on it. The Natives of these Islands are short squat People; they are generally round-visaged, with low Foreheads, and thick Eye-brows; their Eyes of a hazel colour, and small, yet bigger than the *Chinese*; short low Noses, and their Lips and Mouths middle propor-tioned; Their Teeth are white; their Hair is black, and thick, and lank, which they wear but short; it will just cover their Ears, and so it is cut round very even. Their Skins are of a very dark Copper-colour.

They wear no Hat, Cap, nor Turbat, nor any thing to keep off the Sun. The Men for the biggest part have only a small Clout to cover their Nakedness; some of them have Jackets made of Plantain-leaves, which were as rough as any Bear's-skin: I never saw such rugged Things. The Women have a short Petticoat made of Cotton, which comes a little below

William Dampier, "A New Voyage Round the World," in *A Collection of Voyages. In four volumes*, vol. I, London: James and John Knapton, 1729, pp. 425–34, 464–6, 484–6, vol. II 40–3, 50, 52, 56–61, 64–5.

their Knees. It is a thick sort of stubborn Cloth, which they make themselves of their Cotton. Both Men and Women do wear large Ear-rings, made of that yellow Metal before mentioned. Whether it were Gold or no I cannot positively say; I took it to be so, it was heavy and of the colour of our paler Gold. I would fain have brought away some to have satisfied my Curiosity; but I had nothing wherewith to buy any. Captain *Read* bought two of these Rings with some Iron, of which the People are very greedy; and he would have bought more, thinking he was come to a very fair Market, but that the paleness of the Metal made him and his Crew distrust its being right Gold. For my part, I should have ventured on the purchase of some, but having no property in the Iron, of which we had great store on board, sent from *England* by the Merchants along with Captain *Swan*, I durst not barter it away.

These Rings when first polished look very gloriously, but time makes them fade, and turn to a pale yellow. Then they make a soft Paste of red Earth, and smearing it over their Rings, they cast them into a quick Fire, where they remain till they be red hot; then they take them out and cool them in Water, and rub off the Paste; and they look again of a glorious Colour and Lustre.

These People make but small low Houses. The Sides which are made of small Posts, watled with Boughs, are not above 4 Foot and a half high: the Ridge-pole is about 7 or 8 Foot high. They have a Fire-place at one end of their Houses, and Boards placed on the Ground to lye on. They inhabit together in small Villages built on the sides and tops of rocky Hills, 3 or 4 rows of Houses one above another, and on such steep Precipices, that they go up to the first Row with a wooden Ladder, and so with a Ladder still from every Story up to that above it, there being no way to ascend. The Plain on the first Precipice may be so wide, as to have room both for a Row of Houses that stand all along on the Edge or Brink of it, and a very narrow Street running along before their Doors, between the Row of Houses and the Foot of the next Precipice; the Plain of which is in a manner level to the tops of the Houses below, and so for the rest. The common Ladder to each Row or Street comes up at a narrow

Passage left purposely about the middle of it; and the Street being bounded with a Precipice also at each end, 'tis but drawing up the Ladder, if they be assaulted, and then there is no coming at them from below, but by climbing up as against a perpendicular Wall: And that they may not be assaulted from above, they take care to build on the side of such a Hill, whose backside hangs over the Sea, or is some high, steep, perpendicular Precipice, altogether inaccessible. These Precipices are natural; for the Rocks seem too hard to work on; nor is there any sign that Art hath been employed about them. On *Bashee* Island there is one such, and built upon, with its back next the Sea. *Graston* and *Monmouth* Isles are very thick set with these Hills and Towns; and the Natives, whether for fear of Pirates, or Foreign Enemies, or Factions among their own Clans, care not for Building but in these Fastnesses; which I take to be the Reason that *Orange* Isle, though the largest, and as fertile as any, yet being level, and exposed, hath no Inhabitants. I never saw the like Precipices and Towns.

These People are pretty ingenious also in building Boats. Their small Boats are much like our *Deal* Yalls, but not so big; and they are built with very narrow Plank, pinn'd with wooden Pins, and some Nails. They have also some pretty large Boats, which will carry 40 or 50 Men. These they Row with 12 or 14 Oars of a side. They are built much like the small ones, and they row doubled banked; that is, two Men setting on one Bench, but one Rowing on one side, the other on the other side of the Boat. They understand the use of Iron, and work it themselves. Their Bellows are like those at *Mindanao.*

The common Imployment for the Men is Fishing; but I did never see them catch much: Whether it is more plenty at other times of the Year I know not. The Women do manage their Plantations.

I did never see them kill any of their Goats or Hogs for themselves, yet they would beg the Panches of the Goats that they themselves did fell to us: And if any of our surly Seamen did heave them into the Sea, they would take them up again and the Skins of the Goats also. They would not meddle with Hogs-guts, if our Men threw away any besides what they made

Chitterlings and Sausages of. The Goat-skins these People would carry ashore, and making a Fire they would singe off all the Hair, and afterwards let the Skin lie and parch on the Coals, till they thought it eatable; and then they would knaw it, and tear it in pieces with their Teeth, and at last swallow it. The Paunches of the Goats would make them an excellent Dish; they drest it in this manner. They would turn out all the chopt Grass and Crudities found in the Maw into their Pots, and set it over the Fire, and stir it about often: This would smoak and puff, and heave up as it was boiling; Wind breaking out of the Ferment, and making a very savoury Stink. While this was doing, if they had any Fish, as commonly they had two or three small Fish, these they would make very clean (as hating Nastiness belike) and cut the Flesh from the Bone, and then mince the Flesh as small as possibly they could, and when that in the Pot was well boiled, they would take it up, and strewing a little Salt into it, they would eat it, mixt with their raw minced Flesh. The Dung in the Maw would look like so much boil'd Herbs minc'd very small; and they took up their Mess with their Fingers, as the *Moors* do their Pillaw, using no Spoons.

They had another Dish made of a sort of Locusts, whose Bodies were about an Inch and an half long, and as thick as the top of one's little Finger; with large thin Wings, and long and small Legs. At this time of the Year these Creatures came in great Swarms to devour their Potato-leaves, and other Herbs; and the Natives would go out with small Nets, and take a Quart at one sweep. When they had enough, they would carry them home, and parch them over the Fire in an earthen Pan; and then their Wings and Legs would fall off, and their Heads and Backs would turn red like boil'd Shrimps, being before brownish. Their Bodies being full, would eat very moist, their Heads would crackle in one's Teeth. I did once eat of this Dish, and liked it well enough; but their other Dish my Stomach would not take.

Their common Drink is Water; as it is of all other *Indians*: Besides which they make a sort of Drink with the Juice of the Sugar-cane, which they boil, and put some small black sort of Berries among it. When it is well boiled,

they put it into great Jars, and let it stand three or four Days and work. Then it settles, and becomes clear, and is presently fit to drink. This is an excellent Liquor, and very much like *English* Beer, both in Colour and Taste. It is very strong, and I do believe very wholesome: For our Men, who drank briskly of it all day for several Weeks, were frequently drunk with it, and never sick after it. The Natives brought a vast deal of it every Day to those aboard and ashore: For some of our Men were ashore at work on *Bashee*-Island; which Island they gave that Name to from their drinking this Liquor there; that being the Name which the Natives call'd this Liquor by: and as they sold it to our Men very cheap, so they did not spare to drink it as freely. And indeed from the plenty of this Liquor, and their plentiful use of it, our Men call'd all these Islands, the *Bashee* Islands.

What Language these People do speak I know not: for it had no affinity in sound to the *Chinese*, which is spoke much through the Teeth; nor yet to the *Malayan* Language. They called the Metal that their Ear-rings were made of *Bullawan*, which is the *Mindanao* word for Gold; therefore probably they may be related to the *Philippine Indians*; for that is the general Name for Gold among all those *Indians*. I could not learn from whence they have their Iron; but it is most likely they go in their great Boats to the North-end of *Luconia*, and trade with the *Indians* of that Island for it. Neither did I see any thing beside Iron, and pieces of Buffaloes Hides, which I could judge that they bought of Strangers: Their Cloaths were of their own Growth and Manufacture.

These Men had Wooden Lances, and a few Lances headed with Iron; which are all the Weapons that they have. Their Armour is a piece of Buffaloe-hide, shaped like our Carters Frocks, being without Sleeves, and sewed both sides together, with holes for the Head and the Arms to come forth. This Buff-Coat reaches down to their Knees: It is close about their Shoulders, but below it is three Foot wide, and as thick as a Board.

I could never perceive them to worship any thing, neither had they any Idols; neither did they seem to observe any one Day more than other. I could never perceive that one Man was of greater Power than another; but they seemed to be all equal; only every Man ruling in his own House, and the Children respecting and honouring their Parents.

Yet 'tis probable that they have some Law, or Custom, by which they are govern'd; for while we lay here we saw a young Man buried alive in the Earth; and 'twas for Theft, as far as we could understand from them. There was a great deep hole dug, and abundance of People came to the Place to take their last Farewell of him: Among the rest, there was one Woman who made great Lamentation, and took off the condemn'd Person's Ear-rings. We supposed her to be his Mother. After he had taken his leave of her and some others, he was put into the Pit, and covered over with Earth. He did not struggle, but yielded very quietly to his Punishment; and they cramm'd the Earth close upon him, and stifled him.

They have but one Wife, with whom they live and agree very well; and their Children live very obediently under them. The Boys go out a fishing with their Fathers; and the Girles live at home with their Mothers: And when the Girles are grown pretty strong, they send them to their Plantations, to dig Hames and Potatoes, of which they bring home on their Heads every Day enough to serve the whole Family; for they have no Rice nor Maize.

Their Plantations are in the Valleys, at a good distance from their Houses; where every Man has a certain spot of Land, which is properly his own. This he manageth himself for his own use; and provides enough, that he may not be beholding to his Neighbour.

Notwithstanding the seeming nastiness of their Dish of Goats-Maw, they are in their Persons a very neat cleanly People, both Men and Women: And they are withal the quietest and civilest People that I did ever meet with. I could never perceive them to be angry with one another. I have admired to see 20 or 30 Boats aboard our Ship at a time, and yet no difference among them; but all civil and quiet, endeavouring to help each other on occasion: No noise, nor appearance of distaste: and although sometimes cross Accidents would happen, which might have set other Men together by the Ears, yet they were not moved by them. Sometimes they will also drink freely, and warm themselves with their Drink; yet

neither then could I ever perceive them out of Humour. They are not only thus civil among themselves, but very obliging and kind to Strangers; nor were their Children rude to us, as is usual. Indeed the Women, when we came to their Houses, would modestly beg any Rags or small pieces of Cloth, to swaddle their young ones in, holding their Children out to us; and begging is usual among all these wild Nations. Yet neither did they beg so importunately as in other Places; nor did the Men ever beg any thing at all. Neither, except once at the first time that we came to an Anchor (as I shall relate) did they steal any thing; but dealt justly, and with great sincerity with us; and make us very welcome to their Houses with *Bashee* drink. If they had none of this Liquor themselves, they would buy a Jar of Drink of their Neighbours, and sit down with us: for we could see them go and give a piece or two of their Gold for some Jars of *Bashee*. And indeed among wild *Indians*, as these seem to be, I wonder'd to see buying and selling, which is not so usual; nor to converse so freely, as to go aboard Strangers' Ships with so little caution: Yet their own small Trading may have brought them to this. At these Entertainments, they and their Family, Wife and Children, drank out of small Calabashes: and when by themselves, they drink about from one to another; but when any of us came among them, then they would always drink to one of us.

They have no sort of Coin; but they have small Crumbs of the Metal before described, which they bind up very safe in Plantain-Leaves, or the like. This Metal they exchange for what they want, giving a small quantity of it, about two or three Grains, for a Jar of Drink that would hold five or six Gallons. They have no Scales, but give it by guess.

[...]

The Inhabitants of [Australia] are the miserablest People in the World. The *Hodmadods* of *Monomatapa*, though a nasty People, yet for Wealth are Gentlemen to these; who have no Houses, and skin Garments, Sheep, Poultry, and Fruits of the Earth, Ostrich Eggs, &c. as the *Hodmadods* have: And setting aside their Humane Shape, they differ but little from Brutes. They are tall, strait-bodied, and thin, with small long Limbs. They have great Heads, round Foreheads, and great Brows. Their Eye-lids are always half closed, to keep the Flies out of their Eyes; they being so troublesome here, that no fanning will keep them from coming to one's Face; and without the Assistance of both Hands to keep them off, they will creep into ones Nostrils, and Mouth too, if the Lips are not shut very close; so that from their Infancy being thus annoyed with these Insects, they do never open their Eyes as other People: And therefore they cannot see far, unless they hold up their Heads, as if they were looking at somewhat over them.

They have great Bottle-Noses, pretty full Lips, and wide Mouths. The two Fore-teeth of their Upper-jaw are wanting in all of them, Men and Women, old and young; whether they draw them out, I know not: Neither have they any Beards. They are long-visaged, and of a very unpleasing Aspect, having no one graceful Feature in their Faces. Their Hair is black, short and curl'd, like that of the Negroes; and not long and lank like the common *Indians*. The Colour of their Skins, both of their Faces and the rest of their Body, is Coal-black, like that of the Negroes of *Guinea*.

They have no sort of Cloaths, but a piece of the Rind of a Tree tied like a Girdle about their Waists, and a handful of long Grass, or three or four small green Boughs full of Leaves, thrust under their Girdle, to cover their Nakedness.

They have no Houses, but lie in the open Air without any covering; the Earth being their Bed, and the Heaven their Canopy. Whether they cohabit one Man to one Woman, or promiscuously, I know not; but they do live in Companies, 20 or 30 Men, Women, and Children together. Their only Food is a small sort of Fish, which they get by making Wares of Stone across little Coves or Branches of the Sea; every Tide bringing in the small Fish, and there leaving them for a Prey to these People, who constantly attend there to search for them at Low-water. This small Fry I take to be the top of their Fishery: They have no Instruments to catch great Fish, should they come; and such seldom stay to be left behind at Low-water: Nor could we catch any Fish with our Hooks and Lines all the while we lay there. In other Places at Low-water they seek for Cockles, Muscles, and Periwincles: Of these Shell-fish there are fewer still; so that their chiefest dependance is upon what the Sea leaves in their Wares; which, be it much or little they gather up, and march to the Places of their Abode. There the old People that are not able to stir abroad by reason of their Age, and the tender Infants, wait their return; and what Providence has bestowed on them, they presently broil on the Coals, and eat it in common. Sometimes they get as many Fish as makes them a plentiful Banquet; and at other times they scarce get every one a taste: But be it little or much that they get, every one has his part, as well the young and tender, the old and feeble, who are not able to go abroad, as the strong and lusty. When they have eaten they lie down till the next Low-water, and then all that are able march out, be it Night or Day, rain or shine, 'tis all one; they must attend the Wares, or else they must fast: For the Earth affords them no Food at all. There is neither Herb, Root, Pulse nor any sort of Grain for them to eat, that we saw; nor any sort of Bird or Beast that they can catch, having no Instruments wherewithal to do so.

I did not perceive that they did worship any thing. These poor Creatures have a sort of Weapon to defend their Ware, or fight with their Enemies, if they have any that will interfere with their poor Fishery. They did at first endeavour with their Weapons to frighten us, who lying ashore deterr'd them from one of their Fishing-places. Some of them had wooden Swords, others had a sort of Lances. The Sword is a piece of Wood shaped somewhat like a Cutlass. The Lance is a long strait Pole sharp at one end, and hardened afterwards by heat. I saw no Iron, nor any other sort of Metal; therefore it is probable they use Stone-Hatchets.

[...]

Now we were Men enough to defend ourselves against the Natives of this Island, if they should prove our Enemies: though if none of these Men had come ashore to me, I should not have feared any Danger: Nay, perhaps less, because I should have been cautious of giving any Offence to the Natives. And I am of the Opinion, that there are no People in the World so barbarous as to kill a single Person that falls accidentally into their Hands, or comes to live among them; except they have before been injured, by some Outrage or Violence committed against them. Yet even then, or afterwards, if a Man could but preserve his Life from their first Rage, and come to treat with them, (which is the hardest thing, because their way is usually to abscond, and rushing suddenly upon their Enemy to kill him at unawares) one might, by some slight, insinuate one's self into their Favours again; especially by shewing some Toy or Knack that they did never see before: which any *European*, that has seen the World, might soon contrive to amuse them withal: as might be done, generally even with a lit-Fire struck with a Flint and Steel.

As for the common Opinion of *Authropophagi*, or Man-eaters, I did never meet with any such People: All Nations or Families in the World, that I have seen or heard of, having some sort of Food to live on, either Fruit, Grain, Pulse or Roots, which grow naturally, or else planted by them; if not Fish and Land-Animals besides; (yea, even the People of *New-Holland* had Fish amidst all their Penury) and would scarce kill a Man purposely to eat him. I know not what barbarous Customs may formerly have been in the World; and to sacrifice their Enemies to their Gods, is a thing hath been much talked of, with Relation to the Savages of *America*. I am a Stranger to that also, if it be, or have been customary in any Nation there; and yet, if they sacrifice their Enemies, it is not necessary they should eat them too. After all, I will not be peremptory in the Negative, but I speak as to the Compass of my own Knowledge, and know some of these Cannibal Stories to be false, and many of them have been disproved since I first went to the *West-Indies*. At that time how barbarous were the poor *Florida Indians* accounted, which now we find to be civil enough? What strange Stories have we heard of the *Indians*, whose Islands were called the Isles of *Cannibals?* Yet we find that they do trade very civilly with the *French* and *Spaniards*; and have done so with us. I do own that they have formerly endeavoured to destroy our Plantations at *Barbadoes*, and have since hindred us from settling in the Island *Santa Loca* by destroying two or three Colonies successively of those that were settled there; and even the Island *Tabago* has been

often annoyed and ravaged by them, when settled by the *Dutch*, and still lies waste (though a delicate fruitful Island) as being too near the *Caribbees* on the Continent, who visit it every Year. But this was to preserve their own right, by endeavouring to keep out any that would settle themselves on those Islands, where they had planted themselves; yet even these People would not hurt a single Person, as I have been told by some that have been Prisoners among them. I could instance also in the *Indians* of *Bocca Toro*, and *Bocca Drago*, and many other Places where they do live, as the *Spaniards* call it, wild and savage: yet there they have been familiar with Privateers, but by Abuses have withdrawn their Friendship again. As for these *Nicobar* People, I found them affable enough, and therefore I did not fear them; but I did not much care whether I had gotten any more Company or no.

[...]

Of the Natives of Tonquin

Tonquin is very populous, being thick-set with Villages; and the Natives in general are of a middle Stature, and clean limb'd. They are of a Tawny *Indian* colour: but I think the fairest and clearest that I ever saw of that Complexion: for you may perceive a Blush or Change of Colour in some of their Faces, on any sudden Surprize of Passion; which I could never discern in any other *Indians*. Their Faces are generally flattish, and of an oval Form. Their Noses and Lips are proportionable enough, and altogether graceful. Their Hair is black, long and lank, and very thick; and they wear it hanging down to their Shoulders.

Their Teeth are as black as they can make them; for this being accounted a great Ornament, they dye them of that Colour, and are three or four Days doing it. They do this when they are about twelve or fourteen Years old, both Boys and Girls: and during all the Time of the Operation they dare not take any Nourishment, besides Water, Chau, or some liquid Thing, and not much of that neither, for fear, I judge, of being poyson'd by the Dye, or Pigment. So that while this is doing they undergo very severe Penance: but as both

Sexes, so all Qualities, the Poor as well as the rich, must be in this Fashion: they say they should else be like Brutes; and that would be a great Shame to them to be like Elephants or Dogs; which they compare those to that have white Teeth.

They are generally dextrous, nimble, and active, and ingenious in any Mechanick Science they profess. This may be seen by the Multitude of fine Silks that are made here; and the curious Lacker-work, that is yearly transported from thence. They are also laborious and diligent in their Callings; but the Country being so very populous, many of them are extreme poor for Want of Employment: and tho' the Country is full of Silk, and other Materials to work on, yet little is done, but when strange Ships arrive. For 'tis the Money and Goods that are brought hither, especially by the *English* and *Dutch*, that puts Life into them: for the Handicrafts Men have not Money to set themselves to work; and the Foreign Merchants are therefore forced to trust them with Advance-money, to the Value of at least a third, or half their Goods; and this for two or three Months or more, before they have made their Goods, and brought them in. So that they having no Goods ready by them, till they have Money from the Merchant Strangers, the Ships that trade hither must of Necessity stay here all the time that their Goods are making, which are commonly 5 or 6 Months.

The *Tonquinese* make very good Servants; I think the best in *India*. For as they are generally apprehensive and docil, so are they faithful when hired, diligent and obedient. Yet they are low spirited: probably by reason of their living under an Arbitrary Government. They are patient in Labour, but in Sickness they are mightily dejected. They have one great Fault extreme common among them, which is gaming. To this they are so universally addicted, Servants and all, that neither the awe of their Masters, nor any Thing else, is sufficient to restrain them, till they have lost all they have, even their very Cloaths. This is a reigning Vice among the Eastern Nations, especially the *Chinese*, as I said in the 15th Chapter of my former Volume. And I may add, that the *Chinese* I found settled at *Tonquin*, were no less given to it than those I met with elsewhere.

For after they have lost their Money, Goods and Cloaths, they will stake down their Wives and Children: and lastly, as the dearest Thing they have, will play upon tick, and mortgage their Hair upon Honour: And whatever it cost them they will be sure to redeem it. For a free *Chinese* as these are, who have fled from the *Tartars*, would be as much ashamed of short Hair, as a *Tonquinese* of white Teeth.

The Cloaths of the *Tonquinese* are made either of Silk or Cotton. The poor People and Soldiers do chiefly wear Cotton Cloath dyed to a dark tawny Colour. The rich Men and *Mandarins* commonly wear *English* Broad-Cloath: the chief Colours are red or green. When they appear before the King, they wear long Gowns which reach down to their Heels: neither may any Man appear in his presence but in such a Garb. The great Men have also long Caps made of the same that their Gowns are made of: but the middle sort of Men and the poor commonly go bare-headed. Yet the Fishermen, and such Labourers as are by their Employments more exposed to the Weather, have broad-brimm'd Hats made of Reeds, Straw, or Palmeto-Leaves. These Hats are as stiff as Boards, and sit not pliant to their Heads: for which reason they have Band-strings or Necklaces fastened to their Hats; which coming under their Chins are there tied, to keep their Hats fast to their Heads. These Hats are very ordinary Things; they seldom wear them but in rainy Weather. Their other Cloaths are very few and mean: a ragged pair of Breeches commonly sufficeth them. Some have bad Jackets, but neither Shirt, Stockings nor Shooes.

[...]

They are courteous and civil to Strangers, especially the trading People: But the great Men are Proud, Haughty and Ambitious; and the Soldiers very insolent. The poorer sort are very Thievish; insomuch that the Factors and Strangers that Traffick hither are forced to keep good Watch in the Night to secure their Goods, notwithstanding the severe Punishments they have against Thieving. They have indeed great Opportunities of Thieving, the Houses being so slightly built: But they will work a way under Ground, rather than fail; and use many subtle Stratagems. I am a Stranger to any

Ceremonies used by them in Marriage, or at the Birth of a Child, or the like, if they use any: Polygamy is allowed of in this Country, and they buy their Wives of the Parents. The King and great Men keep several, as their Inclinations lead them, and their Ability serves. The Poor are stinted for want of means more than desire: For though many are not able to buy, much less to maintain one Wife; yet most of them make a shift to get one, for here are some very low-prized ones, that are glad to take up with poor Husbands. But then in hard Times, the Man must sell both Wife and Children, to buy Rice to maintain himself.

[...]

When a Man dies he is interr'd in his own Land, for here are no common Burying-places: And within a Month afterwards the Friends of the Deceased, especially if he was the Master of the Family, must make a great Feast of Flesh and Fruit at the Grave. 'Tis a Thing belonging to the Priest's Office to assist at this Solemnity; they are always there, and take care to see that the Friends of the deceased have it duly performed. To make this Feast they are obliged to sell a Piece of Land, tho' they have Money enough otherways: Which Money they bestow in such Things as are necessary for the Solemnity, which is more or less, according to the Quality of the Deceased. If he was a great Man, there is a Tower of Wood erected over the Grave; it may be 7 or 8 Foot square, and built 20 or 25 Foot high. About 20 Yards from the Tower, are little Sheds built with Stalls, to lay the Provisions on, both of Meat and Fruits of all Sorts, and that in great Plenty. Thither the Country People resort to fill their Bellies, for the Feast seems to be free for all Comers, at least of the Neighbourhood. How it is drest or distributed about, I know not; but there the People wait till 'tis ready. Then the Priest gets within the Tower, and climbs up to the Top, and looking out from thence, makes an Oration to the People below. After this the Priest descends, and then they set Fire to the Foundation of the Tower, burning it down to the Ground: and when this is done they fall to their Meat.

[...]

Their Religion is Paganism, and they are great Idolaters: Nevertheless they own an omnipotent, supreme, over-ruling Power, that beholds both them and their Actions, and so far takes Notice of them, as to reward the Good, and punish the Bad in the other World. For they believe the Immortality of the Soul: but the Notion that they have of the Deity is very obscure. Yet by the Figures which they make representing this God, they manifestly shew that they do believe him to excel in Sight, Strength, Courage and Wisdom, Justice, &c. For though their Idols, which are made in humane Shapes, are very different in their Forms; yet they all represent somewhat extraordinary, either in the Countenance, or in the Make of the Body or Limbs. Some are very corpulent and fat, others are very lean; some also have many Eyes, others as many Hands, and all grasping somewhat. Their Aspects are also different, and in some Measure representing what they are made to imitate, or there is somewhat in their Hands or lying by them, to illustrate the Meaning of the Figure. Several Passions are also represented in the Countenance of the Image, as Love, Hatred, Joy, Grief. I was told of one Image that was placed sitting on his Hams, with his Elbows resting on his Knees, and his Chin resting on his two Thumbs, for the supporting his Head, which looks drooping forwards: his Eyes were mournfully lifted up towards Heaven, and the Figure was so lean, and the Countenance and whole Composure was so sorrowful, that it was enough to move the Beholder with Pity and Compassion. My Friend said he was much affected with the Sight thereof.

There are other Images also, that are in the Shape of Beasts, either Elephants or Horses, for I have not seen them in any other Shape. The *Pagodas* or Idol Temples, are not sumptuous and magnificent, as in some of the Neighbouring Kingdoms.

There were many *Pagan* Priests belonging to these *Pagodas*, and 'tis reported that they are by the Laws tied to strict Rules of Living, as Abstinence from Women, and strong Drink especially, and enjoined a poor Sort of Life. Yet they don't seem to confine themselves much to these Rules: but their Subsistence being chiefly from Offerings, and there being many of them, they are usually very poor. The Offerings to the Priest is commonly two or three Handfuls of Rice, a Box of Betle, or some such like Present. One Thing the People resort to them for is Fortune-telling, at which they pretend to be very expert, and will be much offended if any dispute their Skill in that, or the Truth of their Religion. Their Habitations are very little and mean, close by the *Pagodas*, where they constantly attend to offer the Petitions of the poor People, that frequently resort thither on some such Errand. For they have no set Times of Devotion, neither do they seem to esteem one Day above another, except their Annual Feasts. The People bring to the Priest in Writing what Petition they have to make: and he reads it aloud before the Idol, and afterwards burns it in an Incense-pot, the Supplicant all the while lying prostrate on the Ground.

I think the *Mandarins* and rich People seldom come to the *Pagodas*, but have a Clerk of their own, who reads the Petition in their own Courts or Yards: and it should seem by this, that the *Mandarins* have a better Sense of the Deity, than the common People; for in these Yards, there is no Idol, before whom to perform the Ceremony, but 'tis done with Eyes lift up to Heaven. When they make this Petition they order a great deal of good Meat to be drest, and calling all their Servants into the Court, where the Ceremony is to be performed, they place the Food on a Table, where also two Incense-pots are placed, and then the *Mandarin* presents a Paper to the Clerk, who reads it with an audible Voice. In the first Place there is drawn up an ample Account of all that God has blest him withal, as Health, Riches, Honour, Favour of his Prince, &c. and long Life, if he be old; and towards the Conclusion, there is a Petition to God for a Continuance of all these Blessings, and a farther Augmentation of them; especially with long Life and Favour of his Prince, which last they esteem as the greatest of all Blessings. While this Paper is reading, the Master kneels down, and bows his Face to the Earth; and when the Clerk has done reading it, he puts it to the burning Rushes, that are in the Incense-pot, where 'tis consum'd. Then he flings in 3 or 4 little Bundles of sacred Paper, which is very fine and gilded; and when that also is burnt, he bids his Servants eat the Meat.

[...]

They have Schools of Learning and Nurseries to tutor youth. The Characters they write in are the same with the *Chinese*, by what I could judge; and they write with a hair Pencil, not sitting at a Table, as we do, but stand upright. They hold their Paper in one hand, and write with the other: making their Characters very exact and fair. They write their Lines right down from the Top to the Bottom, beginning the first Line from the right Hand, and so proceeding on towards the Left. After they can write they are instructed in such Sciences as their Masters can tutor them in; and the Mathematicks are much studied by them: They seem to understand a little of Geometry and Arithmetick, and somewhat more of Astronomy. They have Almanacks among them: but I could not learn whether they are made in *Tonquin*, or brought to them from *China*.

Since the Jesuits came into these Parts, some of them have improved themselves in Astronomy pretty much. They know from them the Revolution of the Planets; they also learn of them natural Philosophy, and especially *Ethicks*: and when young Students are admitted to make Graduates, they pass through a very strict Examination. They compose something by way of Trial, which they must be careful to have wholly their own, for if it is found out that they have been assisted, they are punished, degraded, and never admitted to a second Examination.

The *Tonquinese* have learnt several Mechanick Arts and Trades, so that here are many Tradesmen, *viz.* Smiths, Carpenters, Sawyers, Joyners, Turners, Weavers, Tailors, Potters, Painters, Money-changers, Paper-makers, Workers on Lacker-Ware, Bell-founders, &c. Their Saws are most in Frames, and drawn forwards and backwards by two Men. Money-changing is a great Profession here. It is managed by Women, who are very dextrous and ripe in this Employment. They hold their Cabals in the Night, and know how to raise their Cash as well as the cunningest Stock-jobber in *London*.

The *Tonquinese* make indifferent good Paper, of two Sorts. One Sort is made of Silk, the other of the Rinds of Trees. This being pounded well with wooden Pestles in large Troughs, makes the best writing Paper.

The vendible Commodities of this Kingdom, are Gold, Musk, Silks, both wrought and raw, some Callicoes, Drugs of many Sorts, Wood for dying, Lacker-Wares, Earthen-Wares, Salt, Anniseed, Wormseed, &c. There is much Gold in this Country: It is like the *China* Gold, as pure as that of *Japan*, and much finer. Eleven or twelve *Tale* of Silver brings one of Gold. A Tale is the Name of a Summ about a Noble *English*. Besides the raw Silk fetched from hence, here are several Sorts of wrought Silks made for Exportation.

[...]

With all these rich Commodities, one would expect the People to be rich; but the Generality are very poor, considering what a Trade is driven here. For they have little or no Trade by Sea themselves, except for Eatables, as Rice, and Fish, which is spent in the Country: but the main Trade of the Country is maintained by the *Chinese*, *English*, *Dutch*, and other Merchant Strangers, who either reside here constantly, or make their annual Returns hither. These export their Commodities, and import such as are vendible here. The Goods imported hither besides Silver, are Salt-peter, Sulphur, *English* Broad-Cloath, Cloath-rashes, some Callicoes, Pepper and other Spices, Lead, great Guns, &c. but of Guns the long Saker is most esteemed. For these Commodities you receive Money or Goods, according to contract: but the Country is so very poor, that, as I formerly observed, the Merchant commonly stays 3 or 4 Months for his Goods after he has paid for them; because the Poor are not employed till Ships arrive in the Country, and then they are set to work by the Money that is brought thither in them. The King buys great Guns, and some pieces of Broad-Cloath: but his pay is so bad, that Merchants care not to deal with him, could they avoid it. But the trading People by all accounts are honest and just.

Part V

The Enlightenment

Section V

(a) The Quarrel of the Ancients and the Moderns

17

Of Heroic Virtue

William Temple

Sect. I

[…]

These four great monarchies, with the smaller kingdoms, principalities, and states that were swallowed up by their conquests and extent, make the subject of what is called ancient story, and are so excellently related by the many Greek and Latin authors still extant and in common vogue, so commented, enlarged, reduced into order of time and place by many more of the modern writers that they are known to all men who profess to study or entertain themselves with reading. The orders and institutions of these several governments, their progress and duration, their successes or decays, their events and revolutions, make the common themes of schools and colleges, the study of learned, and the conversation of idle men, the arguments of histories, poems, and romances. From the actions and fortunes of those princes and lawgivers are drawn the common examples of virtue and honour, the reproaches of vice, which are illustrated by the felicities or misfortunes that attend them. From the events and revolutions of these governments are drawn the usual instructions of princes and statesmen, and the discourses and reflections of the greatest wits and writers upon the politics. From the orders and institutions, the laws and customs of these empires and states, the sages of law and of justice in all countries endeavour to deduce the very common laws of nature and of nations, as well as the particular civil or municipal of kingdoms and provinces. From these they draw their arguments and precedents in all disputes concerning the pretended excellencies or defaults of the several sorts of governments that are extolled or decried, accused or defended; concerning the rights of war and peace, of invasion and defence between sovereign princes, as well as of authority and obedience, of prerogative and liberty, in civil contentions.

Yet the stage of all these empires, and revolutions of all these heroic actions, and these famous constitutions (how great or how wise soever any of them are esteemed) is but a limited compass of earth that leaves out many vast regions of the world, the which, though accounted barbarous and little taken notice of in story or by any celebrated authors, yet have a right to come in for their voice, in agreeing upon the laws of nature and nations (for aught I know) as well as the rest that have arrogated it wholly to themselves; and besides, in my opinion, there are some of them that, upon enquiry, will be found to have equalled or exceeded all the others in the wisdom of their constitutions, the extent of their conquests, and the duration of their empires or states.

William Temple, "Of heroic virtue," in *Five Miscellaneous Essays by Sir William Temple*, ed. Samuel Holt Monk, Ann Arbor, MI: University of Michigan Press, 1963, pp. 98, 104–7, 110–17, 121–3, 126–9, 133–6, 145–7, 151–4, 172.

[...]

Now, if we consider the map of the world as it lies at present before us since the discoveries made by the navigations of these three last centuries, we shall easily find what vast regions there are which have been left out of that ancient scene on all sides: and though passing for barbarous, they have not been esteemed worth the pens of any good authors, and are known only by common and poor relations of traders, seamen, or travellers; yet, by all I have read, I am inclined to believe that some of these outlying parts of the world, however unknown by the ancients, and overlooked by the modern learned, may yet have afforded as much matter of action and speculation, as the other scene so much celebrated in story; I mean not only in their vast extent and variety of soils and climates, with their natural productions, but even in the excellent constitutions of laws and customs, the wise and lasting foundations of states and empires, and the mighty flights of conquests that have risen from such orders and institutions.

Now, because the first scene is such a beaten road and this so little known or traced, I am content to take a short survey of four great schemes of government or empire that have sprung and grown to mighty heights, lived very long, and flourished much in these remote (and, as we will have it, more ignoble) regions of the world; whereof one is at the farthest degree of our eastern longitude, being the kingdom of China. The next is at the farthest western, which is that of Peru. The third is the outmost of our northern latitude, which is Scythia or Tartary. And the fourth is Arabia, which lies very far upon the southern.

[...]

Sect. II

[...]

This empire consists of fifteen several kingdoms, which at least have been so of old, though now governed as provinces by their several viceroys, who yet live in greatness, splendor, and riches, equal to the great and sovereign kings. In the whole kingdom are one hundred and forty-five capital cities, of mighty extent and magnificent building, and one thousand three hundred and twenty-one lesser cities, but all walled round; the number of villages is infinite, and no country in the known world so full of inhabitants, nor so improved by agriculture, by infinite growth of numerous commodities, by canals of incredible length, conjunctions of rivers, convenience of ways for the transportation of all sorts of goods and commodities from one province to another, so as no country has so great trade, though till very lately they never had any but among themselves; and what there is now foreign among them is not driven by the Chineses going out of their country to manage it, but only by the permission of the Portugueses and Dutch to come and trade in some skirts of their southern provinces.

[...]

As other nations are usually distinguished into noble and plebeian, so that of China may be distinguished into learned and illiterate. The last makes up the body and mass of the people who are governed, the first comprehends all the magistrates that govern, and those who may in time or course succeed them in the magistracy; for no other than the learned are ever employed in the government, nor any in the greatest charges that are not of those ranks or degrees of learning that make them termed sages, or philosophers, or doctors among them.

But to comprehend what this government of China is, and what the persons employed in it, there will be a necessity of knowing what their learning is, and how it makes them fit for government, very contrary to what ours in Europe is observed to do, and the reason of such different effects from the same cause.

The two great heroes of the Chinese nation were Fohu and Confuchu, whose memories have always continued among them sacred and adored. Fohu lived about four thousand years ago, and was the first founder of their kingdom; the progress whereof has ever since continued upon their records so clear that they are esteemed by the missionary Jesuits unquestionable and infallible. For, after the death of every king, the successor appoints certain persons to write the memorable actions of his predecessor's reign, and of these an epitome is afterwards drawn and entered into their registers. Fohu first reduced them from the common original lives of mankind, introduced agriculture, wedlock, distinction of sexes by different habits, laws, and orders of government: he invented characters, and left several short tables or writings of astronomy or observations of the heavens, of morality, of physic, and political government. The characters he used seem to have been partly strait lines of different lengths, and distinguished by different points, and partly hieroglyphics; and these in time were followed by characters, of which each expressed one word.

In these several ways were for many centuries composed many books among the Chineses, in many sorts of learning, especially natural and moral philosophy, astronomy, astrology, physic, and agriculture.

Something above two thousand years ago lived Confuchu, the most learned, wise, and virtuous of all the Chineses, and for whom both the king and magistrates in his own age, and all of them in the ages since, seem to have had the greatest deference that has anywhere been rendered to any mortal man. He writ many tracts, and in them digested all the learning of the ancients, even from the first writing or tables of Fohu, at least all that he thought necessary or useful to mankind in their personal, civil, or political capacities; which were then received and since prosecuted with so great esteem and veneration that none has questioned whatever he writ, but admitted it as the truest and best rules of opinion and life; so that it is enough in all argument that Confuchu has said it.

Some time after lived a king, who, to raise a new period of time from his own name and reign, endeavoured to abolish the memory of all that had passed before him, and caused all books to be burnt except those of physic and agriculture. Out of this ruin to learning escaped, either by chance, or some private industry, the epitomes or registers of the several successions of their kings since Fohu, and the works of Confuchu, or at least a part of them, which have lately in France been printed in the Latin tongue, with a learned preface, by some of the missionary Jesuits, under the title of the Works of Confucius.

After the death of this tyrannous and ambitious king, these writings came abroad, and, being the only remainders of the ancient Chinese learning, were received with general applause, or rather veneration: four learned men, having long addicted themselves to the study of these books, writ four several tracts or comments upon them; and one of the succeeding kings made a law that no other learning should be taught, studied, or exercised, but what was extracted out of these five books; and so learning has ever since continued in China, wholly confined to the writings of those five men, or rather to those of their prince of philosophers, the great and renowned Confucius.

The sum of his writings seem to be a body or digestion of ethics, that is, of all moral virtues, either personal, œconomical, civil, or political, and framed for the institution and conduct of men's lives, their families, and their governments, but chiefly of the last: the bent of his thoughts and reasonings running up and down this scale that no people can be happy but under good governments, and no governments happy but over good men; and that for the felicity of mankind, all men in a nation, from the prince to the meanest peasant, should endeavour to be good and wise, and virtuous, as far as his own thoughts, the precepts of others, or the laws of his country can instruct him.

The chief principle he seems to lay down for a foundation and builds upon, is that every man ought to study and endeavour the improving and perfecting of his own natural reason to the greatest height he is capable, so as he may never (or as seldom as can be) err and swerve from the law of nature in the course and conduct of his life: that this, being not to be done without much thought, enquiry, and diligence, makes study and philosophy necessary; which teaches men what is good and what is bad, either in its own nature or for theirs; and consequently what is to be done and what is to be avoided by every man in his several station or capacity. That in this perfection of natural reason consists the perfection of body and mind and the utmost or supreme happiness of mankind; that the means and rules to attain this perfection are chiefly not to will or desire anything but what is consonant to his natural reason, nor anything that is not agreeable to the good and happiness of other men, as well as our own. To this end is prescribed the constant course and practice of the several virtues, known and agreed so generally in the world; among which, courtesy or civility and gratitude are cardinal with them. In short, the whole scope of all Confucius has writ seems aimed only at teaching men to live well and to govern well; how parents, masters, and magistrates should rule, and how children, servants, and subjects should obey.

All this, with the many particular rules and instructions for either personal, œconomical, or political wisdom and virtue, is discoursed by him with great compass of knowledge, excellence of sense, reach of wit, and illustrated with elegance of style and aptness of similitudes and examples, as may be easily conceived by any that can allow for the lameness and shortness of translations out of language and manners of writing infinitely differing from ours. So as the man appears to have been of a very extraordinary genius, of mighty learning, admirable virtue, excellent nature, a true patriot of his country, and lover of mankind.

This is the learning of the Chineses, and all other sorts are either disused or ignoble among them; all that which we call scholastic or polemic is unknown or unpracticed, and serves, I fear, among us, for little more than to raise doubts and disputes, heats and feuds, animosities and factions in all controversies of religion or government. Even astrology and physic, and chymistry are but ignoble studies, though there are many among them that excel in all these; and the astrologers are much in vogue among the vulgar, as well as their predictions; the chymists apply themselves chiefly to the search of the universal medicine for health and length of life, pretending to make men immortal, if they can find it out; the physicians excel in the knowledge of the pulse and of all simple medicines, and go little further, but in the first are so skilful as they pretend not only to tell by it how many hours or days a sick man can last, but how many years a man in perfect seeming health may live, in case of no accident or violence; and by simples they pretend to relieve all diseases that nature will allow to be cured. They never let blood, but say, if the pot boils too fast, there is no need of lading out any of the water, but only of taking away the fire from

under it; and so they allay all heats of the blood by abstinence, diet, and cooling herbs.

But all this learning is ignoble and mechanical among them, and the Confucian only essential and incorporate to their government, into which none enters without having first passed through the several degrees. To attain it is first necessary the knowledge of their letters or characters; and to this must be applied at least ten or twelve years' study and diligence, and twenty for great perfection in it: for by all I can gather out of so many authors as have written of China, they have no letters at all, but only so many characters expressing so many words; these are said by some to be sixty, by others eighty, and by others six score thousand; and upon the whole, their writings seem to me to be like that of shorthand among us, in case there were a different character invented for every word in our language. Their writing is neither from the left-hand to the right like the European, nor from right to left like the Asiatic languages, but from top to bottom of the paper in one straight line, and then beginning again at the top till the side be full.

The learning of China therefore consists first in the knowledge of their language, and next in the learning, study, and practice of the writings of Confucius and his four great disciples; and as every man grows more perfect in both these, so he is more esteemed and advanced; nor is it enough to have read Confucius, unless it be discovered by retaining the principal parts of him in their memories, and the practice of him in their lives.

[...]

Upon these foundations and institutions, by such methods and orders, the kingdom of China seems to be framed and policed with the utmost force and reach of human wisdom, reason, and contrivance; and in practice to excel the very speculations of other men, and all those imaginary schemes of the European wits, the institutions of Xenophon, the republic of Plato, the Utopias, or Oceanas of our modern writers. And this will perhaps be allowed by any that considers the vastness, the opulence, the populousness of this region, with the ease and facility wherewith 'tis governed and the length of time this government has run. The last is three times longer than that of the Assyrian monarchy, which was thirteen hundred years and the longest period of any government we meet with in story. The numbers of people and of their forces, the treasures and revenues of the crown, as well as wealth and plenty of the subjects, the magnificence of their public buildings and works, would be incredible, if they were not confirmed by the concurring testimonies of Paulus Venetus, Martinius, Kercherus, with several other relations, in Italian, Portuguese, and Dutch; either by missionary friars, or persons employed thither upon trade, or embassies upon that occasion: yet the whole government is represented as a thing managed with as much facility, order, and quiet as a common family; though some writers affirm the number of people in China, before the last Tartar wars, to have been above two hundred millions. Indeed the canals cut through the country, or made by conjunctions of rivers, are so infinite, and of such lengths, and so perpetually filled with boats and vessels of all kinds that one writer believes there are near as many people in these and the ships wherewith their havens are filled who live upon the water, as those upon the land.

[...]

The great idea which may be conceived of the Chinese wisdom and knowledge, as well as their wit, ingenuity, and civility, by all we either read or see of them, is apt to be lessened by their gross and sottish idolatry; but this itself is only among the vulgar or illiterate, who worship after their manner whatever idols belong to each city, or village, or family; and the temples and priests belonging to them, are in usual request among the common people and the women. But the learned adore the spirit of the world, which they hold to be eternal; and this without temples, idols, or priests. And the Emperor only is allowed to sacrifice at certain times, by himself or his officers, at two temples in the two imperial cities of Peking and Nanking: one dedicated to heaven and t'other to the earth.

This I mention to shew how the furthest East and West may be found to agree in notions of divinity, as well as in excellence of civil or politic constitutions, by passing at one leap from these of China to those of Peru.

[...]

The kingdom of Peru deduced its original from their great heroes, Mango Copac, and his wife and sister Coya Mama, who are said to have first appeared in that country, near a mighty lake, which is still sacred with them upon this occasion.

Before this time, the people of these countries are reported to have lived like the beasts among them, without any traces of orders, laws, or religion, without other food than from the trees or the herbs, or what game they could catch, without further provision than for present hunger, without any clothing or houses; but dwelt in rocks, or caves, or trees, to be secure from wild beasts, or in tops of hills, if they were in fear of fierce neighbours. When Mango Copac and his sister came first into these naked lands, as they were persons of excellent shape and beauty, so they were adorned with such clothes as continued afterwards the usual habit of the Yncas, by which name they called themselves. They told the people who came first about them, that they were the son and daughter of the Sun, and that their father, taking pity of the miserable condition of mankind, had sent them down to reclaim them from those bestial lives and to instruct them how to live happily and safely, by observing such laws, customs, and orders as their father the Sun had commanded these his children to teach them. The great rule they first taught was that every man should live according to reason, and consequently neither say nor do any thing to others that they were not willing others should say or do to them; because it was against all common reason to make one law for ourselves, and another for other people: and this was the great principle of all their morality. In the next place that they should worship the Sun, who took care of the whole world, gave life to all creatures, and made the plants grow, and the herbs fit for food to maintain them; and was so careful and so good as to spare no pains of his own, but to go round the world every day to inspect and provide for all that was upon it, and had sent these his two children down on purpose for the good and happiness of mankind, and to rule them with the same care and goodness that he did the world. After this, they taught them the arts most necessary for life, as Mango Copac, to sow maize (or the common Indian grain) at certain seasons, to preserve it against others; to build houses against inclemencies of air and danger of wild beasts; to distinguish themselves by wedlock into several families; to clothe themselves, so as to cover at least the shame of nakedness; to tame and nourish such creatures as might be of common use and sustenance. Coya Mama taught the women to spin and weave both cotton and certain coarse wools of some beast among them.

With these instructions and inventions they were so much believed in all they said, and adored for what they did and taught of common utility, that they were followed by great numbers of people, observed and obeyed like sons of the Sun, sent down from heaven to instruct and to govern them. Mango Copac had in his hand a rod of gold about two feet long, and five inches round. He said that his father the Sun had given it him, and bid him, when he travelled northward from the lake, he should, every time he rested, strike this wand down into the ground, and where at the first stroke it should go down to the very top he should there build a temple to the Sun and fix the seat of his government.

This fell out to be in the vale of Cozco, where he founded that city which was head of this great kingdom of Peru.

Here he divided his company into two colonies or plantations, and called one the High Casco, and t'other the Low, and began here to be a lawgiver to those people. In each of these were at first a thousand families, which he caused all to be registered, with the numbers in each: this he did by strings of several colours, and knots of several kinds and colours upon them, by which both accounts were kept of things and times, and as much expressed of their minds as was necessary in government, where neither letters nor money, nor consequently disputes or avarice, with their consequences, ever entered.

He instituted Decurions through both these colonies, that is, one over every ten families, another over fifty, a third over a hundred, a fourth over five hundred, and a fifth over a thousand; and to this last they gave the name of a Curaca or governor. Every Decurion was a

censor, a patron, and a judge or arbiter in small controversies among those under his charge. They took care that every one clothed themselves, laboured, and lived according to the orders given them by the Yncas, from their father the Sun; among which one was that none who could work should be idle more than to rest after labour; and that none who could not work by age, sickness, or invalidity should want, but be maintained by the others' pains. These were so much observed that in the whole empire of Peru, and during the long race of the Ynca kings, no beggar was ever known; and no women ever so much as went to see a neighbour but with their work in their hands, which they followed all the time the visit lasted. Upon this, I remember a strain of refined civility among them, which was that when any woman went to see another of equal or ordinary birth, she worked at her own work in the other's house; but if she made a visit to any of the Pallas (which was the name by which they called all the women of the true royal blood, as Yncas was that of the men) then they immediately desired the Palla to give them a piece of her own work, and the visit passed in working for her. Idleness sentenced by the Decurions was punished by so many stripes in public, and the disgrace was more sensible than the pain. Every colony had one supreme judge, to whom the lower Decurions remitted great and difficult cases, or to whom (in such case) the criminals appealed: but every Decurion that concealed any crime of those under his charge above a day and a night, became guilty of it, and liable to the same punishment. There were laws or orders likewise against theft, mutilations, murders, disobedience to officers, and adulteries (for every man was to have one lawful wife, but had the liberty of keeping other women as he could). The punishment of all crimes was either corporal pains or death, but commonly the last, upon these two reasons which they gave: first, that all crimes, whether great or small, were of the same nature and deserved the same punishment, if they were committed against the divine commands, which were sent them down from the Sun: next, that to punish any man in his possessions or charges, and leave them alive and in strength and liberty, was to leave an ill man more incensed, or necessitated to commit new crimes. On t'other side, they never forfeited the charge or possessions of a son for his father's offences; but the judges only remonstrated to him the guilt and punishment of them for his warning or example. These orders had so great force and effect, that many times a whole year passed without the execution of one criminal.

[...]

I will say nothing of the greatness, magnificence, and riches of their buildings, palaces, or temples, especially those of the Sun; of the splendor of their court, their triumphs after victories, their huntings and feasts, their military exercises and honours; but, as testimonies of their grandeur, mention only two of their highways, whereof one was five hundred leagues, plain and levelled through mountains, rocks, and valleys, so that a carriage might drive through the whole length without difficulty. Another very long and large, paved all with cut or squared stone, fenced with low walls on each side, and set with trees, whose branches gave shade, and the fruits food, to all that passed.

I shall end this survey of their government with one remark upon their religion, which is that, though the vulgar worshiped only the Sun, yet the *Amautas*, who were their sages or philosophers, taught that the Sun was only the great minister of *Pachacamac*, whom they adored in the first place, and to whom a great and sumptuous temple was dedicated. This word is interpreted by the Spaniard, *Animador del mundo*, or *He that animates or enlivens the world*; and seems to be yet a more refined notion of the deity than that of the Chineses, who adored the spirit and soul of the world. By this principle of their religion, as all the others of their government and policy, it must, I think, be allowed that human nature is the same in these remote, as well as the other more known and celebrated parts of the world: that the different governments of it are framed and cultivated by as great reaches and strength of reason and of wisdom as any of ours, and some of their frames less subject to be shaken by the passions, factions, and other corruptions to which those in the middle scene of Europe and Asia have been so often and so much exposed: that the same causes produce every where the same effects; and that the same honours and

obedience are in all places but consequences or tributes paid to the same heroic virtue, or transcendent genius, in what parts soever, or under what climates of the world, it fortunes to appear.

Sect. IV

[...]

'Tis agreed in story that the Scythians conquered the Medes, during the periods of that race in the Assyrian empire, and were masters of Asia for fifteen years, till they returned home upon domestic occasions; that Cyrus was beaten and slain by their fury and revenge under the leading of a woman, whose wit and conduct made a great figure in ancient story; that the Romans were defeated by the Parthians, who were of the Scythian race.

But the great hero of the Eastern Scythians or Tartars I esteem to have been Tamerlane, and, whether he was son of a shepherd or a king, to have been the greatest conqueror that was ever in the world, at least that appears upon any present records of story. His achievements were great upon China, where he subdued many provinces, and forced their King to such conditions of a peace as he was content to impose. He made war against the Muscovites with the same success, and partly by force, partly by consent, he gained a passage through their territories for that vast army which he led against Bajazet (then the terror of the world). He conquered this proud Turk and his whole empire, as far as the Hellespont, which he crossed, and made a visit to the poor Greek Emperor at Constantinople, who had sent to make alliance with him upon his first invasion of Bajazet, at whose mercy this prince then almost lay, with the small remainders of the Grecian Empire. Nothing was greater or more heroical in this victorious Tamerlane than the faith and honour wherewith he observed this alliance with the Greeks; for having been received at Constantinople with all the submissions that could be made him, having viewed and admired the greatness and structure of that noble city, and said it was fit to make the seat for the empire of the world, and having the offer of it freely made him by the Greeks to possess it for his own; yet, after many honours exchanged between these two princes, he left this city in the freedom, and the Greek Emperor in the possessions he found them, went back into Asia, and in his return conquered Syria, Persia, and India, where the Great Moguls have ever since boasted to be the race of Tamerlane. After all these conquests, he went home and passed the rest of his age in his own native kingdom, and died a fair and natural death, which was a strain of felicity, as well as greatness, beyond any of the conquerors of the four renowned monarchies of the world. He was, without question, a great and heroic genius, of great justice, exact discipline, generous bounty, and much piety, adoring one God, though he was neither Christian, Jew, nor Mahometan, and deserves a nobler character than could be allowed by modern writers to any person of a nation so unlike themselves.

[...]

... Their bodies indeed were hard and strong, their minds rough and fierce, their numbers infinite, which was owing perhaps all to their climate: but, besides these advantages, their courage was undaunted, their business was war, their pleasures were dangers, their very sports were martial; their disputes and processes were decided by arms; they feared nothing but too long life, decays of age, and a natural or slothful death – any violent or bloody they desired and pursued; and all this from their opinion of one being succeeded by miseries, the other by felicities, of a future and a longer life.

For my own part, when I consider the force of this principle, I wonder not at the effects of it, their numerous conquests, nor immensity of countries they subdued, nor that such strange adventures should have been finished by such enchanted men. But when Christianity, introduced among them, gave an end to these delusions, the restless humour of perpetual wars and actions was likewise allayed, and they turned their thoughts to the establishment of their several kingdoms, in the provinces they had subdued and chosen for their seats, and applied themselves to the orders and constitutions of their civil or political governments.

Their principle of learning was that all they had among them was applied to the knowledge and distinction of seasons by the course of the stars, and to the prognostics of weather, or else to the praises of virtue, which consisted among them only in justice to their own nation and valour against their enemies; and the rest was employed in displaying the brave and heroic exploits of their princes and leaders, and the prowess and conquest of their nation; all their writings were composed in verse, which were called *Runes* or *Viises*, and from thence the term of wise came: and these poets or writers, being esteemed the sages among them, were, as such, always employed in the attendance upon their princes, both in courts and camps, being used to advise in their conduct, and to record their actions and celebrate their praises and triumphs. The traces of these customs have been seen within the compass of this very age, both in Hungary and Ireland, where, at their feasts, it was usual to have these kind of poets entertain the company with their rude songs or panegyrics of their ancestors' bold exploits; among which the number of men that any of them had slain with their own hands was the chief ingredient in their praises. By these, they rewarded the prowess of the old men among them, and inflamed the courage of the young to equal the boldness and achievements of those that had travelled before them in these paths of glory.

The principle of politic or civil government in these Northern nations seems derived from that which was military among them. When a new swarm was upon the wing, they chose a leader or general for the expedition, and, at the same time, the chief officers to command the several divisions of their troops; these were a council of war to the general, with whom they advised in the whole progress of their enterprise; but upon great occasions, as a pitched battle, any military exploit of great difficulty and danger, the choice of a country to fix their seat, or the conditions of peace that were proposed, they assembled their whole troops, and consulted with all the soldiers or people they commanded. This Tacitus observes to have been in use among the German princes in his time, to consult of smaller affairs with the chief officers, but *de majoribus omnes*.

If a leader of these colonies succeeded in his attempts and conquered a new country, where by common consent they thought fit to reside, he grew a prince of that country while he lived; and when he died another was chosen to succeed him by a general election. The lands of the subdued territory were divided into greater and smaller shares, besides that reserved to the prince and government. The great were given to the chief officers of the army, who had best deserved and were most esteemed; the smaller to the common or private soldiers. The natives conquered were wholly despoiled of their lands, and reckoned but as slaves by the conquerors, and so used for labour and servile offices, and those of the conquering nation were the freemen. The great sharers, as chief officers, continued to be the council of the prince in matters of state, as they had been before in matters of war; but in the great affairs, and of common concernment, all that had the smaller shares in land were assembled and advised with. The first great shares were, in process of time, called baronies, and the small, fees.

[…]

Sect. V

The last survey I propose of the four outlying (or, if the learned so please to call them, barbarous) empires, was that of the Arabians, which was indeed of a very different nature from all the rest, being built upon foundations wholly enthusiastic, and thereby very unaccountable to common reason, and in many points contrary even to human nature; yet few others have made greater conquests or more sudden growths than this Arabian or Saracen Empire; but having been of later date, and the course of it engaged in perpetual wars with the Christian princes, either of the East or West, of the Greek or the Latin churches, both the original and progress of it have been easily observed and are most vulgarly known, having been the subject of many modern writers, and several well digested histories or relations; and therefore I shall give but a very summary account of both.

About the year 600 or near it, lived Mahomet, a man of mean parentage and condition, illiterate, but of great spirit and subtle wit, like those of the climate or country where he was born or bred, which was that part of Arabia called The Happy, esteemed the loveliest and sweetest region of the world…

He was servant to a rich merchant of this country, and after his master's death, having married his widow, came to be possessed of great wealth and of a numerous family: among others, he had entertained in it a Sergian monk, or at least called by that name, whose vicious and libertine dispositions of life had made him leave his enclosure and profession, but otherwise a man of great learning. Mahomet was subject to fits of an epilepsy or falling-sickness, and, either by the customs of that climate, or the necessity of that disease, very temperate and abstaining from wine, but in the rest voluptuous and dissolute. He was ashamed of his disease, and, to disguise it from his wife and family, pretended his fits were trances into which he was cast at certain times by God Almighty, and in them instructed in his will, and his true worship and laws, by which he would be served; and that he was commanded to publish them to the world, to teach them, and see them obeyed.

About this age all the Christian provinces of the East were overrun with Arianism, which, however refined or disguised by its learned professors and advocates, either denied or undermined the divinity of Christ, and allowed only his prophetical office. The countries of Arabia and Ægypt were filled with great numbers of the scattered Jews, who, upon the last destruction of their country in Adrian's time, had fled into these provinces to avoid the ruin and even extinction which was threatening their nation by that emperor, who, after all the desolations he made in Judea, transported what he could of their remaining numbers into Spain. The rest of Arabia and Ægypt was inhabited by Gentiles, who had little sense left of their decayed and derided idolatry, and had turned their thoughts and lives to luxury and pleasure, and to the desires and acquisition of riches, in order to those ends. Mahomet, to humour and comply with these three sorts of men, and by the assistance of the monk his only confident, framed a scheme of religion he thought likely to take in, or at least not to shock, the common opinions and dispositions of them all, and yet most agreeable to his own temper and designs.

He professed one God, creator of the world, and who governed all things in it. That God had in ancient times sent Moses, his first and great prophet, to give his laws to mankind, but that they were neither received by the Gentiles, nor obeyed by the Jews themselves, to whom he was more peculiarly sent. That this was the occasion of the misfortunes and captivities that so often befell them. That in the latter ages he had sent Christ, who was the second prophet, and greater than Moses, to preach his laws and observation of them, in greater purity, but to do it with gentleness, patience, and humility, which had found no better reception or success among men than Moses had done. That for this reason God had now sent his last and greatest prophet Mahomet, to publish his laws and commands with more power, to subdue those to them by force and violence who should not willingly receive them; and for this end to establish a kingdom upon earth that should propagate this divine law and worship throughout the world. That as God had designed utter ruin and destruction to all that refused them, so, to those that professed and obeyed them, he had given the spoils and possessions of his and their enemies as a reward in this life, and had provided a paradise hereafter, with all sensual enjoyments, especially of beautiful women new created for that purpose; but with more transcendent degrees of pleasure and felicity to those that should die in the pursuit and propagation of them, through the rest of the world, which should in time submit or be subdued under them: these, with the severe prohibition of drinking wine, and the principle of predestination, were the first and chief doctrines and institutions of Mahomet, and which were received with great applause, and much confluence of Arians, Jews, and Gentiles in those parts; some contributing to the rise of his kingdom by the belief of his divine mission and authority; many, by finding their chief principles or religious opinions contained or allowed in them; but most, by their voluptuousness and luxury, their passions of avarice, ambition, and revenge being thereby complied with. After his fits or trances, he writ the many several parts or chapters of his Alcoran, as newly inspired and dictated from heaven, and left in them that

which to us, and in its translations, looks like a wild fanatic rhapsody of his visions or dreams, or rather of his fantastical imaginations and inventions, but has ever passed among all his followers as a book sacred and divine; which shews the strange difference of conceptions among men.

To be short, this contagion was so violent that it spread from Arabia into Ægypt and Syria, and his power increased with such a sudden growth as well as his doctrine that he lived to see them overspread both those countries and a great part of Persia; the decline of the old Roman Empire making easy way for the powerful ascent of this new comet that appeared with such wonder and terror in the world, and with a flaming sword made way wherever it came, or laid all desolate that opposed it.

Mahomet left two branches of his race for succession, which was in both esteemed divine among his Mussulmans or followers; the one was continued in the Caliphs of Persia, and th'other of Ægypt and Arabia: both these, under the common appellation of Saracens, made mighty and wonderful progress, the one to the east, and the other to the west.

[...]

After all that has been said of conquerors or conquests, this must be confessed to hold but the second rank in the pretensions to heroic virtue, and that the first has been allowed to the wise institution of just orders and laws, which frame safe and happy governments in the world. The designs and effects of conquests are but the slaughter and ruin of mankind, the ravaging of countries, and defacing the world: those of wise and just governments are preserving and increasing the lives and generations of men, securing their possessions, encouraging their endeavours, and by peace and riches improving and adorning the several scenes of the world.

So the institutions of Moses leave him a diviner character than the victories of Joshua: those of Belus, Osiris, and Janus, than the prowess of Ninus, Cyrus, and Sesostris. And if, among the ancients, some men have been esteemed heroes by the brave achievements of great conquests and victories, it has been by the wise institution of laws and government, that others have been honoured and adored as gods.

18

Of the Origin of Fables[1]

Bernard le Bovier de Fontenelle

We have been so accustomed to Greek fables in our childhood that, when we are at an age where we can reason, we no longer notice how astonishing they are. But if we manage to take off the blindfold of familiarity, we cannot help being horrified to see all of the ancient history of a people reduced to an amalgam of chimeras, dreams, and absurdities. Is it possible that these were ever portrayed as truth? Why would they have been purposefully told as falsehoods? Because the fables of the Greeks are not like novels, which are offered for what they are, and not as historical; there is no other ancient history apart from fables. Let us shed some light, if we can, on this question; let us study the human mind in its strangest creations: this is often the best way it presents itself to our understanding.

In the first centuries of the world, and among nations who had never heard of the traditions of the family of Seth,[2] or else who had forgotten them, ignorance and barbarism were so prevalent that we are hardly capable of representing it. Think of the Kaffirs, the Lapps, and the Iroquois;[3] and we must bear in mind that these people, too, have a long history, and they must have attained a greater degree of learning and politeness than the earliest men.

The more ignorant people are, and the less experience they have, the more they see wonders. Thus, the earliest men saw many; and since fathers naturally tell their children what they have seen and done, the tales of those times consisted only of wonders.

When we tell a surprising story, our imagination gets all excited about the subject, and on its own exaggerates it and adds whatever is lacking to make it entirely marvelous, as if it regretted to let something beautiful remain imperfect. Moreover, we are flattered by the feelings of surprise and admiration we excite among our listeners, and we are inclined to add even more, because it contributes I know not what to our vanity. These two reasons added together explain why a man who has no intention of lying in beginning a somewhat extraordinary story can surprise himself by telling a lie, unless he takes precautions against exaggeration. From this it follows that we need to make an effort and to pay special attention in order to avoid saying anything that is not precisely true. How would this be for those who naturally like to invent things and impress others?

The tales that the earliest men told to their children were often false in themselves because they were told by people who tended to see many things which didn't exist, and having in addition been exaggerated, either in good faith, as we just explained, or in bad faith, it is evident that they were already rotten at the outset. But they certainly would get much worse

Bernard le Bovier de Fontenelle, "*Of the Origin of Fables*," trans. by Robert Launay.

once they were passed from person to person; every teller would remove some true detail and substitute a false one, particularly a marvelous falsehood which would best please the audience. Perhaps, after a century or two, not only would nothing remain of what little truth there was at the beginning, but perhaps not even many of the original falsehoods.

Will anyone believe what I will now assert? There was philosophy even in these crude centuries, and it greatly assisted the production of fables. Those who have a little more intelligence than others are naturally inclined to seek out the cause of what they see. Where can this stream which flows all the time come from, a thinker from those first centuries must have asked? He was a strange sort of philosopher, but he may have been the Descartes of his day. After much meditation, he came to the happy conclusion that there must be someone who pours the water in from a jar. But who provided this water? Our thinker didn't get that far.

We must take into account that these ideas, which might be called the philosophical systems of those ages, were always copied from those things that were best known. They had often seen water poured into a jar. They could easily imagine how a god could pour it into a stream, and from the ease with which they could imagine it, they were all the more inclined to believe it. Thus, to explain thunder and lightning, they readily arrived at a representation of a god in human form who would lance iron arrows in our direction, an idea manifestly drawn from very familiar objects.

This philosophy of the first centuries worked according to a principle so natural that, even today, our philosophy knows no other; that is to say, we explain unknown phenomena in nature by those which we have before our eyes, and we apply in physics the ideas which experience provides us. We have discovered through use, and not by guessing, what levers, weights, and springs can do. Levers, weights and springs are the tools we possess to make Nature do our bidding. These poor savages who were the first to inhabit the world either didn't know these things or didn't pay them any attention. They only explained the effects of Nature by the crudest and most palpable things they knew. What have all of us

ever done? We have always represented the unknown in the guise of what we know; but fortunately we have all the reason in the world to believe that the unknown cannot be entirely unlike what we know at present.

This crude philosophy which necessarily reigned in the earliest centuries gave birth to gods and goddesses. It is curious to see how human imagination created false divinities. Men saw many things which they themselves couldn't do: hurl thunderbolts, stir up winds, and create sea currents, all this was way beyond their capacities. They imagined beings much more powerful than they, capable of producing such powerful effects. Such beings must have been like men; what other form could they have taken? From the moment they had human likenesses, imagination naturally attributed them all that is human; they appeared as human in every respect, with the exception that they were always a little more powerful than men.

This leads us to an issue that has perhaps not yet received much attention; it is that, among all the divinities which the pagans imagined, the idea of power predominated, with almost no regard either for wisdom, justice, nor any of the other attributes of divine nature. Nothing better proves that these divinities are very ancient or better shows the path that the imagination took in forming them. The earliest men knew no feature more desirable than physical strength; wisdom and justice did not even have a name in ancient languages, as they still remain unnamed among the American barbarians. In any case, the first idea that men formulated of some superior being was derived from extraordinary effects, and in no way from the regular order of the universe which they were in no way capable of recognizing or admiring. Thus, they imagined gods at a time where they had nothing more beautiful to bestow on them than power, and were in no way inclined to grant them wisdom. It is consequently not surprising that they imagined several gods, often in conflict with one another, who were cruel, bizarre, and ignorant. All this does not directly contradict the idea of force and power, the only one which they would have adopted. It was necessary that these gods reflect the period in which they had been created and the circumstances which led to their invention. Even so, what was the miserable sort of power which they were given? Mars, the god of war, is wounded in combat with a mortal; this detracts a great deal from his dignity. But in withdrawing from combat, he lets out a shout louder than ten thousand men could make. It is by this vigorous shout that Mars triumphs over Diomedes. This is enough, according to the judicious Homer, to save the god's honor. Given the nature of such imagination, it contents itself with very little, and will always take for a divinity anything which has a bit more power than a human.

Cicero said somewhere that he would have preferred that Homer lent the attributes of gods to men, rather than, as he did, the attributes of men to gods. But Cicero was asking too much; what, in his day, he called the attributes of gods were totally unknown in Homer's time. The pagans always copied divinities after themselves; thus, to the extent that humanity perfected itself, gods too became more perfect. The earliest men were very brutal, and they only respected strength; the gods were almost as brutal, and only a little more powerful; these are the gods of Homer's time. When men begin to acquire ideas of wisdom and justice, the gods improve; they begin to be wise and just, and are always that much more so as these ideas are perfected among humans. These are the gods of Cicero, and they were worth much more than those of Homer's time, because much better philosophers had contributed to their elaboration.

For all intents and purposes, the earliest men deserve no blame for inventing fables. They were ignorant, and they consequently witnessed many marvels. They naturally exaggerated surprising things when telling about them; the stories acquired diverse additional falsehoods when transmitted from person to person. This established systems of philosophy that were very crude and absurd, but it was impossible to come up with any others. We will now see how, with these foundations, men took pleasure to a certain extent in fooling themselves.

What we call philosophy in these early centuries was properly tied to the narration of events. A young man fell into a stream and his body was never recovered. What became of him? The philosophy of that time taught that there were young women in that stream who rule over it. That these young women waylaid the young man seemed perfectly natural; there was no need of proof to believe it. Suppose a man whose ascendance was unknown possessed some extraordinary talent; since there were gods who resembled humans, there was little need to identify his parents; he was the son of one of these gods. When you carefully consider the majority of fables, you find that they are nothing but a hodgepodge of events seen through the lens of the philosophy of those times, which very conveniently explained what was marvelous about these events, to which they were naturally associated. There were only gods and goddesses who resembled us entirely, and who were well matched with humans.

Since the story of true events wedded to imaginary falsehoods was so prevalent, people began to elaborate stories without any foundation. Or, at least, any events which were only somewhat remarkable could not be narrated without adorning them with ornaments which the tellers noticed were apt to please the audience. Such ornaments were false, and perhaps they were even put forth as such; nevertheless, such histories were not considered fabulous. It is easy to understand this if you compare modern to ancient history.

In periods where thought is more developed, as in Augustus' century or our own, we like to reason about the actions of men, to penetrate their motives and know their character. The historians of such centuries accommodated themselves to such tastes. They refrained from relating events straightforwardly and dryly. They accompanied them with motives along with portraits of their main protagonists. Do we think that such portraits or such motives are precisely true? Do we have as much faith in them as in facts? No; we are well aware that historians have made inferences as best as they could, and that it is nearly impossible that these inferences are always true. Nevertheless, we don't find fault with the fact that historians have sought to add such embellishments which are not unrealistic; it is because of this realism that the incorporation of falsehoods which we admit might be included in our histories doesn't make us consider them as fables.

Similarly, in the way we have indicated, if ancient peoples acquired a taste for histories including gods and goddesses, and more generally marvelous occurrences, no one told histories which were not so embellished. They knew that they couldn't be true; but in those times, they were considered realistic, and this sufficed to classify such fables as history.

Even nowadays Arabs fill their histories with prodigies and marvels, most often ridiculous and grotesque ones. Undoubtedly they only take these to be embellishments which will not fool them, because among them it is a sort of convention to write in this manner. But when these kinds of histories are read by other peoples whose taste dictates that narratives of facts be strictly true, either they are taken literally, or at least readers are persuaded that they were taken literally by those who first wrote them and accepted them without contest. This is certainly a considerable misunderstanding. When I stated that the falsehood in these histories was recognized for what it was, I meant by those who were somewhat enlightened; as for the masses, they are destined to be fooled by everything.

In the early centuries, not only was everything surprising in the history of events explained by a chimerical philosophy, but what belonged to philosophy was explained by a narrative of imaginary events. They saw in the north two constellations called the two bears, which were always visible and never sank below the horizon like the others. No one took care to imagine that they inclined in the direction of a pole high above the heads of spectators; they did not know that much. They imagined that, of these two bears, one had once been the mistress and the other the son of Jupiter; that, having been turned into constellations, the jealous Juno begged that the Ocean refuse to let them rest by sinking down like the others into its midst. All these metamorphoses are the physics of the first ages. Blackberries are red because they were stained with the blood of two lovers; the partridge always flies low because Daedalus, who turned into a partridge, remembered the sad fate of his son who flew too high; and so forth. I have never forgotten that I was told in my childhood that elder trees used to have grapes which tasted as good as those on the vine; but because the traitor Judas hanged himself on that tree, its fruit turned bitter. This fable can only have been devised after the advent of Christianity; and it is precisely of the same species as those which Ovid collected, which is to say that men have always had an inclination for this type of story. They have the double advantage of striking the imagination through some marvelous feature and of satisfying curiosity by the explanation they provide for some natural and well-known phenomenon.

Aside from these particular principles explaining the birth of fables, there are two others, more general, which have certainly favored them. The first is the right to invent things that resemble those we have been told, or to draw additional conclusions from them. Some extraordinary event might have led to the belief that a god had been in love with some woman; soon, all histories will be full of amorous deities. If you believe one, why not the others? If gods have children, they love them and wield all their powers on their behalf as needs be; here is an inexhaustible source for marvels which one can only label absurd.

The second principle which reinforces these errors is the blind respect for antiquity. Our forefathers believed this; can we presume to be wiser than they? These two principles taken together make marvels. The first, building on the slightest weakness provided by human nature, infinitely expands some imbecility; the other, granted that it has been established, perpetuates it forever. The one, because we are already in error, engages us to be more and more so; the other forbids us to abandon such errors because they have already been believed for a long time.

This, in all likelihood, is what has elevated fables to the high degree of absurdity which they achieved and in which they were preserved; what nature furnished in its own right was neither so ridiculous nor so widespread; and men are not so mad either that they could all of a sudden have given birth to such fantasies, believed in them, and maintained their credence for so long, unless the two principles we just mentioned were not involved.

If we examine the errors of recent centuries, we will find that the same principles established, exaggerated, and preserved them. It is true that we have not formulated any absurdity as considerable as the ancient Greek fables; but this is because we have not started off from such an absurd state. We are just as apt to expand and preserve our own errors. Fortunately, they are not so big, because we are enlightened by true Religion and, in my opinion, a few rays of true Philosophy.

We usually attribute the origin of fables to the lively imagination of Orientals; but, as for me, I attribute it to the ignorance of the first men. Put a new people on earth, and their first histories will be fables; in fact, aren't the ancient histories of northern lands full of them? They tell only of giants and magicians. I won't deny that hot and lively sunshine won't provide imaginations with an extra ingredient which might perfect their disposition to regale themselves with fables; but all men have had this talent, independent of sunlight. Thus, in all that I have said, I have only taken into account what all men have in common, and which should operate in glacial as well as in torrid zones.

I can even demonstrate, if necessary, an astonishing conformity between the fables of the [native] Americans and those of the Greeks. The Americans consigned the souls of those who had lived evil lives to muddy and unpleasant lakes, just as the Greeks consigned them to the banks of the rivers Styx and Acheron. The Americans believed that rain came when a young girl living in the clouds was playing with her younger brother, and he broke her jar full of water. Doesn't this resemble the fountain nymphs, who pour water out from urns? According to the traditions of Peru, the Inca Manco Guyna Capac, son of the sun, was able by his eloquence to make people who lived like beasts leave the forest and live under reasonable laws. Orpheus did as much for the Greeks, and he too was son of the sun. This shows that the Greeks were for a time as savage as the Americans, and that they were rescued from their barbarity by the same means; and that the imaginations of both peoples, living so far from one another, agreed in believing

that those who possessed extraordinary talents were sons of the sun. The Greeks, subtle thinkers as they were, when they were a young people, did not think any more reasonably than American barbarians who were, in all likelihood, a young enough people when they were discovered by the Spaniards. Thus there is reason to believe that the Americans would in the long run have come to think as reasonably as the Greeks, had they only been given the chance.

We also find among the ancient Chinese the same method that the ancient Greeks had of making up stories to explain natural things. Where do the ebb and the tide come from? You can be sure that they won't think of the effects of the moon's attraction. It is that a princess had a hundred children. Fifty lived on the shores of the sea, and the other fifty in the mountains. This was the origin of two great peoples who are often at war with one another. When the inhabitants of the shores are prevailing over the mountain dwellers, and push them away, it is the tide; when they are repelled, and they flee from the mountains towards the shore, it is the ebb. This manner of philosophizing quite resembles Ovid's metamorphoses; we see how true it is that the same ignorance produced approximately the same effects among all peoples.

It is for this reason that there is no history which does not begin with fables, apart from the Chosen People, among whom Providence preserved the truth.[4] How amazingly slowly did men arrive at any reasonable conclusions, however simple! To preserve the memory of events as they were is no great marvel; nonetheless, several centuries elapsed before they were able to do it, and up to then the events whose memory was preserved were only of visions and dreams. We would be very wrong to be surprised after this that philosophy and modes of reasoning were for many centuries very crude and very imperfect, and that even now progress remains very slow.

Among most peoples, fables were turned into religion; but in addition, among the Greeks, they were turned, so to speak, into entertainment. Poetry and painting, as they furnish ideas which conform to the imagination of the commonest of men, were perfectly suited, and we know what passion the Greeks had for these two arts. Divinities of all sorts all over the place, who make everything lively and animated, who are interested in everything and, most importantly, divinities who often act in surprising ways, cannot fail to make a pleasant impression, either in poems or in paintings, where it is only a matter of seducing the imagination by presenting it with objects it can easily grasp and which are simultaneously striking. How could fables, who owe their origins to this very imagination, not be suitable? When poetry and painting mobilized them to offer a spectacle to our imagination, they just served back its own creations.

Once these errors are established among men, they customarily grow deep roots, and hold on to different things which sustain them. Religion and common sense free us from the fables of the Greeks; but they still survive among us through the media of poetry and painting, where they seem to have found the secret of making themselves indispensable. We are incomparably more enlightened than those whose crude mind invented in good faith the fables they found so agreeable; they delighted in them because they believed them, and we delight in them with as much pleasure without believing them. Nothing demonstrates more effectively that imagination and reason have little truck with one another, and that things which have lost all hold on reason have lost none of their charms for the imagination.

We have until now only taken into account in our history of the origin of fables that which springs from human nature, and this is effectively the most important factor; but there are other influences whose role we must also acknowledge. For example, the Phoenicians and the Egyptians were older peoples than the Greeks. Their fables were passed on to the Greeks and were exaggerated in the transmission, so that even their truest histories became fables. The Phoenician (and perhaps the Egyptian) language was full of words with double meanings; moreover, the Greeks didn't much understand either meaning, which provided a marvelous source of misunderstanding. Two Egyptians, whose name meant "Dove,"

settled in the forest of Dodona in order to tell fortunes. The Greeks understood that there were two doves perched in trees who prophesied, and soon that the trees themselves foretold the future. The Phoenician name for a ship's rudder can also mean "talking"; the Greeks, in their history of the ship *Argo*, imagined a rudder which spoke. Scholars have lately found a thousand other examples, where we clearly see that the origin of several fables consists of what we commonly call a mix-up, and that the Greeks were very prone to making them with Egyptian or Phoenician terms. As for me, I find that the Greeks, who possessed so much intelligence and curiosity, lacked one as well as the other in not taking pains to learn these languages perfectly, or neglecting them. Didn't they know that almost all their towns were Egyptian or Phoenician colonies, and that most of their ancient history came from those lands? Didn't the origins of their languages and their antiquities depend on both these languages? But they were barbarian languages, harsh and disagreeable to the ear. What charming scruples!

Once the art of writing was invented, it served to disseminate fables, enriching one people with all the idiocies of another; but we gained the advantage that uncertain traditions were to some extent fixed, that the stock of fables did not increase so fast, and that they stayed in more or less the state where the invention of writing found them.

Ignorance slowly diminished, and consequently there were fewer miracles, fewer false systems of philosophy, histories grew less fabulous; because all of this follows. Beforehand, the memory of past things was only preserved out of pure curiosity; but once people perceived that it could be useful to maintain it, whether to matters of national pride, or to arbitrate differences which could arise between peoples, or to provide models of virtue; I think that this latter use was the last they thought of, even though it is the one which is most touted nowadays. All this required that history be true; I mean, true by comparison to ancient histories, which were only full of absurdities. Thus several nations began to write history in a more reasonable manner, which was generally realistic.

At this point, no new fables appeared; they were content to preserve the old ones. But of what are minds madly enamored of antiquity not capable? They imagine that these fables contain hidden secrets of physics or morality.[5] Was it possible that the Ancients could have produced such reveries without meaning something intelligent? The name of the Ancients is always imposing; but certainly those who produced fables weren't apt to be people who knew anything of morality or physics, much less of finding the art of disguising them through borrowed images.

Let us not look for anything else in fables than the history of the errors of the human mind. The mind is less capable of error once it realizes precisely what it has achieved. It is not science to stuff one's head with all the extravagances of the Phoenicians and the Greeks; but it is one to know what led the Phoenicians and the Greeks to these extravagances. All men are so much alike that there is no people on earth whose idiocies should not make us tremble.

NOTES

1 Fontenelle uses the word "fable" to refer to what we would now call "myth" (translator's note).

2 The Biblical traditions of the Old Testament; even freethinkers like Fontenelle would be careful to avoid contradicting Biblical authority publicly (translator's note).

3 I have retained the original terminology, although Kaffir and Lapp among other terms are now considered highly offensive (translator's note).

4 Fontenelle took pains in this sentence to insist that he was not contradicting the Scriptural account; he had, in fact, been accused (not improbably) of being a freethinker, and narrowly escaped getting into serious trouble for a satire he wrote which made fun of controversies between Catholics and Protestants (translator's note).

5 Fontenelle is referring to the current practice of his time of interpreting myths as allegories (translator's note).

Section V

(b) Putting Words in Their Mouths: Dialogues and Letters

19

New Voyages
to North America

Baron de Lahontan

I have read some Histories of *Canada*, which were writ at several times by the Monks, and must own that they have given some plain and exact Descriptions of such Countries as they knew; but at the same time they are widely mistaken in their Accounts of the Manners and Customs of the Savages. The Recollets brand the Savages for stupid, gross and rustick Persons, uncapable of Thought or Reflection: But the Jesuits give them other sort of Language, for they intitle them to good Sense, to a tenacious Memory, and to a quick Apprehension season'd [3] with a solid Judgment. The former allege that 'tis to no purpose to preach the Gospel to a sort of People that have less Knowledge than the Brutes.[1] On the other hand the latter (I mean the Jesuits) give it out, that these Savages take Pleasure in hearing the Word of God, and readily apprehend the meaning of the Scriptures. In the mean time, 'tis no difficult matter to point to the Reasons that influence the one and the other to such Allegations; the Mystery is easily unravell'd by those who know that these two Orders cannot set their Horses together in *Canada*.

I have seen so many impertinent Accounts of this Country, and those written by Authors that pass'd for Saints; that I now begin to believe, that all History is one continued Series of Pyrrhonism. Had I been unacquainted with the Language of the Savages, I might have

credited all that was said of them; but the opportunity I had of Conversing with that People, serv'd to undeceive me, and gave me to understand, that the Recollets and the Jesuits content themselves with glancing at things, without taking notice of the (almost) invincible Aversion of the Savages to the Truths of Christianity. Both the one and the other had good reason to be cautious of touching upon that String. In the mean time suffer me to acquaint you, that upon this Head I only speak of the Savages of *Canada*, excluding those that live beyond the River of *Missisipi*, of whose Manners and Customs I could not acquire a perfect Scheme, by reason that I was unacquainted with their Languages, not to mention that I had not time to make any long stay in their Country. In the Journal of my Voyage upon the long River, I acquainted you that they are a very polite People, which you [4] will likewise infer from the Circumstances mention'd in that Discourse.

[...]

The greatest Passion of the Savages consists in the Implacable Hatred they bear to their Enemies; that is, all Nations with whom they are at Open War: They value themselves mightily upon their Valour; insomuch that they have scarce any regard to any thing else. One may say, That they are wholly govern'd by Temperament, and their Society is perfect

Baron de Lahontan, *New Voyages to North America*, ed. Reuben Thwaites, Chicago: A. C. McClurg & Co., 1905, pp. 412–14, 424–6, 551–5, 568–82.

Mechanism. They have neither Laws, Judges, nor Priests; they are naturally inclin'd to Gravity, which makes them very circumspect in their Words and Actions. They observe a certain Medium between Gayety and Melancholy. The *French* Air they could not away with; and there was none but the younger sort of them that approv'd of our Fashions.

I have seen Savages when they've come a great way, make no other Compliment to the Family than, *I am arriv'd, I wish all of you a great deal of* [12] *Honour.* Then they take their Pipe quietly without asking any Questions: When that's done, they'l say, *Heark'e Friend, I am come from such a Place, I saw such a thing, &c.* When you ask a Question, their Answer is exceeding concise, unless they are Members of the Council; otherwise you'll hear 'em say, *That's Good; That signifies nought; That's admirable; That has Reason in it; That's valiant.*

If you tell a Father of a Family that his Children have fignaliz'd themselves against the Enemy, and have took several Slaves, his Answer is short, *That's Good,* without any farther Enquiry. If you tell him his Children are slain, he'll say immediately, *That Signifies nought,* without asking how it happen'd? When a Jesuit preaches to them the Truth of the Christian Religion, the Prophecies, Miracles, &c. they return you, a *That's wonderful,* and no more. When the *French,* tell them of the Laws of a Kingdom; the Justice, Manners and Customs of the *Europeans,* they'll repeat you a hundred times, *That's reasonable.* If you discourse them upon an Enterprise of great importance, or that's difficult to execute, or which requires much thought, they'll say, *That's Valiant,* without explaining themselves, and will listen to the end of your Discourse with great attention: Yet 'tis to be observed, when they're with their Friends in private, they'll argue with as much boldness as those of the Council. 'Tis very strange, that having no advantage of Education, but being directed only by the Pure Light of Nature, they should be able to furnish Matter for a Conference which often lasts above three Hours, and which turns upon all manner of Things; and should acquit themselves of it so well, that I never repented the time I spent with these truly Natural Philosophers.

[...]

Of Laws

Lahontan. Well, my Friend; thou hast heard what the Jesuit had to say; he has set matters in a clear light, and made 'em much plainer than I could do. You fee plainly there's a great difference between his Arguments and mine. We Soldiers of Fortune have only a superficial knowledge of our Religion, tho' indeed we ought to know it better; but the Jesuits have Study'd it to that degree, that they never fail of converting and convincing the most obstinate Infidels in the Universe.

Adario. To be free with thee, my dear Brother, I could scarce understand one tittle of what he meant, and I am much mistaken if he understands it himself. He has repeated the very [122] same Arguments a hundred times in my Hutt; and you might have observ'd, that yesterday I answer'd above twenty times, that I had heard his Arguments before upon several occasions. But, what I take to be most ridiculous, he teazes me every minute to get me to interpret his Arguments, word for word, to my Countrymen; upon the Plea that a Man of my Sense may find out in his own Language, more significant terms, and render the meaning of his Words more Intelligible, than a Jesuit who is not thoroughly Master of the *Huron* Language. You heard me tell him, that he might Baptise as many Children as he pleas'd, tho' at the same time he could not give me to know what Baptism was. He may do what he pleases in my Village; let him make Christians, and Preach, and Baptise if he will; I shall not hinder him. But now, methinks, we have had enough of Religion, let us therefore talk a little of what you call Laws; for you know that we have no such Word in our Language; tho' at the same time, I apprehend the force and importance of the Word, by vertue of the explication I had from you t'other day, together with the examples you mention'd, to make me conceive what you meant. Prithee tell me, are not Laws the same as just and reasonable Things? You say they are. Why then, to observe the Law, imports no more than to observe the measures of Reason and Justice: And at this rate you must take just and reasonable things in another sense than we do;

or if you take 'em in the same sense. 'tis plain you never observe 'em.

Lahontan. These are fine Distinctions indeed, you please your self with idle Flams. Hast not thee the Sense to perceive, after twenty Years Conversation with the *French*, that what the *Hurons* [123] call Reason is Reason among the *French*. 'Tis certain that all Men do not observe the Laws of Reason, for if they did there would be no occasion for Punishments, and those Judges thou hast seen at *Paris* and *Quebec* would be oblig'd to look out for another way of Living. But in regard that the good of the Society consists in doing Justice and following these Laws, there's a necessity of punishing the Wicked and rewarding the Good; for without that Precaution Murthers, Robberies and Defamations would spread every where, and in a Word, we should be the most miserable People upon the Face of the Earth.

Adario. Nay, you are miserable enough already, and indeed I can't see how you can be more such. What sort of Men must the *Europeans* be? What Spacies of Creatures do they retain to? The *Europeans*, who must be forc'd to do Good, and have no other Prompter for the avoiding of Evil than the fear of Punishment. If I ask'd thee, what a Man is, thou wouldst answer me, *He's a Frenchman*, and yet I'll prove that your *Man* is rather a *Beaver*. For *Man* is not intitled to that Character upon the score of his walking upright upon two Legs, or of Reading and Writing, and shewing a Thousand other Instances of his Industry. I call that Creature a *Man*, that hath a natural inclination to do Good, and never entertains the thoughts of doing Evil. You fee we have no Judges; and what's the reason of that? Why? We neither quarrel nor sue one another. And what's the reason that we have no Laws Suits? Why? Because we are resolved neither to receive nor to know Silver. But why do we refuse admission to Silver among us? The reason is this: We are resolv'd to have no Laws, for fince the World [124] was a World our Ancestors liv'd happily without 'em. In fine, as I intimated before, the Word *Laws* does not signifie just and reasonable things as you use it, for the Rich make a Jest of 'em, and 'tis only the poor Wretches that pay any regard to

'em. But, pray, let's look into these *Laws*, or reasonable things, as you call 'em. For these Fifty Years, the Governors of *Canada* have still alledg'd that we are subject to the Laws of their great Captain. We content our selves in denying all manner of Dependance, excepting that upon the Great Spirit, as being born free and joint Brethren, who are all equally Masters: Whereas you are all Slaves to one Man. We do not put in any such Answer to you, as if the *French* depended upon us; and the reason of our silence upon that Head is, that we have no mind to Quarrel. But, pray tell me, what Authority or Right is the pretended Superiority of your great Captain grounded upon? Did we ever fell our selves to that great Captain? Were we ever in *France* to look after you? 'Tis you that came hither to find out us. Who gave you all the Countries that you now inhabit, by what Right do you possess 'em? They always belong'd to the *Algonkins* before. In earnest, my dear Brother, I'm sorry for thee from the bottom of my Soul. Take my advice, and turn *Huron*; for I see plainly a vast difference between thy Condition and mine. I am Master of my own Body, I have the absolute disposal of my self, I do what I please, I am the first and the last of my Nation, I fear no Man, and I depend only upon the Great Spirit: Whereas thy Body, as well as thy Soul, are doom'd to a dependance upon thy great Captain; thy Vice-Roy disposes of thee; thou hast not the liberty of doing what thou hast a mind to; thou'rt affraid of Robbers, [125] false Witnesses, Assassins, &c. and thou dependest upon an infinity of Persons whose Places have rais'd 'em above thee. Is it true, or not? Are these things either improbable or invisible? Ah! my dear Brother, thou feest plainly that I am in the right of it; and yet thou choosest rather to be a *French* Slave than a free *Huron*. What a fine Spark does a *Frenchman* make with his fine Laws, who taking himself to be mighty Wife is assuredly a great Fool; for as much as he continues in Slavery and a state of Dependence, while the very Brutes enjoy that adorable Liberty, and like us fear nothing but Foreign Enemies.

[…]

Adario. [Y]our Judges ought to begin first to observe the Laws, that their example may influence others; they ought to discontinue their Oppression of Widows, Orphans, and poor Creatures; to give dispatch to the Suits of Persons that come an hundred Leagues off for a Hearing; and in a word, to form such Judgments of Causes as the Great Spirit shall do. I can never entertain a good thought of your Laws, till they lessen the Taxes and Duties that poor People are constrain'd to pay, at a time when the Rich of all Stations pay nothing in proportion to their Estates; till [138] you put a stop to the course of Drunkenness that spreads thro' our Villages, by prohibiting the *Coureurs de Bois* to import Brandy among us. Then indeed I shall hope that you'll compleat your Reformation by degrees, that a levelling of Estates may gradually creep in among you; and that at last you'll abhor that thing call'd Interest, which occasions all the Mischief that *Europe* groans under. When you arrive at that pitch, you'll have neither *Meum* nor *Tuum* to disturb you, but live as happily as the *Hurons*. This is enough for one day: I see my Slave coming to acquaint me that I am wanted in the Village. Farewel, my dear Brother, till tomorrow.

Lahontan. I am of the Opinion, my dear Friend, that you would not have come so soon to my Apartment, if you had not design'd to pursue our last Dispute. As for my part, I declare I will not enter the lists farther with you, upon the consideration that you are not capable to apprehend my Arguments. You are so prepossess'd on the behalf of your own Nation, so strongly byass'd to the Savage Customs, and so little sond of a due enquiry into ours; that I shall not daign to kill both my Body and my Soul, in endeavouring to make you sensible of the ignorance and misery that the *Hurons* have always liv'd in. Thou knowest I am thy Friend; and so I have no other view, but to set before thine eyes the Felicity that attends the *French*, to the end that thou and the rest of thy Nation may live as they do. I told you, I do not know how often, that you insist on the Conversation of some *French* Debauchees, and measure all the rest by their Bushel. I acquainted you, that they were punish'd for their Crimes; but these reasons will not go down with you; you obstinately [139] maintain your assertion by throwing in affrontive answers, as if the *French* were not

Men. Upon the whole, I am downright weary of hearing such poor stuff come from the Mouth of a Man that all the *French* look upon as a Man of excellent Sense. The People of thy Nation respect thee not only for thy Sense and Spirit, but for thy Experience and Valour. Thou art the Head of the Warriours, and the President of the Council; and without flattery, I have scarce met with a Man of a quicker apprehension than thy self. 'Tis upon this consideration, that I pity thee with all my heart for not throwing off thy prejudicate Opinions.

Adario. Thou'rt mistaken, my dear Brother, in all thou hast said; for I have not form'd to my self any false Idea of your Religion, or of your Laws. The Example of all the *French* in General, will ever oblige me to look upon all their Actions as unworthy of a Man. So that my Idea's are just; the prepossession you talk of is well grounded; and I am ready to make out all my advances. We talk'd of Religion and Laws, and I did not impart to you above a quarter of what I had to say upon that Head. You insist chiefly upon our way of living, which you take to be Blame-worthy. The *French* in general take us for Beasts; the Jesuits Brand us for impious, foolish and ignorant Vagabonds. And to be even with you, we have the same thoughts of you; but with this difference, that *we* pity you without offering invectives. Pray hear me, my dear Brother, I speak calmly and without passion. The more I reflect upon the lives of the *Europeans*, the less Wisdom and Happiness I find among 'em. These six years I have bent my thoughts upon the State of the *Europeans*: But I can't light on any thing in their Actions that is not [140] beneath a Man; and truly I think 'tis impossible it should be otherwise, so long as you stick to the measures of *Meum* and *Tuum*. I affirm that what you call Silver is the Devil of Devils; the Tyrant of the *French*; the Source of all Evil; the Bane of Souls, and the Slaughter-House of living Persons. To pretend to live in the Mony Country, and at the same time to save one's Soul, is as great an inconsistency as for a Man to go to the bottom of a Lake to preserve his Life. This Mony is the Father of Luxury, Lasciviousness, Intrigues, Tricks, Lying, Treachery, Falseness, and in a word, of all the mischief in the World. The Father sells his

Children, Husbands expose their Wives to Sale, Wives betray their Husbands, Brethren kill one another, Friends are false, and all this proceeds from Mony. Consider this, and then tell me if we are not in the right of it, in refusing to singer, or so much as to look upon that cursed Metal.

Lahontan. What! is it possible that you should always Reason so sorrily! Prithee, do but listen once in thy life time to what I am going to say. Dost not thou see, my dear Friend, that the Nations of *Europe* could not live without Gold and Silver, or some such precious thing. Without that Symbol, the Gentlemen, the Priests, the Merchants, and an infinity of other Persons who have not Strength enough to labour the Earth, would die for Hunger. Upon that lay, our Kings would be no Kings: Nay, what Soldiers should we then have? Who would then Work for Kings or any body else, who would run the hazard of the Sea, who would make Arms unless 'twere for himself? Believe me, this would run us to remediless Ruine,'twould turn *Europe* into a Chaos, and create the most dismal Confusion that Imagination it self can reach.

[141] *Adario.* You sobb me off very prettily, truly, when you bring in your Gentlemen, your Merchants and your Priests. If you were Strangers to *Meum* and *Tuum*, those distinctions of Men would be sunk; a levelling equality would then take place among you as it now do's among the *Hurons*. For the first thirty years indeed, after the banishing of Interest, you would see a strange Desolation; those who are only qualify'd to eat, drink, sleep and divert themselves, would languish and die; but their Posterity would be fit for our way of living. I have set forth again and again, the qualities that make a Man inwardly such as he ought to be; particularly, Wisdom, Reason, Equity, &c. which are courted by the *Hurons*. I have made it appear that the Notion of separate Interests knocks all these Qualities in the Head, and that a Man sway'd by Interest can't be a Man of Reason. As for the outward Qualifications of a Man; he ought to be expert in Marching, Hunting, Fishing, Waging War, Ranging the Forests, Building Hutts and Canows, Firing of Guns, Shooting of Arrows, Working Canows: He ought to be Indefatigable, and able to live

on short Commons upon occasion. In a word, he ought to know how to go about all the Exercises of the *Hurons*. Now in my way, 'tis the Person thus qualify'd that I call a *Man*. Do but consider, how many Millions there are in *Europe*, who, if they were left thirty Leagues off in the Forrests, and provided with Fusees and Arrows, would be equally at a loss, either to Hunt and maintain themselves, or to find their way out: And yet you see we traverse a hundred Leagues of Forrests without losing our way, that we kill Fowl and other Beasts with our Arrows, that we catch Fish in all the places where they are to be had; that we [142] Dog both Men and Wild Beasts by their Footsteps, whether in Woods or in open Fields, in Summer or in Winter; that we live upon Roots when we lye before the Gates of the *Iroquefe*, that we run like Hares, that we know how to use both the Axe and the Knife, and to make a great many useful things. Now since we are capable of such things, what should hinder you to do the same, when Interest is laid aside? Are not your Bodies as large, strong and brawny as ours? Are not your Artisans imploy'd in harder and more difficult Work than ours? If you liv'd after our manner, all of you would be equally Masters; your Riches would be of the same Stamp with ours, and consist in the purchasing of Glory by military Actions, and the taking of Slaves; for the more you took of them the less occasion you would have to Work: In a word, you would live as happily as we do.

Lahontan. Do you place a happy Life, in being oblig'd to lye under a pittiful Hutt of Bark, to Sleep under four sorry Coverlets of Beaver Skins, to Eat nothing but what you Boil and Roast, to be Cloath'd with Skins, to go a Beaver Hunting in the harshest Season of the Year, to run a hundred Leagues on Foot in pursuit of the *Iroquefe*, thro' Marshes and thick Woods, the Trees of which are cut down so as to render 'em inaccessible! Do you think your selves happy when you venture out in little Canows, and run the risque of being drown'd every foot in your Voyages upon the Great Lakes; when you lye upon the ground with the Heavens for your Canopy, upon approaching to the Villages of your Enemies; when you run with full Speed, both days and nights without eating or drinking, as being pursued by your Enemies; when you are sure of being reduc'd to the last extremity, if [143] the *Coureurs de Bois* did not out of Friendship, Charity and Commiseration, supply you with Fire-Arms, Powder, Lead, Thread for Nets, Axes, Knives, Needles, Awls, Fishing-Hooks, Kettles, and several other Commodities?

Adario. Very fine, come, don't let's go so fast; the day is long, and we may talk one after the other at our own leisure. It seems you take all these things to be great hardships; and indeed I own they would be such to the *French*, who like Beasts, love only to eat and to drink, and have been brought up to Softness and Effeminacy. Prithee, tell me what difference there is between lying in a good Hutt, and lying in a Palace; between Sleeping under a Cover of Beaver-Skins, and Sleeping under a Quilt between two Sheets; between Eating Boil'd and Roast Meat, and feeding upon dirty Pies, Ragou's &c. dress'd by your greasy Scullions? Are we liable to more Disorders and Sicknesses than the *French*, who are accommodated with these Palaces, Beds and Cooks? But after all, how many are there in *France* that lye upon Straw in Garrets where the Rain comes in on all hands, and that are hard put to't to find Victuals and Drink? I have been in *France*, and speak from what I have seen with my Eyes. You rally with-out reason, upon our Cloaths made of Skins, for they are warmer, and keep out the Rain better than your Cloth; besides, they are not so ridiculously made as your Garments, which have more Stuff in their Pockets and Skirts, than in the Body of the Garment. As for our Beaver-Hunting, you take it to be a terrible thing; while it affords us all manner of pleasure and diversion; and at the same time, procures us all sorts of Commodities in exchange for the Skins. Besides, our Slaves take all the Drudgery off our hands, (if so be [144] that you will have it to be drudgery.) You know very well that Hunting is the most agreeable Diversion we have; but the Beaver-Hunting being so very pleasant, we prefer it to all the other sorts. You say, we have a troublesome and tedious way of waging War; and indeed I must own that a *French* Man would not be able to bear it, upon the account that you are not accustom'd to such long Voyages on Foot;

but there Excursions do not fatigue us in the leaft, and 'twere to be with'd for the good of *Canada*, that you were possess'd of the same Talent; for if you were, the *Iroquese* would not Cut your Throats in the midst of your own Habitations, as they do now every day. You insist likewise on the risque we run in our little Canows, as an instance of our Misery; and with reference to that Point, 'tis true that sometimes we cannot dispense with the use of Canows, because we are Strangers to the Art of Building larger Vessels; but after all, your great Vessels are liable to be cast away as well as our Canows. 'Tis likewise true, that we lye flat upon the open ground when we approach to the Villages of our Enemies; but 'tis equally true that the Soldiers in *France* are not so well accommodated as your Men are here, and that they are oftentimes forc'd to lye in Marshes and Ditches, where they are expos'd to the Rain and Wind. You object farther, that we betake our selves to a speedy Flight; and pray what can be more natural than to flye when the number of our Enemies is triple to ours. The Fatigue indeed of running night and day without Eating and Drinking, is terrible; but we had better undergo it than become Slaves. I am apt to believe that such extremities are matter of Horrour to the *Europeans*, but we look upon 'em as in a manner, nothing. [145] You conclude, in pretending that the *French* prevent our Misery by taking pity of us. But pray consider how our Ancestors liv'd an hundred years ago: They liv'd as well without your Commodities as we do with 'em; for instead of your Fire-Locks, Powder and Shot, they made use of Bows and Arrows, as we do to this day: They made Nets of the Thread of the Barks of Trees, Axes of Stone; Knives, Needles and Awls of Stag or Elk-Bones; and supply'd the room of Kettles with Earthen Pots. Now, since our Ancestors liv'd without these Commodities for so many Ages; I am of the Opinion, we could dispense with 'em easier than the *French* could with our Beaver Skins; for which, by a mighty piece of Friendship, they give us in exchange Fusees, that burst and Lame many of our Warriors, Axes that break in the cutting of a Shrub, Knives that turn Blunt, and lose their Edge in the cutting of a Citron; Thread which is half Rotten, and so very bad that our Nets are worn out as soon as they are made; and Kettles so thin and slight, that the very weight of Water makes the Bottoms fall out. This, my dear Brother, is the answer I had to give to your Reflexions upon the Misery of the *Hurons*.

Lahontan. 'Tis well; I find you would have me to believe that the *Hurons* are insensible of their Fatigue and Labour; and being bred up to Poverty and Hardships, have another notion of 'em than we have. This may do with those who have never stir'd out of their own Country, and consequently have no Idea of a better Life than their own; who having never visited our Cities and Towns, fancy that we live just as they do. But as for thee, who hast seen *France, Quebec* and *New-England*, methinks thy judgment and relish of things are too much of the Savage [146] Strain; whilst thou prefers the Condition of the *Hurons* to that of the *Europeans*. Can there be a more agreeable and delightful Life in the World, than that of an infinity of rich Men, who want for nothing? They have fine Coaches, Stately Houses adorn'd with Rich Hangings and Magnificent Pictures, Sweet Gardens replenish'd with all sorts of Fruit, Parks Stock'd with all sorts of Animals, Horses and Hounds and good store of Mony, which enables 'em to keep a Sumptuous Table, to frequent the Play-Houses, to Game freely, and to dispose handsomely of their Children. These happy Men are ador'd by their Dependants; and you have seen with your own eyes our Princes, Dukes, Mareshals of *France*, Prelates, and a Million of persons of all Stations, who want for nothing, and live like Kings, and who never call to mind that they have liv'd, till such time as Death alarms 'em.

Adario. If I had not been particularly inform'd of the State of *France*, and let into the knowledge of all the Circumstances of that People, by my Voyage to *Paris;* I might have been Blinded by the outward appearances of Felicity that you set forth: But I know that your Prince, your Duke, your Mareshal, and your Prelate are far from being happy upon the Compaarison with the *Hurons*, who know no other happiness than that of Liberty and Tranquility of Mind: For your great Lords hate one another in their Hearts; they forseit

their Sleep, and neglect even Eating and Drinking, in making their Court to the King, and undermining their Enemies; they offer such Violence to Nature in dissembling, disguising and bearing things, that the Torture of their Soul leaves all Expression far behind it. Is all this nothing in your way? Do you think it such a trisling matter to have fifty [147] Serpents in your Bosom? Had not they better throw their Coaches, their Palaces and their Finery, into the River, than to spend their life time in a continued Series of Martyrdom? Were I in their place, I'd rather choose to be a *Huron* with a Naked Body and a Serene Mind. The Body is the Apartment in which the Soul is lodg'd; and what signifies it, for the Cafe call'd the Body, to be set off with Gold Trappings, or spread out in a Coach, or planted before a Sumptuous Table, while the Soul Galls and Tortures it? The great Lords, that you call Happy, lie expos'd to Disgrace from the King, to the detraction of a thousand sorts of Persons, to the loss of their Places, to the Contempt of their Fellow Courtiers; and in a word, their soft Life is thwarted by Ambition, Pride, Presumption and Envy. They are Slaves to their Passions, and to their King, who is the only *French* Man that can be call'd Happy, with respect to that adorable Liberty which he alone enjoys. There's a thousand of us in one Village, and you see that we love one another like Brethren; that whatever any one has is at his Neighbour's Service; that our Generals and Presidents of the Council have not more Power than any other *Huron;* that Detraction and Quarreling were never heard of among us; and in fine, that every one is his own Master, and do's what he pleases, without being accountable to another, or censur'd by his Neighbour. This, my dear Brother, is the difference between us and your Princes, Dukes, &c. And if those great Men are so Unhappy, by consequence, those of inferiour Stations must have a greater share of Trouble and perplexing Cares.

[148] *Lahontan*. You must know that as your *Hurons* who are brought up in the way of Fatigue and Misery, have no mind to be rid of it; so these great Lords being inur'd from their infancy to ambition, care, &c. can't live without it. As Happiness lies in the imagination, so they

feed themselves with Vanity, and in their hearts think themselves as good as the King. That Tranquility of mind that the *Hurons* enjoy, never car'd for crossing over to *France*, for fear of being confin'd to the little Religious Houses. Tranquility of mind passes in *France* for the Character of a Fool, of a senseless, careless Fellow. To be happy, one must always have somewhat in his view that feeds his Wishes. He that confines his Wishes to what he enjoys, must be a *Huron*, which none will desire to be, if he considers that Life would be a Scene of Uneasyness, if our Mind did not direct us every minute to desire somewhat that we are not yet possess'd of; and 'tis this that makes a Life happy, provided the means imploy'd in the prosecution of such Wishes are lawful and warrantable.

Adario. Is not that Burying a Man alive; to rack his Mind without intermission in the acquisition of Riches and Honour, which cloy us as soon as obtain'd; to infeeble and waste his Body, and to expose his Life in the forming of Enterprises, that for the most part prove Abortive? As for your Allegation, that these great Lords are bred from their Infancy to Ambition and Care, as we are to Labour and Fatigue; I must say, 'tis a fine Comparison for a Man that can Read and Write. Tell me, prithee, if the repose of the Mind and the exercise of the Body are not the necessary Instruments of Health, if the tossing of the Mind and the rest of the Body are not the means to destroy it? What have we [149] in the World that's dearer to us than our Lives, and ought not we to take the best measures to preserve 'em? The *French* murder their Health by a thousand different means, and we preserve ours till our Bodies are worn out, our Souls being so far free from Paffions, that they can't alter or diffurl our Bodies. And after all, you infinuate that the *French* haften the Moment of their Death by lawful means: A very pretty conclusion indeed,

and such as deserves to be took notice of Believe me, my dear Brother, 'tis thy Interest to turn *Huron* in order to prolong thy life. Thou shalt drink, eat, sleep, and Hunt with all the ease that can be; thou shalt be free'd from the Passions that Tyrannise over the *French;* thou shalt have no occasion for Gold or Silver to make thee happy; thou shalt not fear Robbers, Assassins or False Witnesses; and if thou hast a mind to be King of all the World, why, thou shalt have nothing to do but to think that thou art so.

Lahontan. You cannot expect I should comply with your demand, without thinking that I have been guilty of such Crimes in *France*, that I can't return without running the risque of being Burnt: For after all, I can't imagine a more unaccountable *Metamorphosis*, than that of a *French* Man into a *Huron*. How d'ye think I could undergo the Fatigues we talk'd of but now? D'ye think I could undergo the patience to hear the Childish Proposals of your Ancient and your Young Men, without taking them up? Is it feasible that I could live upon Broth, Bread, *Indian* Corn, Roast Meat and Boil'd, without either Pepper or Salt? Could I brook the Larding of my Face like a Fool, with twenty sorts of Colours? What Spirit must I be of, if I drink nothing but Mapple-Water, and go stark Naked all the Summer, [150] and eat out of nothing but Wooden Dishes? Your Meals would never go down with me, since two or three hundred Persons must Dance for two or three hours before and after. I can't live with an uncivilis'd sort of People, who know no other Compliment than, *I honour you.* No, no; my dear *Adario*, 'tis impossible for a *French-Man* to turn *Huron*, but a *Huron* may easily become a *French-Man*.

Adario. At that rate you prefer Slavery to Liberty. But 'tis no Surprisal to me, after what I have heard you maintain.

20

Persian Letters

Montesquieu

Letter XXVIII

*Rica to * * ***

Yesterday I witnessed a most remarkable thing, although it is of daily occurrence in Paris.

In the evening, after dinner, all the people gather together and play at a sort of dramatic game, which I have heard them call comedy. The main performance takes place upon a platform which is called the theatre. On both sides may be seen in little nooks called boxes, men and women who perform in dumb show, something after our own style in Persia.

Here you see a languishing love-sick lady; there, a more animated dame exchanges burning glances with her lover: their faces portray every passion, and express them with an eloquence, none the less fervid because it is mute. The actresses here display only half their bodies, and usually wear a modest muff to hide their arms. In the lower part of the theatre there stands a crowd of people who ridicule those who are seated on high; the latter, in their turn, laugh at those who are below.

But the most zealous and active of all are certain people whose youth enables them to support fatigue. They are obliged to appear everywhere; they move through passages known only to them, mounting with surprising agility from storey to storey; now above, now below, they visit every box. They dive, so to speak; are lost, and reappear; often they leave the place of performance, and carry on the game in another. And there are some who, by a miracle one would hardly have expected from the fact that they carry crutches, perform prodigies similar to those I have described. Lastly, there are the rooms where a private comedy is played. Commencing with salutations, the performers proceed to embrace each other: I am told that the slightest acquaintance gives a man a right to squeeze another to death. The place seems to inspire tenderness. Indeed, it is said that the princesses who reign here are far from cruel; and, with the exception of two or three hours during the day in which they are sufficiently hard-hearted, it must be admitted that they are uniformly very tractable, their hard-heartedness being a species of frenzy, which goes as easily as it comes.

All this that I have described goes on in much the same style at another place called the Opera: the sole difference being, that they speak at the one, and sing at the other. One of my friends took me the other day to a box where one of the principal actresses was undressing. We became so well acquainted, that next morning I received the following letter from her.

"Sir,

"I, who have always been the most virtuous actress at the Opera, am yet the most miserable

Montesquieu, *Persian Letters*, trans. John Davidson, London: privately printed, 1892, pp. 66–74.

woman in the world. About seven or eight months ago, while I was in the box where you saw me yesterday, and in the act of dressing myself as priestess of Diana, a young Abbé broke in upon me. Undismayed by my white robe, my veil, and my frontlet, he stole from me my innocence. I have tried to persuade him of the greatness of the sacrifice I made; but he mocks me, and maintains that he found me very profane. In the meantime my pregnancy is so apparent, that I dare not show myself upon the stage; for I am, in the matter of honour, extremely delicate, and always insist that it is easier for a well-born woman to lose her virtue than her modesty. You will readily believe that the young Abbé would never have overcome such exquisite modesty, had he not given me a promise of marriage. Having such a good reason to do so, I overlooked the usual petty formalities, and began where I should have ended. But, since I am dishonoured by his faithlessness, I do not wish to remain longer at the Opera, where, between you and me, they scarcely give me enough for a livelihood; because now, as I grow older, and, on the one hand, begin to lose my charms, on the other, my salary, which remains stationary, seems to grow less and less every day. I have learned from a member of your suite, that, in your country, they cannot make enough of a good dancer; and that, if I were once at Ispahan, I would quickly realize a fortune. If you would deign to take me under your protection, and carry me with you to your country, you would do yourself the credit of aiding a woman, whose virtuous behaviour renders her not altogether unworthy of your good offices. I am ..."

Paris, the 2nd of the moon of Chalval, 1712.

Letter XXIX

Rica to Ibben, at Smyrna

The Pope is the head of the Christians: an old idol, kept venerable by custom. Formerly he was feared even by princes; for he deposed them as easily as our glorious sultans depose the kings of Irimetta and Georgia. He is, however, no longer dreaded. He declares himself to be the successor of one of the first Christians,

called Saint Peter: and it is certainly a rich succession; for he possesses immense treasures, and a large territory owns his sway.

The bishops are the administrators under his rule, and they exercise, as his subordinates, two very different functions. In their corporate capacity they have, like him, the right to make articles of faith. Individually, their sole duty is to dispense with the observance of these articles. For you must know that the Christian religion is burdened with an immense number of very tedious duties: and, as it is universally considered less easy to fulfil these than to have bishops who can dispense with their fulfilment, the latter method has been chosen for the benefit of the public. Thus, if anyone wishes to escape the fast of Rhamazan, or is unwilling to submit to the formalities of marriage, or wishes to break his vows, or to marry within the prescribed degrees, or even to forswear himself, all he has to do is to apply to a bishop, or to the Pope, who will at once grant a dispensation.

The bishops do not make articles of faith for their own government. There are a very great number of learned men, for the most part dervishes, who raise new questions in religion among themselves: they are left to discuss them for a long time, and the dispute lasts until a decision terminates it.

I can also assure you that there never was a realm in which so many civil wars have broken out, as in the kingdom of Christ.

Those who first propound some new doctrine, are immediately called heretics. Each heresy receives a name which is the rallying cry of those who support it. But no one need be a heretic against his will: he only requires to split the difference, and allege some scholastic subtlety to those who accuse him of heresy; and, whether it be intelligible or not, that renders him as pure as the snow, and he may insist upon his being called orthodox.

What I have told you holds good only in France and Germany: for I have heard it affirmed that in Spain and Portugal there are certain dervishes who do not understand raillery, and who cause men to be burned as they would burn straw. Happy the man, who, when he falls into the hands of these people, has been accustomed to finger little balls of wood while saying his prayers, who has carried on his person two pieces of cloth attached to two ribbons, and who has paid a visit to a province called Galicia. Without that, a poor devil is in a wretched plight. Although he should swear like a Pagan that he is orthodox, they may very likely decline to admit his plea, and burn him for a heretic. Much good his scholastic subtlety will do him! They will none of it; he will be burned to ashes before they would dream of even giving him a hearing.

Other judges assume the innocence of the accused; these always deem them guilty. In dubious cases, their rule is to lean to the side of severity, apparently because they think mankind desperately wicked. And yet, when it suits them, they have such a high opinion of mankind, that they think them incapable of lying; for they accept as witnesses, mortal enemies, loose women, and people whose trade is infamous. In sentencing culprits, they pay them a little compliment. Having dressed them in brimstone shirts, they assure them that they are much grieved to see them in such sorry attire; that they are tender-hearted, abhorring bloodshed, and are quite overcome at having to condemn them. Then these heart-broken judges console themselves by confiscating to their own use all the goods of their miserable victims.

Oh, happy land, inhabited by the children of the prophets! There such woeful sights as these are unknown. There, the holy religion which angels brought protects itself by its innate truth; it can maintain itself without recourse to violent means like these.

Paris, the 4th of the moon of Chalval, 1712.

Letter XXX

Rica to the Same, at Smyrna

The curiosity of the people of Paris exceeds all bounds. When I arrived, they stared at me as if I had dropped from the sky: old and young, men, women, and children, were all agog to see me. If I went abroad, everybody flew to the window. If I visited the Tuileries, I was immediately surrounded by a circle of gazers, the women forming a rainbow woven of a thousand colours. When I went sight-seeing, a hundred lorgnettes were speedily levelled at me: in fact, never was a man so stared at as I have been. I smiled frequently when I heard people who had never travelled beyond their own door, saying to each other, "He certainly looks very like a Persian." One thing struck me: I found my portraits everywhere – in all the shops, on every mantelpiece – so fearful were they lest they should not see enough of me.

So much distinction could not fail to be burdensome. I do not consider myself such a rare and wonderful specimen of humanity; and although I have a very good opinion of myself, I would never have dreamt that I could have disturbed the peace of a great city, where I was quite unknown. I therefore resolved to change my Persian dress for a European one, in order to see if my countenance would still strike people as wonderful. This experiment made me acquainted with my true value. Divested of everything foreign in my garb, I found myself estimated at my proper rate. I had reason to complain of my tailor, who had made me lose so suddenly the attention and good opinion of the public; for I sank immediately into the merest nonentity. Sometimes I would be as much as an hour in a given company, without attracting the least notice, or having an opportunity given me to speak; but, if anyone chanced to inform the company that I was a Persian, I soon overheard a murmur all round me, "Oh! ah! a Persian, is he? Most amazing! However can anybody be a Persian?"

Paris, the 6th of the moon of Chalval, 1712.

21

The *Supplément au Voyage de Bougainville*

Denis Diderot

II

The Old Man's Farewell

The speaker is an old man. He was the father of a large family. When the Europeans arrived he looked upon them with scorn, showing neither astonishment, nor fear, nor curiosity. On their approach he turned his back and retired to his hut. Yet his silence and anxiety revealed his thoughts only too well; he was inwardly lamenting the eclipse of his countrymen's happiness. When Bougainville was leaving the island, as the natives swarmed on the shore, clutching his clothes, clasping his companions in their arms and weeping, the old man made his way forward and proclaimed solemnly, 'Weep, wretched natives of Tahiti, weep. But let it be for the coming and not the leaving of these ambitious, wicked men. One day you will know them better. One day they will come back, bearing in one hand the piece of wood you see in that man's belt, and, in the other, the sword hanging by the side of that one, to enslave you, slaughter you, or make you captive to their follies and vices. One day you will be subject to them, as corrupt, vile and miserable as they are. But I have this consolation. My life is drawing to its close, and I shall not see the calamity I foretell. Oh fellow Tahitians, oh my friends! There is one way to avert a dreadful fate, but I would

rather die than counsel you to take it. Let them leave, and let them live.'

Then turning to Bougainville, he continued, 'And you, leader of the ruffians who obey you, pull your ship away swiftly from these shores. We are innocent, we are content, and you can only spoil that happiness. We follow the pure instincts of nature, and you have tried to erase its impression from our hearts. Here, everything belongs to everyone, and you have preached I can't tell what distinction between "yours" and "mine". Our daughters and our wives belong to us all. You shared that privilege with us, and you enflamed them with a frenzy they had never known before. They have become wild in your arms, and you have become deranged in theirs. They have begun to hate each other. You have butchered one another for them, and they have come back stained with your blood. We are free, but into our earth you have now staked your title to our future servitude. You are neither a god nor a demon. Who are you, then, to make them slaves? Orou, you who understand the language of these men, tell us all, as you have told me, what they have written on that strip of metal: *This land is ours*. So this land is yours? Why? Because you set foot on it! If a Tahitian should one day land on your shores and engrave on one of your stones or on the bark of one of your trees, *This land belongs to the*

Denis Diderot, "*The* Supplément au Voyage de Bougainville," in *Political Writings*, ed. and trans. John Hope Mason and Robert Wokler. Cambridge: Cambridge University Press, 1992, pp. 41–65.

people of Tahiti, what would you think then? You are stronger than we are, and what does that mean? When one of the miserable trinkets with which your ship is filled was taken away, what an uproar you made, what revenge you exacted! At that very moment, in the depths of your heart, you were plotting the theft of an entire country! You are not a slave, you would rather die than be one, and yet you wish to make slaves of us. Do you suppose, then, that a Tahitian cannot defend his own liberty and die for it as well? This inhabitant of Tahiti, whom you wish to ensnare like an animal, is your brother. You are both children of Nature. What right do you have over him that he does not have over you? You came; did we attack you? Have we plundered your ship? Did we seize you and expose you to the arrows of our enemies? Did we harness you to work with our animals in the fields? We respected our own image in you.

'Leave us to our ways; they are wiser and more decent than yours. We have no wish to exchange what you call our ignorance for your useless knowledge. Everything that we need and is good for us we already possess. Do we merit contempt because we have not learnt how to acquire superfluous needs? When we are hungry, we have enough to eat. When we are cold, we have enough to wear. You have entered our huts; what do you suppose we lack? Pursue as far as you wish what you call the comforts of life, but let sensible beings stop when they have no more to gain from their labours than imaginary benefits. If you persuade us to go beyond the strict bounds of necessity, when will we finish our work? When will we enjoy ourselves? We have kept our annual and daily labours within the smallest possible limits, because in our eyes nothing is better than rest. Go back to your own country to agitate and torment yourself as much as you like. But leave us in peace. Do not fill our heads with your factitious needs and illusory virtues. Look at these men. See how upright, healthy and robust they are. Look at these women. See how they too stand up straight, how healthy, fresh and lovely they are. Take this bow; it's mine. Call upon one, two, three, four of your comrades, and together with them try to draw it. I draw it unaided; I till the soil; I climb mountains; I go through the forest; I can run a league across the plain in less than an hour; your young companions can hardly keep up with me, and yet I'm more than ninety years old.

'Woe to this island! Woe to all present Tahitians and to those still to come, from the day of your arrival! We used to know but one disease, old age, to which men, animals and plants were all equally prey, but you have now brought us another. You have infected our blood. Perhaps we shall be forced to wipe out, with our own hands, our daughters, our wives, our children, those who have lain with your women, and those who have been with your men. Our fields will be soaked with the foul blood which has passed from your veins into ours, or our children will be condemned to nourish and perpetuate the evil you inflicted on their fathers and mothers and which shall henceforth be forever passed onto their descendants. Wretched man. You must bear guilt, either for the ravages that will follow the deadly caresses of your people, or for the murders we shall commit to arrest the poison. You speak of crimes. Can you imagine any worse than yours? What is the punishment, where you come from, for the murder of your neighbour? Death by the sword. Where you come from, what is the punishment for the coward who poisons his victim? Death by fire. Compare your own offence to this second crime and tell us, scourge of nations, what punishment you deserve? A short while ago a young maiden of Tahiti would yield blissfully to the embraces of a Tahitian youth, once she had reached the age of marriage; she would wait impatiently for her mother to lift her veil and expose her breasts; she was proud to stir the desires and attract the amorous glances of a stranger, her relatives, her brother. Without fear or shame, in our presence, in the midst of a circle of innocent Tahitians, to the sound of flutes and between the dances, she welcomed the caresses of the youth whom her young heart and the secret promptings of her senses had selected for her. It was you who first brought the idea of crime and the risk of illness to us.

'Our pleasures, once so sweet, are now accompanied with remorse and fear. That man in black by your side, who is listening to me, spoke to our young men; I do not know what he said to our girls, but now they blush and the boys hesitate. If you wish, creep away into the dark forest with the perverse partner of your pleasures, but let the good and simple inhabitants of Tahiti multiply without shame in the light of day under the open sky. What more honest and noble sentiment can you put in the place of the one which we have inspired in them and which nurtures them? When they believe the moment has arrived to enrich the nation and the family with a new citizen, they exalt in it. They eat to live, and to grow; they grow to multiply, and in that they see neither vice nor shame. Take heed of the effects of your offences. You had hardly arrived among them before they became thieves. You had hardly set foot on our soil before it reeked of blood. The Tahitian who ran to meet you, to greet you, who welcomed you crying, "*taïo*, friend, friend", you killed. And why did you kill him? Because he had been tempted by the glitter of your little serpent's eggs. He offered you his fruits, his wife, his daughter, his hut, and you killed him for a handful of beads which he took without asking. At the sound of your murderous weapons the others were seized by terror and fled to the hills. But rest assured that they would soon have returned and, in an instant, but for me, would have destroyed you. Ah! Why did I appease them? Why did I hold them back? Why do I hold them back even now? I don't know, for with your unfeeling heart you can have no sense of pity and do not deserve any.

'You and your men have wandered where you please throughout our island. You were respected; you enjoyed everything; you were neither rebuffed nor obstructed in your way; you were invited; you joined us. We spread out before you the abundance of our country. When you desired young girls, all (except those not yet entitled to show their face and breasts) were placed before you completely naked by their mothers. That was how you took possession of the tender victim of our obligations as hosts; leaves and flowers were strewn upon the ground for her and for you; musicians tuned their instruments; nothing disturbed the sweetness nor interfered with the liberty of her caresses and yours. Hymns were sung, exhorting you to be a man, and our child to be a woman, compliant and voluptuous. We danced around your bed, and, for your part, after

leaving the arms of that woman, after drawing from her breast the sweetest intoxication, you slaughtered her brother, her friend, perhaps her father. You have done worse still. Look over there. See that enclosure bristling with arrows; those arms which had once only menaced our enemies are now turned on our own children. Look upon the unhappy partners of your pleasures. See their sadness, the grief of their fathers, the despair of their mothers. That is where they are condemned to die, either by our hands or from the disease you passed on to them. Go away now, unless your cruel eyes relish the spectacle of death. Go away, leave, and may the seas that spared you on your voyage absolve themselves of their guilt and avenge us by swallowing you up before your return. And you, inhabitants of Tahiti, go back to your huts. Go back and let these unworthy foreigners hear nothing as they depart but the roaring waves. Let them see nothing but the foaming spray as it whitens a deserted shore.'

He had scarcely finished speaking before the crowd of natives disappeared. A great silence stretched over the island. Nothing was to be heard but the dry whistling of the wind and the muffled breaking of the waves, all the length of the coast. It was as if the air and the sea had absorbed the man's words and were moved to obey him.

[...]

III

The Conversation Between the Chaplain and Orou

In the division of Bougainville's crew by the Tahitians, the chaplain was allotted to Orou. They were roughly the same age, around thirty-five or thirty-six years old. At the time Orou had only his wife and three children, who were called Asto, Palli and Thia. They undressed the chaplain, washed his face, hands and feet, and served him a wholesome and frugal meal. When he was about to go to bed, Orou, who had stepped out with his family, reappeared, presented him with his wife and three daughters, each of them naked, and said, 'You have eaten, you are young and in good health; if you go to bed alone, you will sleep badly. At night a man needs a companion beside him. Here is my wife; here are my daughters. Choose whomever you prefer; but if you wish to oblige me you will select the youngest of my daughters, who is still childless.' 'Alas', added the mother. 'I don't hold it against her, poor Thia! It's not her fault.'

The chaplain replied that his religion, his holy orders, morality and decency all prohibited him from accepting Orou's offer.

Orou answered: 'I don't know what you mean by "religion", but I can only think ill of it, since it prevents you from enjoying an innocent pleasure to which Nature, that sovereign mistress, invites every person: that is, of bringing into the world one of your own kind; rendering a service which the father, mother and children all ask of you; repaying a gracious host, and enriching a nation by adding one more subject to it. I don't know what you mean by "holy orders", but your first duty is to be a man and to show gratitude. I'm not asking you to take back the ways of Orou to your country, but Orou, your host and friend, begs that here you accept the ways of Tahiti. Whether the ways of Tahiti are better or worse than yours is an easy question to settle. Has the land of your birth more people than it can feed? In that case your ways are neither worse nor better than ours. Can it feed more than it has? In that case our ways are better than yours. As for the decency which holds you back, I quite understand. I admit I'm wrong and ask that you forgive me. I don't insist that you put your health in danger. If you are tired, you must rest; but I trust that you will not continue to disappoint us. Look at the sorrow you've brought to all these faces. They're afraid you have detected blemishes in them which have aroused your distaste. But even if that were so, wouldn't the pleasure of doing a good deed, of ensuring that one of my daughters was honoured among her companions and sisters – wouldn't that suffice for you? Be generous.'

The chaplain – It's not that. They are all four of them equally beautiful. But my religion! My holy orders!

Orou – They are mine, and I'm offering them to you. They are their own as well and give themselves up to you freely. Whatever purity of conscience is prescribed to you by that thing you call 'religion' and that thing you call 'holy orders', you may accept them without scruple. I am in no way exceeding my authority, and you may be sure that I know and respect the rights of individuals.

At this point the truthful chaplain acknowledges that Providence had never exposed him to such strong temptation. He was young, agitated, vexed. He averted his eyes from the delightful supplicants and then gazed at them again; he raised his eyes and hands to the heavens. Thia, the youngest, threw her arms around his knees and said to him, 'Stranger, do not make my father unhappy, nor my mother, nor me. Honour me in this hut and within my family. Lift me up to the status of my sisters, who make fun of me. Asto, the eldest, already has three children; Palli, the second, has two; but Thia has none. Stranger, good stranger, do not reject me. Make me a mother. Make me bear a child whom I can one day lead by the hand, by my side, in Tahiti, who in nine months' time will be seen suckling at my breast, who will make me proud and who will be a part of my dowry, when I pass from my father's hut to another. I may be more fortunate with you than with our young Tahitians. If you grant me this favour, I shall never forget you. I shall bless you all my life; I shall write your name on my arm and on that of your son. We shall forever utter it with joy; and when you leave these shores my prayers will accompany you across the seas, until you reach your own land.'

The artless chaplain says that she clasped his hands, that she fastened her eyes on his with glances so touching and expressive that she wept, that her father, mother and sisters withdrew, that he remained alone with her, and that, still calling out 'But my religion, but my holy orders', he found himself at dawn lying beside this young girl who overwhelmed him with caresses and who invited her father, mother and sisters, when in the morning they came to his bed, to add their own gratitude to hers.

Asto and Palli, after withdrawing for a time, returned with native food, drinks and fruits. They embraced their sister and wished her good fortune. They breakfasted together; then Orou remained alone with the chaplain and said to him, 'I see that my daughter is pleased with you, and I thank you. But could you tell me just what is the meaning of the word "religion" which you have expressed so many times and with such sadness?'

(The chaplain, after reflecting for a moment, replied,) 'Who made your hut and all the things that furnish it?'

Orou – I did.

The chaplain – Well, we think that this world and everything in it is the work of one craftsman.

Orou – Does he then have feet, hands, a head?

The chaplain – No.

Orou – Where does he live?

The chaplain – Everywhere.

Orou – Here, even?

The chaplain – Here.

Orou – We have never seen him.

The chaplain – He cannot be seen.

Orou – What a pretty poor father. He must be aged, because he must be at least as old as what he's made.

The chaplain – He never grows old. He spoke to our ancestors; he gave them laws; he prescribed the way he wished to be honoured; he ordained that certain actions were good and forbade others as evil.

Orou – I understand. And one of those actions he forbade as evil is to lie with a woman or girl. But why then did he make two sexes?

The chaplain – So that they may be united, but subject to certain conditions, following preliminary ceremonies, by virtue of which a man belongs to a woman and only to her; and a woman belongs to a man and only to him.

Orou – For as long as they live?

The chaplain – For as long as they live.

Orou – So that if a woman should happen to lie with someone other than her husband, or a husband should lie with someone other than his wife ... But that doesn't happen, since he's there and whatever displeases him he knows how to stop.

The chaplain – No, he lets them do it, and so they sin against the law of God, for that is the name we give to the great craftsman. Against the law of the country what we commit is a crime.

Orou – I should be sorry to offend you by what I say, but if you'll permit me, let me tell you what I think.

The chaplain – Speak.

Orou – I find these strange precepts contrary to Nature, an offence against reason, certain to breed crime and bound to exasperate at every turn the old craftsman who, without a head, hand or tools has made everything; and who is everywhere but nowhere to be seen; who exists today and endures tomorrow without ever ageing a single moment; who commands and is not obeyed; who does not prevent occurrences which it is in his power to stop. Contrary to Nature, because they assume that a being which feels, thinks and is free may be the property of another being like himself. On what could such a right be based? Don't you see that in your country you have confused something which cannot feel or think or desire or will; which one takes or leaves, keeps or sells, without it suffering or complaining, with a very different thing that cannot be exchanged or acquired; which *does* have freedom, will, desire; which has the ability to give itself up or hold itself back forever; which complains and suffers; and which can never be an article of exchange unless its character is forgotten and violence is done to its nature. Such rules are contrary to the general order of things. What could seem more ridiculous than a precept which forbids any change of our affections, which commands that we show a constancy of which we're not capable, which violates the nature and liberty of male and female alike in chaining them to one another for the whole of their lives? What could be more absurd than a fidelity restricting the most capricious of our pleasures to a single individual; than a vow of immutability taken by two beings formed of flesh and blood, under a sky that doesn't remain fixed for an instant, beneath caverns poised on the edge of collapse, under a cliff crumbling into dust, at the foot of a tree shedding its bark, beneath a quivering stone? Believe you me, you have made the plight of man worse than that of an animal. I've no understanding of your great craftsman, but I rejoice in his never having addressed our forefathers, and I hope he will never speak to our children; for he might by chance tell them the same nonsense, and they might commit the folly of believing him.

Yesterday at supper you talked to us about magistrates and priests. I don't know what you mean by 'magistrates' and 'priests', who have the authority to regulate your conduct, but tell me, are they masters of good and evil? Can they make what is just unjust, and transform what is unjust into what's just? Can they make harmful actions good, and innocent and useful ones evil? One would hardly think so, since nothing could then be true or false, good or evil, beautiful or ugly, unless it pleased your great craftsman and his magistrates and priests to deem them so; in which case you'd be obliged, from one moment to another, to change your beliefs and conduct. One day, on behalf of one of your three masters you'd be told, 'Kill', and you'd then be obliged in conscience to kill; another day, 'Steal', and you'd then have to steal; or 'Do not eat this fruit', and you wouldn't dare eat it; 'I forbid you this plant or animal', and you'd refrain from touching them. There's nothing good that couldn't be forbidden, nothing evil that might not be required of you. And where would you be if your three masters, out of sorts with one another, took it upon themselves to permit you, command you, and forbid you the very same thing, as I suspect must happen often? Then, to please the priest, you'll be forced to oppose the magistrate; to satisfy the magistrate, you'll be forced to displease the great craftsman; (and to satisfy the great craftsman,) you'll have to abandon Nature. And do you know what will happen then? You'll come to despise all three of them, and you'll be neither a man, nor a citizen, nor a true believer. You'll be nothing. You'll be out of favour with each form of authority, at odds with yourself, malicious, tormented by your heart, miserable and persecuted by your senseless masters, as I saw you yesterday when I offered my daughters (and wife) to you, and you cried out, 'But my religion; but my holy orders!'

Would you like to know what's good and what's bad at all times and in all places? Stick to the nature of things and of actions, to your relations with your fellow-man, to the effect of your conduct on your own well-being and on the general welfare. You're mad if you suppose there can be anything high or low in the universe which can add to or take away from the laws of Nature. Her eternal will is that good should be preferred to evil and the general good to the

particular. You may decree the opposite, but you will not be obeyed. You will merely breed rascals and wretches, inspired by fear, punishment and remorse, depraving their conscience, corrupting their character. People will no longer know what they should do and what they should avoid. Anxious when innocent, calm only in crime, they will have lost sight of the pole star which should have guided their way. Answer me truthfully. Despite the express commands of your three legislators, doesn't a young man in your country ever lie with a young woman without their permission?

The chaplain – I should be lying if I assured you this never happens.

Orou – Doesn't the woman who has sworn to belong to her husband give herself to another?

The chaplain – Nothing is more common.

Orou – Your legislators must be either severe in meting out punishment, or not severe. If severe, they're wild beasts fighting against nature. If not severe, they're imbeciles whose useless prohibitions have subjected their authority to scorn.

The chaplain – Culprits who escape the severity of the laws are punished by public censure.

Orou – This amounts to saying that justice is administered without benefit of the whole nation's common sense, and that in place of laws you adopt the folly of opinion.

The chaplain – A girl who's lost her honour can no longer find a husband.

Orou – Lost her honour! Why?

The chaplain – An unfaithful woman is more or less despised.

Orou – Despised! And why?

The chaplain – The young man is called a cowardly seducer.

Orou – A coward, a seducer! And why?

The chaplain – The father, mother and poor child are disconsolate. The unfaithful husband is a libertine. The betrayed husband shares the shame of his wife.

Orou – What a monstrous web of delirium you describe, and yet you've not told me everything. For as soon as it's permitted to settle ideas of justice and property according to one's fancy, to ascribe or strike out the traits of things as if they were arbitrary, to attribute or deny good and evil to actions on no other grounds than whim, each person blames, accuses, suspects another; everyone tramples upon each other, becomes envious, jealous, deceitful, distressed, secretive, covert, spying upon another to take him or her by surprise; everyone quarrels and lies. Daughters deceive their parents, husbands cheat their wives, wives their husbands. Daughters – yes, I'm sure of it – will suffocate their children, suspicious fathers will scorn and neglect theirs, mothers will abandon them and leave them to the mercy of fate, and the crime of debauchery will appear in every shape and form. I know all this as plainly as if I'd lived among you. It's just so because it could not be otherwise; and the society whose splendid order your leader acclaims will be nothing but a swarm of hypocrites who secretly trample on the laws, or unfortunates who are themselves the willing instruments of their own torture; or imbeciles in whom prejudice has altogether stifled the voice of Nature; or misshapen creatures in whom Nature does not lay claim to her rights.

The chaplain – It's a fair likeness. But do you therefore never marry?

Orou – We marry.

The chaplain – What does your marriage consist of?

Orou – A mutual consent to live in the same hut and to share the same bed, for as long as we find it good to do so.

The chaplain – And when you come to find it bad?

Orou – We separate.

The chaplain – What becomes of the children?

Orou – Oh stranger! That last question reveals to me your country's depths of misery. You must understand, my friend, that here the birth of a child is always a source of joy, and a child's death an occasion for sorrow and tears. A child is a precious thing because it will grow up to be an adult. We thus have an interest in caring for it altogether different from that shown in our plants and animals. The birth of a child brings domestic and public joy. It will mean an increase of wealth for the hut, and of strength for the nation. It means another pair of arms and hands in Tahiti. We see in him a future farmer, fisherman,

hunter, soldier, husband, father. In returning from her husband's hut to that of her parents, a woman brings back the children she had taken with her as a dowry; those born during the companionship are shared, males and females equally, as far as possible, so that each parent has more or less the same number of boys and girls.

The chaplain – But children are a burden for many years before they can make themselves useful.

Orou – For their maintenance and that of the aged we set aside one part in six of all our harvests. This allowance always goes with them. So you see that the larger a Tahitian's family, the richer he is.

The chaplain – One part in six!

Orou – Yes. It encourages the growth of population and respect for the elderly and the welfare of children.

The chaplain – Do your husbands and wives sometimes take each other back?

Orou – Very often. The shortest length of a marriage, however, is one month.

The chaplain – Assuming, of course, that the mother's not with child; for then they must live together for at least nine months.

Orou – You're mistaken. The child's paternity, like its allowance, follows it everywhere.

The chaplain – You speak to me of children which a wife brings to her husband as a dowry.

Orou – Exactly. Take my eldest daughter here, who has three children. They can walk, they're healthy and attractive. They promise to be strong. When she comes to fancy getting married, she'll take them with her; they're hers. Her husband will accept them with joy and could only regard his wife as more dear to him if she were pregnant with a fourth.

The chaplain – By him?

Orou – By him or another. The more our girls have children, the more sought after they are. The more lusty and handsome our boys, the richer they are. Before they're reached the age of sexual maturity, we're careful to keep girls away from men, and boys from intercourse with women, but once they've passed puberty we exhort them to produce children. You can't imagine the importance of the service you will have rendered to my daughter Thia, if she's now with child. Her mother will no longer say to her each month, 'But Thia, what are you thinking of? You never get pregnant. You're nineteen years old; you should already have two children, and you've none. Who will look after you? If you let your youth pass in this way, what will you do in your old age? Thia, there must be something wrong with you that puts men off. Cure yourself of it, my child. At your age, I'd already been a mother three times.'

The chaplain – What precautions do you take to safeguard your adolescent girls and boys?

Orou – That's the main object of domestic education, and the most important item of public morality. Up to the age of twenty-two, that is, two or three years past puberty, our boys wear a long tunic which covers them, their loins clasped by a little chain. Before they become nubile, our girls daren't go out without a white veil. To take off one's chain or remove one's veil is a wrong seldom committed, because we teach our children at an early age what harmful effects will follow. But as soon as the male has attained his full strength, when the symptoms of his virility appear durable, and when the frequent emission and quality of his seminal fluid confirm it; just when the young girl becomes languid, bored and sufficiently mature to feel passion, to inspire and satisfy it usefully; then the father unfastens his son's chain and cuts the nail of the middle finger of his right hand; while the mother removes her daughter's veil. The young man may henceforth seek a woman's favours and be sought out in turn himself; the woman may thereafter walk about freely, her face and breasts uncovered. She may accept or reject a man's caresses. We merely indicate in advance to the boy, which girls, and to the girl, which boys, they should prefer. The (day of) emancipation for a boy or girl is a great holiday. If it's a girl, the young men assemble round her hut the evening before, filling the air the whole night long with their singing and the sound of musical instruments. On the appointed day, she's led by her father and mother into an enclosure where there's dancing and exercises of jumping, wrestling and running. The naked man is displayed before her, from all sides and in all attitudes. If it's a boy, then the girls undertake to please and do the honours of the ceremony, presenting before his eyes the nude female body, without reserve or furtiveness.

The rest of the ceremony is enacted on a bed of leaves, as you saw on your arrival here. At sunset the girl returns to her parents' hut or to the hut of the young man she's chosen, and she remains there as long as she pleases.

The chaplain – So is this ceremony a wedding-day or not?

Orou – Just so.

A – What's that I see there in the margin?

B – It's a note in which the good chaplain says that the parents' precepts on the boys' and girls' choices were full of common sense, and very acute and useful observations, but that he suppressed this catechism, which would have appeared intolerably licentious to people as corrupt and superficial as we are. He adds, nevertheless, that it wasn't without regret that he had deleted details which would have shown, in the first place, how far a nation that pursues an important objective can proceed in its investigations without the help of physics and anatomy; and, secondly, how different are ideas of beauty in a country where its forms reflect the pleasures of a moment, from such ideas in a nation that appreciates them for a more constant utility. In the latter, to be beautiful, a woman must have a striking complexion, a high forehead, large eyes, fine and delicate features, a slender waist, a small mouth, small hands and feet. In the former, almost none of these qualities matters. The woman who attracts admiring glances and is the object of desire is the one who promises many children, like the wife of Cardinal Ossat – children who will be active, intelligent, courageous, healthy and robust. The Venus of Athens and that of Tahiti have next to nothing in common. [One is *Vénus galante*, the other *Vénus féconde*.] A Tahitian woman one day said scornfully to another woman from her country, 'You are pretty; but you bear ugly children. I am ugly, but my children are beautiful, and the men prefer me.'

[...]

IV

Orou – What a happy moment for a young girl and her parents when it's discovered that she's with child! She leaps to her feet, runs and throws her arms round the neck of her mother and father. Beside herself with the delight of mutual joy she tells them the news, and so they learn of the happy event. 'Mother, dear father, kiss me. I am pregnant. – Is it really true? – Quite true. – And who got you with child? – So and so.'

The chaplain – How is she able to tell who's the father of her child?

Orou – Why shouldn't she know? Our love affairs are like our marriages. Each lasts from one moon to the next.

The chaplain – And is this rule strictly observed?

Orou – You can judge for yourself. First, the interval between two moons isn't long; but when two men have a plausible claim to be the father of a child it no longer belongs to its mother.

The chaplain – To whom does it belong then?

Orou – To whichever of the two the mother pleases to give it. That's her sole privilege. And since a child is in itself a source of benefit and riches, you can understand why, among us, lascivious women are rare and young men keep away from them.

The chaplain – So you do have your loose women as well. I feel better for it.

Orou – We even have more than one kind, but that's another matter. When one of our daughters is pregnant, if the father of the child is a good-looking, well-built, brave, intelligent, industrious young man, the hope that it will inherit his qualities renews our joy. Our daughter is only ashamed of making a bad choice. You can understand what value we attach to health, beauty, strength, ingenuity and courage. You can imagine how, even without our interference, the prerogatives of blood are bound to be perpetuated among us. Since you've been in so many countries, tell me, have you ever seen more handsome men and more beautiful women than in Tahiti? Look at me. What do you think of me? Well, there are ten thousand men here who are taller than I am and just as strong, but there's not one as brave. That's why mothers often point me out to their daughters.

The chaplain – But of all the children you've sired outside your hut, how many come back to you?

Orou – A quarter, male or female. We have a circulation of men, women and children, of able-bodied persons of all ages and occupations, which is of far greater importance than the circulation of commodities, which are no more than the product of people's work.

The chaplain – I can understand that. What's the significance of those black veils I've noticed from time to time?

Orou – They're a mark of sterility, either a defect of birth or a consequence of old age. Any woman who takes off that veil and consorts with men is licentious, and so is a man who lifts it and has relations with such a woman.

The chaplain – And those grey veils?

Orou – They're the mark of a woman indisposed by her monthly period. Any woman who takes off that veil and consorts with men is licentious, and so is a man who lifts it and has relations with such a woman.

The chaplain – Have you punishments for such licentiousness?

Orou – Only public censure.

The chaplain – May a father lie with his daughter, a mother with her son, a brother with his sister, a husband with the wife of another man?

Orou – Why not?

The chaplain – To say nothing of fornication, but incest, adultery!

Orou – What do you mean by these words 'fornication', 'incest', 'adultery'?

The chaplain – Crimes, monstrous crimes, for which people are burnt to death in my country.

Orou – Whether or not people are burnt to death in your country matters little to me. You can't condemn the ways of Europe in the light of those of Tahiti, nor consequently the ways of Tahiti in the light of those of your country. We must have a more reliable standard, so what will that be? Do you know a better one than the general welfare and individual utility? Well, tell me, now, how your crime of incest is in conflict with these two aims of our actions? You're mistaken, my friend, if you suppose that once a law is published, a dishonourable word invented, a punishment determined, enough has been said. Tell me, then, what do you mean by 'incest'?

The chaplain – But to commit incest …

Orou – Yes, 'incest'. Has it been a long time since your great crafts-man, without hands, head or tools, made the world?

The chaplain – No.

Orou – Did he make the whole human race at one time?

The chaplain – (No,) he only created one man and one woman.

Orou – Did they have children?

The chaplain – Certainly.

Orou – Suppose that these two original parents only had daughters and that their mother was the first to die. Or that they only had sons and that the wife lost her husband.

The chaplain – You embarrass me. But in spite of all your remarks, incest is a dreadful crime. Let's discuss something else.

Orou – That's easily said, but for my part I shall remain silent, until you've explained to me what this dreadful crime, 'incest', may be.

The chaplain – Very well then, I grant you that incest perhaps does not offend against nature, but isn't it enough to remark that it threatens the political order? How could a state be tranquil and its leader safe if a whole nation made up of several million people were to be split into fifty families, each centred on a different father?

Orou – At worst it would mean that instead of one great society there would be fifty small ones, more happiness overall and one less crime.

The chaplain – I suspect, nevertheless, that even here a son rarely lies with his mother.

Orou – Unless he has so much respect for her, and feels such tenderness, that he forgets the disparity of their ages and prefers a woman of forty to a girl of nineteen.

The chaplain – What about intercourse between fathers and daughters?

Orou – Hardly more frequent, unless the girl's ugly and little sought after by young men. If her father loves her, he takes responsibility for preparing her dowry in children.

The chaplain – This leads me to suppose that in Tahiti the fate of women on whom Nature has not smiled must be difficult.

Orou – Your remark convinces me that you don't have a high opinion of the generosity of our young people.

The chaplain – As for the union of brother and sister, I presume it must be very common.

Orou – And much approved.

The chaplain – To hear you say it, the same passion which produces so many crimes and evils among us would here be altogether innocent.

Orou – Stranger, you lack both judgement and memory. You lack judgement, since whenever something's forbidden there are always people who are tempted to do it and who in fact set about doing it. Your memory fails you, since you no longer recall what I've told you. We do have dissolute old women who go out at night without their black veils, receiving men whose advances can't prove fruitful. If they're recognised or found out, their punishment is either exile to the north of the island, or slavery. We have precocious girls who lift their white veils without their parents' knowledge; for them we reserve a locked corner of the hut. We have young men who remove their chain before the time prescribed by nature and by law; we reprimand their parents. We have women to whom the period of pregnancy seems too long; women and girls none too careful about wearing their grey veils. But, as a matter of fact, we attach no great importance to any of these lapses, and you'd hardly believe how much our morals are actually improved by the extent to which we're inclined to identify private and public gain with the growth of population.

The chaplain – But don't you ever have trouble stemming from the attraction of two men to the same woman or the longing of two women or girls for the same man?

Orou – I've scarcely seen four such examples. The woman's or man's choice settles the matter. An act of violence committed by a man would be a serious offence; but the victim would have to make a public complaint, and it's almost unheard of for a woman or girl to do so. The only thing I've noticed is that our women are a little less considerate of unattractive men than our young men are of illfavoured women, and that doesn't worry us at all.

The chaplain – From what I can see, there's hardly any jealousy here. But what about the powerful and delightful feelings of marital tenderness and paternal care? If these sentiments aren't unknown here, they must be rather weak.

Orou – In their place we've another which is altogether more general, energetic and durable: self-interest. Look candidly into your conscience and leave behind that sanctimonious bluster always foaming from the lips of your comrades but never to be found deep in their hearts; tell me if there's any country in the world in which a father, unless held back by shame, wouldn't rather lose his child, or a husband his wife, than accept the loss of his fortune and the comforts of his life. You can be sure that whenever a man is as attentive to his fellow-creatures as to his bed, health or peace of mind, his hut, harvests or fields, he will do his utmost to ensure their welfare. It's here that you will see tears shed over the bed of a sick child, and mothers nursed through illness. It's here that we prize a fruitful woman, a nubile girl, an adolescent boy. It's here that we take an interest in their upbringing, because in preserving them our fortune grows, while with their loss it is diminished.

The chaplain – I rather fear this savage is right. The wretched peasants of our countries wear out their wives to spare their horses, let their children perish without help and only call the doctor for their oxen.

Orou – I can't grasp what you've just said. But when you return to your country that's so civilised, try to introduce this motive there. Only then will the value of every newborn child, and the importance of population, be recognised. Shall I tell you a secret? Be sure to keep it to yourself. On your arrival, we let you have our wives and daughters. You showed surprise and such gratitude that we laughed. You thanked us for having placed on you and your companions the greatest of all impositions. We didn't ask you for money; we didn't loot your ships; we cared nothing for your produce; but our wives and daughters drew blood from your veins. When you've gone you will have left children. Don't you think that this tribute seized from your person, from your very flesh, surpasses all others? And if you wish to judge its value, imagine that you had still two hundred leagues of coastline to navigate, and that every twenty miles the same tribute was collected from you. We've vast tracts of untilled soil; we lack hands and asked you for them. We've still to recover from calamitous epidemics, and we used you to make good the void they've left. We have nearby enemies to contend with, a need for soldiers, and we asked you to supply us with them. We have a surplus of women and girls over men, and so in our endeavours we enlisted your services. Among these women and girls there are some with whom we've never been able to beget children, and these are the ones we exposed to your first embraces. We're obliged to pay a tribute, in men, to a neighbouring oppressor; you and your comrades will pay off this debt for us, and in five or six years it will be your sons whom we send, if they're less hardy than ours. While more robust and healthy than you, we saw at once that you surpassed us in intelligence, and we immediately marked out for you some of our most beautiful women and girls to receive the seed of a race superior to ours. We tried an experiment which may still bring us success. We've drawn from you and yours the only part which we could take; and, rest assured, however savage we are, we know just how to scheme. Go wherever you will, and you'll almost always find a man as shrewd as yourself. He'll never give you anything but what's worthless to him, and will always ask you for what he finds useful. If he offers you a bit of gold for a bit of iron, it's because he thinks nothing of gold but cares highly for iron. But tell me, by the way, why you're not dressed like the others? What's the significance of this long robe which envelops you from head to foot, and the pointed sack which you let fall behind your shoulders, or which you pull up over your ears?

The chaplain – The reason I dress as I do is that I'm a member of a society of men which in my country is called monks. The most sacred of their vows is to refrain from sexual relations with a woman and to have no children.

Orou – What then do you do?

The chaplain – Nothing.

Orou – And your magistrates put up with that sort of idleness, the worst of all?

The chaplain – They do more; they respect it and see that others do so too.

Orou – My first thought was that Nature, some accident or cruel trick of fate, had deprived you of the ability to reproduce your kind, and that out of compassion you'd been allowed to live rather than been put to death. But, monk, my daughter told me that you are indeed a man, and one as robust as any Tahitian, and that she hoped that your repeated caresses wouldn't prove fruitless. Now that I understand why you cried out yesterday, 'But my religion! But my holy orders!', would you tell me the reason for the favour and respect which magistrates extend to you?

The chaplain – I don't know.

Orou – You must at least know why, as a man, you freely condemned yourself not to be one.

The chaplain – That would take too long and be too hard to explain to you.

Orou – And are monks always faithful to their vows of sterility?

The chaplain – No.

Orou – I thought not. Do you also have female monks?

The chaplain – Yes.

Orou – As wise as the male monks?

The chaplain – More strictly confined, they shrivel away from unhappiness and perish from boredom.

Orou – So that the injury done to Nature is avenged. Oh, what a wretched country! If everything there's managed the way you say, you're more barbarous than we are.

The good chaplain reports that he spent the rest of the day wandering about the island and viewing the huts; and that in the evening, after supper, when the father and mother implored him to lie with the second of their daughters, Palli offered herself to him in the same state of undress as Thia before; that during the night he cried out several times, 'But my religion! But my holy orders!'; that on the third night he was struck by the same remorse in the arms of Asto, the eldest; and that out of courtesy he granted the fourth night to the wife of his host.

Section V

(c) Universal History: France

22

The Spirit of Laws

Montesquieu

Book I

3. – Of positive laws

As soon as man enters into a state of society he loses the sense of his weakness; equality ceases, and then commences the state of war:

Each particular society begins to feel its strength, whence arises a state of war between different nations. The individuals likewise of each society become sensible of their force; hence the principal advantages of this society they endeavour to convert to their own emolument, which constitutes a state of war between individuals.

These two different kinds of states give rise to human laws. Considered as inhabitants of so great a planet, which necessarily contains a variety of nations, they have laws relating to their mutual intercourse, which is what we call the *law of nations*. As members of a society that must be properly supported, they have laws relating to the governors and the governed, and this we distinguish by the name of *politic law*. They have also another sort of laws, as they stand in relation to each other; by which is understood the *civil law*.

The law of nations is naturally founded on this principle, that different nations ought in time of peace to do one another all the good they can, and in time of war as little injury as possible, without prejudicing their real interests.

The object of war is victory; that of victory is conquest; and that of conquest preservation. From this and the preceding principle all those rules are derived which constitute the *law of nations*.

All countries have a law of nations, not excepting the Iroquois themselves, though they devour their prisoners: for they send and receive ambassadors, and understand the rights of war and peace. The mischief is that then law of nations is not founded on true principles.

Besides the law of nations relating to all societies, there is a polity or civil constitution for each particularly considered. No society can subsist without a form of government. *The united strength of individuals*, as Gravina well observes, *constitutes what we call the body politic*.

The general strength may be in the hands of a single person, or of many. Some think that nature having established paternal authority, the most natural government was that of a single person. But the example of paternal authority proves nothing. For if the power of a father relates to a single government, that of brothers after the death of a father, and that of cousin-germans after the decease of brothers, refer to a government

Montesquieu, *The Spirit of Laws*, trans. Thomas Nugent, rev. and ed. J. V. Prichard, vol. I, London: George Bell and Sons, 1878, pp. 5–7, 20–31, 111–12, 133–6.

of many. The political power necessarily comprehends the union of several families.

Better is it to say, that the government most conformable to nature is that which best agrees with the humour and disposition of the people in whose favour it is established.

The strength of individuals cannot be united without a conjunction of all their wills. *The conjunction of those wills*, as Gravina again very justly observes, *is what we call the* CIVIL STATE.

Law in general is human reason, inasmuch as it governs all the inhabitants of the earth: the political and civil laws of each nation ought to be only the particular cases in which human reason is applied.

They should be adapted in such a manner to the people for whom they are framed that it should be a great chance if those of one nation suit another.

They should be in relation to the nature and principle of each government; whether they form it, as may be said of politic laws; or whether they support it, as in the case of civil institutions.

They should be in relation to the climate of each country, to the quality of its soil, to its situation and extent, to the principal occupation of the natives, whether husbandmen, huntsmen, or shepherds: they should have relation to the degree of liberty which the constitution will bear; to the religion of the inhabitants, to their inclinations, riches, numbers, commerce, manners, and customs. In fine, they have relations to each other, as also to their origin, to the intent of the legislator, and to the order of things on which they are established; in all of which different lights they ought to be considered.

This is what I have undertaken to perform in the following work. These relations I shall examine, since all these together constitute what I call the *Spirit of Laws*.

I have not separated the political from the civil institutions, as I do not pretend to treat of laws, but of their spirit; and as this spirit consists in the various relations which the laws may bear to different objects, it is not so much my business to follow the natural order of laws as that of these relations and objects.

I shall first examine the relations which laws bear to the nature and principle of each government; and as this principle has a strong influence on laws, I shall make it my study to understand it thoroughly: and if I can but once establish it, the laws will soon appear to flow thence as from their source. I shall proceed afterwards to other and more particular relations.

[…]

Book III. Of the Principles of the Three Kinds of Government

1. – Difference between the nature and principle of government

Having examined the laws in relation to the nature of each government, we must investigate those which relate to its principle.

There is this difference between the nature and principle of government, that the former is that by which it is constituted, the latter that by which it is made to act. One is its particular structure, and the other the human passions which set it in motion.

Now, laws ought no less to relate to the principle than to the nature of each government. We must, therefore, inquire into this principle, which shall be the subject of this third book.

2. – Of the principle of different governments

I have already observed that it is the nature of a republican government, that either the collective body of the people, or particular families, should be possessed of the supreme power; of a monarchy, that the prince should have this power, but in the execution of it should be directed by established laws; of a despotic government, that a single person should rule according to his own will and caprice. This enables me to discover their three principles; which are thence naturally derived. I shall begin with a republican government, and in particular with that of democracy.

3. – Of the principle of democracy

There is no great share of probity necessary to support a monarchical or despotic government. The force of laws in one, and the prince's arm in the other, are sufficient to direct and maintain the whole. But in a popular state, one spring more is necessary, namely, *virtue*.

What I have here advanced is confirmed by the unanimous testimony of historians, and is extremely agreeable to the nature of things. For it is clear that in a monarchy, where he who commands the execution of the laws generally thinks himself above them, there is less need of virtue than in a popular government, where the person entrusted with the execution of the laws is sensible of his being subject to their direction.

Clear is it also that a monarch who, through bad advice or indolence, ceases to enforce the execution of the laws, may easily repair the evil; he has only to follow other advice; or to shake off this indolence. But when, in a popular government, there is a suspension of the laws, as this can proceed only from the corruption of the republic, the state is certainly undone.

A very droll spectacle it was in the last century to behold the impotent efforts of the English towards the establishment of democracy. As they who had a share in the direction of public affairs were void of virtue; as their ambition was inflamed by the success of the most daring of their members; as the prevailing parties were successively animated by the spirit of faction, the government was continually changing: the people, amazed at so many revolutions, in vain attempted to erect a commonwealth. At length, when the country had undergone the most violent shocks, they were obliged to have recourse to the very government which they had so wantonly proscribed.

When Sylla thought of restoring Rome to her liberty, this unhappy city was incapable of receiving that blessing. She had only the feeble remains of virtue, which were continually diminishing. Instead of being roused from her lethargy by Cæsar, Tiberius, Caius Claudius, Nero, and Domitian, she riveted every day her chains; if she struck some blows, her aim was at the tyrant, not at the tyranny.

The politic Greeks, who lived under a popular government, knew no other support than virtue. The modern inhabitants of that country are entirely taken up with manufacture, commerce, finances, opulence, and luxury.

When virtue is banished, ambition invades the minds of those who are disposed to receive it, and avarice possesses the whole community. The objects of their desires are changed; what they were fond of before has become indifferent; they were free while under the restraint of laws, but they would fain now be free to act against law; and as each citizen is like a slave who has run away from his master, that which was a maxim of equity he calls rigour; that which was a rule of action he styles constraint; and to precaution he gives the name of fear. Frugality, and not the thirst of gain, now passes for avarice. Formerly the wealth of individuals constituted the public treasure; but now this has become the patrimony of private persons. The members of the commonwealth riot on the public spoils, and its strength is only the power of a few, and the licence of many.

Athens was possessed of the same number of forces when she triumphed so gloriously as when with such infamy she was enslaved. She had twenty thousand citizens, when she defended the Greeks against the Persians, when she contended for empire with Sparta, and invaded Sicily. She had twenty thousand when Demetrius Phalereus numbered them, as slaves are told by the head in a marketplace. When Philip attempted to lord it over Greece, and appeared at the gates of Athens, she had even then lost nothing but time. We may see in Demosthenes how difficult it was to awaken her; she dreaded Philip not as the enemy of her liberty, but of her pleasures. This famous city, which had withstood so many defeats, and having been so often destroyed had as often risen out of her ashes, was overthrown at Chæronea, and at one blow deprived of all hopes of resource. What does it avail her that Philip sends back her prisoners, if he does not return her men? It was ever after as easy to triumph over the forces of Athens as it had been difficult to subdue her virtue.

How was it possible for Carthage to maintain her ground? When Hannibal, upon his being made prætor, endeavoured to hinder the magistrates from plundering the republic, did not they complain of him to the Romans? Wretches, who would fain be citizens without a city, and be beholden for their riches to their very destroyers! Rome soon insisted upon having three hundred of their principal citizens as hostages; she obliged them next to surrender their arms and ships; and then she declared war. From the desperate efforts of this defenceless city, one may judge of what she might have performed in her full vigour, and assisted by virtue.

4. – Of the principle of aristocracy

As virtue is necessary in a popular government, it is requisite also in an aristocracy. True it is that in the latter it is not so absolutely requisite.

The people, who in respect to the nobility are the same as the subjects with regard to a monarch, are restrained by their laws. They have, therefore, less occasion for virtue than the people in a democracy. But how are the nobility to be restrained? They who are to execute the laws against their colleagues will immediately perceive that they are acting against themselves. Virtue is therefore necessary in this body, from the very nature of the constitution.

An aristocratic government has an inherent vigour, unknown to democracy. The nobles form a body, who by their prerogative, and for their own particular interest, restrain the people; it is sufficient that there are laws in being to see them executed.

But easy as it may be for the body of the nobles to restrain the people, it is difficult to restrain themselves. Such is the nature of this constitution, that it seems to subject the very same persons to the power of the laws, and at the same time to exempt them.

Now such a body as this can restrain itself only in two ways; either by a very eminent virtue, which puts the nobility in some measure on a level with the people, and may be the means of forming a great republic; or by an inferior virtue, which puts them at least upon a level with one another, and upon this their preservation depends.

Moderation is therefore the very soul of this government; a moderation, I mean, founded on virtue, not that which proceeds from indolence and pusillanimity.

5. – That virtue is not the principle of a monarchical government

In monarchies, policy effects great things with as little virtue as possible. Thus in the nicest machines, art has reduced the number of movements, springs, and wheels.

The state subsists independently of the love of our country, of the thirst of true glory, of self-denial, of the sacrifice of our dearest interests, and of all those heroic virtues which we admire in the ancients, and to us are known only by tradition.

The laws supply here the place of those virtues; they are by no means wanted, and the state dispenses with them: an action performed here in secret is in some measure of no consequence.

Though all crimes be in their own nature public, yet there is a distinction between crimes really public and those that are private, which are so called because they are more injurious to individuals than to the community.

Now in republics private crimes are more public, that is, they attack the constitution more than they do individuals; and in monarchies, public crimes are more private, that is, they are more prejudicial to private people than to the constitution.

I beg that no one will be offended with what I have been saying; my observations are founded on the unanimous testimony of historians. I am not ignorant that virtuous princes are so very rare; but I venture to affirm, that in a monarchy it is extremely difficult for the people to be virtuous.

Let us compare what the historians of all ages have asserted concerning the courts of monarchs; let us recollect the conversations and sentiments of people of all countries, in respect to the wretched character of courtiers, and we shall find that these are not airy speculations, but truths confirmed by a sad and melancholy experience.

Ambition in idleness; meanness mixed with pride; a desire of riches without industry; aversion to truth; flattery, perfidy, violation of engagements, contempt of civil duties, fear of the prince's virtue, hope from his weakness, but, above all, a perpetual ridicule cast upon virtue, are, I think, the characteristics by which most courtiers in all ages and countries have been constantly distinguished. Now, it is exceedingly difficult for the leading men of the nation to be knaves, and the inferior sort to be honest for the former to be cheats, and the latter to rest satisfied with being only dupes.

But if there should chance to be some unlucky honest man among the people, Cardinal Richelieu, in his political testament, seems to hint that a prince should take care not to employ him. So true is it that virtue is not the spring of this government! It is not indeed excluded, but it is not the spring of government.

6. – In what manner virtue is supplied in a monarchical government

But it is high time for me to have done with this subject, lest I should be suspected of writing a satire against monarchical government. Far be it from me; if monarchy wants one spring, it is provided with another. Honour, that is, the prejudice of every person and rank, supplies the place of the political virtue of which I have been speaking, and is everywhere her representative: here it is capable of inspiring the most glorious actions, and, joined with the force of laws, may lead us to the end of government as well as virtue itself.

Hence, in well-regulated monarchies, they are almost all good subjects, and very few good men; for to be a good man, a good intention is necessary, and we should love our country, not so much on our own account, as out of regard to the community.

7. – Of the principle of monarchy

A monarchical government supposes, as we have already observed, pre-eminences and ranks, as likewise a noble descent. Now since it is the nature of honour to aspire to preferments and titles, it is properly placed in this government.

Ambition is pernicious in a republic. But in a monarchy it has some good effects; it gives life to the government, and is attended with this advantage, that it is in no way dangerous, because it may be continually checked.

It is with this kind of government as with the system of the universe, in which there is a power that constantly repels all bodies from the centre, and a power of gravitation that attracts them to it. Honour sets all the parts of the body politic in motion, and by its very action connects them; thus each individual advances the public good, while he only thinks of promoting his own interest.

True it is, that philosophically speaking it is a false honour which moves all the parts of the government; but even this false honour is as useful to the public as true honour could possibly be to private persons.

Is it not very exacting to oblige men to perform the most difficult actions, such as require an extraordinary exertion of fortitude and resolution, without other recompense than that of glory and applause?

8. – That honour is not the principle of despotic government

Honour is far from being the principle of despotic government: mankind being here all upon a level, no one person can prefer himself to another; and as on the other hand they are all slaves, they can give themselves no sort of preference.

Besides, as honour has its laws and rules; as it knows not how to submit; as it depends in a great measure on a man's own caprice, and not on that of another person; it can be found only in countries in which the constitution is fixed, and where they are governed by settled laws.

How can despotism abide with honour? The one glories in the contempt of life; and the other is founded on the power of taking it away. How can honour, on the other hand, bear with despotism? The former has its fixed rules, and peculiar caprices; but the latter is directed by no rule, and its own caprices are subversive of all others.

Honour, therefore, a thing unknown in arbitrary governments, some of which have not even a proper word to express it, is the prevailing principle in monarchies; here it gives life to the whole body politic, to the laws, and even to the virtues themselves.

9. – Of the principle of despotic government

As virtue is necessary in a republic, and in a monarchy honour, so fear is necessary in a despotic government: with regard to virtue, there is no occasion for it, and honour would be extremely dangerous.

Here the immense power of the prince devolves entirely upon those whom he is pleased to intrust with the administration. Persons capable of setting a value upon themselves would be likely to create disturbances. Fear must therefore depress their spirits, and extinguish even the least sense of ambition.

A moderate government may, whenever it pleases, and without the least danger, relax its springs. It supports itself by the laws, and by its own internal strength. But when a despotic prince ceases for one single moment to uplift his arm, when he cannot instantly demolish those whom he has intrusted with the first employments, all is over: for as fear, the spring of this government, no longer subsists, the people are left without a protector.

It is probably in this sense the Cadis maintained that the Grand Seignior was not obliged to keep his word or oath, when he limited thereby his authority.

It is necessary that the people should be judged by laws, and the great men by the caprice of the prince, that the lives of the lowest subject should be safe, and the pasha's head ever in danger. We cannot mention these monstrous governments without horror. The Sophi of Persia, dethroned in our days by Mahomet, the son of Miriveis, saw the constitution subverted before this resolution, because he had been too sparing of blood.

History informs us that the horrid cruelties of Domitian struck such a terror into the governors, that the people recovered themselves a little during his reign. Thus a torrent overflows one side of a country, and on the other leaves fields untouched, where the eye is refreshed by the prospect of fine meadows.

10.   – Difference of obedience in moderate and despotic governments

In despotic states, the nature of government requires the most passive obedience; and when once the prince's will is made known, it ought infallibly to produce its effect.

Here they have no limitations or restrictions, no mediums, terms, equivalents, or remonstrances; no change to propose: man is a creature that blindly submits to the absolute will of the sovereign.

In a country like this they are no more allowed to represent their apprehensions of a future danger than to impute their miscarriage to the capriciousness of fortune. Man's portion here, like that of beasts, is instinct, compliance, and punishment.

Little does it then avail to plead the sentiments of nature, filial respect, conjugal or parental tenderness, the laws of honour, or want of health; the order is given, and that is sufficient.

In Persia, when the king has condemned a person, it is no longer lawful to mention his name, or to intercede in his favour. Even if the prince were intoxicated, or *non compos*, the decree must be executed; otherwise he would contradict himself, and the law admits of no contradiction. This has been the way of thinking in that country in all ages; as the order which Ahasuerus gave, to exterminate the Jews, could not be revoked, they were allowed the liberty of defending themselves.

One thing however, may be sometimes opposed to the prince's will, namely, religion. They will abandon, nay they will slay a parent, if the prince so commands; but he cannot oblige them to drink wine. The laws of religion are of a superior nature, because they bind the sovereign as well as the subject. But with respect to the law of nature, it is otherwise; the prince is no longer supposed to be a man.

In monarchical and moderate states, the power is limited by its very spring, I mean by honour, which, like a monarch, reigns over the prince and his people. They will not allege to their sovereign the laws of religion; a courtier would be apprehensive of rendering himself ridiculous. But the laws of honour will be appealed to on all occasions. Hence arise the restrictions necessary to obedience; honour is naturally subject to whims, by which the subject's submission will be ever directed.

Though the manner of obeying be different in these two kinds of government, the power is the same. On which side soever the monarch turns, he inclines the scale, -and is obeyed. The whole difference is, that in a monarchy the prince receives instruction, at the same time that his ministers have greater abilities, and are more versed in public affairs, than the ministers of a despotic government.

11. – Reflections on the preceding chapters

Such are the principles of the three sorts of government: which does not imply that in a particular republic they actually are, but that they ought to be, virtuous; nor does it prove that in a particular monarchy they are actuated by honour, or in a particular despotic government by fear; but that they ought to be directed by these principles, otherwise the government is imperfect.

[...]

Book IV

9. – Of the condition or state of women in different governments

In monarchies women are subject to very little restraint, because as the distinction of ranks calls them to court, there they assume a spirit of liberty, which is almost the only one tolerated in that place. Each courtier avails himself of their charms and passions, in order to advance his fortune: and as their weakness admits not of pride, but of vanity, luxury constantly attends them.

In despotic governments women do not introduce, but are themselves an object of, luxury. They must be in a state of the most rigorous servitude. Every one follows the spirit of the government, and adopts in his own family the customs he sees elsewhere established. As the laws are very severe and executed on the spot they are afraid lest the liberty of women should expose them to danger. Their quarrels, indiscretions, repugnancies, jealousies, piques, and that art, in fine, which little souls have of interesting great ones, would be attended there with fatal consequences.

Besides, as princes in those countries make a sport of human nature, they allow themselves a multitude of women; and a thousand considerations oblige them to keep those women in close confinement.

In republics women are free by the laws and restrained by manners; luxury is banished thence, and with it corruption and vice.

In the cities of Greece, where they were not under the restraint of a religion which declares that even amongst men regularity of manners is a part of virtue; where a blind passion triumphed with a boundless insolence, and love appeared only in a shape which we dare not mention, while marriage was considered as nothing more than simple friendship; such was the virtue, simplicity, and chastity of women in those cities, that in this respect hardly any people were ever known to have had a better and wiser polity.

[...]

21 – Of the empire of China

[...]

Our missionaries inform us that the government of the vast empire of China is admirable, and that it has a proper mixture of fear, honour, and virtue. Consequently I must have given an idle distinction in establishing the principles of the three governments.

But I cannot conceive what this honour can be among a people who act only through fear of being bastinadoed.

Again, our merchants are far from giving us any such accounts of the virtue so much talked of by the missionaries; we need only consult them in relation to the robberies and extortions of the mandarins. I likewise appeal to another unexceptionable witness, the great Lord Anson.

Besides, Father Perennin's letters concerning the emperor's proceedings against some of the princes of the blood who had incurred his displeasure by their conversion, plainly show us a settled plan of tyranny, and barbarities committed by rule, that is, in cold blood.

We have likewise Monsieur de Mairan's, and the same Father Perennin's, letters on the government of China. I find therefore that after a few proper questions and answers the whole mystery is unfolded.

Might not our missionaries have been deceived by an appearance of order? Might not they have been struck with that constant exercise of a single person's will – an exercise by which they themselves are governed, and which they are so pleased to find in the courts of the Indian princes; because as they go thither only in order to introduce great changes, it is much easier to persuade those princes that there are no bounds to their power, than to convince the people that there are none to their submission.

In fine, there is frequently some kind of truth even in errors themselves. It may be owing to particular and, perhaps, very extraordinary circumstances that the Chinese government is not so corrupt as one might naturally expect. The climate and some other physical causes may, in that country, have had so strong an influence on their morals as in some measure to produce wonders.

The climate of China is surprisingly favourable to the propagation of the human species. The women are the most prolific in the whole world. The most barbarous tyranny can put no stop to the progress of propagation. The prince cannot say there like Pharaoh, *Let us deal wisely with them, lest they multiply.* He would be rather reduced to Nero's wish, that mankind had all but one head. In spite of tyranny, China by the force of its climate will be ever populous, and triumph over the tyrannical oppressor.

China, like all other countries that live chiefly upon rice, is subject to frequent famines. When the people are ready to starve, they disperse in order to seek for nourishment; in consequence of which, gangs of robbers are formed on every side. Most of them are extirpated in their very infancy; others swell, and are likewise suppressed. And yet in so great a number of such distant provinces, some band or other may happen to meet with success. In that case they maintain their ground, strengthen their party, form themselves into a military body, march up to the capital, and place their leader on the throne.

From the very nature of things, a bad administration is here immediately punished. The want of subsistence in so populous a country produces sudden disorders. The reason why the redress of abuses in other countries is attended with such difficulty is, because their effects are not immediately felt; the prince is not informed in so sudden and sensible a manner as in China.

The Emperor of China is not taught like our princes, that if he governs ill he will be less happy in the other life, less powerful and less opulent in this. He knows that if his government be not just he will be stripped both of empire and life.

As China grows every day more populous, notwithstanding the exposing of children, the inhabitants are incessantly employed in tilling the lands for their subsistence. This requires a very extraordinary attention in the government. It is their perpetual concern that every man should have it in his power to work, without the apprehension of being deprived of the fruits of his labour. Consequently this is not so much a civil as a domestic government.

Such has been the origin of those regulations which have been so greatly extolled. They wanted to make the laws reign in conjunction with despotic power; but whatever is joined to the latter loses all its force. In vain did this arbitrary sway, labouring under its own inconveniences, desire to be fettered; it armed itself with its chains, and has become still more terrible.

China is therefore a despotic state, whose principle is fear. Perhaps in the earliest dynasties, when the empire had not so large an extent the government might have deviated a little from this spirit; but the case is otherwise at present.

23

A Discourse on Inequality

Jean-Jacques Rousseau

[The] savage man, wandering in the forests, without work, without speech, without a home, without war, and without relationships, was equally without any need of his fellow men and without any desire to hurt them, perhaps not even recognizing any one of them individually. Being subject to so few passions, and sufficient unto himself, he had only such feelings and such knowledge as suited his condition; he felt only his true needs, saw only what he believed it was necessary to see, and his intelligence made no more progress than his vanity. If by chance he made some discovery, he was all the less able to communicate it to others because he did not even recognize his own children. Every art would perish with the inventor. There was neither education nor progress; the generations multiplied uselessly, and as each began afresh from the same starting-point, centuries rolled on as underdeveloped as the first ages; the species was already old, and man remained eternally a child.

If I have dwelled so long on the hypothesis of this primitive condition, it is because, having ancient errors and inveterate prejudices to eliminate, I thought I ought to dig down to the roots, and provide a picture of the true state of nature, to show to what extent inequality, even in its natural form, is far from having in that state as much reality and influence as our writers claim.

In fact, it is easy to see that among the differences which distinguish between men that several are taken to be natural which are solely the product of habit and of the various ways of life that man adopts in society. Thus a robust or a delicate temperament, together with the strength or weakness attaching to it, often derives from the manly or the effeminate manner in which one has been raised rather than from the original constitution of the body. The same is true of the powers of the mind; and not only does education establish a difference between cultivated minds and those which are not, but it increases the differences among cultivated minds in proportion to their culture; for when a giant and a dwarf walk the same road, every step each takes gives an extra advantage to the giant. Now if we compare the prodigious diversity of upbringings and of ways of life which prevail among the different classes in the civil state with the simplicity and uniformity of animal and savage life, where everyone eats the same foods, lives in the same style and does exactly the same things, it will be understood how much less the difference between man and man must be in the state of nature than it is in society, and how much natural inequality must be increased in the human species through the effects of instituted inequality.

But even if nature did exhibit in the distribution of her gifts as much partiality as is

Jean-Jacques Rousseau, *A Discourse on Inequality*, trans. Maurice Cranston, London: Penguin Books, 1984, pp. 104–9, 114–23, 159–61.

claimed, what advantage would the most favoured draw from it, to the detriment of the others, in a state of affairs which permitted almost no relationship between persons? There, where there is no love, what would be the use of beauty? What is intelligence to people who do not speak, or cunning to those who have no commerce with others? I hear it constantly repeated that the stronger will oppress the weak, but I would like someone to explain to me what is meant by the word 'oppression'. Does it mean some men dominating with violence, and others groaning in slavish submission to their whims? Such is precisely what I observe among us, but I do not see how the same situation could be attributed to savage men, who could hardly even be brought to understand what servitude and domination are. A savage may well seize the fruits which another has gathered, seize the game he has killed, or the cave he is using as his shelter; but how will he ever be able to exact obedience? And what sort of chains of dependence could exist among men who possess nothing? I am chased from one tree, I am free to go to the next; if I am tormented in one place, who will prevent my moving some-where else? Is there a man who is so much stronger than me and who is, moreover, depraved enough, lazy enough and fierce enough to compel me to provide for his sustenance while he remains idle? He must resolve not to lose sight of me for a single moment, and keep me very carefully bound while he sleeps, for fear that I should escape or kill him: that is to say, he is obliged to expose himself voluntarily to much worse trouble than the trouble he wishes to avoid, or gives to me. After all this, suppose his vigilance slackens for a moment? An unexpected noise makes him turn his head? I slip twenty paces into the forest, my chains are broken, and he will never see me again in his life.

Without expanding uselessly on these details, anyone must see that since the bonds of servitude are formed only through the mutual dependence of men and the reciprocal needs that unite them, it is impossible to enslave a man without first putting him in a situation where he cannot do without another man, and since such a situation does not exist in the state of nature, each man there is free

of the yoke, and the law of the strongest is rendered vain.

Having proved that inequality is hardly perceived in the state of nature, and that its influence there is almost nil, it remains for me to explain its origin and its progress in the successive developments of the human mind. After having shown that *improvability*, the social virtues and other faculties that natural man received as potentialities could never have developed by themselves, that in order to develop they needed the fortuitous concurrence of several alien causes which might never have arisen and without which man would have remained forever in his primitive condition, I must now consider and bring together the different chance factors which have succeeded in improving human reason while worsening the human species, making man wicked while making him sociable, and carrying man and the world from their remote beginnings to the point at which we now behold them.

Since the events I have to describe might have happened in several ways, I admit I can make the choice between those possibilities only by means of conjecture: but beside the fact that those conjectures become rational when they are the most probable that can be inferred from the nature of things and constitute the only means one can have for discovering the truth, the conclusions I want to deduce from mine will not thereby be conjectural, since, on the basis of the principles I have established, it would be impossible to formulate any other system which would not yield the same results and from which I could not draw identical conclusions.

This will exempt me from elaborating my thoughts about the way in which the passage of time makes up for the slender probability of events, or about the surprising potency of very trivial causes when they operate without interruption; or about the impossibility, on the one hand, of demolishing certain hypotheses, and, on the other hand, of giving them the measure of certainty of facts; or again about how, when two facts given as real are to be connected by a series of intermediary facts which are either unknown or regarded as unknown, it is for history, when it exists, to furnish the facts that do connect them, and when history cannot, for philosophy to determine the kind of facts that might connect them. Finally, I will be excused from considering how similarity, in reference to events, reduces facts to a much smaller number of different classes than is usually imagined. It is enough for me to offer these subjects for the consideration of my critics; it is enough for me also to have set things out in such a way that the common reader has no need to consider them at all.

Part Two

The first man who, having enclosed a piece of land, thought of saying 'This is mine' and found people simple enough to believe him, was the true founder of civil society. How many crimes, wars, murders; how much misery and horror the human race would have been spared if someone had pulled up the stakes and filled in the ditch and cried out to his fellow men: 'Beware of listening to this impostor. You are lost if you forget that the fruits of the earth belong to everyone and that the earth itself belongs to no one!' But it is highly probable that by this time things had reached a point beyond which they could not go on as they were; for the idea of property, depending on many prior ideas which could only have arisen in successive stages, was not formed all at once in the human mind. It was necessary for men to make much progress, to acquire much industry and knowledge, to transmit and increase it from age to age, before arriving at this final stage of the state of nature. Let us therefore look farther back, and try to review from a single perspective the slow succession of events and discoveries in their most natural order.

[...]

As soon as men learned to value one another and the idea of consideration was formed in their minds, everyone claimed a right to it, and it was no longer possible for anyone to be refused consideration without affront. This gave rise to the first duties of civility, even among savages: and henceforth every intentional wrong became an outrage, because together with the hurt which might result from the injury, the offended party saw an insult to his person which was often more unbearable than the hurt itself. Thus, as everyone punished the contempt shown him by another in a manner proportionate to the esteem he accorded himself, revenge became terrible, and men grew bloodthirsty and cruel. This is precisely the stage reached by most of the savage peoples known to us; and it is for lack of having sufficiently distinguished between different ideas and seen how far those peoples already are from the first state of nature that so many authors have hastened to conclude that man is naturally cruel and needs civil institutions to make him peaceable, whereas in truth nothing is more peaceable than man in his primitive state; placed by nature at an equal distance from the stupidity of brutes and the fatal enlightenment of civilized man, limited equally by reason and instinct to defending himself against evils which threaten him, he is restrained by natural pity from doing harm to anyone, even after receiving harm himself: for according to the wise Locke: 'Where there is no property, there is no injury.'

But it must be noted that society's having come into existence and relations among individuals having been already established meant that men were required to have qualities different from those they possessed from their primitive constitution; morality began to be introduced into human actions, and each man, prior to laws, was the sole judge and avenger of the offences he had received, so that the goodness suitable to the pure state of nature was no longer that which suited nascent society; it was necessary for punishments to be more severe to the extent that opportunities for offence became more frequent; and the terror of revenge had to serve in place of the restraint of laws. Thus although men had come to have less fortitude, and their natural pity had suffered some dilution, this period of the development of human faculties, the golden mean between the indolence of the primitive state and the petulant activity of our own pride, must have been the happiest epoch and the most lasting. The more we reflect on it, the more we realize that this state was the least subject to revolutions, and the best for man; and that man can have left it only as the result of some fatal accident, which, for the common good, ought never to have happened.

The example of savages, who have almost always been found at this point of development, appears to confirm that the human race was made to remain there always; to confirm that this state was the true youth of the world, and that all subsequent progress has been so many steps in appearance towards the improvement of the individual, but so many steps in reality towards the decrepitude of the species.

As long as men were content with their rustic huts, as long as they confined themselves to sewing their garments of skin with thorns or fish-bones, and adorning themselves with feathers or shells, to painting their bodies with various colours, to improving or decorating their bows and arrows; and to using sharp stones to make a few fishing canoes or crude musical instruments; in a word, so long as they applied themselves only to work that one person could accomplish alone and to arts that did not require the collaboration of several hands, they lived as free, healthy, good and happy men so far as they could be according to their nature and they continued to enjoy among themselves the sweetness of independent intercourse; but from the instant one man needed the help of another, and it was found to be useful for one man to have provisions enough for two, equality disappeared, property was introduced, work became necessary, and vast forests were transformed into pleasant fields which had to be watered with the sweat of men, and where slavery and misery were soon seen to germinate and flourish with the crops.

Metallurgy and agriculture were the two arts whose invention produced this great revolution. For the poet it is gold and silver, but for the philosopher it is iron and wheat which first civilized men and ruined the human race. Both metallurgy and agriculture were unknown to the savages of America, who have always therefore remained savages; other peoples seem to have remained barbarians, practising one of these arts and not the other; and one of the best reasons why Europe, if not the earliest to be civilized, has been at least more continuously and better civilized than other parts of the world, is perhaps that it is at once the richest in iron and the most fertile in wheat.

It is very difficult to suggest how men came first to know and to use iron; for it is impossible to believe they would think on their own of drawing ore from the mine and undertaking the necessary preparations for smelting before they knew what the outcome would be. On the other hand, we can even less easily attribute this discovery to some accidental fire, since mines are formed only in barren places, denuded of trees and plants, so that one might say that nature had taken pains to hide this deadly secret from us. There remains, therefore, only the faint possibility of some volcano, by pouring out metallic substances in fusion giving those who witnessed it the idea of imitating this operation of nature. What is more, we would have to assume those men having enough courage to undertake such arduous labour and enough foresight to envisage from afar the advantages they might derive from it – an assumption hardly to be made even of minds more developed than theirs.

As for agriculture, the principle of it was known long before the practice of it was established, and it is indeed hardly conceivable that men who were ceaselessly occupied drawing their subsistence from trees and plants did not fairly promptly acquire an idea of the means used by nature to propagate plants. Even so men's industry probably turned in that direction only very late – possibly because trees, which together with hunting and fishing provided their food, needed no husbandry, or because men had no knowledge of the use of wheat, or because they had no implements for cultivating it, or for lack of foresight into future needs, or, finally, for lack of the means of preventing others taking possession of the fruits of their labour. As soon as they became more skilled, we can believe that men began, with sharp stones and pointed sticks, to cultivate a few vegetables or roots around their huts; although it was long before they knew how to process wheat or had the implements necessary for largescale cultivation; they had also to learn that in order to devote oneself to that activity and sow seeds in the soil, one must resign oneself to an immediate loss for the sake of a greater gain in the future – a forethought very alien to the turn of mind of the savage man, who, as I have said, is hard pressed to imagine in the morning the needs he will have in the evening.

The invention of other arts must therefore have been necessary to compel the human race to apply itself to agriculture. As soon as some men were needed to smelt and forge iron, other men were needed to supply them with food. The more the number of industrial workers multiplied, the fewer hands were engaged in providing the common subsistence, without there being any fewer mouths to consume it; and as some men needed commodities in exchange for their iron, others finally learned the secret of using iron for the multiplication of commodities. From this arose, on the one hand, ploughing and agriculture, and, on the other, the art of working metals and of multiplying their uses.

From the cultivation of the land, its division necessarily followed, and from property once recognized arose the first rules of justice: for in order to render each his own, each must be able to have something; moreover, as men began to direct their eyes towards the future and all saw that they had some goods to lose, there was no one who did not fear reprisals against himself for the injuries he might do to another. This origin is all the more natural, in that it is impossible to conceive of the idea of property arising from anything other than manual labour, for one cannot see what besides his own labour a man can add to things he has not actually made in order to appropriate them. It is his labour alone which, in giving the cultivator the right to the product of the land he has tilled, gives him in consequence the right to the land itself, at least until the harvest, which, being repeated from year to year, brings about a continued occupation, easily transformed into property. Grotius says that when the ancients gave Ceres the title of Legislatrix, and the festival celebrated in her honour the name of Thesmophoria, they implied that the division of the earth had produced a new sort of right: that is to say, the right to property different from the one derived from natural law.

Things in this state might have remained equal if talents had been equal, and if, for example, the use of iron and the consumption of foodstuffs had always exactly balanced each other, but this equilibrium, which nothing maintained, was soon broken: the stronger did more productive work, the more adroit did better work, the more ingenious devised ways of abridging his labour: the farmer had greater need of iron or the smith greater need of wheat, and with both working equally, the one earned plenty while the other had hardly enough to live on. It is thus that natural inequality merges imperceptibly with inequality of ranks, and the differences between men, increased by differences of circumstance, make themselves more visible and more permanent in their effects, and begin to exercise a correspondingly large influence over the destiny of individuals.

Things having once arrived at this point, it is easy to imagine the rest. I shall not pause to describe the successive invention of the other arts, the progress of language, the testing and employment of talents, the inequality of fortunes, the use and abuse of riches, and all the details which follow from this and which anyone can easily supply. I shall simply limit myself to casting a glance over the human race as it is placed in this new order of things.

Behold, then, all our faculties developed, memory and imagination brought into play, pride stimulated, reason made active and the mind almost at the point of the perfection of which it is capable. Behold all the natural qualities called into action, the rank and destiny of each man established, not only as to the quantity of his possessions and his power to serve or to injure, but as to intelligence, beauty, strength, skill, merit or talents; and since these qualities were the only ones that could attract consideration it soon became necessary either to have them or to feign them. It was necessary in one's own interest to seem to be other than one was in reality. Being and appearance became two entirely different things, and from this distinction arose insolent ostentation, deceitful cunning and all the vices that follow in their train. From another point of view, behold man, who was formerly free and independent, diminished as a consequence of a multitude of new wants into subjection, one might say, to the whole of nature and especially to his fellow men, men of whom he has become the slave, in a sense, even in becoming their master; for if he is rich he needs their services; if he is poor he needs their aid; and even a middling condition does not enable him to do without them. He must therefore seek constantly to interest others in his lot and make them see an advantage, either real or apparent, for themselves in working for his benefit; all of which makes him devious and artful with some, imperious and hard towards others, and compels him to treat badly the people he needs if he cannot make them fear him and does not judge it in his interest to be of service to them. Finally, a devouring ambition, the burning passion to enlarge one's relative fortune, not so much from real need as to put oneself ahead of others, inspires in all men a dark propensity to injure one another, a secret jealousy which is all the more dangerous in that it often assumes the mask of benevolence in order to do its deeds in greater safety; in a word, there is competition and rivalry on the one hand, conflicts of interest on the other, and always the hidden desire to gain an advantage at the expense of other people. All these evils are the main effects of property and the inseparable consequences of nascent inequality.

Before the invention of symbols to represent it, wealth could hardly consist of anything except land and livestock, the only real goods that men could possess. But when estates became so multiplied in number and extent as to cover the whole of the land and every estate to border on another one, no estate could be enlarged except at the expense of its neighbour; and the landless supernumeraries, whom weakness or indolence had prevented from acquiring an estate for themselves, became poor without having lost anything, because, while everything around them changed they alone remained unchanged, and so they were obliged to receive their subsistence – or to steal it – from the rich; and out of this situation there was born, according to the different characters of the rich and the poor, either dominion and servitude, or violence and robbery. The rich, for their part, had hardly learned the pleasure of dominating before they disdained all other pleasures, and using their old slaves to subdue new ones, they dreamed only of subjugating and enslaving their neighbours; like those ravenous wolves, which, having once tasted human flesh, refuse all other nourishment and desire thenceforth only to devour men.

Hence, as the strongest regarded their might, and the most wretched regarded their need as giving them a kind of right to the possessions of others, equivalent, according to them, to the right of property, the elimination of equality was followed by the most terrible disorder. The usurpations of the rich, the brigandage of the poor and the unbridled passions of everyone, stifling natural pity and the as yet feeble voice of justice, made men greedy, ambitious and bad. There arose between the right of the stronger and the right of the first occupant a perpetual conflict which ended only in fights and murders (Q). Nascent society gave place to the most horrible state of war; the human race, debased and desolate, could not now retrace its path, nor renounce the unfortunate acquisitions it had made, but labouring only towards its shame by misusing those faculties which should be its honour, brought itself to the brink of ruin.

> Shocked at a new-found evil, at once rich and wretched,
> He wants to flee from his wealth, and hates what he once prayed for.
> Ovid, *Metamorphosis*. XI. 127

It is impossible that men should not eventually have reflected on so melancholy a situation, and on the calamity which had over-whelmed them. The rich above all must have perceived how disadvantageous to them was a perpetual state of war in which they bore all the costs, and in which the risk of life was universal but the risk of property theirs alone. Furthermore, whatever disguises they might put upon their usurpations, they knew well enough that they were founded on precarious and bogus rights and that force could take away from them what force alone had acquired without their having any reason for complaint. Even those who had been enriched by their own industry could not base their right to property on much better titles. In vain would one say: 'I built this wall; I earned the right to this field by my own labour.' For "Who gave you its extent and boundaries?' might be the answer. 'And in virtue of what do you claim payment from us for work we never instructed you to do? Do you not know that a multitude of your brethren perish or suffer from need of what you have to excess, and that you required the express and unanimous consent of the whole human race in order to appropriate from the common subsistence anything beyond that required for your own subsistence?' Destitute of valid reasons to justify himself and of forces adequate to defend himself; easily crushing an individual but crushed himself by troupes of bandits; alone against all, and unable because of mutual jealousies to form alliances with his equals against enemies united by the common hope of plunder, the rich man under pressure of necessity conceived in the end the most cunning project that ever entered the human mind: to employ in his favour the very forces of those who attacked him, to make his adversaries his defenders, to inspire them with new maxims and give them new institutions as advantageous to him as natural right was disadvantageous.

To this end, having demonstrated to his neighbours the horror of a situation which set each against all, made men's possessions as burden-some to them as their needs, and afforded no security either in poverty or in riches, he invents specious reasons to lead his listeners to his goal.

'Let us unite', he says, 'to protect the weak from oppression, to restrain the ambitious, and ensure for each the possession of what belongs to him; let us institute rules of justice and peace to which all shall be obliged to conform, without exception, rules which compensate in a way for the caprice of fortune by subjecting equally the powerful and the weak to reciprocal duties. In a word, instead of directing our forces against each other, let us unite them together in one supreme power which shall govern us all according to wise laws, protect and defend all the members of the association, repulse common enemies, and maintain us in everlasting concord.'

It needed much less than the equivalent of this speech to win round men so uncultivated and so easily seduced, especially as they had too many disputes to settle among themselves to be able to do without umpires, and too much avarice and ambition to be able to do for long without masters. All ran towards their chains believing that they were securing their liberty; for although they had reason enough to discern the advantages of a civil order, they

did not have experience enough to foresee the dangers. Those most capable of predicting the abuses were precisely those who expected to profit from them; and even the wisest saw that men must resolve to sacrifice one part of their freedom in order to preserve the other, even as a wounded man has his arm cut off to save the rest of his body.

Such was, or must have been, the origin of society and of laws, which put new fetters on the weak and gave new powers to the rich (R), which irretrievably destroyed natural liberty, established for all time the law of property and inequality, transformed adroit usurpation into irrevocable right, and for the benefit of a few ambitious men subjected the human race thenceforth to labour, servitude and misery. It is easy to see how the foundation of one society made the establishment of all the rest unavoidable, and how, being faced with united forces, it was necessary for others to unite in turn. Societies, as they multiplied and spread, soon came to cover the whole surface of the earth, and it was no longer possible to find a single corner of the universe where one might free oneself from the yoke and withdraw one's head from beneath the sword, often precariously held, which every man saw perpetually hanging over him. Positive law having thus become the common rule over citizens, there was room for natural law only as between the various societies where, under the name of international law, it was moderated by certain tacit conventions designed to make intercourse possible and to supplement natural compassion, which having lost as between society and society nearly all the force it had as between man and man, no longer dwells in any but a few great cosmopolitan souls, who, breaking through the imaginary barriers that separate peoples, and following the example of the Sovereign Being who created them, include the whole human race in their benevolence.

The bodies politic, thus remaining in the state of nature in their relationship to each other, soon experienced the same disadvantages that had forced individuals to quit it; the state of nature proved indeed even more harmful to these large bodies than it had previously been for the individuals of whom they were composed. From this there arose wars between nations, battles, murders, reprisals which make nature tremble and offend reason, and all those horrible prejudices which count the honour of shedding human blood a virtue. The most decent men learned to regard the killing of their fellows as one of their duties; and in time men came to massacre one another by thousands without knowing why, committing more murders in a single day's battle and more atrocities in the sack of a single city than were committed in the state of nature throughout entire centuries over the whole face of the earth. Such are the first effects we note of the division of the human race into different societies.

[...]

In the two or three centuries since the inhabitants of Europe have been flooding into other parts of the world, endlessly publishing new collections of voyages and travel, I am persuaded that we have come to know no other men except Europeans; moreover it appears from the ridiculous prejudices, which have not died out even among men of letters, that every author produces under the pompous name of the study of man nothing much more than a study of the men of his own country. Individuals go here and there in vain; it seems that philosophy does not travel and that the philosophy of one nation proves little suited to another. The cause of this is obvious, at least in the case of distant countries. There are hardly more than four sorts of men who make long-distance voyages: sailors, merchants, soldiers and missionaries. Now it can hardly be expected that the first three classes should yield good observers, and as for the fourth, taken up with the sublime vocation to which they have been called, even if they are not subject to the same prejudices of rank as are all the others, one must believe that they would not lend themselves willingly to researches that would look like pure curiosity and distract their attention from the more important labours to which they have committed themselves. Besides, to preach the Gospel usefully, it is only necessary to have zeal and God supplies the rest; but to study man it is necessary to have talents that God is not obliged to give to anyone, and which are not always possessed by saints. One does not open a book of voyages without finding descriptions of characters and customs, but one is altogether amazed

to find that these authors who describe so many things tell us only what all of them knew already, and have only learned how to see at the other end of the world what they would have been able to see without leaving their own street, and that the real features which distinguish nations, and which strike eyes made to see them, have almost always escaped their notice. Hence that fine adage of ethics, so often repeated by the philosophistical throng: that men are everywhere the same, and since they all have the same passions and the same vices, it is pretty useless to seek to characterize different peoples – which is as reasonable as saying that one cannot distinguish Pierre from Jacques, since they both have a nose, a mouth and eyes.

Shall we never see reborn those happy times when the people did not meddle in philosophy, but when a Plato, a Thales, a Pythagoras, impelled by an ardent desire for knowledge, undertook the most extensive voyages solely to instruct themselves, and travelled far in order to shake off the yoke of national prejudices, to learn to study men by their resemblances and their differences, and to acquire a universal knowledge which was not that of one century or one country exclusively, but being that of all times and all places, was, so to speak, the universal science of the wise?

We admire the magnificence of several men whose curiosity has made them undertake, or have undertaken, at great expense expeditions to the East with scholars and artists, to make drawings of ruins there or to decipher and copy inscriptions; but I find it hard to imagine why in a century which prides itself on its fine sciences, we do not find two well-matched men, rich, the one in money, the other in genius, both loving glory and aspiring to immortality, two men who would sacrifice, in the one case twenty thousand crowns of his property, in the other, ten years of his life, so as to make a glorious voyage round the world in order to study, not eternally plants and stones, but for once men and customs; and who, after all the centuries that have been spent measuring and appraising the house, should finally decide that they would like to have knowledge of the inhabitants.

The Academicians who have travelled to the northern parts of Europe and the southern parts of America have gone to visit those places rather as geometers than as philosophers. However, since some have been both, we cannot regard as entirely unknown the regions seen and described by such as La Condamine and Maupertuis. The jeweller Chardin, who travelled like Plato, has left nothing more to be said about Persia; China seems to have been well observed by the Jesuits. Kaempfer gives a tolerable idea of the little he saw of Japan. Apart from these narratives, we know nothing of the peoples of the East Indies, visited only by Europeans eager to fill their purses rather than their minds. The whole of Africa with its numerous inhabitants, as remarkable in character as in colour, is yet to be studied. The entire world is covered with peoples of whom we know only the names, and yet we amuse ourselves judging the human race! Suppose a Montesquieu, a Buffon, a Diderot, a Duclos, a D'Alembert, a Condillac and other men of that stamp were to travel to instruct their compatriots, observing and describing as only they know how, Turkey, Egypt, Barbary, the Empire of Morocco, Guinea, the land of the Kaffirs, the interior and the East coast of Africa, the Malabars, Mogul, the banks of the Ganges, the kingdoms of Siam, Pegu and Ava. China, Tartary and above all Japan, and then in the other hemisphere, Mexico, Peru, Chile, and Magellan lands, not forgetting the Patagonias, true and false; Tucamen, Paraguay if possible, Brazil; finally the Caribbean islands, Florida and all the savage countries – the most important voyage of all, and the one that would have to be undertaken with the greatest possible care. Suppose that these new Hercules, on their return from these memorable journeys, then wrote at leisure the natural, moral and political history of what they had seen, we ourselves would see a new world spring from under their pens, and we should learn thereby to know our own world. If such observers as these were to assert of an animal that it is a man and of another animal that it is a beast, then I say we must believe them; but it would be excessively naïve to accept the authority of uncultured travellers about whom one is sometimes tempted to ask the very question that they take it upon themselves to answer in the case of other animals.

24

The Philosophy of History

Voltaire

VII. Of Savages

By "savages," do you mean villagers living in huts with their women and a few animals, perpetually exposed to the seasonal extremes of the weather; who know nothing but the land which feeds them and the market where they occasionally go to sell a few items in order to purchase their crude clothing; speaking jargon incomprehensible to townsmen; holding few ideas and consequently having little to say; subject, without their knowing why, to some scribe to whom each year they bring half of what they have garnered through the sweat of their brows; assembling on certain days in a sort of barn where they celebrate ceremonies about which they comprehend nothing, listening to a man dressed differently from them and whom they do not understand; leaving their huts from time to time to the sound of a drumbeat in order to enroll and to get themselves killed in some foreign land while slaughtering their fellow men, for a quarter of what they might earn working at home? There are savages like this throughout Europe. It must be noted that the peoples of Canada and the Kaffirs, whom we readily call "savages," are infinitely superior to our own variety. The Huron, the Algonquin, the Illinois, the Kaffir, the Hottentot all have the art of making whatever they need themselves, a skill lacking among our own rustics. The peoples of

American and Africa are free, and our savages do not even have the slightest notion of liberty.

The so-called savages of America are sovereign nations to whom we send ambassadors from our own colonies, which we, thanks to our own greed and incomprehension, have transplanted in their vicinity. They understand honor, about which our European savages have never heard. They have a fatherland, they love it, they defend it, they make treaties; they fight with courage, and often speak with heroic energy. Is there a nobler reply in all of Plutarch's *Great Men* than that of the chief of the Canadians whom a European nation proposed to relocate? "We were born on this land, our fathers are buried here; what shall we tell the bones of our fathers: Get up and come with us to a foreign place?"

These Canadians were Spartans, compared to the rustics who vegetate in our villages and the sybarites who infest our cities.

Do you mean by "savages" animals with two legs, walking if need be on their hands, isolated, wandering in forests, *Salvatici, Salvaggi*; mating occasionally, forgetting the women with whom they have coupled, recognizing neither their sons nor their fathers; living like brutes, without either the instincts or the resources of brutes? It has been written[1] that this is the true state of humanity, and that we have just miserably degenerated when we

Voltaire, *The Philosophy of History*, trans. Robert Launay.

abandoned it. I do not believe that this solitary life, attributed to our forefathers, is part of human nature.

We are, if I am not mistaken, in the first rank (if I may be allowed to say so) of animals who live in groups, such as bees, ants, beavers, geese, chickens, sheep, etc. If we find a lone bee, should we conclude that this bee is in the pure state of nature, and that those who work together in the hive have degenerated? ...

VIII. Of America

Can we still ask ourselves from where the men came who populated America? We should assuredly ask the same question for the nations of southern lands. They are much further away from the port from which Christopher Columbus took sail than are the Antilles. We find men and animals everywhere where the earth is inhabitable: who put them there? We have already said that it is He who makes the grass grow in the fields: one shouldn't be more surprised to find men in America than to find flies.

It is quite amusing that the Jesuit Lafitau asserts, in his preface to the *History of the American Savages*, that only atheists can say that God created Americans.

They still print maps of the Old World where America appears under the name of the Atlantic Isle, the Cap Verde Islands as the Gorgades, the Caribbean islands as the Hesperides. All this is only based on the ancient discovery by the Phoenicians and the Carthaginians of the Canary Islands and possibly Madeira; these islands are almost adjacent to Africa, and were possibly even closer in ancient times than nowadays.

Let us allow Father Lafitau to suggest that the Caribs came from Caria, because of the resemblance between these names, and above all because Carib women cooked for their husbands just as did Carian women. Let him imagine that Caribs are born red, and Negresses black, only because their fathers once had the habit of painting themselves black or red.

It happened, he states, that Negresses were so struck with seeing their husbands all black that the race was forever altered. The same happened to Carib women who, through the same power of imagination, gave birth to red children. He cites the examples of Jacob's lambs, who were born mottled thanks to the care which this patriarch took to place before their eyes branches from which half the bark had been stripped, appearing bicolor; on the strength of such appearances, the patriarch's lambs had two. But our Jesuit should know that everything doesn't happen nowadays the way they happened in Jacob's time.

If we had asked Laban's son-in-law [Jacob] why his ewes, who always had grass before their eyes, didn't give birth to green lambs, he would have been at quite a loss to reply.

Finally, Lafitau has the Americans descend from ancient Greeks on these grounds. The Greeks had fables, the Americans too. The first Greeks were hunters, and the Americans also hunt. The early Greeks had oracles, the Americans sorcerers [i.e., shamans]. The Greeks danced on holidays, the Americans dance too. We have to admit that such arguments are convincing.

We can draw a conclusion about these peoples of the New World that Father Lafitau failed to draw: those populations who live far from the tropics have always been invincible, and that those closer to the tropics have almost always been subjected to monarchical rule. It was long the case in our own continent. But it would be hard to imagine that the peoples of Canada ever set out to conquer Mexico, in the way that the Tartars spread throughout Asia and Europe. It would seem that the Canadians were never numerous enough to establish colonies elsewhere.

In general, America can never have been as populated as Europe and Asia; it is full of immense swamps which render the air unhealthy; the land produces a prodigious number of poisons; arrows dipped in the sap of these venomous grasses always make mortal wounds. Nature also supplied Americans with fewer industries than the men of the Old World. All these causes taken together were of great harm to the population.

Among all the physical observations that we have been able to make about this fourth potion of our world, so long unknown, the strangest perhaps is that we only find one people with beards: the Eskimo. They live north of the fifty-second parallel, where the cold is bitterer than the sixty-sixth on our own continent. Their neighbors are beardless. Here are thus two absolutely different races of men living side by side, supposing that Eskimos are really bearded. But later travelers assert that the Eskimo are actually beardless, that we mistook their dirty hair for beards. Whom should we believe?

Near the isthmus of Panama lives a race of Darians, almost like albinos, who flee from light and who vegetate in caves, a feeble race and consequently not at all populous.

The lions of America are diminutive and cowardly; the wool-bearing animals are so large and vigorous that they are also used to carry loads. All the rivers are at least ten times bigger than ours. Finally, the natural productions of this land are not those of our hemisphere. Thus we find variety everywhere; and the same Providence which created the elephant, the rhinoceros and the Negroes gave rise in another world to moose, condors, animals whom we long imagined had navels on their backs, and men of a different character from ours.

[...]

XVIII.   Of China

Dare we write about the Chinese without citing their own annals? They are confirmed by the unanimous testimony of travelers of different sects – Jacobins, Jesuits, Lutherans, Calvinists, Anglicans, all eager to contradict one another. It is evident that the empire of China dates to more than four thousand years ago. This ancient people never heard of those natural upheavals, those floods and fires whose feeble memory was preserved and altered in the fables of Deucalion's flood and Phaeton's fall. The climate of China was thus preserved from these disasters, as it was spared from the plague which so often ravaged Africa, Asia and Europe.

If any annals can be taken for certain, they are those of the Chinese who united, as I have written elsewhere, the history of the sky with that of the earth. Alone among peoples they have constantly marked their epochs by eclipses and by the conjunction of planets; and our

own astronomers, who have examined all their calculations, were astonished to verify almost all of them. Other nations invented allegorical fables; the Chinese wrote their history, pen and astrolabe in hand, with a simplicity which we find nowhere else in Asia.

The history of each reign of their emperors was written by contemporaries. There were no different ways of counting among them, no contradictory chronologies. Our missionary travelers candidly mention that, when they were explaining to the emperor Kang Xi the considerable variations between the chronologies of the Vulgate, the Septuagint, and the Samaritan Pentateuch,[2] Kang Xi answered them, "Is it possible that the books in which you believe conflict with one another?"

The Chinese wrote on light bamboo tablets while the Chaldeans were still writing on crude bricks; and they still possess some of these ancient tablets whose varnish has preserved them from rotting. These are possibly the world's oldest monuments. There is no history among them before their emperors; almost no fictions, no prodigies, no inspired personage who claims to be a demigod, as among the Egyptians and the Greeks. As soon as this people wrote, they wrote reasonably.

They differ above all from other nations in that their history never mentions any corps of priests who influenced their laws. The Chinese do not hearken back to savage times when men needed to be tricked in order to be led. Other peoples begin their history with the origin of the world: the Persian *Zend*, the Hindu *Shastas* and *Vedas*, Sanchoniathon, Manetho, and finally Hesiod,[3] all go back to the origin of things and the creation of the universe. The Chinese never had this folly; their history is only that of historical times.

Here, we must apply the principle that a nation whose first chronicles attest the existence of a vast, powerful and wise empire must have been assembled as a people centuries beforehand. Here is a people who, for over four thousand years, wrote down its annals every day. Once again, wouldn't it be demented not to see that, for them to become accomplished in all the arts that human society requires, and to learn not only to write but to write well, it must have taken more time than the duration of the Chinese empire itself, from the emperor Fo-hi down to our own time? There is not a single mandarin in China who doubts that the five *Kings* were written two thousand three hundred years before the present era. This monument is thus four hundred years older than the first observations of Babylon sent to Greece by Callisthenes. Are there still scholars in Paris who contest in good faith the antiquity of a Chinese book considered authentic by every tribunal in China?

The first rudiments are, in every endeavor, slower among men than great strides of progress. Do we still remember that five hundred years ago almost no one knew how to write, neither in the North, nor in Germany, nor among ourselves? The notches that our bakers still use were once our hieroglyphs and our account books. There was no other arithmetic for levying taxes, as the word "*taille*" (notch) still attests in our countryside.[4] Our capricious customs, which we only began to commit to writing four hundred and fifty years ago, show us how rare the art of writing was in those times. There is no nation in Europe which hasn't ultimately made more progress in every endeavor in the past half century than it had made from the barbarian invasions down to the fourteenth century.

I will not here examine why the Chinese, who have managed to know and practice all that is useful to society, have not progressed as far as we have today in the sciences. They are, I must confess, as poor physicists as we were two hundred years ago and as were the Greeks and Romans; but they have perfected morality, the first among the sciences.

Their vast and populous empire was already governed like a family in which the monarch was the father, and whose forty legislative tribunals were considered like big brothers, at a time when we were a small horde wandering in the forest of Ardennes.

Their religion was simple, wise, august, and free from all superstition and all barbarity when we didn't yet even acknowledge Teutates,[5] to whom the Druids sacrificed the children of our ancestors in big baskets.

Twice a year, the Chinese emperors personally offered the first fruits of the harvest (and what harvests!) which they had sown with their own hands up to the God of the Universe, to Chang-ti, to Tien, to the first principle of everything. This practice was maintained for forty centuries, even in the midst of revolutions and the most horrible calamities.

Never was the religion of the emperors and the tribunals dishonored by falsifications, never troubled by quarrels between the priesthood and the empire, never loaded with absurd innovations which contradict one another, supported by arguments even more absurd and whose insanity eventually placed daggers in the hands of assassins misled by partisan schemers. It is most of all in this way that the Chinese are ahead of all the other nations in the world.

Their Confutzée, whom we call Confucius, neither dreamt up new opinions nor new rites; he was neither divinely inspired nor a prophet; he was a wise magistrate who taught the ancient laws. We speak sometimes, and quite inaccurately, about the Confucian religion. He had no religion other than that of the emperor and the tribunals, none other than that of the first sages. He only recommended virtue; he preached no mysteries. He says in his first book that, in order to learn to govern, one must spend each day correcting oneself. In the second, he proves that God himself engraved virtue into the hearts of men; he says that man is not born wicked, and becomes so only through his own fault. The third book is a collection of maxims, where one finds nothing in bad taste and no ridiculous allegories. He had five thousand disciples. He could have led a powerful faction but instead preferred teaching men to governing them.

We already argued in the *Essai sur les Mœurs* against the audacity we have had, from our corner of the world in the West, to judge this eastern court and accuse it of atheism. By what madness, in effect, have some of us been able to call an empire atheist when almost all its laws are founded on the knowledge of a Supreme Being who rewards and punishes? The inscriptions on their temples, of which we possess authentic copies,[6] are "The first principle, without beginning and end. He created all and governs all; He is infinitely good, infinitely just; he enlightens, he upholds, he rules over all nature."

In Europe, they reprimanded the Jesuits, whom they hated, for flattering the Chinese atheists.[7] A Frenchman called Maigrot, named titular bishop of Conon in China by the Pope, was sent by this same Pope to China to judge the issue. This Maigrot didn't know a word of Chinese. Nevertheless, he qualified Confucius as an atheist, citing the words of this great man: *Heaven has granted me virtue, man cannot harm me.* The greatest of our saints has never uttered a more celestial maxim. If Confucius was an atheist, so were Cato and the Chancellor de l'Hopital.[8]

Let us repeat here, in order to make the slanderers blush, that the same persons who argue contra Bayle that a society of atheists is an impossibility simultaneously hold the opinion that the oldest government in the world was a society of atheists. We cannot shame the authors of such contradictions enough.

Let me repeat here that the Chinese literati, who adored a single God, abandoned the people to the superstition of the bonzes.[9] They adopted the sect of Laokium [Lao-Tzu] and that of Fo [Buddha], and several others. The magistrates felt that the people could have different religions from the religion of State, just as it ate grosser food; they tolerated the bonzes and restricted their activities. Almost everywhere else [in Asia], practicing bonzes were in charge.

It is true that the laws of China do not mention punishments and rewards after death; they didn't want to affirm what they didn't know. This difference between them and all the other great civilized peoples is quite astonishing. The doctrine of hell was useful, and the Chinese government never adopted it. They contented themselves with exhorting men to worship heaven and to act justly. They thought that an efficient and perpetually vigilant police would have more effect than opinions that may be contested, and that people would always fear laws in the present more than laws in the hereafter …

Let us summarize by stating that the Chinese empire subsisted with splendor while the Chaldeans were just beginning their nineteen years of astronomical observations, as reported in Greece by Callisthenes. The Brahmans then reigned over part of India; Arabs in the south, Scythians in the north, lived in tents; and Egypt … was a powerful kingdom.

NOTES

1 The reference here is obviously to Rousseau's depiction of the State of Nature.

2 Different translations of the Old Testament.

3 Sanchoniathon was a Phoenician historian, Manetho an Egyptian. Hesiod, roughly a contemporary of Homer, was the author of *Works and Days* and of the *Theogony* to which Voltaire alludes.

4 The word *taille*, literally "notch," also referred to (highly unpopular) taxes in eighteenth-century France from which the nobility and clergy, but not the third estate, were exempt.

5 A deity of ancient Gaul.

6 See the engravings in the collection of the Jesuit Du Halde [Voltaire's note].

7 Voltaire is alluding to the Quarrel of the Chinese rites. The Jesuits, who were the most successful order in China and closest to the emperor, were accused by rival orders of complacency towards Confucian rites and of watering down the Christian message in order to win converts and influence. Maigrot was a member of the French Missions Etrangères, the "foreign missions," who were fiercely antagonistic to the Jesuits.

8 Michel de l'Hopital (1505–1573), a French statesman.

9 Buddhist and Taoist monks.

25

The A, B, C

Voltaire

A

What do you think of [Montesquieu's] *Spirit of the laws*?

B

It's given me great pleasure because there are a lot of jokes in it, a lot of bold, hard-hitting truths, and whole chapters worthy of the *Persian letters*. Chapter 26 of Book XIX is a portrayal of your England, drawn in the style of Paolo Veronese. I can see bright colours, skillful brush strokes, and a few errors in costume. The portrayal of the Inquisition and of negro slaves, is greatly superior to Callot. Everywhere he fights despotism, depicts financiers as being odious, courtiers despicable, monks ridiculous. Thus those who are neither monks, financiers or public servants, or with no aspirations to be, have been enchanted, especially in France.

I find it annoying that this book is a labyrinth with no route [through it], and no method [in it]. I'm even more surprised that a man who writes about the laws should say in his preface that 'no flashes of wit will be found in his work', and it's stranger still that the book should be a collection of witticisms. It's Michel Montaigne as legislator; and what's more, he was from Michel Montaigne's part of the country.

I can't help laughing when I skip through more than a hundred chapters containing less than a dozen lines, and several with only two. The author always seems to have wanted to play with the reader when dealing with the most serious subject-matter.

You don't think that you're reading a serious work when, after having quoted Grecian and Roman law, he talks about the laws of Bantam, Cochin–China, Tonkin, Acham, Borneo, Jakarta, Formosa as if he had accurate information on the governments of all those countries. He mixes up truth and error too frequently in physics, morality and history. He tells you, following Pufendorf, that in the age of King Charles IX there were twenty million people in France. Pufendorf even goes as far as to say twenty-nine million: he was speaking very much off the top of his head. Nobody has ever taken a count of the population in France. People were too ignorant then to even suspect that you could estimate the number of inhabitants by the number of births and deaths. In those days, France didn't possess Lorraine, Alsace, Franche-Comté, Roussillon, Artois, the area around Cambrai, half of Flanders; and today, when she possesses all these provinces, it has been proved, from the fairly accurate count of homesteads taken in 1751, that she only has about twenty million souls at the most.

Voltaire, "The A, B, C, or Dialogue between A, B, C," in *Political Writings*, ed. and trans. David Williams, Cambridge: Cambridge University Press, 1994, pp. 89–99.

The same author assures us, on the strength of Chardin's word, that the only navigable river in Persia is the little river Cyrus. Chardin did not make that blunder. He says in chapter I, volume II, that 'there is no river open to boats in the central part of the kingdom'; but excluding the Euphrates, the Tigris and the Indus, all the frontier provinces are awash with rivers which help to facilitate trade and make the land fertile. The Zin crosses Isfahan; the Aras joins the Kura, etc. And then what connection can there be between the *Spirit of the laws* and the rivers of Persia?

The reasons that he gives for the founding of the great empires of Asia, and for the multitude of small powers in Europe, seem as wrong as his statements on the rivers of Persia. 'In Europe', he says, 'great empires have never been able to survive.' Roman power survived there, however, for more than five hundred years; and, he continued, 'the reason for the duration of these great empires lies in the fact that there are great plains'. It did not occur to him that Persia is interspersed with mountains; he did not remember the Caucasus, the Taurus mountains, Mount Ararat, the Himalayas, Mount Sharon, whose branches cover Asia. One must neither give reasons for things that don't exist, nor wrong reasons for the things that do exist.

His theory of so-called climatic influence on religion is taken from Chardin, and is no truer for that. The Mohammedan religion, born in the hot, arid earth of Mecca, flourishes today in the beautiful lands of Asia minor, Syria, Egypt, Thrace, Mysia, North Africa, Serbia, Bosnia, Dalmatia, Epirus, Greece. It has held sway in Spain. It only just failed to reach Rome. The Christian religion was born in the stony earth of Jerusalem, and in a land of lepers where pork was an almost lethal food, forbidden by law. Jesus never ate pork, yet it's eaten by Christians. Today their religion is dominant in countries with lots of mud and dirt where people live on pork alone, as in Westphalia. You would never get to the end if you wanted to examine this sort of error with which this book is littered.

What's still more shocking to a reasonably well-educated reader is that nearly all the quotations are wrong. He almost always mistakes his imagination for his memory.

He claims that in the *Testament* attributed to Cardinal Richelieu it is said that 'if among the people there is some unfortunate who is an honest man, you must never use him; which only goes to prove that virtue is not the motivating force of monarchic government'.

The wretched *Testament*, falsely attributed to Cardinal Richelieu, says precisely the opposite. Here are its words in chapter 4: 'You can be as bold as to say that of two people of equal merit, the one who is more comfortably off is preferable to the other, in the certainty that a poor magistrate will need to have a very strongly tempered moral conscience if it is not to be weakened by considerations of self-interest. Thus experience teaches us that rich men are less likely to misappropriate public funds than poor men, and that poverty compels an officer to pay careful attention to the income [to be gained] from looting a town.'

It must be said that Montesquieu is no better at quoting Greek authors than French. Often he makes them say the opposite to what they did say.

Talking about the condition of women under various systems of government, or rather, promising to talk about it, he puts forward the view that with the Greeks 'love took only one form whose name one dare not speak'. He doesn't hesitate to take Plutarch as his authority. He makes Plutarch say that 'women have no part to play in true love'. He doesn't pause to reflect that Plutarch is putting words into the mouths of several interlocutors: there is Protogenes who rails against women, but Daphneus who takes their side. Plutarch decides in favour of Daphneus; he composes a very fine eulogy of celestial love and conjugal love; he concludes by recording several examples of the faithfulness and courage of women. It is in this dialogue even that the story of Camma is to be found, as well as that of Epponina, Sabinus' wife, whose virtues have been used for themes in plays.

In short, it's clear that in the *Spirit of the laws* Montesquieu has slandered the spirit of Greece by taking an objection that Plutarch refutes for a law that Plutarch recommends.

'Cadis maintained that the Grand Sultan did not have to keep his word or his oath when, in so doing, he would restrict his authority.'

Ricaut, who is referred to at this point, just says on page 18 of the 1671 Amsterdam edition: 'There are even some people there who maintain that the Grand Sultan can set aside promises made on oath when, in order to fulfil them, limits must be placed on his authority.'

These words are very vague. The Sultan of the Turks can only make promises to his subjects or to neighbouring states. If they are promises made to his subjects, no oath is involved; if they are peace treaties, he has to keep them like any other prince, or make war. The Koran says nowhere that one's oath can be broken, and says in a hundred places that it must be kept. It's possible that, to wage an unjust war, as nearly all of them are, the Great Turk might assemble a council to guide his conscience, as several Christian princes have done, in order to do evil in good conscience. It's possible that some Muslim scholars have imitated those Catholic scholars who said that one's word of honour need not be kept either with infidels or with heretics, but whether the Turks have this philosophy of law has yet to be ascertained.

The author of the *Spirit of the laws* offers this alleged decision by the Cadis as proof of the Sultan's despotism. It would appear, on the contrary, to be proof that he is subject to the laws, since he would have to consult scholars in order to put himself above the laws. We are neighbours of the Turks, and we do not know them. Count Marsigli, who lived so long among them, says that no author has displayed true knowledge of either their empire or their laws. We did not even have a tolerable translation of the Koran until the Englishman Sale gave us one in 1734. Nearly everything that has been said about their religion and their system of laws is wrong, and the conclusions that are drawn every day to their detriment are too ill-founded. When examining laws only laws that are understood should be referred to.

'With the Greeks all low commerce was vile.' I don't know what Montesquieu means by low commerce, but I do know that in Athens every citizen engaged in trade, that Plato sold oil, and that the father of the demagogue Demosthenes was an ironmonger. The majority of workers were foreigners or slaves. It's important for us to note that a trade was not incompatible with high rank in the Greek republics, except in the case of the Spartans, who did not have commercial interests.

'Several times I have heard people deplore', he says, 'the lack of vision on the part of Francis I's Council, which rebuffed Christopher Columbus, who had proposed the India project to it.' You will note that Francis I hadn't been born when Columbus discovered the islands of America.

Since the subject here is commerce, let's note that the author condemns an order issued by the Council of Spain forbidding the use of gold and silver in gilding. 'Such a decree', he says, 'would resemble one made by the Dutch states if they were to forbid the use of cinnamon.' It doesn't occur to him that the Spanish, having no factories, would have bought gold braid and dress material from abroad, and that the Dutch could not buy cinnamon. What was quite reasonable in Spain would have been quite ridiculous in Holland.

If a king votes in matters of criminal procedure, 'he would lose the finest attribute of his sovereignty, namely that of granting mercy. It would be sheer madness for him to make and unmake his judgements. He would not wish to be at odds with himself. Apart from the fact that this would overturn accepted theory, you would not know whether a man was being acquitted or whether he was receiving mercy.'

All that is clearly mistaken. Who would stop the sovereign from granting mercy after having been himself among the judges? How is one at odds with oneself by judging according to the law, and granting pardons in accordance with one's sense of leniency? In what way would accepted theory be overturned? How could you be unaware that the King had publicly pardoned the man after he had been convicted?

In the trial of a French peer, the Duke of Alençon, in 1458, the *parlement*, which the King had consulted in order to ascertain whether he had the right to be present at the trial and judgement of a peer of France, replied that it had discovered from its records that not only did the kings of France have this right, but that their presence was necessary in their capacity as first peers [of the realm].

This practice has been retained in England. The kings of England delegate their seat on these occasions to a Grand *Steward*, who represents them. The Emperor can be present at the trial of a prince of the Empire. No doubt it's much better for a sovereign not to be present at criminal trials: men are too weak and too cowardly. The breath of the prince alone would be enough to tip the scales.

'The English, to encourage liberty, have removed all the intermediary powers that made up their monarchy.'

It's accepted that the opposite is the case. They have made their House of Commons into an intermediary power balancing that of the Lords. They never stop undermining the power of the Church, which ought to be an organisation that prays, edifies and exhorts, and not one that wields power.

'It is not enough for a monarchy to have intermediary ranks. A repository of the laws is also needed. ... The natural ignorance of the nobility, its negligent ways, its contempt for civil government necessitate the existence of a body that continually makes laws emerge from the dust in which they would otherwise be buried.'

However, the repository of the Empire's laws is in the hands of princes at the Diet of Regensberg; in England this repository is in the Upper Chamber; in Sweden it's in the Senate which is composed of nobles; and last but not least Empress Catherine II locates this repository, under her new code, in the Senate, made up of the greatest people in her empire.

Shouldn't we distinguish between political laws and distributive justice? Shouldn't political laws have as their guardians the most important members of the State? The laws of what is *mine* and what is *yours*, [and] the [1670] decree on criminal procedure, need only to be well formulated and well printed; the repository for them should be with booksellers. Judges must conform with them, and when the laws are bad, as is very often the case, then judges must protest to the supreme authority in order to have them changed.

The same author claims that in Tonkin all magistrates and senior military officers are eunuchs, and in the case of the Lamas the law allows women to have several husbands. Even if these stories were true, so what? Would our magistrates want to become eunuchs, and be only the fourth or fifth husband in line for the good lady councillors?

Why waste time making errors about the fleets that Solomon is supposed to have sent from Ezion-geber to Africa, and about the fanciful voyages from the Red Sea to the Sea of Bayonne, and about the even more fanciful treasures of Sofala? What is the link between these erroneous digressions and the *Spirit of the laws?*

I expected to see how the *Decretals* changed the whole jurisprudence of the old Roman code, with what laws Charlemagne governed his empire, and by what anarchical process feudal government overthrew it, by what art and what boldness Gregory VII and his successors crushed the laws of kingdoms and great fiefdoms beneath the fisherman's ring, the upheavals that succeeded in destroying papal legislation. I hoped to see the origin of the bailiff's courts that dispensed justice almost everywhere from the time of the Ottonians, and the origin of the tribunals called *parlements*, or of *hearings*, or of the *King's bench*, or *exchequer*. I wanted to know the history of the laws under which our forefathers and their children lived, the reasons for their introduction, neglect, destruction and renewal. Unfortunately, I found only cleverness, witticisms, fantasies and errors.

How was it that the Gauls, conquered and plundered by the Romans, continued to live under Roman law when they were reconquered and plundered by a horde of Francs? What exactly were the laws and customs of these new brigands?

What rights did the Gallic bishops arrogate to themselves when the Francs became their masters? Did they not occasionally have a part to play in public administration before the rebel Pépin made room for them in the nation's parliament?

Were there hereditary fiefdoms before Charlemagne? A host of such questions spring to mind. Montesquieu does not resolve any of them.

What was this abominable law court set up by Charlemagne in Westphalia, a tribunal stained in blood called the Vehmic Council, a court even more horrible than the Inquisition, composed of unknown judges who condemned people to death on the reports of its spies alone, and whose executioner was the youngest councillor in this little senate of murderers. Good Grief! Montesquieu talks to me about the laws of Bantam, and he doesn't know the laws of Charlemagne; he takes him to be a good legislator!

I looked for a guide on a difficult road. I found a travelling companion who was hardly any better informed than I was. I found the spirit of the author, who has plenty, and rarely the spirit of the laws. He hops rather than walks; he shines more often than he illuminates; sometimes he satirises more than he assesses, and he makes you wish that such a fine genius had made more attempt to instruct rather than to surprise.

This highly defective book is full of admirable things from which detestable copies have been made. Lastly, fanatics have insulted him for those very parts that deserve the thanks of the human race.

In spite of its faults, this work will always be valued by men because the author has said sincerely what he thinks, whereas the majority of writers from his country, starting with the great Bossuet, have very often said what they were not thinking. Everywhere in the book he has reminded men that they are free. He presents human nature with its rights, rights lost in most parts of the world. He fights superstition, he inspires morality.

I'll admit to you how distressed I am that a book that could be so useful should be based on a chimerical principle. Virtue, he says, is the principle of republics, honour that of monarchies. You can be sure that republics have never been created by virtue. Public interest opposed rule by a single man; the property ethos, the ambition of each individual, acted as a curb on the urge to loot. The pride and arrogance of each citizen keeps close watch on the pride and arrogance of his neighbour. Nobody wished to be the slave of someone else's capricious whims. This is what establishes a republic, and this is what keeps it going. It's ridiculous to imagine that a Grison needs more virtue than a Spaniard!

That honour should be the principle of monarchies alone is an equally chimerical idea; he makes this very clear himself unconsciously. 'The nature of honour', he says in chapter 7, Book III, 'is to ask for marks of preference and distinction. Things being what they are, it is thus located in monarchical government.'

Certainly, things being what they are, people would ask for praetorships, consulships, acclamations, triumphal arches: those are marks of preference and distinction well worth the titles of rank often bought in monarchies at a fixed price. There is another principle behind his book that's just as misleading: this is the division of governments into republics, monarchies and despotisms.

Our authors have been pleased (I don't know why) to call the sovereigns of Asia and Africa *despots*. In days gone by, it was understood that by despot was meant a minor European prince, a vassal of the Turk, a disposable vassal, a kind of crowned slave governing other slaves. Originally this word *despot* had meant with the Greeks, *master of the house, father*. Today we make free with this title for the Emperor of Morocco, the Great Turk, the Pope, the Emperor of China. At the start of the second book (ch. 1), Montesquieu defines despotic government thus: 'A single man, without laws or rules, who carries everyone along by willpower and impulse.'

Now it's quite wrong to think that such a government exists and, it seems to me, quite wrong to think that it could exist. The Koran and the authorised commentaries are the laws of the Muslims. All monarchs of this religion swear on the Koran to observe these laws.

The old officer corps and the lawyers have immense privileges, and when the sultans wished to break those privileges they were all strangled, or at least solemnly deposed.

I've never been to China, but I've seen more than twenty people who have made the journey, and I think that I've read all the authors who have spoken about that country. I know, with far more certainty than Rollin knew ancient history, I know from the unanimous reports from our missionaries of various sects, that China is governed by laws, and not by a single arbitrary will. I know that in Peking there are six supreme courts with jurisdiction over forty-four other courts. I know that when these six supreme courts address remonstrations to the Emperor it has the force of law. I know that at the far outposts of the Empire a street porter or a charcoal-burner are not executed without the trial proceedings having been sent to the supreme court at Peking, which reports them to the Emperor. Is that an arbitrary and tyrannical government? The Emperor is more revered there than the Pope is in Rome; but to be respected, must one reign without the curb of the law? One proof that the laws reign in China is that the country is more heavily populated than the whole of Europe. We've transported to China our holy religion, and it's been a failure. We might well have taken its laws in exchange, but perhaps we don't know how to trade like that.

It's an absolute certainty that the Bishop of Rome is more despotic than the Emperor of China, for he is infallible and the Chinese Emperor is not. However, that bishop is still subject to the law.

Despotism is just the abuse of monarchy, a corruption of a fine system of government. I could more easily accept highwaymen in political office than I can tyrants as kings.

A

You say nothing to me about the venality of judgeships, this fine trade in the law that only the French in the whole wide world know about. Those people must be the biggest traders in the universe since they sell and buy even the right to judge men. Devil take it! If I had the honour to have been born in Picardy or in Champagne, and to be the son of a tax-farmer or royal victualler, I could, with the help of twelve or fifteen thousand *écus*, become absolute master of the lives and fortunes of my fellow citizens! I would be called *monsieur* in accordance with the protocol used by my colleagues, and I would call litigants by their plain surnames, whether they be Châtillons or Montmorencys and, to get my money's worth, I would be a Guardian of Kings! It's an excellent deal. In addition, I would have the pleasure of having every book that displeased me burnt by someone whom Jean-Jacques Rousseau wishes to make the Dauphin's stepfather. It's a great right.

B

True, Montesquieu does have the weakness to say that the venality of offices *is good in monarchical states*. What do you expect? He was a high court president complete with mortar. I've never seen a mortar, but I imagine that it's a superb adornment. It's very difficult for the most philosophical mind not to pay tribute to pride. If a spice merchant talked about legislation, he would want everyone to buy cinnamon and nutmeg.

A

All that doesn't stop the *Spirit of the laws* from having some excellent bits in it. I like thinking people who make me think. How would you rank this book?

B

With works of genius that make you yearn for perfection. It appears to me to be a building with poor foundations, and an irregular structure, in which there are a lot of fine, well-polished, gilded apartments.

(d) Universal History: Scotland

26

Lectures on Jurisprudence

Adam Smith

Monday Febry. 21st 1762

4... In the age of hunters there can be very little government of any sort, but what there is will be of the democraticall kind. A nation of this sort consists of a number of independent families, no otherwise connected than as they live together in the same town or village and speak the same language. With regard to the judicial power, this in these nations as far as it extends is possessed by the community as one body. The affairs of private families, as long as they concern only the members of one family, are left to the determination of *the members of that* family. Disputes betwixt others can in this state but rarely occur, but if they do, and are of such a nature as would be apt to disturb the community, the whole community then interferes to make up the difference; which is ordinarily all the length they go, never daring to inflict what is properly called punishment. The design of their intermeddling is to preserve the public quiet and the safety of the individualls; 5they therefore endeavour to bring about a reconcilement betwixt the parties at variance. This is the case amongst the savage nations of America, as we are informed by Father Charlevoix and Monsieur Laffitau who give us the most distinct account of the manners of those nations. They tell us also that if one has committed any very heinous crime against

another, they will sometimes put him to death; but this is not in a judicial way, but thro' the resentment or indignation the crime has raised in each individuall. In such cases the whole body of the people lie in wait for him and kill him by an assassination in the same manner as they would an enemy. A very common method in these cases is to invite him to a feast and have some 3 or 4 persons appointed before hand who dispatch him. The power of making peace and war in such nations belongs to the whole people. A treaty of peace amongst them is no more than an agreement to cease hostili-6ties against each other, and to | make such an agreement compleat it is necessary that the consent of every individuall in the society should be obtain, every one thinking he has a title to continue hostilities till he has obtained sufficient satisfaction. And in the same manner an injury done to any individuall is sufficient to make him commence hostilities against the injurious person, which will commonly bring on a generall quarrell. The legislative power can hardly subsist in such a state; there could be occasion but for very few regulations, and no individuall would think himself bound to submit to such regulations as were made by others, even where the whole community was concerned. – The whole of the government in this state, as far as there is any, is democraticall. There may indeed be some persons in this

Adam Smith, *Lectures on Jurisprudence,* ed. R. L. Meek, D. D. Raphael and P. G. Stein, Oxford: Oxford University Press, 1978, pp. 200–6.

state who have a superior weight and influence with the rest of the members; but this does not derogate from the democraticall form, as such persons will only have this influence by their 7 superior wisdom, valour, or such | like qualifications, and over those only who incline of themselves to be directed by him. In the same manner as in every club or assembly where the whole members are on an equall footing there is generally some person whose counsil is more followed than any others, and who has generally a considerable influence in all debates, and is as it were the king of the company.

The age of shepherds is that where government properly first commences. And it is at this time too that men become in any considerable degree dependent on others. The appropriation of flocks and herds renders subsistence by hunting very uncertain and pr(e)carious. Those animalls which are most adapted for the use of man, as oxen, sheep, horses, camels, etc. which are also the most numerous, are no longer common but are the property of certain individualls. The distinctions of rich and poor then arise. Those who have not any possessions in flocks and herds can find no way of maintaining themselves but by procuring it 8 from the rich. The rich | therefore, as they maintain and support those of the poorer sort out of the large possessions which they have in herds and flocks, require their service and dependance. And in this manner every wealthy man comes to have a considerable number of the poorer sort depending and attending upon him. And in this period of society the inequality of fortune makes a greater odds in the power and influence of the rich over the poor than in any other. For when luxury and effeminacy have once got a footing in a country, one may expend in different manners a very large fortune without creating one single dependent; his taylor, his [illegible word], his cook, etc. have each a share of it, but as they all give him their work in recompense for what he bestows on them, and that not out of necessity, they do not look upon themselves as any (?way) dependent on him. They may reckon that they are obliged to him, but not one of them would go 9 so far as to fight for him. But | in the early periods, when arts and manufactures are not known and there is hardly any luxury amongst

mankind, the rich man has no way of spending the produce of his estate but by giving it away to others, and these become in this manner dependent on him. The patriarchs we see were all a sort of independent princes who had their dependents and followers attending them, being maintain'd by the produce of the flocks and herds which were committed to their care. Over these they would naturally have considerable power, and would be the only judges amongst the people about them.

{The authority of the rich men would in this manner soon come to be very great; let us therefore consider its progress.} In this way of life there are many more opportunities of dispute betwixt the different persons of a tribe or nation than amongst a nation of hunters. Property is then introduced, and many disputes on that head must inevitably occur. Let us suppose then a nation of shepherds living together in a village or town. {We will find that the form of government which would take place here will also be democraticall. Let us therefore consider the severall parts of the supreme power, and we will find they are all in the hands of the body of the people. 1st, with regard to the judiciall power,} the way they would most readily think of, and which the severall individualls would most readily agree to, of accommodating any such differences as might arise would be to refer them to the 10 assembly of the whole | people. There would no doubt as I said above be many more disputes in this stage of society than in that of hunters, but not near so great a number as there afterwards are in the farther advances of society. For the great sources of debate, and which give ground to the far greater part of lawsuits, were not known in the earlier periods of society. The most of those which now employ the courts arise either 1st, from some question concerning the meaning of the will of a deceased person; this they at that time had not, for as I observed before no testaments were allowed or thought of in the first periods of society; or 2dly, from marriage settlements: these also are unknown in the early periods of society; or 3dly, from voluntary contracts, which do not sustain action nor are they supported by the community at this time. The business therefore would not be very great; nor would the inhabitants be so much engaged as not to have leisure to attend these meetings. – But as in every society there is some persons who take the lead and are of influence over the others, so there would without question be some persons 13 of eminence who would have some influence over the[m]| deliberations of the others. The rich men who have large possessions in flocks and herds would as I observed have many dependents who would follow their council and direction, and in this manner they would have the greatest influence over the people. – As these persons would be the most eminent among the old people, so would their sons be amongst the younger one(s), as their fathers eminence would convey respect to their character, and as they would be thus respected in their fathers life time they would naturally fill his place after his death. If there were two sons the authority would be divided amongst them, as well as the estate. And tho nothing can be more in convenient than a government thus split when the king or monarch comes to be of considerable authority, yet it is not attended with the same in convenience in these periods. We see that at the time of the Trojan wars there were severall nations who were led on by different chiefs. Sarpedon and Glaucus led on the Cretans, Diomedes and Idomeneus the Beotians, Menestheus and 5 others the people of Attica. It generally happened indeed that 12 some one | was more respected than the others, as we see these Grecian leaders were in the same order as those of each country here are mentioned. The authority therefore of these chief men in this state would soon become hereditary, and when in the farther advances of society they would find thes(e) inconveniences attending on these divided, the right of primogeniture and the other regulations of succession would be brought in (in) the manner I mentioned when treating on that subject. But this was not an infringement of the democraticall form of government, as these persons had not any authority more than was acquired by their private influence. The community would also have it in their power to punish in some manner any heinous offences. They may perhaps sometimes assassinate any of these, in the manner I mentioned before with regard to the North Americans, and they would have it also in their power to punish them by turning from out of the society. The members of any club have it in their power to turn out any member, and so also have the members of such a com- 13 munity. This, tho it would be no great grievance on | the first commencement of a society when the members had formed no connections or friendships with each other, would be a very great one when they had lived together some time and perhaps been born and educated in the society. When they were turned out they would have no friends, no acquaintances else where; commerce does not then take place, so that they would have no opportunity of communication with others. They would be banished from all their friends and connections. So that this would be one of the most severe punishments that could be inflicted.

With regard to the executive power, or that of making peace and war, this also as far as it would extend would be in the same hands as the former. Wars betwixt nations of this sort are generally undertaken on a sudden, and decided by one or two set skirmishes. The whole people would rush out when they were attack'd, or make an incursion on their neighbours in a body. Their leaders would not be any regular commanders; their army | would be 14 rather an unruly band than a disciplined body. … The legislative is never met with amongst people in this state of society. Laws and regulations are the product of more refind manners and improved government, and are never 15 found | till it is considerably advanced.

When mankind have made some farther advances, the determination of causes becomes an affair of more difficulty and labour. Arts and manufactures are then cultivated, and the people are by this means less able (to) spare their time and attendance at the tryalls. Besides this the causes of dispute also multiply. Testaments come to be in use, contracts of marriage, etc. gradually come in, so that on the one hand the business is increased and on the other hand the people has less time to spare. So that one of two things must happen: either the causes or disputes must lie undetermined, or some persons must be appointed who shall judge in these matters. The 1st of this alternative can never be allowed, as confusion and quarrels must inevitably follow on it. The latter therefore is always taken. A certain number of men are chosen by the body of the people, whose business it is to attend on the causes and settle all disputes. The chief and leading men of the nation will necessarily make a part of this 16 council. Their authority will still | continue, and they will become a sort of head or president in the court. His authority in this station will grow very fast; much faster than in proportion to the advances made by the society. For in all thes(e) early countries the custom is altogether contrary to that now in use. The rich now make presents to the poor, but in (the) beginnings of society the rich rec(e)ive presents from their dependents. They will never enter on the consideration of a cause without a gratuity. No one can have access to the Mogul unless he have a present in his hand, and so in all other rude and barbarous nations. A Tartar prince can not be spoke to without you open his ears by a gift. As this will soon increase their riches, so the number of their dependents and their power must increase proportionably, and their influence on the council will also be increased. This number is originally pretty large in all countries. They dont think it safe to trust themselves and their property in the hands of a few persons, but think they are much safer when they are under the management of a considerable body. | The sovereign court of Athens 17 consisted of 500 persons. The affairs and debates relating to peace and war are originally very simple and soon determined, but when the affairs of the state multiply, and any extraordinary provision is to be made, this is a matter of too tedious a nature to be determined by the whole people, who can not detach themselves so long from their private affairs as these matters would require. It here again becomes absolutely necessary for the safety of the state either to give the management of these affairs [either] to the same court as that to which the determination of private causes was before committed, or to appoint a new one.

27

An Essay on the History of Civil Society

Adam Ferguson

Part Second. Of the History of Rude Nations

Section I

Of the informations on this subject which are derived from antiquity

The history of mankind is confined within a limited period, and from every quarter brings an intimation that human affairs have had a beginning. Nations, distinguished by the possession of arts, and the felicity of their political establishments, have been derived from a feeble original, and still preserve in their story the indications of a slow and gradual progress, by which this distinction was gained. The antiquities of every people, however diversified, and however disguised, contain the same information on this point.

In sacred history, we find the parents of the species, as yet a single pair, sent forth to inherit the earth, and to force a subsistence for themselves amidst the briars and thorns which were made to abound on its surface. Their race, which was again reduced to a few, had to struggle with the dangers that await a weak and infant species; and after many ages elapsed, the most respectable nations took their rise from one or a few families that had pastured their flocks in the desert.

The Grecians derive their own origin from unsettled tribes, whose frequent migrations are a proof of the rude and infant state of their communities; and whose warlike exploits, so much celebrated in story, only exhibit the struggles with which they disputed the possession of a country they afterwards, by their talent for fable, by their arts, and their policy, rendered so famous in the history of mankind.

Italy must have been divided into many rude and feeble cantons, when a band of robbers, as we are taught to consider them, found a secure settlement on the banks of the Tiber, and when a people, yet composed only of one sex, sustained the character of a nation. Rome, for many ages, saw, from her walls, on every side, the territory of her enemies, and found as little to check or to stifle the weakness of her infant power, as she did afterwards to restrain the progress of her extended empire. Like a Tartar or a Scythian horde, which had pitched on a settlement, this nascent community was equal, if not superior, to every tribe in its neighbourhood; and the oak which has covered the field with its shade, was once a feeble plant in the nursery, and not to be distinguished from the weeds by which its early growth was restrained.

Adam Ferguson, *An Essay on the History of Civil Society*. Philadelphia: A. Finley, 1819. pp. 135–9, 148–78, 324–30, 334–41.

The Gauls and the Germans are come to our knowledge with the marks of a similar condition; and the inhabitants of Britain, at the time of the first Roman invasions, resembled, in many things, the present natives of North America: they were ignorant of agriculture; they painted their bodies; and used for clothing the skins of beasts.

Such, therefore, appears to have been the commencement of history with all nations, and in such circumstances are we to look for the original character of mankind. The inquiry refers to a distant period, and every conclusion should build on the facts which are preserved for our use. Our method, notwithstanding, too frequently, is to rest the whole on conjecture; to impute every advantage of our nature to those arts which we ourselves possess; and to imagine, that a mere negation of all our virtues is a sufficient description of man in his original state. We are ourselves the supposed standards of politeness and civilization; and where our own features do not appear, we apprehend, that there is nothing which deserves to be known. But it is probable that here, as in many other cases, we are ill qualified, from our supposed knowledge of causes, to prognosticate effects, or to determine what must have been the properties and operations, even of our own nature, in the absence of those circumstances in which we have seen it engaged. Who would, from mere conjecture, suppose that the naked savage would be a coxcomb and a gamester? that he would be proud or vain, without the distinctions of title and fortune? and that his principal care would be to adorn his person, and to find an amusement? Even if it could be supposed that he would thus share in our vices, and, in the midst of his forest, vie with the follies which are practised in the town; yet no one would be so bold as to affirm, that he would likewise, in any instance, excel us in talents and virtues; that he would have a penetration, a force of imagination and elocution, an ardour of mind, an affection and courage, which the arts, the discipline, and the policy of few nations would be able to improve. Yet these particulars are a part in the description which is delivered by those who have had opportunities of seeing mankind in their rudest condition; and beyond the reach of such testimony, we can neither safely take, nor pretend to give, information on the subject.

If conjectures and opinions formed at a distance, have not sufficient authority in the history of mankind, the domestic antiquities of every nation must, for this very reason, be received with caution. They are, for the most part, the mere conjectures or the fictions of subsequent ages; and even where at first they contained some resemblance of truth, they still vary with the imagination of those by whom they are transmitted, and in every generation receive a different form. They are made to bear the stamp of the times through which they have passed in the form of tradition, not of the ages to which their pretended descriptions relate. The information they bring, is not like the light reflected from a mirror, which delineates the object from which it originally came; but, like rays that come broken and dispersed from an opaque or unpolished surface, only give the colours and features of the body from which they were last reflected.

[...]

Section II

Of rude nations prior to the establishment of property

From one to the other extremity of America; from Kamtschatka westward to the river Oby; and from the Northern Sea, over that length of country, to the confines of China, of India, and Persia; from the Caspian to the Red Sea, with little exception, and from thence over the inland continent and the western shores of Africa; we every where meet with nations on whom we bestow the appellations of barbarous or savage. That extensive tract of the earth, containing so great a variety of situation, climate, and soil, should, in the manners of its inhabitants, exhibit all the diversities which arise from the unequal influence of the sun, joined to a different nourishment and manner of life. Every question, however, on this subject, is premature, till we have first endeavoured to form some general conception of our species in its rude state, and have learned to distinguish mere ignorance from dulness, and the want of arts from the want of capacity.

Of the nations who dwell in those, or any other of the less cultivated parts of the earth, some entrust their subsistence chiefly to hunting, fishing, or the natural produce of the soil. They have little attention to property, and scarcely any beginnings of subordination or government. Others, having possessed themselves of herbs, and depending for their provision on pasture, know what it is to be poor and rich. They know the relations of patron and client, of servant and master, and by the measures of fortune determine their station. This distinction must create a material difference of character, and may furnish two separate heads, under which to consider the history of mankind in their rudest state; that of the savage, who is not yet acquainted with property; and that of the barbarian, to whom it is, although not ascertained by laws, a principal object of care and desire.

It must appear very evident, that property is a matter of progress. It requires, among other particulars, which are the effects of time, some method of defining possession. The very desire of it proceeds from experience; and the industry by which it is gained, or improved, requires such a habit of acting with a view to distant objects, as may overcome the present disposition either to sloth or to enjoyment. This habit is slowly acquired, and is in reality a principal distinction of nations in the advanced state of mechanic and commercial arts.

In a tribe which subsists by hunting and fishing, the arms, the utensils, and the fur, which the individual carries, are to him the only subjects of property. The food of to-morrow is yet wild in the forest, or hid in the lake; it cannot be appropriated before it is caught; and even then, being the purchase of numbers, who fish or hunt in a body, it accrues to the community, and is applied to immediate use, or becomes an accession to the stores of the public.

Where savage nations, as in most parts of America, mix with the practice of hunting some species of rude agriculture, they still follow, with respect to the soil and the fruits of the earth, the analogy of their principal object. As the men hunt, so the women labour together; and, after they have shared the toils of the seed time, they enjoy the fruits of the harvest in common. The field in which they have planted, like the district over which they are accustomed to hunt, is claimed as a property by the nation, but is not parcelled in lots to its members. They go forth in parties to prepare the ground, to plant and to reap. The harvest is gathered into the public granary, and from thence, at stated times, is divided into shares for the maintenance of separate families. Even the returns of the market, when they trade with foreigners, are brought home to the stock of the nation.

As the fur and the bow pertain to the individual, the cabin and its utensils are appropriated to the family; and as the domestic cares are committed to the women, so the property of the household seems likewise to be vested in them. The children are considered as pertaining to the mother, with little regard to descent on the father's side. The males, before they are married, remain in the cabin in which they are born; but after they have formed a new connection with the other sex, they change their habitation, and become an accession to the family in which they have found their wives. The hunter and the warrior are numbered by the matron as a part of her treasure; they are reserved for perils and trying occasions; and in the recess of public councils, in the intervals of hunting or war, are maintained by the cares of the women, and loiter about in mere amusement or sloth.

While one sex continue to value themselves chiefly on their courage, their talent for policy, and their warlike achievements, this species of property which is bestowed on the other, is, in reality, a mark of subjection; not, as some writers allege, of their having acquired an ascendant. It is the care and trouble of a subject with which the warrior does not choose to be embarrassed. It is a servitude, and a continual toil, where no honours are won; and they whose province it is, are in fact the slaves and the helots of their country. If in this destination of the sexes, while the men continue to indulge themselves in the contempt of sordid and mercenary arts, the cruel establishment of slavery is for some ages deferred; if, in this tender, though unequal alliance, the affections of the heart prevent the severities practised on slaves;

we have in the custom itself, as perhaps in many other instances, reason to prefer the first suggestions of nature, to many of her after refinements.

If mankind, in any instance, continue the article of property on the footing we have now represented, we may easily credit what is further reported by travellers, that they admit of no distinctions of rank or condition; and that they have in fact no degree of subordination different from the distribution of function, which follows the differences of age, talents, and dispositions. Personal qualities give an ascendant in the midst of occasions which require their exertion; but in times of relaxation, leave no vestige of power or prerogative. A warrior who has led the youth of his nation to the slaughter of their enemies, or who has been foremost in the chase, returns upon a level with the rest of his tribe; and when the only business is to sleep, or to feed, can enjoy no pre-eminence; for he sleeps and he feeds no better than they.

Where no profit attends dominion, one party is as much averse to the trouble of perpetual command, as the other is to the mortification of perpetual submission. "I love victory, I love great actions," says Montesquieu, in the character of Sylla; "but have no relish for the languid detail of pacific government, or the pageantry of high station." He has touched perhaps what is a prevailing sentiment in the simplest state of society, when the weakness of motive suggested by interest, and the ignorance of any elevation not founded on merit, supplies the place of disdain.

The character of the mind, however, in this state, is not founded on ignorance alone. Men are conscious of their equality, and are tenacious of its rights. Even when they follow a leader to the field, they cannot brook the pretensions to a formal command: they listen to no orders; and they come under no military engagements, but those of mutual fidelity, and equal ardour in the enterprise.

This description, we may believe, is unequally applicable to different nations, who have made unequal advances in the establishment of property. Among the Caribbees, and the other natives of the warmer climates in America, the dignity of chieftain is hereditary,

or elective, and continued for life: the unequal distribution of property creates a visible subordination. But among the Iroquois, and other nations of the temperate zone, the titles of *magistrate* and *subject*, of *noble* and *mean*, are as little known as those of *rich* and *poor*. The old men, without being invested with any coercive power, employ their natural authority in advising or in prompting the resolutions of their tribe: the military leader is pointed out by the superiority of his manhood and valour; the statesman is distinguished only by the attention with which his counsel is heard; the warrior by the confidence with which the youth of his nation follow him to the field; and if their concerts must be supposed to constitute a species of political government, it is one to which no language of ours can be applied. Power is more than the natural ascendancy of the mind; the discharge of office no more than a natural exercise of the personal character; and while the community acts with an appearance of order, there is no sense of disparity in the breast of any of its members.

In these happy, though informal proceedings, where age alone gives a place in the council; where youth, ardour, and valour in the field, give a title to the station of leader; where the whole community is assembled on any alarming occasion, we may venture to say, that we have found the origin of the senate, the executive power, and the assembly of the people; institutions for which ancient legislators have been so much renowned. The senate among the Greeks, as well as the Latins, appears, from the etymology of its name, to have been originally composed of elderly men. The military leader at Rome, in a manner not unlike to that of the American warrior, proclaimed his levies, and the citizen prepared for the field, in consequence of a voluntary engagement. The suggestions of nature, which directed the policy of nations in the wilds of America, were followed before on the banks of the Eurotas and the Tyber; and Lycurgus and Romulus found the model of their institutions, where the members of every rude nation find the earliest mode of uniting their talents, and combining their forces.

Among the North American nations, every individual is independent; but he is engaged by his affections and his habits in the cares of a family. Families, like so many separate tribes, are subject to no inspection or government from abroad; whatever passes at home, even bloodshed and murder, are only supposed to concern themselves. They are, in the mean time, the parts of a canton; the women assemble to plant their maize; the old men go to council; the huntsman and the warrior joins the youth of his village in the field. Many such cantons assemble to constitute a national council, or to execute a national enterprise. When the Europeans made their first settlements in America, six such nations had formed a league, had their amphyctiones or states general, and, by the firmness of their union and the ability of their councils, had obtained an ascendant from the mouth of St. Lawrence to that of the Mississippi. They appeared to understand the objects of the confederacy, as well as those of the separate nation; they studied a balance of power; the statesman of one country watched the designs and proceedings of another; and occasionally threw the weight of his tribe into a different scale. They had their alliances and their treaties, which, like the nations of Europe, they maintained, or they broke, upon reasons of state; and remained at peace from a sense of necessity or expediency, and went to war upon any emergence of provocation or jealousy.

Thus, without any settled form of government, or any bond of union, but what resembled more the suggestion of instinct, than the invention of reason, they conducted themselves with the concert and the force of nations. Foreigners, without being able to discover who is the magistrate, or in what manner the senate is composed, always find a council with whom they may treat, or a band of warriors with whom they may fight. Without police or compulsory laws, their domestic society is conducted with order, and the absence of vicious dispositions, is a better security than any public establishment for the suppression of crimes.

Disorders, however, sometimes occur, especially in times of debauch, when the immoderate use of intoxicating liquors, to which they are extremely addicted, suspends the ordinary caution of their demeanour, and, inflaming their violent passions, engages them in quarrels and bloodshed. When a person is slain, his murderer is seldom called to an immediate account; but he has a quarrel to sustain with the family and the friends; or, if a stranger, with the country-men of the deceased; sometimes even with his own nation at home, if the injury committed be of a kind to alarm the society. The nation, the canton, or the family endeavour, by presents, to atone for the offence of any of their members; and, by pacifying the parties aggrieved, endeavour to prevent what alarms the community more than the first disorder, the subsequent effects of revenge and animosity. The shedding of blood, however, if the guilty person remain where he has committed the crime, seldom escapes unpunished: the friend of the deceased knows how to disguise, though not to suppress, his resentment; and even after many years have elapsed, is sure to repay the injury that was done to his kindred or his house.

These considerations render them cautious and circumspect, put them on their guard against their passions, and give to their ordinary deportment an air of phlegm and composure superior to what is possessed among polished nations. They are, in the mean time, affectionate in their carriage, and in their conversations, pay a mutual attention and regard, says Charlevoix, more tender and more engaging, than what we profess in the ceremonial of polished societies.

This writer has observed, that the nations among whom he travelled in North America, never mentioned acts of generosity or kindness under the notion of duty. They acted from affection, as they acted from appetite, without regard to its consequences. When they had done a kindness, they had gratified a desire; the business was finished, and it passed from the memory. When they received a favour, it might, or it might not, prove the occasion of friendship: if it did not, the parties appeared to have no apprehensions of gratitude, as a duty by which the one was bound to make a return, or the other entitled to reproach the person who had failed in his part. The spirit with which they give or receive presents, is the same which Tacitus observed among the ancient Germans; they delight in them, but do not consider them as matter of obligation. Such gifts are of little consequence, except when employed as the seal of a bargain or treaty.

It was their favourite maxim, that no man is naturally indebted to another; that he is not, therefore, obliged to bear with any imposition, or unequal treatment. Thus, in a principle apparently sullen and inhospitable, they have discovered the foundation of justice, and observe its rules, with a steadiness and candour which no cultivation has been found to improve. The freedom which they give in what relates to the supposed duties of kindness and friendship, serves only to engage the heart more entirely, where it is once possessed with affection. We love to choose our object without any restraint, and we consider kindness itself as a task, when the duties of friendship are exacted by rule. We therefore, by our demand for attentions, rather corrupt than improve the system of morality; and by our exactions of gratitude, and our frequent proposals to enforce its observance, we only shew that we have mistaken its nature; we only give symptoms of that growing sensibility to interest, from which we measure the expediency of friendship and generosity itself; and by which we would introduce the spirit of traffic into the commerce of affection. In consequence of this proceeding, we are often obliged to decline a favour, with the same spirit that we throw off a servile engagement, or reject a bribe. To the unrefined savage every favour is welcome, and every present received without reserve or reflection.

The love of equality, and the love of justice, were originally the same; and although, by the constitution of different societies, unequal privileges are bestowed on their members; and although justice itself requires a proper regard to be paid to such privileges; yet he who has forgotten that men were originally equal, easily degenerates into a slave; or, in the capacity of a master, is not to be trusted with the rights of his fellow creatures. This happy principle gives to the mind its sense of independence, renders it indifferent to the favours which are in the power of other men, checks it in the commission of injuries, and leaves the heart open to the affections of generosity and kindness. It gives to the untutored American that sentiment of candour, and of regard to the welfare of others, which, in some degree, softens

the arrogant pride of his carriage, and in times of confidence and peace, without the assistance of government or law, renders the approach and commerce of strangers secure.

Among this people, the foundations of honour are eminent abilities, and great fortitude; not the distinctions of equipage and fortune: the talents in esteem are such as their situation leads them to employ, the exact knowledge of a country, and stratagem in war. On these qualifications, a captain among the Caribbees underwent an examination. When a new leader was to be chosen, a scout was sent forth to traverse the forests which led to the enemy's country, and upon his return, the candidate was desired to find the track in which he had travelled. A brook, or a fountain, was named to him on the frontier, and he was desired to find the nearest path to a particular station, and to plant a stake in the place. They can, accordingly, trace a wild beast, or the human foot, over many leagues of a pathless forest, and find their way across a woody and uninhabited continent, by means of refined observations, which escape the traveller who has been accustomed to different aids. They steer in slender canoes, across stormy seas, with a dexterity equal to that of the most experienced pilot. They carry a penetrating eye for the thoughts and intentions of those with whom they have to deal; and when they mean to deceive, they cover themselves with arts which the most subtile can seldom elude. They harangue in their public councils with a nervous and a figurative elocution; and conduct themselves in the management of their treaties with a perfect discernment of their national interests.

Thus being able masters in the detail of their own affairs, and well qualified to acquit themselves on particular occasions, they study no science, and go in pursuit of no general principles. They even seem incapable of attending to any distant consequences, beyond those they have experienced in hunting or war. They entrust the provision of every season to itself; consume the fruits of the earth in summer; and, in winter, are driven in quest of their prey, through woods, and over deserts covered with snow. They do not form in one hour those maxims which may prevent the errors of the next; and they fail in those apprehensions, which, in the intervals of passion, produce ingenuous shame, compassion, remorse, or a command of appetite. They are seldom made to repent of any violence; nor is a person, indeed, thought accountable in his sober mood, for what he did in the heat of a passion, or in a time of debauch.

Their superstitions are groveling and mean; and did this happen among rude nations alone, we could not sufficiently admire the effects of politeness; but it is a subject on which few nations are entitled to censure their neighbours. When we have considered the superstitions of one people, we find little variety in those of another. They are but a repetition of similar weaknesses and absurdities, derived from a common source, a perplexed apprehension of invisible agents, that are supposed to guide all precarious events to which human foresight cannot extend.

In what depends on the known or the regular course of nature, the mind trusts to itself; but in strange and uncommon situations, it is the dupe of its own perplexity, and, instead of relying on its prudence or courage, has recourse to divination, and a variety of observances, that, for being irrational, are always the more revered. Superstition being founded in doubts and anxiety, is fostered by ignorance and mystery. Its maxims, in the mean time, are not always confounded with those of common life; nor does its weakness or folly always prevent the watchfulness, penetration, and courage, men are accustomed to employ in the management of common affairs. A Roman consulting futurity by the pecking of birds, or a king of Sparta inspecting the entrails of a beast, Mithridates consulting his women on the interpretation of his dreams, are examples sufficient to prove, that a childish imbecility on this subject is consistent with the greatest military and political conduct.

Confidence in the effect of charms is not peculiar to any age or nation. Few, even of the accomplished Greeks and Romans, were able to shake off this weakness. In their case, it was not removed by the highest measures of civilization. It has yielded only to the light of true religion, or to the study of nature, by which we are led to substitute a wise providence operating by physical causes, in the place of phantoms that terrify or amuse the ignorant.

The principal point of honour among the rude nations of America, as indeed in every instance where mankind are not greatly corrupted, is fortitude. Yet their way of maintaining this point of honour, is very different from that of the nations of Europe. Their ordinary method of making war is by ambuscade; and they strive, by overreaching an enemy, to commit the greatest slaughter, or to make the greatest number of prisoners, with the least hazard to themselves. They deem it a folly to expose their own persons in assaulting an enemy, and do not rejoice in victories which are stained with the blood of their own people. They do not value themselves, as in Europe, on defying their enemy upon equal terms. They even boast, that they approach like foxes, or that they fly like birds, not less than they devour like lions. In Europe, to fall in battle is accounted an honour; among the natives of America it is reckoned disgraceful. They reserve their fortitude for the trials they abide when attacked by surprise, or when fallen into their enemies' hands; and when they are obliged to maintain their own honour, and that of their own nation, in the midst of torments that require efforts of patience more than of valour.

On these occasions, they are far from allowing it to be supposed that they wish to decline the conflict. It is held infamous to avoid it, even by a voluntary death; and the greatest affront which can be offered to a prisoner, is to refuse him the honours of a man, in the manner of his execution. "Withhold," says an old man, in the midst of his torture, "the stabs of your knife; rather let me die by fire, that those dogs, your allies, from beyond the seas, may learn to suffer like men." With terms of defiance, the victim, in those solemn trials, commonly excites the animosities of his tormentors, as well as his own; and whilst we suffer for human nature, under the effect of its errors, we must admire its force.

The people with whom this practice prevailed, were commonly desirous of repairing their own losses, by adopting prisoners of war into their families; and even, in the last moment, the hand which was raised to torment, frequently gave the sign of adoption, by which the prisoner became the child or the brother of his enemy, and came to share in all the privileges of a citizen. In their treatment of those who suffered, they did not appear to be guided by principles of hatred or revenge; they observed the point of honour in applying as well as in bearing their torments; and, by a strange kind of affection and tenderness, were directed to be most cruel where they intend the highest respect; the coward was put to immediate death by the hands of women; the valiant was supposed to be entitled to all the trials of fortitude that men could invent or employ. "It gave me joy," says an old man to his captive, "that so gallant a youth was allotted to my share; I proposed to have placed you on the couch of my nephew, who was slain by your countrymen; to have transferred all my tenderness to you; and to have solaced my age in your company; but, maimed and mutilated as you now appear, death is better than life; prepare yourself therefore to die like a man."

It is perhaps with a view to these exhibitions, or rather in admiration of fortitude, the principle from which they proceed, that the Americans are so attentive, in their earliest years, to harden their nerves. The children are taught to vie with each other in bearing the sharpest torments; the youth are admitted into the class of manhood, after violent proofs of their patience; and leaders are put to the test by famine, burning, and suffocation.

It might be apprehended, that among rude nations, where the means of subsistence are procured with so much difficulty, the mind could never raise itself above the consideration of this subject; and that man would, in this condition, give examples of the meanest and most mercenary spirit. The reverse, however, is true. Directed in this particular by the desires of nature, men, in their simplest state, attend to the objects of appetite no further than appetite requires; and their desires of fortune extend no further than the meal which gratifies their hunger: they apprehend no superiority of rank in the possession of wealth, such as might inspire any habitual principle of covetousness, vanity, or ambition: they can apply to no task that engages no immediate passion, and take pleasure in no occupation that affords no dangers to be braved, and no honours to be won.

It was not among the ancient Romans alone that commercial arts, or a sordid mind, were held in contempt. A like spirit prevails in every rude and independent society. "I am a warrior, and not a merchant," said an American to the governor of Canada, who proposed to give him goods in exchange for some prisoners he had taken; "your clothes and utensils do not not tempt me; but my prisoners are now in your power, and you may seize them: if you do, I must go forth and take more prisoners, or perish in the attempt; and if that chance should befal me, I shall die like a man; but remember, that our nation will charge you as the cause of my death." With these apprehensions, they have an elevation, and a stateliness of carriage, which the pride of nobility, where it is most revered by polished nations, seldom bestows.

They are attentive to their persons, and employ much time, as well as endure great pain, in the methods they take to adorn their bodies, to give the permanent stains with which they are coloured, or preserve the paint, which they are perpetually repairing, in order to appear with advantage.

Their aversion to every sort of employment which they hold to be mean, makes them pass great part of their time in idleness or sleep; and a man who, in pursuit of a wild beast, or to surprise his enemy, will traverse a hundred leagues on snow, will not, to procure his food, submit to any species of ordinary labour. "Strange," says Tacitus, "that the same person should be so much averse to repose, and so much addicted to sloth."

Games of hazard are not the invention of polished ages; men of curiosity have looked for their origin in vain, among the monuments of an obscure antiquity; and it is probable that they belonged to times too remote and too rude even for the conjectures of antiquarians to reach. The very savage brings his furs, his utensils, and his beads, to the hazard table: he finds here the passions and agitations which the applications of a tedious industry could not excite; and while the throw is depending, he tears his hair, and beats his breast, with a rage which the more accomplished gamester has sometimes learned to repress: he often quits the party naked and stripped of all his possessions; or where slavery is in use, stakes his freedom to have one chance more to recover his former loss.

With all these infirmities, vices, or respectable qualities, belonging to the human species in its rudest state; the love of society, friendship, and public affection, penetration, eloquence, and courage, appear to have been its original properties, not the subsequent effects of device or invention. If mankind are qualified to improve their manners, the materials to be improved were furnished by nature; and the effect of this improvement is not to inspire the sentiments of tenderness and generosity, nor to bestow the principal constituents of a respectable character, but to obviate the casual abuses of passion; and to prevent a mind, which feels the best dispositions in their greatest force, from being at times likewise the sport of brutal appetite, and of ungovernable violence.

[...]

Section III

Of rude nations under the impressions of property and interest

It was a proverbial imprecation in use among the hunting nations on the confines of Siberia, that their enemy might be obliged to live like a Tartar, and have the folly of troubling himself with the charge of cattle. Nature, it seems, in their apprehension, by storing the woods and the desert with game, rendered the task of the herdsman unnecessary, and left to man only the trouble of selecting and of seizing his prey.

The indolence of mankind, or rather their aversion to any application in which they are not engaged by immediate instinct and passion, retards the progress of industry and of impropriation. It has been found, however, even while the means of subsistence are left in common, and the stock of the public is yet undivided, that property is apprehended in different subjects; that the fur and the bow belong to the individual; that the cottage, with its furniture, are appropriated to the family.

When the parent begins to desire a better provision for his children than is found under the promiscuous management of many copartners, when he has applied his labour and his skill apart, he aims at an exclusive possession, and seeks the property of the soil, as well as the use of its fruits.

When the individual no longer finds among his associates the same inclination to commit every subject to public use, he is seized with concern for his personal fortune; and is alarmed by the cares which every person entertains for himself. He is urged as much by emulation and jealousy, as by the sense of necessity. He suffers considerations of interest to rest on his mind, and when every present appetite is sufficiently gratified, he can act with a view to futurity, or rather finds an object of vanity in having amassed what is become a subject of competition, and a matter of universal esteem. Upon this motive, where violence is restrained, he can apply his hand to lucrative arts, confine himself to a tedious task, and wait with patience for the distant returns of his labour.

Thus mankind acquire industry by many and by slow degrees. They are taught to regard their interest; they are restrained from rapine; and they are secured in the possession of what they fairly obtain; by these methods the habits of the labourer, the mechanic, and the trader, are gradually formed. A hoard, collected from the simple productions of nature, or a herd of cattle, are, in every rude nation, the first species of wealth. The circumstances of the soil, and the climate, determine whether the inhabitant shall apply himself chiefly to agriculture or pasture; whether he shall fix his residence, or be moving continually about with all his possessions.

In the west of Europe; in America, from south to north, with a few exceptions; in the torrid zone, and every where within the warmer climates; mankind have generally applied themselves to some species of agriculture, and have been disposed to settlement. In the north and middle region of Asia, they depended entirely on their herds, and were perpetually shifting their ground in search of new pasture. The arts which pertain to settlement have been practised, and variously cultivated, by the inhabitants of Europe. Those which are consistent with perpetual migration, have, from the earliest accounts of history, remained nearly the same with the Scythian or Tartar. The tent pitched on a moveable carriage, the horse applied to every purpose of labour, and of war, of the dairy, and of the butcher's stall, from the earliest to the latest accounts, have made up the riches and equipage of this wandering people.

Part Fourth. Of Consequences That Result from the Advancement of Civil and Commercial Arts

Section I

Of the separation of arts and professions

It is evident, that, however urged by a sense of necessity, and a desire of convenience, or favoured by any advantages of situation and policy, a people can make no great progress in cultivating the arts of life, until they have separated, and committed to different persons, the several tasks which require a peculiar skill and attention. The savage, or the barbarian, who must build and plant, and fabricate for himself, prefers, in the interval of great alarms and fatigues, the enjoyments of sloth to the improvement of his fortune: he is, perhaps, by the diversity of his wants, discouraged from industry; or, by his divided attention, prevented from acquiring skill in the management of any particular subject.

The enjoyment of peace, however, and the prospect of being able to exchange one commodity for another, turns, by degrees, the hunter and the warrior into a tradesman and a merchant. The accidents which distribute the means of subsistence unequally, inclination, and favourable opportunities, assign the different occupations of men; and a sense of utility leads them, without end, to subdivide their professions.

The artist finds, that the more he can confine his attention to a particular part of any work, his productions are the more perfect, and grow under his hands in the greater quantities. Every undertaker in manufacture finds, that the more he can subdivide the tasks of his workmen, and the more hands he can employ on separate articles, the more are his expenses diminished, and his profits increased. The consumer too requires, in every kind of commodity, a workmanship more perfect than hands employed on a variety of subjects can produce; and the progress of commerce is but a continued subdivision of the mechanical arts.

Every craft may engross the whole of a man's attention, and has a mystery which must be studied or learned by a regular apprenticeship. Nations of tradesmen come to consist of members, who, beyond their own particular trade, are ignorant of all human affairs, and who may contribute to the preservation and enlargement of their commonwealth, without making its interest an object of their regard or attention. Every individual is distinguished by his calling, and has a place to which he is fitted. The savage, who knows no distinction but that of his merit, of his sex, or of his species, and to whom his community is the sovereign object of affection, is astonished to find, that in a scene of this nature, his being a man does not qualify him for any station whatever: he flies to the woods with amazement, distaste, and aversion.

By the separation of arts and professions, the sources of wealth are laid open; every species of material is wrought up to the greatest perfection, and every commodity is produced in the greatest abundance. The state may estimate its profits and its revenues by the number of its people. It may procure, by its treasure, that national consideration and power, which the savage maintains at the expense of his blood.

The advantage gained in the inferior branches of manufacture by the separation of their parts, seem to be equalled by those which arise from a similar device in the higher departments of policy and war. The soldier is relieved from every care but that of his service; statesmen divide the business of civil government into shares; and the servants of the public, in every office, without being skilful in the affairs of state, may succeed, by observing forms which are already established on the experience of others. They are made, like the parts of an engine, to concur to a purpose, without any concert of their own: and equally blind with the trader to any general combination, they unite with him, in furnishing to the state its resources, its conduct, and its force.

[...]

Who could anticipate, or even enumerate, the separate occupations and professions by which the members of any commercial state are distinguished; the variety of devices which are practised in separate cells, and which the artist, attentive to his own affair, has invented, to abridge or to facilitate his separate task? In coming to this mighty end, every generation, compared to its predecessors, may have appeared to be ingenious; compared to its followers, may have appeared to be dull: and human ingenuity, whatever heights it may have gained in a succession of ages, continues to move with an equal pace, and to creep in making the last, as well as the first, step of commercial or civil improvement.

It may even be doubted, whether the measure of national capacity increases with the advancement of arts. Many mechanical arts, indeed, require no capacity; they succeed best under a total suppression of sentiment and reason; and ignorance is the mother of industry as well as of superstition. Reflection and fancy are subject to err; but a habit of moving the hand, or the foot, is independent of either. Manufactures, accordingly, prosper most where the mind is least consulted, and where the workshop may, without any great effort of imagination, be considered as an engine, the parts of which are men.

The forest has been felled by the savage without the use of the axe, and weights have been raised without the aid of the mechanical powers. The merit of the inventor, in every branch, probably deserves a preference to that of the performer; and he who invented a tool, or could work without its assistance, deserved the praise of ingenuity in a much higher degree than the mere artist, who, by its assistance, produces a superior work.

But if many parts in the practice of every art, and in the detail of every department, require no abilities, or actually tend to contract and to limit the views of the mind, there are others which lead to general reflections, and to enlargement of thought. Even in manufacture, the genius of the master, perhaps, is cultivated, while that of the inferior workman lies waste.

The statesman may have a wide comprehension of human affairs, while the tools he employs are ignorant of the system in which they are themselves combined. The general officer may be a great proficient in the knowledge of war, while the skill of the soldier is confined to a few motions of the hand and the foot. The former may have gained what the latter has lost; and being occupied in the conduct of disciplined armies, may practise on a larger scale all the arts of preservation, of deception, and of stratagem, which the savage exerts in leading a small party, or merely in defending himself.

[...]

In every commercial state, notwithstanding any pretension to equal rights, the exaltation of a few must depress the many. In this arrangement, we think that the extreme meanness of some classes must arise chiefly from the defect of knowledge, and of liberal education; and we refer to such classes, as to an image of what our species must have been in its rude and uncultivated state. But we forget how many circumstances, especially in populous cities, tend to corrupt the lowest orders of men. Ignorance is the least of their failings. An admiration of wealth unpossessed, becoming a principle of envy, or of servility; a habit of acting perpetually with a view to profit, and under a sense of subjection; the crimes to which they are allured, in order to feed their debauch, or to gratify their avarice, are examples, not of ignorance, but of corruption and baseness. If the savage has not received our instructions, he is likewise unacquainted with our vices. He knows no superior, and cannot be servile; he knows no distinctions of fortune, and cannot be envious; he acts from his talents in the highest station which human society can offer, that of the counsellor, and the soldier of his country. Toward forming his sentiments, he knows all that the heart requires to be known; he can distinguish the friend whom he loves, and the public interest which awakens his zeal.

The principal objections to democratical or popular government, are taken from the inequalities which arise among men in the result of commercial arts. And it must be confessed, that popular assemblies, when composed of men whose dispositions are sordid, and whose ordinary applications are illiberal, however they may be intrusted with the choice of their masters and leaders, are certainly, in their own persons, unfit to command. How can he who has confined his views to his own subsistence or preservation, be intrusted with the conduct of nations? Such men, when admitted to deliberate on matters of state, bring to its councils confusion and tumult, or servility and corruption; and seldom suffer it to repose from ruinous factions, or the effect of resolutions ill formed or ill conducted.

[...]

Section III

Of the manners of polished and commercial nations

Mankind, when in their rude state, have a great uniformity of manners; but when civilized, they are engaged in a variety of pursuits; they tread on a larger field, and separate to a greater distance. If they be guided, however, by similar dispositions, and by like suggestions of nature, they will probably in the end, as well as in the beginning of their progress, continue to agree in many particulars; and while communities admit, in their members, that diversity of ranks and professions which we have already described as the consequence or the foundation of commerce, they will resemble each other in many effects of this distribution, and of other circumstances in which they nearly concur.

Under every form of government, statesmen endeavour to remove the dangers by which they are threatened from abroad, and the disturbances which molest them at home. By this conduct, if successful, they in a few ages gain an ascendant for their country; establish a frontier at a distance from its capital; they find, in the mutual desires of tranquillity, which

come to possess mankind, and in those public establishments which tend to keep the peace of society, a respite from foreign wars, and a relief from domestic disorders. They learn to decide every contest without tumult, and to secure, by the authority of law, every citizen in the possession of his personal rights.

In this condition, to which thriving nations aspire, and which they in some measure attain, mankind having laid the basis of safety, proceed to erect a superstructure suitable to their views. The consequence is various in different states; even in different orders of men of the same community; and the effect to every individual corresponds with his station. It enables the statesman and the soldier to settle the forms of their different procedure; it enables the practitioner in every profession to pursue his separate advantage; it affords the man of pleasure a time for refinement, and the speculative, leisure for literary conversation or study.

[...]

This description may be applied equally to Athens and Rome, to London and Paris. The rude, or the simple observer, would remark the variety he saw in the dwellings and in the occupations of different men, not in the aspect of different nations. He would find, in the streets of the same city, as great a diversity, as in the territory of a separate people. He could not pierce through the cloud that was gathered before him, nor see how the tradesman, mechanic, or scholar, of one country, should differ from those of another. But the native of every province can distinguish the foreigner; and when he himself travels, is struck with the aspect of a strange country, the moment he passes the bounds of his own. The air of the person, the tone of the voice, the idiom of language, and the strain of conversation, whether pathetic or languid, gay or severe, are no longer the same.

Author Index

Acosta, José de   12, 14, 26, 27, 131–42
Alvarez, Francisco   121
Aristotle   1, 107, 116, 126

Bachofen, Johann Jakob   3
Bodin, Jean   10, 26, 114–24
Bossuet, Jacques-Bénigne   20, 269
Brébeuf, Jean de   162–3

Caesar, Julius   5
Chardin, John   15, 21, 26, 173–82, 266
Comte, Auguste   2
Cooper, James Fenimore   25

Dampier, William   15, 183–92
Darwin, Charles   1
De Bry, Theodor   8
Descartes, René   1–2, 208
Diderot, Denis   18–19, 27, 228–39
Duran, Diego   11
Durkheim, Emile   2

Evans-Pritchard, E.E.   2

Ferguson, Adam   24–5, 26, 27, 277–88
Fontenelle, Bernard le Bovier de   16–17,
   207–13

Goldsmith, Oiver   19
Graffigny, Françoise de   19

Hackluyt, Richard   8

Hegel, Georg Wilhelm Friedrich   1, 2
Herder, Gottfried   16
Herodotus   3–5, 20, 26, 27, 31–7
Hobbes, Thomas   11, 21
Hume, David   24

Ibn Battuta   2, 7, 73–83
Ibn Khaldun   2, 7–8, 26, 84–91

John of Plano Carpini   6
Johnson, Samuel   15

Kant, Immanuel   15

Lafitau, Joseph François   2, 3, 14–15, 17,
   20, 23, 24, 26, 27, 159–69, 261, 273
Lahontan, Baron de   17–18, 22, 27, 217–24
La Popelinière, Henri Lancelot Voisin
   de   10–11, 15, 27, 125–6
Landa, Diego de   11
Le Comte, Louis   13–14, 26, 151–8
Leibniz, Gottfried Wilhelm   14
Le Jeune, Paul   12–13, 143–50, 162
Léry, Jean de   9, 95–105
Leo Africanus   118, 121
Lobo, Jeronimo   15
Locke, John   11, 21
Lubbock, John   1

Maine, Henry Sumner   1
Mandeville, John   2, 6–7, 26, 63–9
Marana, Giovanni   19

Marx, Karl   2, 26
McLennan, John   1, 2
Montaigne, Michel de   9, 27, 106–13, 265
Montesquieu, Charles Louis de Secondat,
    Baron de   2, 15, 19, 20–1, 22, 23,
    24, 25, 26, 225–7, 243–50,
    265–70, 280
Morgan, Lewis Henry   2

Odoric of Pordenone   6

Perrault, Charles   15–16
Plato   108, 123, 126, 138, 200
Polo, Marco   2, 6, 7, 26, 51–62, 125

Quesnay, François   19

Radcliffe-Brown, A.R.   2
Ramusio, Givoanni Batista   8

Rousseau, Jean-Jacques   21–2, 23, 27,
    251–9
Rustichello of Pisa   6

Sahagun, Bernardino de   11, 17
Scott, Walter   25
Smith, Adam   24, 26, 273–6
Spencer, Herbert   1
Swift, Jonathan   7, 16, 17

Tacitus   5, 26–7, 38–45, 114, 115, 116, 117,
    204, 281, 284
Tax, Sol   2
Temple, William   16, 26, 197–206
Tylor, Edward B.   1, 2

Voltaire   17, 18, 19, 20, 22–4, 260–70

William of Rubruck   6

Subject Index

Abyssinia   121, 124
Africa   2, 7, 10, 115, 123, 260
    see also Abyssinia
alcohol *see* drinking
Americans, native   3, 11, 17, 22, 23,
        211, 260, 261–2, 273, 278, 279–85
    see also Huron, Iroquois, Mexico,
        Montagnais, Peru, Tupi
antiquity, classical   1, 2, 3–5, 8, 9, 16, 20, 125,
        126, 138, 159, 197, 260, 266, 280, 288
    mythology   159, 207, 209, 210, 211–13
    religion   132, 159–61, 283
    see also Greece, ancient; Rome, ancient
Arabs   16, 84–91, 205–6, 210
Asians   1, 11, 19, 21, 23, 25, 115, 125
    see also Arabs, China, India, Mongols, Persia,
        Scythians, Tonkin
Australia   15, 186–7
    material culture   187
    food   187

"barbarians"   5, 26, 278
    meaning of term   3, 9, 106, 108
Bashee (or Batanes) Islands   183–6
    boats   184
    clothing   183–4
    drink   186
    food   184–5
    houses   184
    justice   186
    kinship   186
    material culture   183–5

    money   186
    religion   185–6
baths
    China   58
    Scythian   38
Brazil   8–9, 95–105, 106, 108–13
    see also Tupi
Buddhism   13

calendar
    Mexico   139–40
Canada
    see Quebec
cannibalism   6, 98, 111–12, 188
Cathay
    see China
chiefs
    German   41–2
    Mongols   52–3
    Iroquois   164–5
China   6, 7, 12, 16, 20, 23, 25, 27,
        54–62, 66–8, 78–83, 156–8,
        198–201, 262–4, 269–70
    art   80
    cities   57–62
    clothing   79
    coal   7, 55, 80
    Confucianism   13, 199–200, 263
    commerce   54–5, 58, 59, 79–80
    divination   61
    drink   157–8
    education   200

China (*Cont'd*)
  empire   6, 13–14, 66–8, 151–3
  etiquette   156–8
  filial peity   153–5
  food   6, 58, 59, 79, 157–8
  funeral rites   61, 154
  government   23, 27, 56, 82, 142, 151–3,
    154–5, 249–50, 262, 269–70
  justice   56
  kinship   153–5
  mandarins   152, 153, 155
  markets   58, 59
  money   6, 7, 54–5, 59, 79–80
  Muslims   81
  mythology   211
  porcelain   79
  prostitution   59
  religion   56, 79, 201, 263–4
  silk   79, 80
  tea   157
  writing   200
  see also Hangzhou
Christianity   6, 7, 8–9, 26, 226–7
  Roman Catholic   8, 9, 10 11–15, 18,
    239; *see also* Dominicans,
    Franciscans, Jesuits
  Protestant   8, 9, 10
chronology   13–14
cities   7–8
  Arabs   86–8
  China   57–62
climate, theory of   10, 26, 114–22, 266
clothing
  Bashee Islands   183–4
  German   42
  Chinese   79
  Montagnais   149
commerce   267, 284
  Germans   39
  China   54–5, 58–9, 79–80
  Persians, modern   180–1
  Tonkin   189, 191–2
Confucius   13. 199–200
councils
  German   41
  Iroquois   166–9

diet *see* food
divination
  Chinese   61
  Germans   40–1
  Huron   162–3
  Scythians   37, 109

  Tupi   109
drinking
  Bashee Islands   186
  Chinese   157–8
  Germans   44
  Montagnais   147
  Tupi   97–9
Dominicans   11, 13

education
  China   200
  Tahiti   235
  Tonkin   191
Egypt, ancient   3, 4, 26, 31–4, 118
  food   31, 32
  funeral rites   3, 33–4
  peculiarities   31
  religion   3, 31–4
  sacrifice   32–3
empires   197–206, 266
  Chinese   6, 13–14, 16, 26, 66–8, 151–3,
    198–201, 249–50, 262–4
  Egyptian   4, 26
  Islamic   90, 205–6
  Mexican   12
  Persian   3–5, 26, 34–5
  Peruvian   12, 16, 201–3
etiquette
  China   156–8
  Persia, modern   176–9
  Tupi   101–5
Ethiopia *see* Abyssinia

fables *see* Mythology
family *see* kinship, marriage
feasting
  Germans   43–4
  Chinese   157–8
  Tupi   97–9, 2
food
  Abyssinia   121
  Australians   187
  Bashee Islands   184–5
  Chinese   6, 58, 59, 79, 157–8
  Egypt   31, 32
  India   74
  Mongols   51, 52, 53
  Montagnais   144, 146–7, 149–50
  Tupi   95–7, 98, 108, 109
  see also cannibalism, feasting, drinking
Franciscans   11, 12, 13
  Recollets   12, 17, 218
funeral rites

Callatians 3, 35
Chinese 61, 154–5
Egypt 3, 33–4
Germans 45
Mexico 134–5
Mongol 83
Peru 134
Scythians 37–8
Tonkin 190

Germans, ancient 5, 39–45, 114, 115,
    116, 117, 204–5, 278, 281
  cattle 39
  chiefs 41–2
  cities, absence of 42
  clothing 42
  commerce 39
  councils 41
  divination 40–1
  drinking 44
  feasts 43–4
  funeral rites 45
  government 40, 41–2
  justice 41
  kinship 43
  marriage 42–3
  property 39, 44–5
  religion 40–1
  warfare 39–40, 41–2
  women 40, 42–3
Germans, modern 10, 123–4
government 10, 20–1, 244–9
  Arabs 90
  aristocracy 246
  China 23, 27, 82, 142, 151–3, 198–201,
    249–50, 262–3, 269–70
  democracy 244–6, 273–4
  "despotism" 4, 20–1, 25, 26, 34–5,
    247–9, 250, 267, 269–70
  German (ancient) 40, 41–2
  Greek 4, 5, 26
  India 73–5, 77–8
  Huron 163–9
  Iroquois 14–15, 24, 163–9
  Mexico 142, 163
  monarchies 20–1, 123–4, 163, 246–7, 249,
    269, 270
  Mongols 52–3
  Peru 163, 201–3
  republics 20–1, 244–6, 249, 269
  theories of 7–8, 10, 11, 20–1, 23,
    26, 89–91, 242–9, 253–8, 265–70,
    273–6, 277–88

Turkey 266–7
  see also chiefs, councils, empires, kings
Greece, ancient 1, 2, 3–5, 35, 245, 261, 277
  government 4, 5, 26, 275–6
  women 249
  writing 31
  see also antiquity, classical

Hang-chow see Hangzhou
Hangzhou 7, 57–62, 81–2
hospitality
  Germans 43–4
  Mongols 55–6, 68
  Montagnais 145
  Persia, modern 174
  Tupi 102–4
houses
  Bahsee Islands 184
  Montagnais 149
  Tupi 100, 109
Huguenots see Christianity, Protestant
humanism 8, 9–10
hunting 12–13, 24, 144, 273–4, 279
Huron 13, 17, 18, 23, 27
  Diviners 162–3
  Justice 218–24
  Material culture 221–3
  Kinship 164
  Religion 161, 162–3

incest 236–7
India 16, 25, 73–8
  Callatians 3, 35
  Brahmins 7, 68–9, 75
  food 74
  government 73–5, 77–8
  Islam 76–7
  kings 73–4, 77–8
  religion 75–6
  sati 75–6
inequality see property
Iroquois 14–15, 23
  chiefs 164–5
  councils 166–9
  government 14–15, 24, 164–9
  kinship 164
  religion 161, 162
Islam 63–6, 87–8, 205–206, 266, 267
  India 76–7
  Sufis 77

Jesuits 11–15, 17, 18, 131–69, 217, 218
  quarrel of the Chinese rites 13, 14, 264

Jews   7, 10, 14, 205, 211, 248
justice
    Bashee Islands   186
    China   56
    Germans   41
    Peru   202–3

kings
    dynasties   89–91
    German   40
    Indian   73–4, 77–8
    Persian   34–5
    Peru   133
kinship
    Bashee Islands   186
    Bedouins   88–9
    Chinese   13, 153–5
    Fictive   54
    German   43
    Huron   164
    Iroquois   164
    matrilineal   3–4, 12–13, 14, 147–8
    Montagnais   145, 147–8
    Tonkin   190
    Tupi   110
    see also marriage
Khansá, Kinsai see Hangzhou

labor, division of   286–8
liquor see drinking
Livelihood, modes of   7–8, 24, 26
Lycians
    matrilineal kinship   3–4, 14

maize   96–7
manioc   95–7, 109
manners see etiquette
markets
    China   58, 59
marriage
    Germans   42–3
    Mongols   51–2, 54
    Montagnais   144
    Tahiti   234
    Tupi   112
    see also kinship
material culture
    Australians   187
    Bashee Islands   183–5
    Bedouins   85
    China   59, 78–80
    Egypt   31
    Germans   39, 42

Huron   221–3
Mongols   51
Montagnais   149–50
Persians, modern   181
Scythians   38
Tupi   95–101, 108–9
Mexico   11–12, 132, 134–41
    calendar   139–40
    funeral rites   134–5
    government   142, 163
    religion   11, 12, 132, 134–5, 136–8, 161
    temples   136–7
    writing   140–1
money   221
    Bashee Islands   186
    Chinese   6, 7, 54–5, 59, 79–80
    Germans   41
Mongols   6, 51–4, 203–4
    chiefs   52–3
    food   51, 52, 53
    funeral rites   83
    justice   53–4
    marriage   51–2, 54
    nomadism   51, 285
    property   53–4
    religion   52, 56
    warfare   52–3
    women   51–2
Montagnais   12–13, 143–9
    clothing   149
    drink   147
    food   144, 146–7, 149–50
    houses   149
    hospitality   145
    kinship   145, 147–8
    marriage   144
    religion   162
Morocco   118, 121
Muhammad (Mahomet in French)   205–6
mummification   3, 33–4
Muslims   6, 7, 10, 63–6, 81
    see also Islam
mythology   17, 159, 207–13
    American   211
    Chinese   211
    classical   159, 207, 209, 210, 211–13
    Peruvian   211

Nature
    "natural" society   18, 21, 27, 232–4
    state of   21–2, 27, 251–3, 261
New France see Quebec
nomads   7–8, 24, 174, 285–6

Bedouins 86–9
Mongols 6, 51
Montagnais 12–13
Scythians 4, 35

Paris 225–7
Pastoralists *see* nomads
Persia, ancient 3, 4, 5, 26, 203
 madness of Cambyses, 34–5
Persia, modern 15, 19, 21, 23, 26, 173–82
 education 176
 etiquette 176–9
 hospitality 174
 material culture 181
 names 181–2
 property 174
 titles 182
Peru 12, 16, 23, 131–6, 138–9, 141–2,
 201–3
 funeral rites 134
 government 142, 163, 201–3
 justice 202–3
 kings 133
 quipus 141–2
 religion 131–4, 136–7, 161, 203, 211
 temples 135–6
Philippines
 see Bashee Islands
politeness
 see etiquette
progress 25, 279, 285–8
property 22, 24, 25, 253–8, 285–8
 and development of government 273–6,
 285–8
 Germans 39, 44–5
 Mongols 53–5
 Native Americans 279
 Pastoralists 274, 285–6
 Persians, modern 174
 see also money

Quebec 12–13, 14–15, 143–50, 161–9,
 217–18

Recollets *see* Franciscans
religion 10, 26, 121, 159–63, 231
 American 17, 283
 Bashee Islands 185–86
 Chinese 13, 56, 79, 201, 263–4
 Egyptian 3, 31–4
 Germans 40–1
 Greeks and Romans 132, 159–61, 283
 Huron 161, 162–3

Iroquois 161, 162
India 75–6
Mexican 11, 14, 17, 132, 136–8, 161
Mongols 52, 56
Montagnais 162
Peru 131–4, 161, 203
Scythian 35–6, 37
Tonkin 190–1
Tupi 109
see also Buddhism, Christianity, Confucius,
 divination, funeral rites, Islam, Jews,
 Muslims, mythology
Rome, ancient 2, 5, 203, 245, 246, 248, 277,
 280, 284
law 9–10
see also antiquity, classical

sacrifice
 Egyptian 32–3
 Human 36, 38
 Scythian 36, 38
"savages" 1, 9, 12, 14, 15, 18, 19, 21, 22, 23,
 24, 25, 27, 108, 125, 251–3, 260–1, 273,
 279
Scythians 3, 4, 16, 26, 35, 114, 115, 116, 117,
 118, 119, 121, 122, 123, 203
 contracts 37
 diviners 37, 109
 funeral rites 37–8
 nomadism 35, 285
 religion 35–6, 37
 sacrifice 3, 36, 38
 steam baths 38
 warfare 36–7
sexuality
 Germans (ancient) 42–3
 Tahitian, 18–19

Tahiti 18–19, 27, 228–39
 education 235
 marriage 234
 sexuality 230–9
Tamerlane 203–4
Tatars, Tartars *see* Mongols
Tonkin 15, 188–92
 commerce 189, 191–2
 education 191
 funeral rites 190
 kinship 190
 religion 190–1
 writing 191
Tupi 9
 cannibalism 9, 98, 111–12

Tupi (*Cont'd*)
  cotton   100, 109
  diviners   109
  drink   97–9, 109
  etiquette   101–5
  feasting   97–9, 102
  fighting   99
  food   95–7, 98, 108, 109
  houses   100, 109
  kinship   110
  marriage   112
  material culture   95–101, 108–9
  poetry   112
  property   99–100
  religion   109
  warfare   109–10
Turkey   266–7

urban life *see* cities

Viet Nam *see* Tonkin

warfare   24
  Germans   39–40, 41–2
  Mongols   52–3
  Tupi   109–10
  Scythian   36–7
wealth *see* property
women   249
  Germany   40, 42–3
  Mongols   51–2
writing   31
  China   200
  Mexico   140–1
  Tonkin   191